INDIA and the UNITED STATES:
ESTRANGED DEMOCRACIES
1941 - 1991

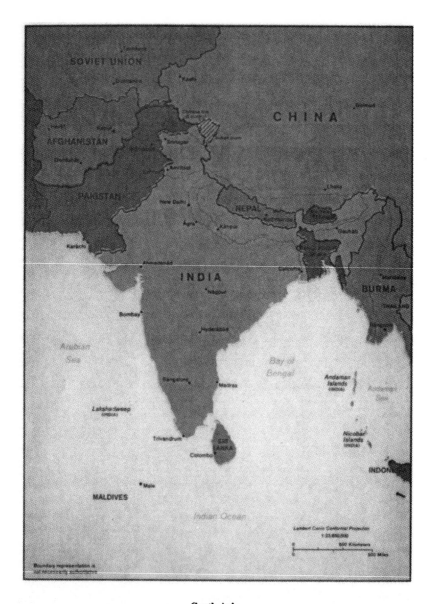

South Asia

INDIA and the UNITED STATES:
ESTRANGED DEMOCRACIES
1941 - 1991

INDIA and the UNITED STATES:
ESTRANGED DEMOCRACIES

1941 - 1991

DENNIS KUX

Introduction by Senator Daniel P. Moynihan

University Press of the Pacific
Honolulu, Hawaii

India and the United States:
Estranged Democracies 1941-1991

by
Dennis Kux

Introduction by
Senator Daniel P. Moynihan

ISBN: 0-89875-825-4

Reprinted from the 1993 edition

University Press of the Pacific
Honolulu, Hawaii
http://www.universitypressofthepacific.com

CONTENTS

MAPS

FOREWORD

Since India achieved independence in 1947, political relations between India and the United States have never been close, and today a number of formidable obstacles hinder progress along the pathway toward closer ties between these two populous democracies. To understand why such obstacles remain, one needs to review—among other matters—the more recent history of India's close ties with the former Soviet Union, even as she proclaimed a policy of nonalignment. To understand why both governments feel there is hope for improved relations today, one should examine the entire history, beginning with the World War II and postwar years during which the United States supported Indian independence from Great Britain, America's closest wartime ally.

Although several books describing elements of this history have been written by Indian and American scholars, no American specialist had undertaken the complete story until Ambassador Dennis Kux decided to analyze the entire five-decade relationship. In this volume, he describes the major issues, events, and personalities that have influenced India-US relations from the Roosevelt administration through the Bush administration. Although the book is arranged by the sequence of US administrations, it clearly addresses audiences in both nations.

Ambassador Kux wrote this book while a Visiting Fellow at the National Defense University. It was his feeling—and one we wholeheartedly support—that only by understanding the ebb and flow of relations over the entire half century may both governments intelligently address the remaining impediments to friendlier relations.

PAUL G. CERJAN
Lieutenant General, US Army
President, National Defense University

AUTHOR'S PREFACE

In 1957, when I was ready to head overseas for my first assignment as a young American Foreign Service Officer, India's struggle to develop under the democratic system caught my imagination and I asked to be sent there. The vagaries of the State Department personnel process assigned me next door, as a third secretary and economic officer at the US Embassy in Karachi. During two years in Pakistan and a follow-on tour in India, I learned much about the problems of the subcontinent and the emotion-laden tensions between the two countries. I also came to admire and respect the ancient cultures of South Asia— a part of the world vastly different in tradition, history, and outlook on life from the United States.

At the time, whether the democratic West could do a better job than the Communist East in addressing the "revolution of rising expectations" in India and elsewhere in the developing world was a question high on the US foreign policy agenda. Now, with the Cold War happily history, India has slid down the ladder of US priorities, although its continuing effort to develop as a democracy does remain significant. One can hardly make support for democracy a guiding principle of American foreign policy yet ignore what happens to democracy in a country where today 860 million people live—one out of every six human beings on earth.

For the better part of twenty years, from late 1957 until mid-1977, my Foreign Service work mainly concerned South Asia, four years on Pakistan and seven on India. During this period, one of the things that most puzzled and frustrated me was the uneven pattern of US-India relations, the swings between periods of cooperation and antagonism, and the often emotional character of the relationship. Why was it that these democracies seemed to have so much trouble in getting along? What caused these two countries to have such volatile relations, occasionally friendly, sometimes hostile, more often than not estranged?

In the decade after 1977, Foreign Service duties sent me far afield from South Asia—an assignment in Turkey, responsibilities for intelligence and management matters in the State Department, and then three years as US Ambassador to the Ivory Coast in West Africa. But the subcontinent was never far from my thoughts. When offered a chance to become a Senior Fellow at the National Defense University, I decided to use the opportunity to write a book exploring the puzzling character of US-India relations.

Once into the research, I found my own knowledge spotty. Some periods I knew well from personal observation or previous study. Others were largely blanks. Trying to fill in the empty spaces, I realized, somewhat to my surprise, that in recent years no American had prepared a comprehensive historical account of the relationship, although numerous Indians had. Since knowing "what" happened before considering "why" seemed logical, I shifted course, deciding to tackle the task of telling the story of India-US diplomatic relations rather than trying to explain what lay behind the many ups and downs.

1941, the eve of the US entry into World War II, seemed the appropriate starting point for the book. That pivotal year 1941 was when New Delhi and Washington established direct diplomatic relations, despite India's membership in the British Empire. It was also the year when the United States first became seriously engaged in the subcontinent. The history closes fifty years later, in mid-1991, with the assassination of Rajiv Gandhi and the end of the Cold War. Since this global struggle between the United States and the Soviet Union, as well as the reaction to it of the three generations of Nehrus—Jawaharlal, Indira, and Rajiv—who led India for 39 of its 45 years as an independent nation, was a defining factor in India-US relations, the termination of the US-Soviet contest and the passing of the Nehru dynasty seemed a fitting point to conclude the book.

My purpose was not to explain the tangled nature of the relationship, but as the story unfolds over the five decades, the major reasons for the mutual estrangement become apparent. India and the United States were *not* at odds because, as some assert, there was too little dialogue, or a lack of mutual understanding, or were serious misperceptions, or because Indians and Americans have trouble getting along with each other. On the contrary, I believe that Washington and New Delhi fell out because they disagreed on national security issues of fundamental importance to each. In the late 1940s, India decided to pursue a neutralist foreign policy, staying apart from the two power blocs then emerging; then, after 1954, the US decided to arm India's enemy Pakistan as part of a global policy of containing communism through a system of military alliances; finally, in the late 1960s and especially after the 1971 Treaty of Friendship, India decided to establish a close political-security relationship with the Soviet Union. India was thus lined up with America's principal foe while, at the same time, Washington was itself aligned with India's major enemy. Not a recipe for amicable relations.

The narrative focuses on the diplomatic interaction between the Indian and American governments and tries to let the story largely tell itself without much attempt at theorizing. Other facets of the bilateral relationship—economic assistance, trade and commerce, and cultural, for example—are discussed mainly as they impact on the political-security ties. Although I have tried to present the Indian, as well as the American, perspective of the story, after three decades as a US diplomat, my understanding of how the United States conducted its diplomacy toward India inevitably is greater than my ability to elaborate the Indian viewpoint. The fact that declassified US official records are far more available reinforced this tendency. (US documents are largely declassified through the 1960s). On the Indian side—even though New Delhi supposedly follows a 30-year rule in releasing documents—little has, in fact, been made available after 1948, except for Prime Minister Nehru's letters to state chief ministers. Originally sent every two weeks, these are of great help for the first decade of independence, but unfortunately become much less frequent in the late 1950s. One hopes India will follow the US lead in opening up its archives so that both sides of the relationship can be better understood.

In keeping with the chronological nature of the study, I have organized the history around the terms of US presidents, with a chapter for each president from Roosevelt to Bush—and two for the busy Eisenhower years. The first six chapters, through the

Johnson presidency, are based on declassified official documents, mainly American, as supplemented by memoirs, biographies, academic studies of various periods or facets of the relationship, and interviews. The final five chapters, from Nixon through the first two years of the Bush presidency, draw more on interviews, my own personal recollections, press accounts, and other secondary sources. Relatively few US documents have been declassified from this period. Although these chapters are necessarily more anecdotal, I hope they are not less accurate in relating the history of relations.

I am indebted to many, many people for their help and encouragement during the two years I spent researching and writing this book. Dr. Fred Kiley, the Director of the National Defense University Press, was an ever wise and cheery source of editorial advice. I am equally appreciative, for her friendly help and counsel, to Dr. Dora Alves, my patient editor at the NDU Press. Mr. Bruce Martin and his colleagues were unfailingly pleasant and efficient in helping me tap the valuable materials at the Library of Congress.

To Professors Thomas Thornton of the School of Advanced International Studies at Johns Hopkins University and Stephen Cohen of the University of Illinois, I am enormously indebted for their generous review of the chapter drafts and their willingness to draw on their own profound knowledge of US relations with South Asia to suggest ways to improve the manuscript. I am similarly appreciative for the many helpful suggestions from Walter Andersen, William Barnds, Peter Galbraith, John Shultz, George Sherman, Sidney Sober, Ambassador Howard Schaffer, Ambassador Jagat Mehta, Ambasador Eric Gonsalves, and Professors Joseph Goldberg, Garry Hess, and Raju G. C. Thomas, who were kind enough to review all or parts of the manuscript. I am especially thankful to Warren Unna, retired *Washington Post* and *Statesman* correspondent, not only for reviewing the manuscript but for making available his newspaper files dating back to the 1960s. I owe the phrase "estranged democracies" to Dr. Gary Hess, Professor of History at Bowling Green University, who employed this in a paper prepared for a January 1991 conference on Indo-US Relations in New Delhi, and kindly agreed to my using it in the title of the book. Naturally, I am also deeply grateful to the more than fifty Indians and

Americans who agreed to share their remembrances and perceptions with me, almost invariably on the record. Their names are listed at the end of the book and their remarks appropriately footnoted in the text.

Finally, I want to thank my wife Marie and my children, Leslie, Sally, and Brian, who provided so much help and encouragement, especially during the inevitable periods of discouragement. Without their support, I am not sure I would have stayed the long course involved in preparing this history, which I dedicate to them with much love and affection. The opinions expressed are, of course, my own and do not reflect the views of the Department of State or the US government.

Washington, DC
November 1992

INTRODUCTION

Early in 1992, *The New York Times* obtained a copy of the United States Defense Planning Guide for the post-cold war era. The planners in the office of the Undersecretary for Policy at the Pentagon had looked about the world for suspicious characters. This used to be called threat analysis. At the height of the Cold War it would have been "threat analysis in worst possible case condition." This time, there were fewer threats on the horizon. But wait! There's India! Fearsome hegemon. There's Pakistan, beleaguered friend of yore! The draft document declared:

> We will seek to prevent the further development of a nuclear arms race on the Indian subcontinent. In this regard, we should work to have both countries, India and Pakistan, adhere to the Nuclear Non-Proliferation Treaty and to place their nuclear energy facilities under International Atomic Energy Agency safeguards. We should discourage Indian hegemonic aspirations over the other states in South Asia and on the Indian Ocean. With regard to Pakistan, a constructive U.S.-Pakistani military relationship will be an important element in our strategy to promote stable security conditions in Southwest Asia and Central Asia. We should therefore endeavor to rebuild our military relationship given acceptable resolution of our nuclear concerns.

This was only a draft. The Undersecretary for Policy had not seen it. But it was for that reason even more of an epiphany. After half a century of relations between what were now the world's two largest democracies, the US government defense planners could routinely assume that there was an American interest in suppressing Indian "hegemonic aspirations" in South Asia, and once again arming its worst enemy and neighbor, Pakistan.

Suppose a comparable Indian document declared a national purpose to keep down US hegemonic aspirations in North America, and to arm Mexico, possibly with the new Indian missile, "Agni." We would not be amused; somehow we are always surprised when Indians are exasperated.

This episode, precisely because it was of so little consequence, will serve as a metaphor for the half-century of misunderstandings, miscues, and mishaps recorded in Ambassador Kux's luminous narrative. At the end of half a century of formal relations, the United States and India, the world's two largest democracies—the two largest *ever* democracies—were still, or once again, or soon to be at odds. The term "estranged" nicely captures the sense on both sides that affection has not been returned, or has somehow lapsed, or has found new outlets. In consequence of which the relationship is no longer the same. But then it never has been.

That, at all events, is the general perception. All rather hazy and soft as of a summer afternoon. Also, all wrong. The United States and India are estranged democracies not because we have failed to understand each other, but because of conflicting policies we and they have pursued with regard to the most elemental of national interests, military security. The supreme virtue of Dennis Kux's history is the way in which bedrock reality shows through at every stage in a half-century of on and off relations.

According to its constitution, India is a "sovereign, socialist, secular, democratic republic." It is surely sovereign, and defiantly democratic. It has a fair amount of socialism of the Fabian sort. The Nehru dynasty, which governed for 37 of the first 42 years of Independence, was surely secular. But all this leaves out *the* great fact, which is that with the coming of independence, for the first time in nearly a millenium, Islamic invaders no longer ruled Hindu India. Well, yes, there had been the British. Here and there, and briefly. (The last Moghul emperor was deposed in 1858.) But the great fact was the endless succession of nomadic horsemen pouring through the Himalayan passes onto the Gangetic plain. Now it was all over. Rather, *almost* all over, for with the creation of an independent Pakistan, the invaders retained their mountain redoubts and no small portion of the plain. Notably Lahore, which Babur had secured before marching on Delhi, and a new capital, Islamabad.

In other words, it was not necessarily over: a millenium of subjugation, defeat, near irrelevance. (Much of what is thought of in the West as Indian history, as for example the advent of the

Moghuls under Babur, is really about the clashes of successive Islamic marauders, some of whom settled down.) Partition had been traumatic. Something like ten million persons were killed by hand. The aftermath was anything but tidy, with the dispute over Kashmir present at the creation, and alive to this day. And so when the United States commenced in the 1950s to provide arms to Pakistan, estrangement with India was inevitable. Indian fear of Pakistan may have been "irrational", as Ambassador Kux suggests. It was no less real. That we had supported independence and welcomed it and promptly set about helping with the associated chores was something Indians understood well enough. Hence, estrangement rather than enmity, but estrangement for certain.

The United States did not intend this. Our concern, early and late, was with the threat, as we saw it, of Soviet expansion. We never quite got it clear in our heads whether by expansion we referred to the Red Army or the Communist party. But at all events, it had to be contained. Pakistan was on the Soviet perimeter and was an early and eager participant in the alliance system that developed in the 1950s under President Eisenhower and his Secretary of State John Foster Dulles. This did not at first imply any disregard for India. When the Chinese Red Army crossed her borders in the early 1960s, American military aid was promptly offered and accepted. When monsoons failed, wheat was forthcoming in continental quantities. There would follow moments of intense attachment which can only be described as infatuation.

Consider this episode. At the height of the Great Society, the Johnson administration was looking for projects worldwide, not just in Appalachia, or inner cities. There was the Mekong Delta to fix up. And there was India to educate. The Indians had paid for our wheat in rupees, of which we came to hold a vast proportion (something like 20 percent of money in circulation). We would use the money to set up a foundation to finance higher education. There would be a joint US/Indian board, and an American executive director. Americans would end up owning a very significant portion of Indian culture as embodied in its universities. Here is the conclusion of President Lyndon B. Johnson's toast at a White House dinner for Prime Minister Indira Gandhi on 28 March 1966:

So may we, Madam Prime Minister, with the permission of your Government and the American Congress, launch a new and imaginative venture. We shall call it an Indo-American Foundation. I would propose that this Foundation be established in India, and that it be endowed with $300 million in Indian currency owned by the United States. Other foundations all over the world will cooperate, I am sure, with an enterprise of this kind.

I would suggest that this Foundation be organized as an independent institution—with distinguished citizens of both our countries on its board of directors. I would propose that the new Foundation be given a broad charter to promote progress in all fields of learning—to advance science—to encourage research—to develop new teaching techniques on the farms and in the factories—to stimulate, if you please, new ways to meet old problems.

The journey to our future is over a very long and very winding road. Every mile will be challenged by doubt. But together, Madam Prime Minister, we must avoid the detours that intrude on our safe journey toward a time when, as your father promised, life will be better for all of our people.

So, ladies and gentlemen, let us honor those who are so welcome here tonight. Let us ask you to join in honoring the Chief of State whose wise and gifted Prime Minister we have enjoyed so much today, and that we welcome so warmly this evening.

I should like to ask those of you who are assembled here to join me now in raising your glass in toast to the great President of India.

Here is the concluding portion of the Prime Minister's reply

India very definitely is on the move. Mr. President, the United States has given India valuable assistance in our struggle against poverty, against hunger, against ignorance, and against disease. We are grateful for this act of friendship. But we also know that our own "Great Society" must and can only rest securely on the quality and the extent of our own effort.

This effort we are determined to make: we owe it to our friends, and even more so we owe it to ourselves.

Nevertheless, I believe that it is of the greatest importance, to use your own words, to bring into closer union the spirit and courage of both our countries. I welcome your intention to set up an Indo-American Foundation, which will give tangible shape and form to this union.

The present-day world offers the possibility of bringing together one people with another. The young men and women of your Peace Corps are well known and well loved in our country. Every endeavor to sustain and enlarge this people-to-people partnership is a good effort and is welcome.

Friendship with America is not a new thing for us.

Those of us in India who have been involved with the struggle for freedom have known from our earliest days your own struggle here. We have been taught the words of your leaders, of your past great Presidents, and above all we were linked in friendship because of the friendship which President Roosevelt showed us and the understanding which he showed during some of the most difficult days of our independence struggle. I have no doubt it was also this understanding and friendly advice given to the British Government which facilitated and accelerated our own freedom.

But there again the major effort had to be on our own, and this is what we want today: that we should bear our burden, as indeed we are doing, but that a little bit of help should come from friends who consider it worthwhile to lighten the burden.

Because, Mr. President, India's problems today are her own, but they are also the world's problems. India has a position in Asia which is an explosive position. India, if it is stable, united, democratic, I think can serve a great purpose. If India is not stable, or if there is chaos, if India fails, I think it is a failure of the whole democratic system. It is a failure of many of the values which you and we both hold dear.

That is why, Mr. President, I welcome your words and I welcome this meeting with you, which has been most valuable to me.

I invite you, ladies and gentlemen, to join with me in drinking a toast to the President and Mrs. Johnson, our friends, the American people, and the Great Society, not just for America, but for all who dream of it, for all who struggle to transform those dreams into reality.*

Not 5 years later, these same two nations looked like they were about to go to war. Pakistan broke up. India invaded "East Bengal." The President of the United States, Richard M. Nixon, would write in his diary of Prime Minister Gandhi's "duplicitous action toward us at the time she saw me in Washington and assured me she would not." He sent the carrier *Enterprise* into the Bay of Bengal. The United States Permanent Representative to the United Nations, George Bush, acting under orders from President Nixon, told the Security Council that India was responsible for the war. The Soviets vetoed the American resolution of condemnation. Prime Minister Gandhi signed a treaty of friendship with the Soviet Union and set off a nuclear explosion. After having sent the Peace Corpsmen home.

Once again, the United States was thinking about the Soviet Union and not about India. Pakistan was arranging for Secretary of State Henry Kissinger to fly to Peking to prepare for a visit of President Nixon that would bring China into play as part of a "global balance of power". Hence we would "tilt" toward Islamabad. The events of the Bangladesh war, as it came to be known, are set forth in great detail in Chapter 7. Nor does the author hesitate to offer a harsh assessment of the American role. In their memoirs, Nixon and Kissinger assert:

> their handling of events scared the Soviets into calling off
> their South Asian proxy, India, from attacking West Paki-
> stan and showed the Chinese that the United States was
> willing to offer steadfast help to a friend during an unpopu-
> lar crisis. Kissinger went so far as to claim that administra-
> tion policy saved "a major American initiative of
> fundamental importance to the global balance of power"
> and that the "very structure of international order was
> endangered by the naked recourse to force by a Soviet
> partner."

---

* Fortunately for all concerned, on further consideration India decided not to go ahead with the foundation for higher education. But it had at first seemed a feasible idea. Toasts of the President and Prime Minister Indira Gandhi of India, March 28, 1966, *Public Papers of the Presidents, Lyndon B. Johnson, 1966,* Volume I.

It is hard to agree with these assertions. Far from a diplomatic victory, the whole affair proved an unnecessary and embarrassing diplomatic setback for the United States. Through their misreading of the crisis, and their pro-Pakistan bias, Richard Nixon and Henry Kissinger succeeded in needlessly transforming a regional dispute into one which threatened to become a great power showdown. The main consequences were severe and long-lasting damage to US relations with India and enhanced Soviet influence with New Delhi.

That is about how matters rested for the remainder of the first half-century of Indo-US relations. At the end, however, a most surprising event occurred. The Soviet Union broke up! This was a blow to India, which had invested far more than she ought to have done in that relationship. But if the United States were left the world's only superpower, the price of victory was considerable. We would have been well advised to learn from the subcontinent as we pursued that protracted conflict. By the 1970s, the United States had opted for a "global balance of power" strategy, the sort of thing seminars are made of, but not the real world. The strategy simply assumed the continued existence and viability of the USSR. Whereas that should have been the first question to be raised. Would the USSR remain intact? Was it not another of those vast empires that had been breaking up all through the twentieth century? Wasn't the Indian subcontinent another such empire? Wasn't it breaking up? Along religious and linguistic and ethnic lines? (In the interest of full disclosure, I should state that by the late 1970s, I was arguing in the Senate that the Soviet Union would break up in the 1980s.) And mind, ought not India have given some thought to this possibility? Prime Minister Gandhi and her son Rajiv Gandhi both cruelly, mindlessly assassinated, but not by instrumentalities of the cold war. Rather, by agents of indigenous nationalisms.

All that is now past. In his closing chapter, the Ambassador remarks that all things considered, "it is surprising the estrangement has not been worse." Things surely are better than they have been, not least owing to a marvelous migration that has brought nearly one million Indians to the United States, with no sign of stopping, such is the welcome accorded these remarkably gifted individuals. The United States has cut off all military aid to Pakistan; it is hard to imagine any resumption. Certainly, there would be no strategic grounds for anything of the sort, Pentagon planners to the contrary. Whatever injuries we have done India, we never intended them, save possibly in that sclerotic interval in 1971. In a sense, then, it is now India's turn. Kux writes: "Relations are unlikely to become more cooperative if India decides almost viscerally that opposing the United States is the natural state of affairs for Indian foreign policy." May a friend suggest that that *is* a temptation which needs watching. As for the United States, there is a related disposition to assume that estrangement is the natural state of this relation. It is nothing of the sort, and *we* should watch *that* temptation!

Daniel Patrick Moynihan
United States Senate

INDIA and the UNITED STATES:
ESTRANGED DEMOCRACIES

1941 - 1991

Chapter I

Roosevelt: The United States Meets India

This history of Indo-US relations begins on the eve of America's entry into World War II. Before then, the United States had scant contact with India even though, in 1792, only three years after he became President, George Washington appointed Benjamin Joy as consul in Calcutta, then the capital of British India.[1] Over the next century and a half, with India part of the British Empire, political relations were virtually non-existent. Economic relations were also insignificant, except for a brief flourishing of trade during the Napoleonic Wars.[2] In the late 1930s, for example, US investment in India amounted to less than $50 million, with half in missionary schools, hospitals, or other non-business activities.[3] US missionaries were, in fact, the principal link to India, yet numbered only a few thousand, far fewer than the Americans active in China.

In the period between the two world wars, India's struggle for independence won the support of American progressives, but did not gain widespread public backing. After Mohandas K. Gandhi—familiarly called the Mahatma, Hindi for "great spirit"—assumed the leadership of the Indian National Congress, the major nationalist organization, his non-violent protest campaigns against British rule generated considerable press coverage. The spindly figure wrapped in a bedsheetlike garb became a sympathetic—if rather puzzling—figure for Americans. On the negative side, Katherine Mayo's 1927 book, *Mother India*, dealt a heavy blow to India's image. This withering depiction of Indian society as depraved, squalid, and without redeeming virtues sold a phenomenal 256,697 copies in 27 editions.[4]

When Franklin D. Roosevelt entered the White House in 1933, New Deal liberals, influenced by the anti-imperialist tradition of the Democratic Party, sympathized with India's desire for independence. Neither Roosevelt nor Secretary of State Cordell Hull, however, actively engaged US influence in support of the Indian nationalist cause in the 1930s. On the eve of World War II, India remained a country about which the United States had limited knowledge and with which the United States had had little contact. American images of India flickered between exotic Hollywood portrayals-of the British Raj and the adventure tales of Rudyard Kipling. Bejewelled maharajahs and British colonial sahibs, impoverished beggars and fakirs, massive demonstrations of Indian nationalists, and the complex problems of untouchability, caste, and Hindu-Muslim communalism all made for a bewildering mélange.

For Indians, the United States was equally unfamiliar terrain, a distant land that seemed vastly different from their own dusty, impoverished sub-continent. Few people of Indian origin lived in the United States—as late as 1940, the census counted only 2,400—mostly Sikh farmers who had immigrated to California from the Punjab in northwest India at the turn of the century.[5]

Educated Indians tended to look at the United States through the often critical British lens, as a country dominated by materialism and crime. Racial discrimination against non-whites, especially segregation in the US South, added to the unflattering picture. Indians, like other Asians, deeply resented US laws barring them from immigrant status and citizenship. Well-publicized incidents further tarnished the American image. Rabindranath Tagore, for example, cut short a lecture tour in 1929 when the Nobel prize winner felt insulted by a US immigration official.[6]

Pandit Jawaharlal Nehru, who in the late 1920s became one of Gandhi's principal lieutenants and foreign policy spokesman for the Indian National Congress,[7] initially found the United States not only racist, but imperialist. In 1927, the Indian leader joined in criticizing US foreign policy toward Latin America at the Brussels International Congress against Colonial Oppression and Imperialism. A year later Nehru wrote, "It is the United States which offers us the best field for the study of economic imperialism."[8]

After the Democrats came to power in 1933, Indian nationalists, including Nehru, gradually developed a less negative attitude. Franklin D. Roosevelt gained popularity in India for his New Deal domestic reforms and his anti-colonialist attitude. The President's decision to grant independence to the Philippines in 1946 impressed Indians; Roosevelt's action sharply contrasted with British refusal to offer a timetable for Indian self-rule. By the late 1930s, Nehru and other nationalists began to look to the United States as a potentially powerful supporter in their struggle for freedom from colonialism. Nehru, who had gained favorable attention in America as an articulate and sensitive Asian leader through his well-received autobiography, presented India's case for independence for the informed US audience in articles in *Foreign Affairs* in 1938 and the *Atlantic Monthly* in 1940.

By this time, the British were slowly—and grudgingly— reforming the Indian political structure to permit greater self-government. Following periodic civil disobedience movements organized by the Indian National Congress, and lengthy negotiations with Mahatma Gandhi and other Indian political leaders, the Government of India Act of 1935 introduced democratically elected governments at the provincial level. Winston Churchill, then a Conservative Party backbencher, bitterly opposed the reforms.

After faring well in 1937 in the first provincial elections under the reforms, the Congress Party was able to form governments in eight of eleven provinces. A brief period of cooperation followed between the Congress, assuming genuine responsibility at the provincial level, and the British imperial authorities, who continued to control the Government of India in New Delhi. The chief executive remained the British Viceroy, who in turn reported to the Secretary of State for India, a member of the British cabinet and head of the India Office in London.

When World War II broke out between Britain and Germany in September 1939, the Viceroy, Lord Linlithgow, declared war for India with little semblance of consultation with nationalist political leaders. Reacting against the Viceroy's unilateral action, the Congress Party refused to give its blessing to the war effort despite the fact that many of its leaders, including Nehru, emotionally supported the Allied cause against the Nazis. Congress Party members of provincial governments resigned their posts in protest against the Viceroy's disregard of Indian sensitivities. A dour, unimaginative old-style man of Empire, Linlithgow thoroughly disliked—even despised—key Indian National Congress leaders like Mahatma Gandhi and Pandit Nehru. Leo Amery, the Secretary of State for India, shared Linlithgow's staunchly conservative views and his dislike for Indian nationalist politicians.

After the Nazis swept through Western Europe in mid-1940—and Winston Churchill succeeded Neville Chamberlain as Prime Minister—Britain sought to allay the nationalists by offering a pledge of "eventual" dominion status after the war. This gesture failed to mollify Congress leaders, who wanted more tangible steps toward self-government in return for full backing for the war effort. The Indian Congress Party's unwillingness to support the struggle against Nazi Germany infuriated the British, who were fighting for their national survival against Hitler.

Prime Minister Churchill's views on India remained rigid. From the start of the war, he warned against "the slippery slope of concessions" and welcomed Hindu-Muslim differences as a "bulwark of British rule in India."[9] Even the firmly colonialist Secretary of State for India, Leo Amery, was at times critical of Churchill's old-fashioned imperialism. "He has never really sympathized with the development of self-government in the Empire," Amery commented," . . . as regards India (Churchill) has never got beyond the early Kipling stage."[10]

The United States Develops an Interest in India

In Washington, the question of India's status became a matter of interest at the senior levels of government in early 1941. Although anti-war sentiment remained strong in the United States, the sympathy of the President and his administration for the allied cause was clear. The initiation of Selective Service, the provision of 50 destroyers to Britain, and the start of Lend-Lease assistance were all signs that the United States was gearing up to become the "arsenal of democracy" in the fight against fascism.

As American leaders looked more closely at India, they saw possibilities of the subcontinent's making a major contribution to the war effort, but soon became disenchanted with the British attitude. According to Secretary of State Cordell Hull, he and President Roosevelt "were convinced that the Indians would cooperate better with the British if they were assured of independence, at least after the war." At the same time, however, Hull said he and Roosevelt accepted that it was "a delicate question" as to how far the United States could push for Indian independence in view of London's sensitivities on this issue. With Britain fighting for its life against Nazi Germany, US policy was to "take no step and utter no words that would impede her struggle."[11] What Hull called the "delicate question" became the policy dilemma for US leadership in dealing with India during the war: how hard could the United States push the British on Indian independence without impairing the alliance?

In order to facilitate US support for the war effort in India—by then ruled eligible to receive Lend-Lease assistance—the British in April 1941 took the initiative in proposing to send an Indian representative to Washington to deal directly with the US authorities. Until then, the Government of India followed the cumbersome procedure of channeling views through the India and Foreign Offices in London and then the British Embassy in Washington. The State Department quickly accepted the British proposal, in turn suggesting a reciprocal arrangement under which the United States would establish an office in New Delhi. Washington found it highly unsatisfactory having to deal with the Government of India through the Consulate General in Calcutta, nearly a thousand miles away from New Delhi. As US interest in India mounted, the United States wanted easier access to British authorities and Indian nationalist leaders.

At first, Lord Linlithgow balked—worried that an official US presence in New Delhi would be inconsistent with India's status as part of the Empire. After a number of exchanges on the subject, Washington, London, and New Delhi finally agreed on an arrangement conveying something less than full diplomatic status to the envoys. In Washington, the Viceroy's representative was to be called the Agent-General of India and attached to the British Embassy. In New Delhi, the United States would establish an office, the head of which would be called the Commissioner. The Viceroy designated a senior Indian civil servant, Sir Girja Shankar Bajpai, as Agent-General in Washington;[12] the State Department named career diplomat Thomas Wilson, the Consul General in Calcutta, to become US Commissioner in New Delhi. In keeping with their unusual semi-diplomatic status, Bajpai and Wilson presented President Roosevelt and Viceroy Linlithgow personal letters of introduction rather than the usual diplomatic letters of credence.[13]

The first expression of discontent with British policy toward India came in a May 1941 proposal by Assistant Secretary of State for Economic Affairs Adolph A. Berle—a New Deal liberal—for pressure on London "to explore the possibility of making India equal of other members of the British Commonwealth." Berle argued that with India's vast pool of manpower, the country could achieve "a dominant position in supplying certain strategic war materials" if it became an "active rather than a passive partner" in the war effort.[14] Despite the fact that Under Secretary of State Sumner Welles convinced Hull "it was undesirable to upset the Indian apple cart" by a formal démarche, Hull informally raised the subject of India with the British Ambassador, Lord Halifax.

Having served as Viceroy from 1926 until 1931—when he was known as Lord Irwin—Halifax was obviously far more knowledgeable about India than US officials. Although regarded as a liberal Viceroy, in 1941 Halifax shared the prevailing Conservative Party view that it was preferable to stand pat on Indian political arrangements and make no political gestures towards the Indian National Congress. Halifax's predictable response to Hull: it was not "feasible or even necessary now to make further liberalizing concessions" to the Indian nationalists.[15]

US interest in India, nonetheless, continued to grow. Just before the August 1941 mid-Atlantic summit between Roosevelt and Churchill, John Winant, the American Ambassador in London, suggested urging the British to set a date for granting India dominion status. Winant's recommendation won the warm endorsement of Assistant Secretary Berle but foundered, like Berle's own earlier suggestion, with Sumner Welles, who opposed telling London "what the status of India should be."

Under Secretary Welles commented, "Were the President disposed to take the matter up, I should imagine he would wish to discuss it in a very personal and confidential way with Mr. Churchill."[16]

The President was quite ready—according to his son Elliot Roosevelt—to raise the topic of India with Prime Minister Churchill when the two leaders met in the mid-Atlantic Ocean in August 1941. Roosevelt took the opportunity during an after-dinner talk the second evening of the conference to criticize British colonialism.[17] British imperial policies, the President charged, represented 18th, not 20th, century views, taking resources out of colonies and giving nothing back to the people. When Roosevelt stressed the need to develop industry, to improve sanitation, and to raise educational levels and standards of living in colonies, Churchill's anger rose. Beginning to look apoplectic, the Prime Minister growled, "You mentioned India."

"Yes," the President responded, "I can't believe that we can fight a war against fascist slavery, and at the same time not work to free people from all over the world from a backward colonial policy." According to Elliot Roosevelt, the two leaders continued to argue over colonialism at length and without agreement.[18]

In the closing statement of the conference on 14 August, Roosevelt and Churchill issued the Atlantic Charter, the declaration of principles that served as the basic statement of Allied war aims. Their difference over colonialism was apparent in later arguments about the meaning of the third article of the Charter, dealing with the right of self-determination. This article stated that the United States and Great Britain "respect the right of all peoples to choose the form of government under which they will live; and that they wish to see sovereign rights and self-government restored to those who have been forcibly deprived of them."

The Americans held that the article's concept of self-determination had universal application, including the right of colonies to become independent. The President, Secretary Hull, and Under Secretary Welles all made this point in public statements the following year. The British took a narrower view. Speaking in Parliament on 9 September 1941, Churchill stated that—as far as Britain was concerned—the article applied only to territories seized by the Nazis, and not to the Empire. Just before entering the House of Commons, the Prime Minister heard a plea from Ambassador Winant not to make the statement. Rebuffing the US envoy, Churchill proceeded with his restrictive interpretation of the Charter.[19]

The Prime Minister's statement caused bitter disappointment in India and dissatisfaction in Washington. Although the State Department's Near Eastern Division recommended that the President press Churchill to extend the Atlantic Charter to India, Under Secretary Sumner Welles again proved the stumbling block. Welles agreed the Atlantic Charter should apply to India, but argued strenuously that the US government should not press Churchill, during that difficult time, to take a step on India he consistently opposed.[20]

US entry into the war in December 1941 vastly raised India's strategic importance in Washington as well as American willingness to express its views on the Indian political situation to the British. US war planners saw the subcontinent as a key bastion for supporting China and a potentially enormous source of manpower and war goods for the Allied cause. The Assistant Chief of the Army's War Plans Division, Dwight D. Eisenhower, then a brigadier general, wrote "We've got to keep Russia in the war—and hold India!!! Then we can get ready to crack Germany through England."[21]

When Prime Minister Churchill visited Washington during Christmas 1941, Roosevelt apparently brought up India "on the usual American lines." There is no US record of the discussion, but Churchill wrote, "I reacted so strongly and at such length that he never raised it (India) verbally again."[22] Roosevelt's closest adviser, Harry Hopkins, said no American suggestions during the war were "so wrathfully received as those relating to the solution of the Indian problem."

> It was indeed one subject on which the normally broad-minded, good-humored, give-and-take attitude which prevailed between the two statesmen was stopped cold. It may be said that Churchill would see the Empire in ruins and himself buried under them before he would concede the right of any American, however great and illustrious a

friend, to make any suggestion as to what he should do about India.[23]

Perhaps sensitized to Churchill's outlook, Roosevelt did not directly react to Britain's initial refusal to allow India to sign the United Nations declaration, although, agreeing with Harry Hopkins, he did not "understand why they don't include it." At Hopkins' suggestion, he asked Secretary of State Hull to "prod them a little." Two days later, Lord Halifax advised the State Department that the Viceroy and the War Cabinet had changed their minds.[24] On New Year's Day 1942, Indian Agent-General Bajpai was among the twenty-six signers of the United Nations Declaration.

As 1942 began, officials in Washington continued to worry about the prospects for rallying Indian support for the war effort. With the allies reeling in Asia, the fall of Singapore on 15 February triggered new concerns. A Senate Foreign Relations Committee hearing ten days later made clear that Congress shared administration anxieties. Assistant Secretary of State Breckenridge Long, noting a "serious undercurrent of anti-British feeling," reported to Secretary Hull that the Senators demanded "India be given a status of autonomy. . . .The only way to get the people of India to fight was to get them to fight for India." The Senators declared, "Gandhi's leadership became part of America's military equipment."[25]

On 25 February, Roosevelt took the initiative, instructing Averell Harriman, his Special Representative in London, to sound Churchill out about a "new relationship between Britain and India." After talking with the Prime Minister, Harriman cabled that the British leader remained strongly opposed to "stirring the pot." The United States, Churchill asserted, was misreading the Indian situation: The war effort was tied to the support of the Muslims, not the Congress Party and the Hindus. The Prime Minister claimed (wrongly) that 75 percent of the Indian Army were Muslims and largely opposed to the Indian Congress Party. Making a gesture toward the Congress would only offend the Muslims and not aid the war effort, the British leader argued.[26]

Appeals from China's President Chiang Kai-shek added to the pressure on a reluctant Churchill. During a visit to India in mid-February, Chiang strongly urged Britain to grant India independence—much to the dismay of the Viceroy Lord Linlithgow. The presence of the British Labour Party as a coalition partner in the war cabinet added further weight to the calls for action on India. Long at odds with the Conservatives over the pace of colonial reform, Labour Party India specialist and Lord Privy Seal, Sir Stafford Cripps, challenged Secretary of State for India Amery to rethink the policy of sitting tight.[27]

Under mounting pressure, the War Cabinet approved the idea—pressed vigorously by Cripps—of issuing a firm offer of post-war independence and of taking steps to give Indian political leaders a substantially larger governmental role during the war. Out of concern for the Muslim minority, about a quarter of India's four hundred million population, and the agitation by its major political grouping, the Muslim League, for a separate homeland—Pakistan—the Cabinet declaration left open the possibility of creating more than one independent state.[28]

The War Cabinet decided to send a senior figure to India to discuss the declaration rather than simply issuing the proposal. Not one to lack self-confidence, Cripps offered to take on the task, reasonably hopeful he could gain the agreement of his many Indian friends, including Gandhi and Nehru. In New Delhi, the Viceroy heartily disliked the whole idea. Upset that the Cabinet in effect pushed him aside by designating Cripps to present the proposals, Linlithgow offered to resign. He agreed to stay on only after a personal plea from Churchill. The Prime Minister explained, "It would be impossible, owing to . . . the general American outlook to stand on a purely negative attitude and Cripps' Mission is indispensable to prove our honesty of purpose."[29]

Just before Sir Stafford left for India, Churchill informed Roosevelt about the War Cabinet proposals. Hardly sounding enthusiastic, the British leader reiterated that Britain must not "on any account" break with the Muslims, the main element in the army. Churchill commented, "Naturally we do not want to throw India into chaos on the eve of an invasion."[30] With Burma having fallen to the Japanese, an attack on India loomed as a real threat.

Roosevelt's response should have shaken the Prime Minister's composure. Disagreeing with the cautious, lawyer-like approach of the Cabinet proposals, the President suggested the

British should immediately establish a "temporary dominion government" on the lines of the US Articles of Confederation.

> Perhaps the analogy of some such method to the travails and problems of the U.S. between 1783 and 1789 might give a new slant in India itself, and it might cause the people there to become more loyal to the British Empire and to stress the danger of Japanese domination, together with the advantage of peaceful evolution as against chaotic revolution.[31]

Surely aware that these words would not make his friend Winston very happy, Roosevelt ended his message diplomatically, "For the love of heaven, don't bring me into this, though I want to be of help. It is, strictly speaking, none of my business, except insofar as it is a part and parcel of the successful fight that you and I are waging."[32]

The Johnson Mission: Roosevelt Tries "To Be Of Help"

Circumstances soon provided the President a chance "to be of help." Discussions about how the United States could aid Indian production of war goods, initiated by Indian Agent General Bajpai, resulted in a decision to send a war production mission to India. On 6 March 1942, the State Department announced that Colonel Louis Johnson, a former Assistant Secretary of War and prominent West Virginia Democrat, would head the mission, supported by former Assistant Secretary of State Henry Grady and three other industry specialists.[33]

Before Johnson departed three weeks later, his role dramatically changed. Instead of leading the mission, the colonel became Franklin Roosevelt's Personal Representative to India. Although the documentary record is lacking, it is reasonable to assume the President switched Johnson's assignment so that the United States would play a more active role in helping the British and Indians reach a political settlement in order to engage Indian energies more fully behind the war effort.[34]

A former national commander of the American Legion and Washington wheeler dealer, Johnson was an unlikely candidate for a sensitive diplomatic mission—and later an unexpected convert to Indian nationalism. A strong supporter of preparedness as Assistant Secretary of War, Johnson was well qualified for the war production mission. His knowledge of India, however, was nil; Johnson admitted the only books he read on the subcontinent were Kipling's *Kim* and Henty's *With Clive in India.*[35]

By the time Johnson arrived in New Delhi on 3 April, the Cripps Mission seemed near failure. Several weeks of intensive talks failed to win the Congress Party's agreement. Mahatma Gandhi was the main obstacle—disliking the loophole permitting the creation of Pakistan. With the Allied position crumbling in Asia, moreover, Gandhi spoke of a British political pledge as a check drawn on a failing bank. Although Gandhi had a majority within the Congress Party leadership, a substantial minority, including South Indian leader C. Rajagopalachari, urged acceptance of the Cripps plan and full support for the war against the Axis. Congress President Maulana Azad, a respected Muslim, and Jawaharlal Nehru were sitting on the fence.

About to leave India in failure, a depressed Cripps delayed his departure after Shiva Rao, a prominent pro-Congress journalist, thought a compromise on the management of India's defense might salvage the negotiations.[36] Although not optimistic, Cripps asked authorization to try to work out a revised arrangement on defense, subject to agreement of the Viceroy and the Commander-in-Chief of the Indian Army, General Wavell.[37]

Churchill replied he would seek agreement of the War Cabinet, expressing satisfaction that Cripps's effort had been "most beneficial in the U.S. and in large circles here." By offering the proposals, Churchill believed the British received a better press in the United States, allaying criticism of Britain's policy toward India.[38] One American who did not share the Prime Minister's appraisal was President Franklin Roosevelt. Talking with Indian Agent-General Bajpai on 2 April, Roosevelt criticized the Cripps proposals as not going far enough, expressing the view that the British should have offered India virtually complete autonomy.[39]

Roosevelt's Personal Representative in India, Louis Johnson, was, in any event, not about to give up without a fight. As soon as the former Assistant Secretary of War arrived in New Delhi, he plunged into the middle of the negotiations. Delivering a message from Roosevelt to Congress President Maulana Azad urging acceptance of the British proposals, Louis Johnson found the Congressites and Cripps eager for his assistance. Delighted to have help, Sir Stafford told a colleague that Roosevelt had sent Johnson post-haste, to "lend a hand in achieving an Indian settlement."[40] And lend a hand Johnson did, shuttling between Cripps and Pandit Nehru in a desperate effort to shape a compromise. Although the Viceroy at first found Johnson engaging—he liked the fact that Johnson bluntly warned the Congress leadership that India would lose US support if it rejected the British offer—Linlithgow worried that Roosevelt's Personal Representative was "concerning himself too closely in detailed negotiations between HMG and Indian politicians."[41]

Just two days after reaching New Delhi, Johnson cabled Roosevelt and Hull to recommend that the President intercede with Churchill. In Johnson's view, both the Viceroy and General Wavell opposed an enlarged Indian defense role, a step the US envoy believed was the key to an agreement. To save the negotiations, Johnson believed the President had to deal directly with Churchill. The answer from Washington was a polite turndown. After considering the Colonel's request, the President decided against a further personal appeal to the Prime Minister. Under Secretary Welles cabled, "You know how earnestly the President has tried to be of help . . . it is feared that if at this moment he interposed his own views, the result would complicate further an already overcomplicated situation."[42]

Not easily deterred, Johnson continued his whirlwind efforts in New Delhi. With Sir Stafford's concurrence, he redrafted the defense proposals to retain full British control but to provide a better sounding Indian role. When both sides seemed agreeable to the revisions, Congress acceptance suddenly seemed possible, indeed likely. Johnson sent off an enthusiastic cable to Washington on 9 April stating that Nehru was going to accept his modified defense proposal and that Wavell and Linlithgow also agreed. Ending with a patriotic flourish, Johnson cabled euphorically, "Both Nehru and Cripps have expressed their appreciation for the revival of negotiations. The magic name over here is Roosevelt; the land, the people would follow and love, America."[43] An elated Cripps reported to Churchill—in less flamboyant language—that as a result of Johnson's help he now hoped to gain Indian agreement. Sir Stafford urged the

Prime Minister to send thanks to the President for Johnson's assistance.[44]

Neither Johnson nor Cripps realized that Linlithgow, fuming over being elbowed aside, and increasingly incensed by Johnson's involvement, was bombarding London with back channel telegrams. The Viceroy was furious that Cripps had allowed Johnson to show the revised defense formulation to Nehru before the Viceroy saw the proposal. Linlithgow also raised a more fundamental problem lurking in the shadows of the Cripps discussions: what would the role of the Viceroy be under the revised governmental arrangements? Cripps had implied he would become a constitutional head of state, with the cabinet, dominated by Indians, possessing genuine authority. Was this really what London wanted, the Viceroy asked? Linlithgow worried that it would be hard for the British to reject the Cripps-Johnson formula if the Congress Party leadership accepted. "We cannot run the risk of the Governor-General (Viceroy), the (Commander-in) Chief and HMG's being unwilling to honour a formula agreed between HMG's emissary and Roosevelt's personal representative," an anxious Linlithgow cabled the Prime Minister.[45]

At this point, with the prospects for success of the Cripps Mission brightening, the fates intervened. Presidential aide Harry Hopkins was in London with US Army Chief of Staff General George C. Marshall for discussions on wartime strategy. The Prime Minister unexpectedly called Hopkins to No. 10 Downing Street on 9 April to talk about India. Brandishing a cable from the Viceroy, Churchill told Hopkins an awkward situation had developed in New Delhi. The Prime Minister claimed the Indians were going to accept the original British proposal, but Cripps and Louis Johnson developed new ideas without consulting the Viceroy. This development badly upset Linlithgow, who was also disturbed by the fact that Johnson was acting and talking as though the President sent him to India to mediate an Indian political settlement. It was possible, Churchill continued, the War Cabinet would reject Johnson's proposal, something that would be embarrassing for the President.

Believing it important to downplay Johnson's role rather than risk a public relations problem for Roosevelt, Hopkins promptly responded that he was very sure Johnson "was not acting as the representative of the President in mediating the Indian business." Hopkins said Roosevelt's instructions on India discouraged becoming engaged in trying to resolve matters unless both sides so requested, and unless India and Britain assured him they would accept his ideas. The President did not want to be placed in the public position where the contending parties turned down his proposals. Hopkins assumed, "Cripps was using Johnson for his own ends, Cripps being very anxious to bring Roosevelt's name into the picture."[46]

In Hopkins' presence, Churchill immediately wrote out a message to New Delhi that Johnson was not Roosevelt's Personal Representative except for munitions questions, and that the President was opposed to anything like intervention or mediation. Later that day, Churchill persuaded the War Cabinet to reprimand Cripps for exceeding instructions and to raise questions about the appropriateness of Johnson's role in the discussions.[47]

A reined-in Cripps met for a final session with Congress leaders Maulana Azad and Pandit Nehru. Instead of crowning the negotiations with success, the 10 April meeting marked the final collapse of Sir Stafford's mission. When the Indians pressed for elaboration on the Viceroy's role under the plan, a depressed Cripps could only temporize. He was unable to give even verbal assurance that the ministers in the new government would possess real authority. Nehru made clear the Congress Party's reluctance to work with the Viceroy and the traditional Government of India machinery—for the nationalists the very symbol of British imperialism. Cripps left dejected. Nehru, in turn, sent a gloomy letter to Johnson, describing the meeting as "entirely unsatisfactory" and indicating that the "very premises" of the discussions were unjustified.[48]

Apparently unaware of Hopkins' session with Churchill, Johnson reported the collapse of the talks to Washington, praising Cripps as sincere but lacking authority for even minor concessions. Roosevelt's Personal Representative charged that London, in effect, wanted the Congress to refuse, painting the British as defeatists, ready to lose India during the war to reclaim it at the peace treaty. Johnson praised Nehru as "magnificent in his cooperation with me. The President would like him and on most things they agree . . . He is our hope here."[49]

Faced with the collapse of the negotiations, Roosevelt reversed field. Although he had rebuffed Johnson's earlier appeal for help, he now instructed Harry Hopkins—still in England—to convey a blunt personal message urging Churchill to make every effort to prevent a breakdown in the talks. Refusing to agree with Churchill's assessment that "public opinion in the U.S. believes that the negotiations have broken down on general broad issues," Roosevelt stated:

> The general impression here is quite the contrary. The feeling is almost universally held that the deadlock has been due to the British Government's unwillingness to concede to the Indians the right of self-government, notwithstanding the willingness of the Indians to entrust technical, military and naval defense control to the competent British authorities.[50]

The President warned that if, after the failure of the talks, Japan successfully invaded India, "the prejudicial reaction on American public opinion can hardly be over-estimated." Asking that Churchill have Cripps postpone his departure, Roosevelt reiterated his suggestion that the British offer the Indians something like the Articles of Confederation. If the Indians rejected this proposal, Roosevelt said responsibility for failure "must clearly be placed on the Indian people and not upon the British Government."[51]

Such a strong message from Roosevelt required a careful response from the Prime Minister. Drafted with Hopkins' advice, Churchill's reply avoided the main thrust of the President's argument—that the British offer was not good enough. Churchill, instead, stated (incorrectly) that he could not do anything further since Cripps had already left India.[52] Churchill also asserted that he would have to place the issue before the War Cabinet. "He could not take responsibility for the defense of India if everything has again to be thrown into the melting pot at this critical juncture." Leaning on the private nature of Roosevelt's cable to "the former naval person," the Prime Minister said he would not bring the message to the Cabinet's attention unless the President asked. Appealing emotionally to Roosevelt, Churchill said, "Anything like a serious difference between you and me would break my heart and surely injure both our countries at the height of this terrible struggle."[53]

A day later, Roosevelt received his first and only communication from Jawaharlal Nehru. Sent through Louis Johnson, the message expressed sentiments not far from the President's own views. Although Indians preferred full "freedom and independence," Nehru said they were ready to accept a "truly national government that "could organize resistance on a popular basis." Nehru stressed, "How anxious and eager we were, and still are, to do our utmost for the defense of India. Our sympathies," Nehru wrote Roosevelt, are "with the forces fighting against fascism and for democracy and freedom."[54] Roosevelt sent Nehru a friendly and prompt reply. Saying he "was deeply gratified by the message," the President assured Nehru the United States would "to the utmost extent of its ability" help India "resist Japanese aggression." Roosevelt, however, made no mention of Indian independence.[55]

Although developments clearly upset the President, he felt able to press Churchill only so far on India without damaging the wartime alliance. When Secretary of the Interior Harold Ickes urged support for Indian independence, the President replied, "You are right about India, but it would be playing with fire if the British Empire told me to mind my own business."[56] Perhaps had Roosevelt intervened sooner with Churchill, heeding Johnson's 4 April plea, or had the fates not placed Harry Hopkins in England on 9 April, Johnson's compromise formula on defense arrangements might have won acceptance. Still the gap between what the British were willing to offer and what the Indian Congress wanted was so wide—and there was so much mistrust between the two sides—that an agreement over defense matters might soon have foundered over more fundamental differences. As Nehru told Louis Johnson in a frank private note, "It is exceedingly difficult to find a formula" to satisfy both Indian nationalists and the British for "between the two there is ineradicable and permanent conflict." Nehru wrote further, "The two cannot exist together or cooperate with each other, for each dislikes and distrusts the other."[57]

Quit India: British Arrest Congress Leadership

The failure of the Cripps mission left everyone despondent, except Winston Churchill, pleased that the effort improved the

British image in the United States without his having to relinquish any power to the Indians. In India, the nationalists regarded the British offer as inadequate and insincere, a view that has been echoed in later assessments by Nehru, Azad, and others.[58] Sir Stafford Cripps placed the blame for failure mainly on Mahatma Gandhi. Cripps believed the Congress Working Committee was prepared to accept Johnson's formulation on defense but after a two-hour telephone conversation with Gandhi voted 8–4 against the proposal.[59] The Labour Party leader refused to blame Churchill or Linlithgow for undercutting him, either from loyalty to the war effort or from ignorance of what happened behind his back.

Johnson remained in active contact with Nehru during the month after Cripps' departure, desperately trying to find some way to restart the negotiations. When Washington rejected a proposal by Johnson for a statement of Pacific War aims that would appeal to Indian nationalists,[60] he again urged the President to intervene with Churchill. "America alone can save India for the United Nations cause," Johnson cabled Roosevelt on 4 May.[61] Presumably with his earlier inability to move Churchill in mind, the President accepted the State Department's appraisal that Johnson's proposal was unlikely to succeed and would only make matters worse in India. He cabled back a polite but firm rejection.[62]

Johnson, who developed medical problems from the dust in India, underwent surgery in New Delhi before returning to the United States in mid-May to recuperate.[63] Once back in Washington, he stressed his opinion that the British, rather than the Indian Congress Party, were to blame for the political impasse. State Department officials, agreeing that Churchill may have been pleased with the breakdown of the talks, questioned that he actively undercut Cripps, as Johnson alleged.[64]

Once London got wind of Johnson's criticisms, Churchill countered his charges, cabling Harry Hopkins, "Frankly we do not think his comments have very much weight. . . .We do not at all relish the prospect of Johnson's return to India." When Hopkins replied that Johnson was sick and had no plans to go back to India, the British were relieved.[65] Two months later, Johnson resigned from the State Department to become head of General Dyestuffs Corporation. After the war, in the Truman administration, he returned to public life to become Secretary of Defense, losing this job after the start of the Korean War.

The British were, on the whole, more than satisfied with the impact of the Cripps Mission on American opinion, especially the shift in the US press from being critical of the British to criticizing the Indian Congress for rejecting the proposals. Graham Spry, a Canadian member of Cripps' party, toured the United States for two months to put across the British viewpoint. In his assessment, Spry asserted that Americans liked the Cripps proposals and thought that Congress should have accepted them.[66]

One person who seemed not to share this view, however, was the President. When Spry called at the White House on 1 May 1942, Roosevelt pointedly asked if the British Cabinet switched instructions during the later stages of the Cripps negotiations. Regarding Louis Johnson's role, Roosevelt stated he sent the Colonel to India to be "helpful." Smiling broadly, the President said, "Perhaps some of your people over there thought he was interfering."[67] Roosevelt also criticized the Cripps proposals when British Embassy Minister Sir Ronald Campbell came to lunch at the President's home at Hyde Park during the summer. Roosevelt told the British diplomat that London would have been wiser not to have proposed a post-war constitutional procedure, but—reiterating the view he put to Churchill in March—should have followed the American example of an interim system settling on constitutional forms only after a period of trial and error. The idea of offering parts of India the right to secede, the President said, "sounded terrible" to American ears after the Civil War.[68]

In the wake of the failure of the Cripps Mission, there was a widespread sense of gloom among Indians. Reflecting his frustration, Mahatma Gandhi unsettled Washington by a number of critical comments about the United States in his journal *Harijan*. "A never-ending stream of soldiers from America. . . . amounts in the end to American influence, if not American rule added to British," Gandhi wrote on 26 April.[69] A month later, the US Mission heard Gandhi was planning to launch a mass civil disobedience movement, apparently "unmoved" by warnings that such a movement could "cause absolute chaos, and make India an easy prey for the Japanese."[70] A worried

Nehru, just back from a holiday in the Himalayas, sent a message to Louis Johnson in Washington, warning that "events seem to be marching towards internal crisis."[71]

On 4 June, Nehru cabled Colonel Johnson that Gandhi did not want to "embarrass the present war effort. . . . American opinion should not misunderstand him; he has emphasized Indian independence as this is the only way for India and progressive nations to utilize India's great resources in cause of world freedom."[72] Fresh calls by Gandhi for the British to withdraw their troops from India and criticism of the moral basis for American participation in the war because of US race policies hardly reassured Washington, whatever Nehru might say about Gandhi's intentions.[73]

Apparently aware of the negative impact of his remarks, Gandhi began to modify his position in talking with American journalists and in his statements. In the 14 June *Harijan*, he wrote that an independent India would permit the Allies to stay. Gandhi also asked the United States to use its influence to help India with the British and followed up with a personal letter to President Roosevelt, which he sent through journalist Louis Fischer. Speaking as a "friend and well wisher of the Allies," Gandhi reiterated India's willingness to cooperate with the Allies—if given freedom. Gandhi probably spoiled the positive impact of his letter by undiplomatically saying Allied support for freedom and democracy seemed "hollow so long as . . . America has the Negro problem in her own home."[74]

The President's short reply to Gandhi, dated 1 August 1942, skirted the Mahatma's call for help. Roosevelt, instead, expressed the hope that "our common interest in democracy and righteousness will enable your countrymen and mine to make common cause against a common enemy."[75] By the time the President's message reached India, Gandhi was in jail. The letter rested for two years undelivered in the US Mission until the British released the Congress leader in late 1944.

As events in India headed toward crisis, the continuing flow of unfavorable war news placed an even greater premium on Allied unity and reduced the chances that Roosevelt would risk Churchill's ire by pressing him to make concessions to the Indian National Congress. In the Middle East, General Rommel's forces were advancing to within 100 miles of Alexandria, threatening to capture the Suez canal. Soviet armies were reeling under renewed Nazi attacks. Although the Japanese had yet to invade India, the threat remained.

On 14 July, the Congress Working Committee, despite strong opposition by Nehru, decided in favor of the civil disobedience campaign—known as the Quit India movement. The next step would be formal adoption of the proposal by the All-India Congress Committee. With the United States closely following developments, Nehru told US Mission Political Officer Lampton Berry that the Congress would be willing to cooperate in the war effort if Britain declared India independent and established a provisional government.[76] Nehru's ideas sounded surprisingly like President Roosevelt's own pet solution for India: form a provisional government and work out the details later.

Following up Nehru's comments and remarks to the press by Congress President Maulana Azad, the Mission on 21 July made a last ditch proposal to avert the civil disobedience campaign. The Mission suggested that the United States stand guarantor to a British pledge of Indian independence immediately after the war, and help the Indian political parties in setting up a provisional wartime government.[77] The medicine was too strong for the State Department, aware of the President's disinclination to challenge Churchill further on India. The proposal never made it out of the Near Eastern Division.[78] Roosevelt gave another sign of his unwillingness to intervene over India when he rejected a plea from Chiang Kai-shek.[79] The President cabled Churchill after turning down the Chinese leader, "We would not of course wish to pursue any course which undermines the authority of the Government of India at this critical time."[80]

Meeting in Bombay on 8 August, the All-India Congress Committee formally adopted the Quit India resolution, calling on Britain to withdraw or face a mass civil disobedience campaign. The day before, Acting Prime Minister Attlee informed President Roosevelt that the Government of India would arrest all Congress leaders as soon as the Congress adopted the resolution.[81] Despite some domestic pressure for US action, Washington remained silent about the arrests of the Congress Party leadership, in effect acquiescing in the British crackdown.

The American leadership could hardly fathom Gandhi's tactic of mounting the Quit India campaign—certain to disrupt the war effort—at the moment the struggle against the Axis hung in the balance. In US eyes, it was one thing to launch a civil disobedience movement as part of a peacetime struggle for freedom, quite another in the midst of world-wide war against fascism. Harry Hopkins told British Embassy Minister Campbell several days later that Roosevelt remained anxious about India, although he did not see what could be done. Even if Pandit Nehru might say all the right things, Roosevelt's adviser commented, "It would be Gandhi who would decide, and we all knew what Gandhi was."[82]

In India, the British authorities, to their dismay, faced widespread violence and sabotage after the arrests. A shaken Viceroy spoke alarmingly of the most serious challenge to the Raj since the 1857 mutiny.[83] By the end of August, however, the government regained control, with official statistics indicating more than 1,000 dead and 3,000 seriously injured in the Quit India disturbances. The British arrested over 100,000 nationalists, many for the duration of the war.[84] The summer of 1942 marked the high water mark of the Axis powers. On the frontiers of India, after the Japanese advance stalled in the jungles of Assam, the threat of invasion receded. In the Middle East, Montgomery defeated Rommel at El Alamein, driving him out of Egypt. The Russians stopped the Nazi tide at Stalingrad. Preparations went forward for the invasion of North Africa.

By this time, the US military build-up of India as a major staging area to supply the China theater and to reconquer Burma was beginning to move into gear. The United States established the China-Burma-India (CBI) command under the inspired, albeit acerbic, leadership of Lt. General Joseph Stilwell. With his headquarters in New Delhi, Stilwell planned the campaign for China, trained troops for the fight against the Japanese, and dispatched supplies for Chiang Kai-shek's forces by air over the Himalayan mountains, the famous "over-the-hump" route. By war's end, the United States had assigned 250,000 American soldiers to India, almost entirely in supply and engineer functions and mainly concentrated in eastern India, in Bengal, and Assam, where they built numerous airfields. Sensitive to potential Indian criticism that this large military presence meant US

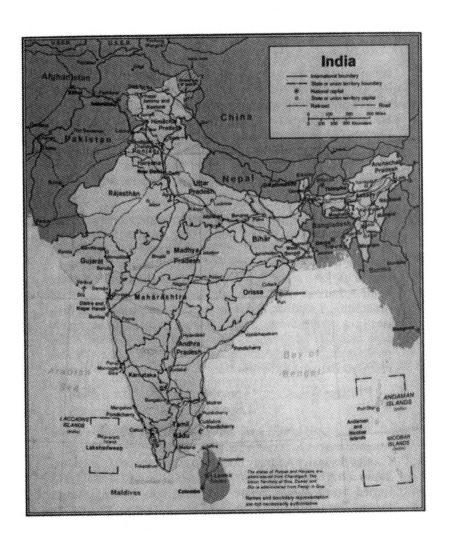

support for British policy, the President approved the State Department's statement, on 12 August, that US forces were not to become involved in Indian internal affairs and were in India only to fight the war against the Axis.[85]

Washington found it difficult to deal with this large-scale American military presence—by far the most extensive contact the United States had ever had with India. Although the war effort remained the primary concern, the US government did not want the presence of so many troops to suggest support for the way the British were dealing with India. Roosevelt never really found a satisfactory way around this problem—how to show America's backing for Indian aspirations for independence without offending the British, his principal wartime ally and partner.

Personal impressions of Americans about India and Indians of Americans were mixed. Many, like General Stilwell, depressed by what they found, unfavorably compared the Indians and the Chinese. "In China they have their heads up . . . appear to have an object in life. India is hopeless," Stilwell wrote.[86] Indians, in turn, found the American GIs more approachable, friendlier, and informal than the stand-offish British. They were, however, put off by US racial policies that rigidly separated GIs into segregated units according to color. A few publicized racial incidents against Indians by white GIs also offended Indian sensitivities.[87]

Phillips Mission: "Amazingly Radical for a Man Like Bill"

While Lord Linlithgow, in New Delhi, had a frosty view of Americans after his experience with Louis Johnson,[88] Churchill, Foreign Secretary Anthony Eden, and others thought the United States could be brought around if properly handled. The Viceroy fretted when White House aide Lauchlin Currie, passing through New Delhi, met with Shiva Rao, a leading pro-Congress journalist. For once, even a diehard like Churchill grew unsympathetic about the Viceroy's complaints. The Prime Minister commented that even though the British could probably block visits by Americans, couldn't the Viceroy "captivate and convert them?" The Prime Minister went on, "I always make a point of seeing these prominent Americans and make sure they get a good show, and the results have been most satisfactory."[89]

Anthony Eden considered Linlithgow's sour reaction to Currie mistaken. The Foreign Secretary, indeed, believed the United States should send a high-caliber envoy to India to replace Louis Johnson. "I am very doubtful whether we can expect to get the results we want unless the tale (about India) is told to the President and to America by an American," Eden wrote Leo Amery, head of the India Office.[90] The War Cabinet agreed with the idea of "more authoritative U.S. representation" in India on the understanding that the new envoy—unlike Louis Johnson—not become involved in the Indian political situation.[91]

During the fall, the British pressed the idea on Washington, and also on the reluctant Viceroy. After the Johnson episode, the British had had enough of political emissaries and wanted a senior career diplomat, preferably someone with entrée to President Roosevelt. London's favored choices were two of America's top diplomats, Joseph Grew, former Ambassador to Japan, and William Phillips, former Ambassador to Rome, then serving as the head of the London office of the Office of Strategic Services (OSS), the US wartime intelligence service. Within the State Department, officials were urging the same two names on the President, who seemed in no hurry to replace Johnson, perhaps—as Gary Hess wrote—because he was unsure how to handle India.[92]

In the meanwhile, pressure in Washington for doing something about India was building up. Although the US press approved the suppression of the "Quit India" movement, public opinion shortly swung in favor of a fresh effort by the British to negotiate with Indian nationalists. After Churchill virtually slammed the door in a bitter attack on the Indian Congress in parliament on 10 September, Roosevelt came under increasing pressure.[93] In October, the pot boiled over. In a nationwide radio address, former 1940 Republican presidential candidate Wendell Willkie—reporting on his around-the-world tour—focussed attention on India. During his talks in Asia, Willkie said:

> Many asked: what about India . . . by our silence on India
> we have already drawn heavily on the reservoir of good-will

in the East . . . They cannot ascertain from our government's wishy washy attitude toward the problem of India what we are likely to feel at the end of the war about the other hundred of millions of Eastern peoples.[94]

The Willkie speech forced Roosevelt's hand. Talking to the press the next day, the President reaffirmed that the Atlantic Charter's right of self-determination applied to all peoples— those subject to colonial rule as well as to Axis conquest. Secretary of State Hull told newsmen the United States was looking for ways to deal with the Indian problem. The President acted to fill the vacancy in New Delhi, selecting William Phillips to replace Johnson as his new Personal Representative. In early December, Roosevelt announced the Phillips appointment, playing down the idea the envoy was on anything than a normal diplomatic mission.[95]

If Louis Johnson typified the back-slapping, rough and tumble American politician, William Phillips personified the American East Coast aristocracy. Having spent his youth in a baronial mansion on Boston's Commonwealth Avenue, Phillips graduated from Harvard in 1902. He entered the diplomatic service a year later as private secretary to Joseph Choate, the Ambassador to London. Advancing rapidly up the diplomatic ladder, Phillips caught the eye of President Theodore Roosevelt and later served Woodrow Wilson as Assistant Secretary of State. Phillips and Franklin Roosevelt, Wilson's Assistant Secretary of the Navy, became friends.

In the 1920s, Phillips reached the top of the career service, becoming Under Secretary, the No. 2 post in the State Department, and later serving as envoy to the Netherlands, Belgium, and Canada. Roosevelt reappointed Phillips as Under Secretary in 1933, and four years later sent the Bostonian to the sensitive post of ambassador to Mussolini's Italy. After Phillips retired in 1941, Colonel William Donovan asked the diplomat to head the OSS's London office. Phillips had a reputation as cautious, conservative, and pro-British. It was hard to imagine "someone less likely than William Phillips to sympathize with the Indian nationalist leaders, much less with the masses."[96]

Before leaving London, Phillips talked with a wide circle of Indians and British, including V. K. Krishna Menon, the Congress Party's representative and a close friend of Jawaharlal

Nehru. Foreign Secretary Anthony Eden urged Phillips to "get the whole picture and report it to the President."[97] Winston Churchill followed his own advice about giving Americans a good show. Hosting a lunch for Phillips, he spoke with "great earnestness" about the assignment, saying "much might come of it," but offering few specifics. In a personal touch, the Prime Minister sent the new envoy his tattered copy of *Twenty-one Days in India*, a book Churchill himself read on the eve of his departure for India as a young cavalryman nearly half a century before.[98]

Phillips' instructions from Secretary Hull posed a difficult challenge: he was to try to move the British toward a political settlement with Indian nationalists without appearing to exert pressure or to suggest US intervention. Although Phillips thought the reference to a political settlement was "naive", he recognized that this task was the heart of his assignment.[99] The envoy arrived in India in January 1943. When his plane touched down at Karachi airfield, at India's western edge, the scope of American military operations at the air base surprised Phillips.

After reaching New Delhi, Phillips spent his initial days in viceregal luxury as Linlithgow's guest at the Viceroy's vast palace. The Viceroy hosted a formal dinner in Phillips' honor the night of his arrival. With Indian footmen standing behind each of the 38 guests at the long dining table, a five-man bagpipe orchestra provided music for the occasion. Taken aback, Phillips wrote in his diary, "Linlithgow had obviously adopted the outward forms of royalty to a pronounced degree."[100]

At first, the Viceroy reacted positively to Phillips. "It is hard," he wrote Amery, "to imagine a greater contrast to Johnson . . . (Phillips) seems to me better really than anything we could reasonably have hoped for."[101] Gradually this attitude changed as Phillips developed his personal views on India and the British role there. The first jolt came two weeks after the American's arrival. In a talk with the Viceroy, Phillips expressed his opinion that progress toward a provisional government and a political settlement would be a good thing. Phillips added that British officials in London encouraged him to help this process along. The discussion triggered a frantic exchange of telegrams between the Viceroy and India Office chief Amery, who assured the worried Linlithgow that somehow Phillips had misinterpreted what he heard in London, namely that the British would welcome his views, but not his intervention.[102]

Had the Viceroy been reading Phillips' letters to President Roosevelt, Linlithgow would have had even more grounds for discontent. Describing his initial impressions, on 22 January 1943, Phillips wrote that both Hindus and Muslims lacked confidence in British promises to free India. Although Phillips found many in Britain ready to grant independence if the Indians agreed among themselves, he was unsure if Churchill and the Viceroy—"old colonialists"—shared this view.[103]

In a February letter, Phillips was gloomier. "Reluctantly," he wrote the President, "I am coming to the conclusion that the Viceroy, presumably responsive to Churchill, is not in sympathy with any change in Britain's relationship with India."[104] The Ambassador worried that the presence of so many American troops in India, as well as his own assignment there, was creating the impression among Indians that the United States supported British imperialist policy. It was important, Phillips stressed, to correct this impression. When Phillips requested policy guidance from Washington, the State Department replied that the President wanted the envoy to return to Washington for consultations in May.[105]

On 10 February, Mahatma Gandhi who, along with the rest of the Congress leadership was in prison, commenced one of his famous fasts in order to attract world attention to the political situation in India. Despite the fact that Churchill belittled the impact that the fast would have in America, official Washington became agitated. On 16 February, Hull called in Halifax to express concern lest Gandhi die in custody. Two days later, he instructed Phillips to make an informal démarche with the Viceroy. Linlithgow took a rigid line; he was convinced "their present policy was right" and "faced with equanimity the possibility of Gandhi's death."[106]

When doubts mounted about the survival of the 73-year-old Gandhi, Secretary Hull called Lord Halifax again to the State Department. During that 20 February meeting, President Roosevelt telephoned to emphasize his "extreme embarrassment" about "sitting with hands folded doing nothing on an issue that was likely to have grave international reactions."

Stressing the undesirable consequences should the Indian leader die, Roosevelt wondered if it were not better to release Gandhi from prison. Although Halifax urged Hull not to publicize the démarche, the State Department let the press know that the Secretary had conveyed US concerns about Gandhi's condition.[107]

Writing the President a day after Gandhi ended the fast—defying predictions that he would die—Phillips said he was deeply moved by Gandhi's willingness to sacrifice himself for Indian independence and found unfeeling the Viceroy's cold reaction. He added that most Indians, believing Great Britain had no intention of granting independence, were turning to the United States for help in breaking the deadlock.

Phillips then proposed that the United States should respond positively by assisting Indian political groups in settling their differences. He suggested that Roosevelt, with British blessing, convene an all-party conference. Failure of the meeting would show that India was not ready for self-government. Phillips wrote he would discuss the idea further with the President when he returned to the United States.[108]

Surprised by Phillips' criticism of the British and sympathy for the Indian nationalist cause, Roosevelt told Harry Hopkins that Phillips' suggestion was "amazingly radical for a man like Bill." Although the President did not respond directly, he asked Hopkins to show the message from Phillips to the visiting Anthony Eden.[109] One can only surmise that Eden, after reading the letter, may have regretted having promoted the assignment of Phillips so vigorously.

In order to gain more detailed impressions of India before returning for consultations, Phillips traveled widely in March and April. The fact that the Congress Party leadership was in jail limited the scope of his contacts with the nationalists. The American envoy made a point, nonetheless, of seeing Congress supporters whenever possible. Before visiting Bombay, Phillips requested permission to see Gandhi, who was still in jail. When the Viceroy refused, the envoy accepted the turndown in apparent good grace.

Among the political figures Phillips met was Mohammed Ali Jinnah, the leader of the Muslim League, the principal political organization for India's 100 million Muslims. Although Jinnah impressed the American diplomat as being highly articulate and intelligent during their nearly four-hour session, Phillips disliked his proposal for Pakistan—the separate Muslim homeland that Jinnah was demanding. "The more I studied Jinnah's Pakistan, the less it appealed to me as the answer to India's communal problem," Phillips wrote, "To break India into two separate nations would weaken both."[110] History has proven him right.

As the date for Phillips' departure drew nearer, he renewed the request to see Mahatma Gandhi. Phillips believed a meeting with the jailed Indian leader would help "make Indians feel that America is with them and in a position to go beyond mere public assurances of friendship." Phillips concluded his usefulness would be over if the record did not show he seriously tried to meet Gandhi.[111]

Tipped off to Phillips' intention by the indiscreet American Minister in Afghanistan, Cornelius Van Engert, the Viceroy informed London he would not agree to a Phillips-Gandhi meeting. Increasingly exasperated, Linlithgow asserted, "I am quite sure that the only possible line to adopt with the Americans over this Indian affair is that it is our affair and not theirs." Although Linlithgow personally found Phillips friendly and distinguished, the Viceroy worried about the envoy's talks with numerous Indian political leaders. London reassured the Viceroy. Anthony Eden promised to take a tough line during an upcoming visit to Washington. Churchill was ready to cable Harry Hopkins.[112]

In exchanges with the State Department, Phillips was skeptical of the Viceroy's agreeing to his request, but pressed for official authorization. He wanted to make clear that America and the British were not marching together on the question of self-government for India. Sumner Welles remained stubbornly negative, arguing that the British would interpret an official request for a meeting as a change in US policy toward India. In the end, Secretary Hull gave half a loaf, agreeing that Phillips make the request to see Gandhi on a "personal" basis.[113]

Although annoyed by Washington's lukewarm backing, Phillips pressed ahead. An unusual opportunity presented itself when Linlithgow invited the American for a tiger hunt in the Himalayan foothills near the Viceroy's mountain lodge at Dehra

Dun. Swaying back and forth together on top of an elephant for three hours during the tiger hunt, the envoy pressed Linlithgow to agree to his seeing Gandhi. The Viceroy refused to budge although he did assent to Phillips' telling the press about the request. "My visit to Dehra Dun," the envoy wrote, "had been a hunt for Gandhi rather than a tiger. I had failed in my principal objective and had to be content with second best."[114]

Disappointed but not surprised, Phillips returned to New Delhi. At a cocktail party for the press before Phillips' departure, Herbert Matthews of the *New York Times*, primed by the envoy, asked about the Gandhi meeting.[115] Phillips lost most of his guests as soon as he responded that he had asked the Viceroy to see Gandhi and had been turned down. "There was an immediate rush for the doors to break the news," Phillips wrote, "My mission was over."[116] As he hoped, the news of his attempt to meet Gandhi received positive press play in India, improving the US image as well as Phillips' own.[117]

Nonetheless, the envoy left India frustrated. Phillips summed up his pessimistic impressions in a 19 April letter to the President. The British were sitting "pretty." They had locked up the Congress leaders and would agree to no political change during the war. Militarily, the British in India were not likely to offer more than "token assistance" for the war effort. The United States would have to bear the burden. Looking to the future, Phillips worried that, in Asian eyes, America seemed to be supporting British imperialism. He voiced concern about a "vast bloc of Oriental peoples" with a "growing dislike and distrust of the Occidental." The only remedy, Phillips argued, was "to try with every means in our power to make Indians feel that America is with them and in a position to go beyond mere public assurances of friendship."[118]

On 14 May, Phillips arrived in Washington, briefly met the President, and then drafted a summary report for Roosevelt. This report forcefully argued that India was unlikely to cooperate fully in the war effort unless the British made a major gesture toward independence. The United States should have a voice, Phillips asserted, not mutely accept the British view that "this is none of your business."[119] Roosevelt agreed with Phillips' analysis, but knowing Churchill's views on India, was reluctant to intervene directly. If a year earlier during the Cripps mission—

when the United States possessed far greater leverage—Roosevelt failed to budge the Prime Minister, there was no realistic prospect he could do so in May 1943 with the tide beginning to turn in favor of the Allies and India no longer in imminent danger of invasion. Phillips was sufficiently persuasive that the President agreed to recommend that Churchill send Eden to India to take soundings with all leaders, including Gandhi. Roosevelt later passed on the idea to British press baron Lord Beaverbrook, who agreed to raise it with Churchill—apparently without result.[120]

Since Churchill happened to be visiting Washington at the time, Roosevelt asked Phillips to present his views frankly to the Prime Minister. Their meeting at the British Embassy was not pleasant. After Phillips outlined his ideas, the Prime Minister paced back and forth across the room and angrily confronted the American: "My answer to you is this: Take India if that is what you want. Take it by all means! But I warn you that if I open the door a crack there will be the greatest bloodbath in all history. Mark my words," he said, shaking a finger at Phillips, "I prophesied the present war, and I prophesy a bloodbath."[121] Phillips wrote in his diary, "It was helpless to argue. It is only too clear he has a complex on India from which he will not and cannot be shaken."[122]

After his stormy session with Churchill, Phillips lunched at the White House with the President. Although the Ambassador was taken aback by Churchill's angry reaction, Roosevelt seemed "rather amused but glad that I had spoken so frankly." Without the President's having to risk a direct clash with Churchill over India, the message had been put across. That evening Phillips saw Roosevelt again over drinks "as two old friends." Phillips raised the question of his returning to India, saying he saw little point unless a change in the British attitude enabled him to be of help in negotiating a settlement.[123] Roosevelt agreed; he knew there was little the United States could do as long as Churchill continued to dig in his heels.

Phillips never went back to New Delhi, although he technically remained the President's Personal Representative for India until his retirement in March 1945, just weeks before Roosevelt's death. In the fall of 1943, Phillips returned to London, assuming new responsibilities as General Eisenhower's

Political Adviser, a function he filled until his retirement. Phillips maintained an active interest in Indian developments—and sympathy for nationalist aspirations. In keeping with Roosevelt's policy, he undertook no initiatives with the British authorities.[124]

The war produced two unusual US envoys to India, Louis Johnson and William Phillips. Despite their radically different backgrounds and styles—Johnson, the political wheeler-dealer who hardly knew where India was, and Phillips, the consummate diplomat, four times a US envoy and twice Under Secretary of State—they reached the same conclusions: Both believed the British did not want to give up India. Both thought the United States should actively press for Indian independence. Both ultimately failed to move President Roosevelt into a battle that he was likely to lose with the closest wartime ally of the United States.

1943-1945: Roosevelt Remains Inactive on India

In Phillips' absence, leadership of the American diplomatic mission in New Delhi fell to George Merrell, a more junior career diplomat. Even though the staff continued to report closely on the Indian situation, remaining critical of the British attitude, US diplomats in India—like Phillips in London—were passive, rather than active, observers. In late 1943, Linlithgow retired, replaced by Lord Wavell, the previous Commander-in-Chief. Although more liberal, Wavell was kept on a tight leash by Churchill, who remained adamantly opposed to political concessions. Thus, a new Viceroy brought no change in Britain's policy of standing pat on India.

By the end of 1943, President Roosevelt was becoming uneasy about reports in the press and from the Mission in New Delhi that the US unwillingness or inability to influence British policy—and the large-scale presence of American troops—was causing growing anti-American sentiments among Indian nationalists. To counter this, the President took the initiative on 4 February 1944 to declare again that the sole reason for the American military presence in India was to defeat the Japanese.[125]

Roosevelt's action helped to some extent in allaying Indian disappointment about US policy. A few months later, a leak of

William Phillips' final report to the President gave an even stronger boost to US standing with Indians. After columnist Drew Pearson on 25 July published parts of the envoy's report to Roosevelt, the story created a sensation in India and in Britain—although it caused little reaction in the United States. Phillips' scathing comments about the British and his support for nationalist aspirations delighted Indians. The British were furious about Phillips' depiction of them as unbending imperialists scarcely concerned about winning the war against Japan.[126]

When the British pressed for an official disavowal by the US government, Hull successfully argued with Roosevelt against this on the grounds that the State Department agreed with Phillips' views.[127] The US refusal to repudiate Phillips angered the British, boosting US stock further in India. Roosevelt told Phillips' wife that he assumed Sumner Welles was the source of the leak. After leaving the State Department in 1943, Welles became highly critical of the British handling of India—in contrast to his strongly pro-British stance when he was Under Secretary.[128]

Pearson and Senator "Happy" Chandler of Kentucky stirred additional controversy by leaking some Government of India telegrams, including one that said Phillips would be persona non grata if he tried to return to India. Word of this message—apparently leaked by an Indian member of Bajpai's staff—proved enormously embarrassing to all concerned. When Phillips tried to retire in August 1944, supposedly for family reasons, Roosevelt decided the envoy should remain as his Personal Representative for India in view of the fuss. By underscoring the continuing policy difference with the British, the President's refusal to accept Phillips' resignation provided a further fillip to US standing in India.[129]

Just before Christmas 1944, the Indian nationalist cause in the United States received a substantial boost from the extended visit of Jawaharlal Nehru's sister, Vijaya Lakshmi Pandit—her flight to New York arranged by US air force commander General Stratemeyer with the blessing of the State Department.[130] Although Mrs. Pandit's ostensible purpose was to see two daughters at college in New England and to attend a Pacific Affairs conference, prominent friends of the Indian nationalist cause, such as author Pearl Buck and *Time-Life* publisher Henry Luce, introduced Mrs. Pandit to many top Americans. Nehru's sister also undertook a well-publicized and successful cross-country speaking tour on behalf of Indian independence. Partly in response to the pressure Mrs. Pandit generated, the State Department reaffirmed US interest in a political settlement in India. Acting Secretary of State Joseph Grew told the press on 29 January 1945 that the United States "would be happy to contribute in any appropriate manner to a satisfactory settlement. We have close ties of friendship, both with the British and with the people of India."[131] When the President was attending the Yalta conference, Mrs. Eleanor Roosevelt invited Mrs. Pandit to lunch at the White House—a further sign of US desire to keep on good terms with Indian nationalists.[132]

Just a month before his death, Roosevelt spoke again of his concern about colonialism in Asia, this time in a talk with State Department adviser Charles Taussig. The President commented that much of the Orient is "ruled by a handful of whites and they resent it." The President told Taussig, "Our goal must be to help them achieve independence—1,100,000,000 potential enemies are dangerous. Churchill doesn't understand this."[133]

"Churchill Doesn't Understand This"

These words—"Churchill doesn't understand this"—summed up the problem Roosevelt faced throughout the war in dealing with India. Supporting nationalist hopes for independence and worried about post-war Asian attitudes toward the United States, the President strongly disagreed with the standpat imperialism of his ally Winston Churchill. At the time of the Cripps Mission—when India itself was threatened with invasion—Roosevelt pressed Churchill hard to grant India de facto independence. Their written exchanges over India are among the sharpest between the two wartime leaders who so admired and respected each other.

Gandhi's tactics—appalling to Americans—of launching the Quit India civil disobedience campaign at the height of the war in August 1942 and his earlier criticism of the United States played into the hands of British hardliners. Winning the war came first in Washington. Those opposing the war effort—in effect what Gandhi was doing although he claimed he was not—got short shrift. Had the Indian National Congress not launched the Quit India movement, Roosevelt might have been willing to press more vigorously for further negotiations. With the entire Congress leadership in jail, there was, instead, little Roosevelt could do given Churchill's rigidly imperialist attitude.

Aware US standing among the nationalists was slipping, Roosevelt worried about the implications for future US-Indian relations. The President succeeded—to some extent—in distancing the United States from the British through symbolic gestures, such as statements on the role of the US military in 1942 and 1944, sending Phillips in 1943, and then refusing to disown the leaked Phillips report in 1944.

If the US attitude toward Indian nationalism was ambivalent—support for independence yet disappointment over the attitude of the nationalists toward the war effort—the Indian reaction to US policy was similarly ambiguous. The Indians appreciated the indications of US support for the nationalist cause. Johnson's and Phillips' views were known during the war. Roosevelt's sharp exchanges with Churchill were revealed in later years. At the same time, Indians felt let down by the United States, especially after Roosevelt refused to intervene in August 1942 over the Quit India movement and thereafter remained unwilling to press the British to make further political concessions.

Between Indian nationalists and Americans, the priorities ultimately differed. For Indian Congress Party leaders, even for those like Nehru who were emotionally supportive of the Allied cause, the top priority remained that of ending British rule and gaining India's independence. For Roosevelt, winning the war was the top order of business. Everything else came second, including independence for India if—as was the case—this would risk a serious rupture with his British allies. Because Indians and Americans expected—and thought they deserved—each other's support, the course of events during the war sharpened the mutual disappointment. This first extended interaction between the United States and India foreshadowed the frustrations that would follow during the next five decades.

NOTES

1. Gary Hess, *America Encounters India, 1941-1947* (Baltimore: Johns Hopkins, 1971), pp. 5-6.

2. G. Bhagat, *Americans in India, 1784-1860* (New York: NYU Press, 1970), pp. 3-84.

3. Harold Isaacs, *Scratches on Our Mind* (White Plains, NY: M.E. Sharpe, 1980), p. 265.

4. Ibid., p. 269.

5. Ibid., pp. 283-85; Hess, p. 159.

6. Ibid., p. 14.

7. The term "Pandit," an indication of respect for a learned man in India, was applied to Nehru because of his caste—the Kashmiri Brahmins—and because he was in his own right a person of unusual erudition. He wrote his sensitive autobiography and the later *Discovery of India* while detained in British prisons.

8. Kenton Clymer, "Jawaharlal Nehru and the United States, the Preindependence Years," *Diplomatic History* 14 (Spring 1990): p. 147. Clymer's interesting article stressed the influence of Roger Baldwin, founder of the American Civil Liberties Union, on Nehru's early thinking about US foreign policy. An outspoken radical, Baldwin castigated US dollar diplomacy in Latin America in the 1920s. After Nehru and Baldwin became close friends, many of Baldwin's criticisms about US foreign policy were reflected in Nehru's writings and statements.

9. Christopher Thorne, *Allies of a Kind, The United States, Britain and the War Against Japan, 1941-1945* (London: Hamish Hamilton, 1978), p. 62.

10. Ibid., pp. 62-63.

11. Cordell Hull, *Memoirs,* vol. II (New York: Macmillan, 1948), p. 1482.

12. A member of the prestigious Indian Civil Service, the elite cadre that filled key positions in the Indian government, Bajpai found himself in an awkward situation as Agent-General. The British regarded him with some suspicion as favoring independence; the nationalists considered him a British stooge. After a period in limbo after the war, Nehru named Bajpai the first Secretary General of the External Affairs ministry. His son, K. Shankar Bajpai, served in Washington as Indian Ambassador in the 1980s.

13. *Foreign Relations of the United States (FRUS), 1941,* vol. III, pp. 170-74; British Embassy Aide-Mémoire, 17 April 1941; letter from Ambassador Lord Halifax to Under Secretary Welles, 28 June 1941; Welles letter to Halifax, 2 July 1941; Halifax letter to Welles, 15 July 1941; State Department press release, 21 July 1941; and telegram from the State Department to Ambassador Winant (London), 16 September 1941.

14. Ibid., pp. 176-77, memorandum by Assistant Secretary A.A. Berle, 5 May 1941.

15. Ibid., p. 178; Memorandum by Secretary Hull of a conversation with Lord Halifax, 7 May 1941; Cordell Hull, *Memoirs,* vol. II, p. 1483.

16. *FRUS, 1941,* vol. III, pp. 178-81; telegram from Ambassador Winant to State Department, 1 August 1941; Memorandum from Assistant Secretary Berle to Under Secretary Welles, 5 August 1941; and Memorandum from Welles to Secretary Cordell Hull, 6 August 1941.

17. Elliott Roosevelt, *As He Saw It* (New York: Duell, Sloan, and Pearce, 1946), pp. 35-37. Some historians have questioned Elliot Roosevelt's version since other accounts of the Atlantic Charter meetings—by Robert Sherwood, Sumner Welles, or Churchill himself—failed to speak of a sharp exchange over India. Hess, at first shared this skepticism, but told the author he has since changed his mind and has accepted Elliot Roosevelt's report as accurately conveying the flavor of the discussion regarding India.

18. Ibid.

19. *FRUS, 1941,* vol. III, pp. 181-84, telegram from Ambassador Winant to State Department, 4 November 1941.

20. Ibid., pp. 184-87, memorandum by Wallace Murray, Near East Division Chief, 7 November 1941, and memorandum from Welles to Hull, 15 November 1941.

21. Ray S. Cline, *US Army in World War II. Washington Command Post: The Operations Division* (Washington: Government Printing Office, 1951), pp. 144-45, quoted in M.S. Vekataramani and B.K. Shrivastava, *Quit India, The American Response to the 1942 Struggle* (New Delhi: Vikas, 1979), pp. 53-54.

22. Winston S. Churchill, *The Hinge of Fate* (Boston: Houghton Miflin Company, 1950), pp. 208-09.

23. Robert S. Sherwood, *Roosevelt and Hopkins* (New York: Harper & Brothers, 1950), p. 512.

24. *FRUS, The Conferences at Washington and Casablanca, 1942 and 1943,* pp. 368-70, memoranda from Hopkins to Roosevelt, and Roosevelt to Hull, 27 December 1941.

25. *FRUS, 1942,* vol. I, pp. 606-07, memorandum from Assistant Secretary Long to Secretary Hull, 25 February 1942.

26. Ibid., p. 608, Harriman to the President, 26 February 1942; W. Averell Harriman and Elie Abel, *Special Envoy to Churchill and Stalin, 1941-1946* (New York: Random House, 1975), pp. 129-30.

27. Nicholas Mansergh, ed., *The Transfer of Power,* vol. I (London: His Majesty's Stationary Office, 1970-1983), pp. 110-12, memorial on India sent by Cripps to the War Cabinet, 2 February 1942.

28. Robin J. Moore, *Churchill, Cripps and India, 1939-1945* (Oxford: Clarendon Press, 1979), provides an excellent account of the Cripps Mission.

29. Mansergh, vol. 1, pp. 394-95, Churchill to Linlithgow, 10 March 1942.

30. *FRUS, 1942*, vol. I, p. 612, Churchill to Roosevelt, 4 March 1942.

31. Ibid., pp. 615-16; Roosevelt to Churchill, 10 March 1942.

32. Robert Sherwood, wartime speech writer for the President, wrote later that probably the only part of the cable with which Churchill agreed was the final sentence that India was none of Roosevelt's business. (*Sherwood*, p. 512.)

33. *FRUS, 1942*, vol. I, p. 613, Department of State Press Release, 6 March 1942.

34. The State Department originally suggested Johnson be called Commissioner, like his predecessor Thomas Wilson, but the West Virginian balked. In the Virginias, he explained, the title of Commissioner "meant one thing and one thing only: a conspicuously unsuccessful lawyer." As an alternative, Johnson readily accepted the title of President's Personal Representative. *FRUS, 1942*, vol. I, pp. 616-17; Memorandum by Assistant Secretary of State Howland Shaw of Conversation with Colonel Louis A. Johnson, 11 March 1942.

35. M.S. Vekataramani and B.K. Shrivastava, *Quit India, The American Response to the 1942 Struggle* (New Delhi: Vikas, 1979), p. 104.

36. Moore, pp. 92-93.

37. Mansergh vol. I, pp. 600-02, Cripps to Churchill, 1 April 1942.

38. Ibid., p. 607, Winston Churchill to Cripps, 2 April 1942.

39. Ibid., p. 619, Bajpai to Viceroy, 2 April 1942.

40. Moore, p. 106.

41. Mansergh, vol. I, pp. 665-66, 691, Olaf Caroe record of meeting with Colonel Johnson, 6 April 1942, and Linlithgow to Amery, 7 April 1942.

42. *FRUS, 1942*, vol. I, pp. 626-27, 628, Johnson to Secretary Hull and President Roosevelt, 4 April 1942, and Under Secretary Welles to Johnson, 4 April 1942.

43. Ibid., p. 630, Johnson to Hull, 9 April 1942.

44. Mansergh, vol. I, p. 697. Cripps to Churchill, 8 April 1942.

45. Ibid., pp. 697-98, Linlithgow to Amery, 9 April 1942; Moore, pp. 101-03, 112.

46. Sherwood, p. 524. Sherwood's account is based on Hopkins' notes of his conversation with Churchill. Hopkins cabled the President he felt it important to play down Johnson's role because of the danger the British might reject a proposal the public thought came from Roosevelt. *FRUS, 1942*, vol. I, p. 629, Hopkins to Roosevelt, 9 April 1942.

47. *Transfer of Power,* vol. I. pp. 704-07. Churchill to Cripps, 9 April 1942; conclusions of 9 April 1942 War Cabinet meeting; and cable from War Cabinet to Cripps, 9 April, 1942.

48. Moore, pp. 115-19.

49. *FRUS, 1942* vol. I, pp. 631-32. Johnson to Roosevelt and Hull, 11 April 1942.

50. Ibid., pp. 633-34, Roosevelt to Harry Hopkins, 11 April 1942.

51. Ibid.

52. Ibid., pp. 634-35, Churchill to Roosevelt, 12 April 1942; Moore, pp. 130. When Churchill received Roosevelt's message, Cripps was, in fact, just departing Delhi for Karachi where he was to overnight before leaving India. In other words, had Churchill wished, he could have instructed Cripps to return to Delhi to resume the discussions.

53. *FRUS, 1942,* vol. I, p. 635, Churchill to Roosevelt, 12 April 1942.

54. Ibid., pp. 635-37, telegram from Johnson to Roosevelt, transmitting message from Nehru, 13 April 1942.

55. Ibid., p. 637, message from Roosevelt to Nehru, 15 April 1942.

56. Hess, p. 82, quoting correspondence between Roosevelt and Ickes, 10 August and 12 November 1942.

57. *Selected Works of Jawaharlal Nehru,* vol. 12, (New Delhi: Orient Longman, 1979), p. 301; Confidential Note sent by Nehru to Louis Johnson, 11 May 1942.

58. See *inter alia* Maulana Abul Kalam Azad, *India Wins Freedom* (New York: Longmans, Green and Co., 1960), pp. 54-81; Jawaharlal Nehru, *Discovery of India* (London: Meridan Books, 1956), pp. 456-74; and V.P. Menon, *The Transfer of Power* (Princeton: Princeton University Press, 1957), pp. 114-38.

59. *Mansergh, 1942,* vol. II, pp. 341-43, Sir Stafford Cripps' report on his Mission to the War Cabinet, 6 July 1942.

60. *FRUS, 1942,* vol. I, pp. 644-45, State Department to Johnson, 27 April 1942.

61. Ibid., pp. 648-49, Johnson to the President and the Secretary, 4 May 1942.

62. Ibid., pp. 642, 648-49, 650, Johnson to President and Hull, 25 April, 4 May 1942 and Roosevelt to Johnson, 8 May 1942; Hess, pp. 54-58.

63. *FRUS, 1942,* vol. I, pp. 651, 653, 654: Johnson to Hull, 9 May 1942; Hull to Johnson, 13 May 1942; and Johnson to Roosevelt and Hull, 14 May 1942.

64. Ibid., p. 658-62. Memorandum of 26 May 1942 meeting in the State Department with Louis Johnson, drafted by Calvin Oakes of the Near Eastern Division.

65. *Mansergh, 1942*, vol. II, pp. 145, 156, 164: Churchill to Hopkins, 28 May 1942; Churchill to Linlithgow, 31 May 1942; Churchill to Hopkins, 31 May 1942; and Hopkins to Churchill, 1 June 1942.

66. Ibid., pp. 471-73, Spry's report of his ten weeks in the United States which Cripps transmitted to the War Cabinet, 27 July 1942.

67. Ibid., pp. 89-92, note by Graham Spry after his meeting with President Roosevelt, 1 May 1942.

68. Ibid., pp 576-77, Sir Ronald Campbell to Alexander Cadogan, 5 August 1942.

69. *Harijan,* 26 April 1942.

70. *FRUS, 1942*, vol. I, p. 663, US Mission New Delhi to the President, Secretary, and Colonel Johnson, 21 May 1942

71. Ibid., pp. 664-65, US Mission in New Delhi to the President, Secretary, and Louis Johnson, 25 May 1942.

72. Ibid., pp. 667-69, Nehru to Louis Johnson, 4 June 1942.

73. *Harijan,* 3, 24, and 31 May 1942.

74. *FRUS, 1942*, vol. I, pp. 677-78, letter from Gandhi to President Roosevelt, 1 July 1942.

75. Ibid., pp. 702-03, Roosevelt's 1 August letter to Gandhi transmitted on 5 August from the State Department to the US Mission in New Delhi.

76. Ibid., pp. 685-89, telegrams from US Mission New Delhi to the State Department, 17 and 18 July 1942.

77. Ibid., pp. 690-94, US Mission New Delhi to State Department, 21 July 1942.

78. Hess, p. 73.

79. *FRUS, 1942*, vol. I, pp. 698-700, 705: Message from Chiang Kai-shek, 28 July 1942; Roosevelt to Churchill, 29 July 1942, and Roosevelt to Chiang Kai-shek, 8 August 1942.

80. Churchill, p. 508, Roosevelt to Churchill, 9 August 1942. Roosevelt's message referred to his correspondence with Chiang Kai-shek.

81. *FRUS, 1942*, vol. I, pp. 703-05, Attlee to Roosevelt, 7 August 1942.

82. *Transfer of Power. 1942*, vol. II, pp. 674-75, Campbell to Eden, 12 August 1942.

83. Ibid., pp. 853-54, Linlithgow to Churchill, 31 August 1942.

84. Hess, pp. 87-88.

85. Ibid., p. 82; Hull, p. 1489; *FRUS, 1942*, vol. I, pp. 720-21.

86. *Stilwell Papers*, 4 January 1943, quoted in Thorne, p. 239.

87. Hess, pp. 136-37.

88. *Mansergh, 1942*, vol. III, pp. 15-19, Linlithgow to Churchill, 22 September 1942.

89. Ibid., pp. 909-10, 933-34, Churchill to Linlithgow, 5 September 1942 and Linlithgow to Churchill, 10 September 1942.

90. Ibid., pp. 785-86, Eden to Amery, 22 August 1942.

91. Ibid., pp. 35-36, conclusions of the 24 September 1942 meeting of the War Cabinet.

92. Hess, p. 95.

93. *Mansergh,* vol. II, pp. 969-70, Halifax to Eden, 16 September 1942; Hess, pp. 88-89.

94. *New York Times,* 27 October 1942.

95. Although the British fought unsuccessfully to downplay Phillips' diplomatic status, they finally conceded him ambassadorial rank as the President's Personal Representative in charge of the US diplomatic mission in New Delhi. In view of Phillips' seniority and prior diplomatic experience, the British efforts seemed petty but illustrated their continuing sensitivity about the American official presence in India. (*Mansergh,* vol. III, pp. 287, 292, 300, and 332, Eden to Halifax, 20 November 1942, and Halifax to Eden, 22 and 25 November and 3 December 1942.

96. Kenton Clymer, "The Education of William Phillips," *Diplomatic History 8* (Winter 1984): p. 19.

97. William Phillips, *Ventures in Diplomacy* (Boston: Beacon Press, 1952), p. 345.

98. Ibid., pp. 345-47.

99. Ibid., p. 344.

100. Ibid., pp. 348-50.

101. *Mansergh,* vol. III, p. 487, Linlithgow to Amery, 11 January 1943.

102. Ibid., pp. 554-56, 560-61, 569-70, 586: Linlithgow to Amery, 26 January 1943; Amery to Linlithgow, 29 January 1943; Amery to Linlithgow, 1 February 1943; and Linlithgow to Amery, 5 February 1943.

103. *FRUS, 1943,* vol. IV, pp. 180-84, letter from Phillips to Roosevelt, 22 January 1943.

104. Ibid., p. 187, Phillips to State Department, 10 February 1943.

105. Phillips, pp. 362-65. *FRUS, 1943,* vol. IV, pp. 187-92, 194: letter from Phillips to Roosevelt, 11 February 1943; telegram from Phillips to State Department, 12 February 1943; and telegram from State Department to Phillips, 16 February 1943.

106. Ibid., pp. 195-96, Phillips to State Department, 18 February 1943; vol. III, pp. 687-90, Mansergh Linlithgow to Amery, 19 February 1943.

107. *FRUS, 1943,* vol. IV, pp. 196-97, 199-200, Hull to Phillips and memorandum of conversation between Hull and Halifax, 20 February

1943; Mansergh, vol III, pp. 687-92, 694-96, 709-10, 712-13: Linlith-gow to Amery, 19 February 1943; Amery to Linlithgow, 19 February 1943; Amery to Linlithgow, 21 February 1943; and Halifax to Eden, 21 February 1943.

108. Phillips, pp. 379-80.

109. Hess, p. 106.

110. Phillips, p. 359; *FRUS, 1943,* vol. IV, pp. 213-14, Phillips to State Department, 7 April 1943.

111. Phillips, pp. 379-80.

112. *Mansergh,* vol. III, pp. 768, 783, 817-19: Linlithgow to Amery, 8 March 1943; Amery to Linlithgow, 11 March 1943, and Linlithgow to Amery, 16 March 1943.

113. *FRUS, 1943,* vol. IV, pp. 211-15: Phillips to State Department, 2 April 1942; memo from Political Affairs Adviser Murray to Welles, 6 April 1943; memo from Welles to Hull, 6 April 1943; Phillips to State Department, 14 April 1943; and Hull to Phillips, 14 April 1943.

114. Phillips, pp. 382-83.

115. Clymer, pp. 30-31.

116. Phillips, p. 383.

117. Clymer, p. 31.

118. *FRUS, 1943,* vol. IV, pp. 217-20, Phillips to Roosevelt, 17 April 1943.

119. Ibid., pp. 220-22, Phillips to Roosevelt, 14 May 1943; Phillips, pp. 387-88.

120. Clymer, p. 31.

121. Phillips, pp. 389-90. Churchill's own report to London differed in tone but not substance from Phillips's account. The session was "most depressing and unsatisfactory," Churchill cabled Attlee and Amery. A "weak, agreeable man . . . Mr. Phillips is a friend of the President and will I have no doubt do a certain amount of harm. He does not think he will return to India. I hope he is right." *Mansergh Transfer of Power,* vol. III, pp. 1003-04, Churchill to Attlee and Amery, 23 May 1943.

122. William Phillips Diary, 22 May 1943. Phillips Papers, Hough-ton Library, Harvard University.

123. Phillips, p. 391.

124. Hess, p.112.

125. Hull, p. 1494, and Hess, p. 137.

126. Ibid., pp. 142-46.

127. *FRUS, 1944,* vol. V, pp. 241-42, letter from British Minister Campbell to Under Secretary Stettinius, 8 August 1944, and memoran-dum from Secretary Hull to Roosevelt, 15 August 1944.

128. Hess, p. 142.

129. Ibid., pp. 144-48; Thorne, p. 476; *FRUS, 1944,* vol. V, pp. 243-47: memorandum of conversation of meeting with British Ambassador Halifax, 2 September 1944; text of UPI News Report Extract regarding Senator Chandler's release of British telegram about Phillips, 2 September 1944; and Mission New Delhi telegram to State Department, 4 September 1944.

130. Vijaya Lakshmi Pandit, *The Scope of Happiness: A Personal Memoir* (New York: Crown Publishers, 1979), pp. 186-87.

131. *FRUS, 1945,* vol. VI, p. 249, text of Grew's 29 January 1945 press conference remarks.

132. Hess, p. 152.

133. *FRUS, 1945,* vol. I, pp. 121-24, memorandum of conversation with Roosevelt. 15 March 1945.

Chapter II

Truman: Dealing with Neutralism

Harry S. Truman—even the name sounded unfamiliar—assumed the presidency with the nation, and indeed the world, stunned by the death of Franklin D. Roosevelt, who led the United States for twelve difficult years through the Depression and World War II. A compromise candidate for Vice President, Truman was in office barely a month when he became the President. The former Senator from Missouri had little experience in foreign affairs and no special knowledge of Asia or India.

One of his first tasks, just ten days after Roosevelt's death, was to convene the San Francisco Conference to establish the United Nations, the post-war organization on which Roosevelt placed such high hopes as a mechanism for keeping the peace. Thanks to Roosevelt's pressure in December 1941, India was a founder-member—although still under British rule in April 1945. The Indian delegation, selected by the Viceroy Lord Wavell, included Indian supporters of the British Raj, but no Congress nationalists. Except for Gandhi, released in late 1944, the party leadership was still languishing in prison.

To protest the composition of the Indian delegation, Nehru's sister, Vijaya Lakshmi Pandit, who was visiting the United States, led a nationalist delegation to San Francisco, claiming to be the true representatives of India. Although Mrs.

Pandit's attempt to challenge the official Indian delegation appointed by the Viceroy got nowhere, the effort proved a public relations success. Representatives of France, the Philippines, and, most important, the Soviet Union, called on Mrs. Pandit. Soviet Foreign Minister Molotov won friends in India by declaring her delegation the true voice of India. Although the United States gave no sign of support for the nationalists at San Francisco, President Truman invited Mrs. Pandit to meet with him at the White House before she left for India. The gesture was appreciated.[1]

The State Department also accepted the advice of William Phillips to urge the British to adopt a more liberal approach toward the subcontinent. Secretary of State Edward Stettinius and Under Secretary Joseph Grew raised the India question with visiting Foreign Secretary Anthony Eden in April and May 1945. Although the Americans received a noncommittal response, US pressure may have played a role in the British offer of an interim government in June 1945.[2]

Just before the Allied victory in Europe on 8 May 1945, the British released Nehru and other Congress Party leaders from jail. During the nearly three years the Congressites were imprisoned, Mohammed Ali Jinnah and other Muslim League leaders, who remained free, won much increased support for the goal of a separate Muslim homeland—Pakistan. Two months later, in July 1945, after the British Labour Party defeated the Conservatives, Clement Attlee replaced Winston Churchill as Prime Minister. Unlike Churchill, Attlee and the Labour Party favored an early handover of power in India.

With Labour in power, Indian independence was no longer in doubt. Although the United States continued to follow events closely, pressure from Washington on London to end colonial rule was not needed. US officials believed it was up to Indian political leaders and the British to work out the modalities, and did not see the need for trying to influence the process. In fact, as the Truman administration grappled with a host of post-war domestic and foreign policy problems, South Asia was scarcely visible on the radar screen.

As the US military presence in India wound down after the Japanese surrender in August 1945, some GIs found themselves entangled in heightened Indian domestic tensions. One US serviceman died and more than thirty were injured in riots in Calcutta in November 1945 to protest trials of Indian National Army (INA) members—the captured Indian troops that fought for the Japanese. In February 1946 following the conviction of an INA officer, some 37 Americans were among 400 casualties in Calcutta riots. In Bombay, a mob waving the Congress Party flag burned the US Information Service Office.[3]

These troubles were the exception. On the whole, the 250,000 US troops in the CBI Theater departed India without problems. Except for stray racial incidents, they left behind a good impression. The GIs seemed friendlier and less standoffish than the British. The US soldiers, however, carried away remarkably few positive memories from this first extensive contact between the United States and India. For most GIs, India was an ordeal in which the jungles of Assam and the slums of Calcutta erased any Hollywood stereotypes of glamour and romance in the mysterious East. The India theater during World War II, according to political scientist Harold Isaacs, produced hardly any nostalgia at all, let alone any significant literature or movies.[4]

From New Delhi, American diplomats began to report signs of dissatisfaction about post-war US policy toward Asia. After President Truman reaffirmed US support for self-determination for all peoples in October 1945, Pandit Nehru welcomed the statement, but added his hope that it represented "something more than an expression of vague goodwill." Although "everywhere in Asia and Africa people looked up to America," Nehru commented critically, "There has been some disillusionment in India in regard to American championing independence for freedom."[5] Commissioner George Merrell, who succeeded Phillips as head of the New Delhi office, kept Washington informed regarding on-going Indian criticism of the US failure to press British, French, and Dutch allies for decolonization of their remaining holdings in Asia.[6] When the Philippines formally gained their independence on the fourth of July 1946, Pandit Nehru sent a barbed message of congratulations. "Some countries that are called independent are far from free and are under the economic or military domination of some great power," Nehru cabled, "We hope that is not so with the Filipinos."[7]

Within the Congress Party leadership, an aging Gandhi played a less active role. Nehru and the more conservative Sardar Vallabhbhai Patel—like Gandhi from Gujarat in western India—emerged as the two senior leaders. Although in domestic matters, the two shared authority, in foreign policy, Nehru, because of his longstanding position as Congress spokesman and his unusually broad knowledge, was unchallenged. During 1946, Pandit Nehru was at first somewhat vague in talking about the foreign policy an independent India would pursue, but the seeds for neutralism were already germinating. "We want to be friendly with the three principal powers—America, Russia, and England—it is impossible for me to say what military and other alliances a free India may approve. Generally speaking, it would not like to entangle itself in other people's feuds and imperialist rivalries," he told journalists in March.[8] In August 1946, talking with the *New York Times*, he took much the same approach, mainly stressing Indian support for decolonization in Africa and Asia.[9] A month later, in September, after the formation of the Interim Government, in which Nehru served as Deputy Leader and Foreign Minister, he was more precise, declaring "India will follow an independent policy, keeping away from the power politics of groups aligned one against another."[10] The concept of neutralism was thus articulated a year before independence.

In the period of intense negotiations in 1946-47 between the British, the Congress, and the Muslim League over the future of British India, the United States watched with interest and generally supported British efforts hoping, like London, that some compromise—such as that envisaged by the British Cabinet Mission Plan of May 1946—could be found to permit an independent India to remain united. The battle lines were, however, sharply drawn following the 1946 Indian general elections. In contrast to the balloting in 1937, the League swept the seats reserved for Muslims, lending far greater credibility to its demand for a separate Muslim homeland—Pakistan. After the British formed an interim government in September 1946, which the Congress, but not the League, initially joined, Acting Secretary of State Dean Acheson sought and received President Truman's approval to raise the US and Indian diplomatic missions to full embassy status, a move designed to bolster the standing of the interim government.[11]

Technically still under British rule, India made its de facto international debut in the fall of 1946. Ironically, Mrs. Vijaya Lakshmi Pandit—an outsider in 1945 at San Francisco—became the leader of the official Indian delegation to the UN's first General Assembly session at Lake Success, New York. Her instructions from Nehru, her brother and the foreign minister, called for India's steering clear of the democratic and communist power groups. Although stressing "we have to be on friendly terms with both Russia and America," Nehru added—foreshadowing his later slant on nonalignment—"Personally I think that in this worldwide tug-of-war there is on the whole more reason on the side of Russia, not always of course."[12]

Also revealing of Nehru's sensitivities and pride was the advice he gave Asaf Ali, a senior Muslim member of the Congress Party, who became India's first Ambassador to the United States in late 1946. "The United States are a great power," Nehru wrote, "and we want to be friendly with them for many reasons. Nevertheless I should like to make it clear that we do not propose to be subservient to anybody . . . . We have plenty of good cards in our hands and there is no need whatever for us to appear as suppliants before any country."[13]

When the Indian envoy paid his initial protocol call on Secretary of State George Marshall on 26 February 1947,[14] Asaf Ali seemed to have forgotten Nehru's advice. His remarks—as recorded by Marshall—were at some variance from the Nehru line. Asaf Ali urged India's political and economic development so that "it would be a bastion for the world against the great northern neighbor which now casts its shadow over two continents, Asia and Europe." Asaf Ali also referred to India's need for economic help. "A number of 'Tennessee Valley Authorities' were projected for India and it was especially in regard to these that the Ambassador would call upon me for assistance," Marshall recalled.[15]

A more accurate preview of the troubled relationship occurred on 14 January 1947, when John Foster Dulles—a Republican Party adviser to the US delegation to the United Nations—criticized alleged Communist influence in the Indian interim government in a speech to the National Publishers' Association in New York City. Nehru reacted with "surprise and regret," telling the press Dulles' comments "show lack of knowledge of

facts and want of appreciation of the policy we are pursuing."[16]
The State Department promptly instructed the New Delhi Embassy to tell Nehru the US government did not share Dulles'
views and, indeed, was "favorably impressed with India's
avowed intention to pursue (an) independent but cooperative
policy."[17] In a letter to State Department official Henry Villard,
Dulles explained he did not mean to suggest India was a Soviet
puppet but based his comments "on his impression of the Indian
delegation to the United Nations and particularly of delegate
Krishna Menon, who he thought a 'confirmed Marxian' and a
protégé not only of Nehru but of Soviet Foreign Minister Vyacheslav Molotov."[18]

As the impasse between the Congress and the League continued, Washington became increasingly concerned about the
future of India. "Any halt in the constitutional process there
may well cause widespread chaos similar China which would
last for many years and could have worldwide repercussions," a
worried State Department cabled the US Embassies in London
and New Delhi on the eve of a last-ditch British effort to break
the deadlock by flying Nehru, Jinnah, and other top Indian
leaders for talks in London.[19] On 3 December 1946, Dean Acheson, then Acting Secretary, spoke out strongly during a press
conference in favor of mutual concessions to permit a united
India. Acheson urged both the Indian National Congress and the
Muslim League to accept the British Cabinet Mission Plan for a
federation. Acheson expressed confidence that the plan would
permit "an Indian federal union in which all elements of the
population have ample scope to achieve their legitimate political
and economic aspirations."[20] The Department instructed the
Embassy in London to convey Acheson's words to Nehru and
Jinnah, and the Embassy in New Delhi to review the text with
Sardar Patel.[21]

For the next several weeks, US diplomats in London, New
Delhi, and Karachi forcefully pressed League leader Jinnah and
his chief lieutenant, Liaquat Ali Khan, and Congress leaders
Nehru and Patel to accept the Cabinet plan without qualifications. The efforts led nowhere. Saying it was up to the Congress
to take the initiative, the League refused to move. The Congress
leaders, in turn, spurned the nudge from the United States,

expressing doubts about the sincerity of the League—and of the British.[22]

In February 1947, disheartened by failure to achieve a compromise formula on independence, the British decided upon shock treatment. Prime Minister Attlee announced Britain's intention to depart from India not later than June 1948 with or without agreement on the future political structure. He named Lord Louis Mountbatten to replace Wavell as the Viceroy to implement the new policy. As a courtesy—and a sign of the US global leadership role—the British Ambassador in Washington, Lord Inverchapel, informed Secretary George Marshall of the decision a day in advance and also left a top secret analysis of the background to the British decision.[23] Four months later, in June 1947, Attlee called in Lewis Douglas, the US envoy in London, to give him advance word of the decision to move the date of independence ahead to August 1947 and, if a last try by Mountbatten failed to attain agreement on a united India, to accept partition into a "Hindustan dominion and a Pakistan dominion." Attlee, Douglas reported, was "in sober mood, at times tinged with sorrow."[24]

In the spring of 1947, the State Department sent career diplomat Raymond Hare, slated to assume charge of South Asian affairs, to spend three months learning about the subcontinent. Within the Department, the former Near Eastern Division became an Office, covering the Near East, South Asia, and Africa, with Loy Henderson, a former specialist in Soviet affairs, named as the first Director. Meeting leading political personalities, the Viceroy, Gandhi, Nehru, Patel, Jinnah, and others, and traveling widely through the subcontinent, Hare had an unusual opportunity to witness the last days of the British India and to ponder how the United States should deal with independent India.

Hare's meeting with Mahatma Gandhi began with a lengthy discussion by the Indian leader on the "beneficial mental effect" of spinning cotton "in times of emotional stress such as the present." When Hare commented he found little enthusiasm in his travels for independence, Gandhi replied the American was right. "The reason was simple," the Mahatma stated, "It was partition." When Hare asked how sympathies between the United States and India could be deepened, Gandhi answered,

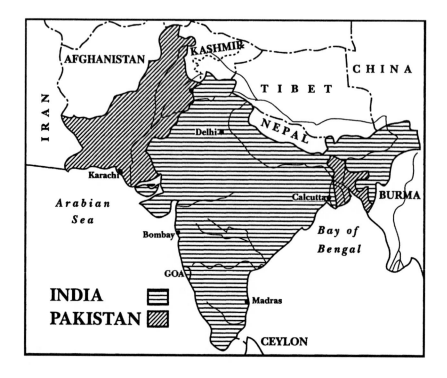

India and Pakistan—the dotted line demarcates that portion of Kashmir in Indian possession from the part possessed by Pakistan

"By the employment of unselfishness, hitherto unknown in international relations."[25]

During talks with Nehru, Hare enquired about India's post-independence foreign policy. The Congress leader, expected to become India's prime minister, said the country would stay "out of entanglement in the current power struggle in the belief that such was best for India and best for world peace." Nehru added there was "a general fear of American economic penetration," but he thought "India would have to depend on the United States for certain types of support." Overall, he emphasized India's desire for friendly relations with the United States.[26]

Hare puzzled about what the US role should be in dealing with an independent India. His thoughts foreshadowed many of the questions that would occupy US foreign policy planners dealing with India in later years:

> In the past our policy had been largely a Revolutionary War hang-over of anti-imperialism and helping colonial peoples to gain their independence; in other words, we had needled the British to take a more liberal attitude vis-à-vis the Indians . . . . But things had changed; India was apparently getting its break but, more important, we had graduated from the role of kibitzing and were playing the hand ourselves. How should we play the Indian trick? Could we do anything to bring them in actively on our side? If not, did it make any particular difference? Could the Russians make any real headway in India? Might it be too much for them to handle as it might be for us?[27]

When India finally gained freedom on 15 August 1947, sadness over the turmoil and bloodshed that followed partition mingled with the joy of freedom from British rule. Washington paid only limited attention to the dramatic events in the subcontinent. At the very moment India and Pakistan were emerging as independent nations, the United States was shaping the concept of containment of communism that became the driving force behind US national security policy for the next 44 years. During the summer of 1947, the US foreign policy focus lay on the mounting difficulties in relations with the Soviet Union. In April, President Truman announced the policy of aid for Greece and Turkey after Britain decided it could no longer shoulder the burden. In June, Secretary of State George Marshall launched the economic recovery program for Europe that bears his name.

India's already expressed desire to have a foreign policy independent of the two power blocs that were then forming did not create too many worries in the State Department. The main American concern in Asia related to the sinking fortunes of China's Nationalist leader, Chiang Kai-shek, and the growing strength of his Chinese Communist rivals. In India, as expected, Pandit Nehru, in addition to his duties as Prime Minister, continued as Foreign Minister. In his many speeches and writings on international issues over the years, and especially in 1946 and 1947, Nehru had already articulated the broad outlines of the foreign policy India would follow.

First, and uppermost at independence, was India's support for rapid decolonization—the end of European overseas empires. Free after its long struggle with the British, India wanted the rest of Asia and Africa to gain freedom from Western colonialism. Foot dragging by the West European colonial powers, especially by the Dutch in Indonesia and the French in Indo-China—and US reluctance to press its European friends too hard—disappointed Prime Minister Nehru. The Indians, on the other hand, were pleased by consistent Soviet support on decolonization although they recognized this was hardly disinterested.

Second was Nehru's desire that Asia's destiny rest in Asian hands and that Europe play a reduced role. Nehru envisaged a close partnership with China and its leader Chiang Kai-shek, a supporter of Indian independence during the difficult war years. The Indian Prime Minister soon became free Asia's best known and most articulate spokesman, sponsoring a pan-Asian conference in New Delhi in 1947.

Third was deep Indian resentment about racial prejudice and discrimination, particularly against non-whites in South Africa, where a million Indians lived, and also racial segregation in the US South. Nehru made South Africa India's top issue at the very first UN General Assembly in 1946.[28]

Finally, there was Nehru's desire that India play an active role in world affairs without joining either of the two power blocs. Nehru favored a policy of "non-entanglement"—the term he used at the time—to ensure that India would not see its independence abridged by joining one of the two blocs, presumably the US-led Western group. By standing apart, Nehru believed India would preserve its freedom of action, increase its international stature, and reduce the possibility that foreign affairs would emerge as a divisive domestic issue. In any case, as the strongest power in South Asia, India did not need external support to bolster its foreign policy position.[29]

The first US Ambassador to India was Dr. Henry Grady, a businessman and former Assistant Secretary of State. No stranger to the subcontinent from his service as head of the 1942 war production mission, Grady arrived in New Delhi in June 1947, two months before independence with the interim government still in office. In a July meeting, Nehru gave Grady his thoughts on policy questions:

- India desired to avoid involvement with either of the power blocs, but, at the same time, wished warm relations with the United States.

- The Soviet Union held attraction for India as an example of how a backward country could develop rapidly. Politically, however, India disliked the undemocratic and totalitarian nature of the Soviet regime.

- India had concerns American economic power would in some way impinge on her sovereignty. At the same time, India needed and desired US capital goods to help the country's development.

- India's economy would probably broadly follow the British Socialist model. As in Britain, basic heavy industries would be nationalized.[30]

Four months after independence, in December 1947, State Department officials dealing with South Asia and Paul Alling and Henry Grady, the Ambassadors to Pakistan and India, met in Washington to review the situation. The record of their discussions indicated less concern about US relations with India and Pakistan than about their relations with each other—strained by the continued exodus of Hindu and Muslim refugees and the outbreak of fighting over Kashmir. The consensus of the meeting was that the United States should promote some sort of loose economic cooperation between the two states.[31] Beyond expressions of good-will and friendship, US policy toward South Asia remained nebulous. Independent India was not a matter of high priority in Washington.

The Kashmir Dispute: US Reaction Disappoints India

Neither the Cold War, dollar diplomacy, nor anti-colonialism caused the first major bilateral difference between the United States and independent India. The problem arose over the unfinished business of partition—the dispute over the princely state of Jammu and Kashmir. Under the British ground rules, the rulers of the several hundred princely states were encouraged to join either India or Pakistan, taking into account factors such as geography and the religious make-up of their populations. By August 1947, all but three of more than 350

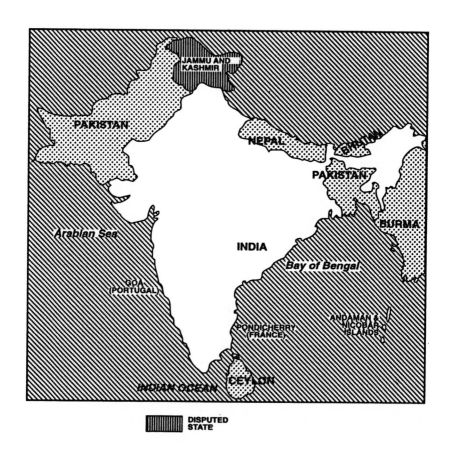

Jammu and Kashmir, 1950

states had acceded to India or Pakistan. Two of the three still standing apart were, unfortunately, the largest states, Kashmir and Hyderabad.

Strategically located in the Himalayas in the northwest portion of the subcontinent, Kashmir had a Hindu ruler and Muslim majority population. The natural beauty and cool climate of the central valley or Vale of Kashmir had attracted the Mughal Emperors and then the British as a haven from the searing heat of Indian summers. When the temperature mounted in May to over 100 degrees on the plains, the British flocked to houseboats on the lakes near the 5,000 foot high capital of Srinagar, where the soaring Himalayas provided a magnificent backdrop.

The Hindu ruler of Kashmir, an unpopular despot, hesitated. Before the British relinquished power, he took a preliminary step toward Pakistan but failed to complete the act of accession. Communal disorders broke out in many parts of the state in mid-summer. In October 1947—two months after independence—as the Maharajah continued to dither about accession, Pathan tribesmen from Pakistan's Northwest Frontier Province, known for their fierce fighting qualities and their Islamic fanaticism, swept into the state, advancing swiftly toward the capital of Srinagar. In panic, the Maharajah appealed for Indian help. Under pressure from Delhi, he executed the documents of accession to India.

Governor General Lord Mountbatten convinced Nehru that Kashmir's accession should be conditional until the people of the state could vote on the final status. Mountbatten's acceptance of accession for the Government of India stated explicitly that when law and order were restored and the invaders gone, "the question of the state's accession should be settled by a reference to the people." A few days later, in a 2 November radio broadcast, Prime Minister Nehru similarly stated that a plebiscite would settle the state's fate.[32]

A dramatic airlift of Indian troops secured the Srinagar airport, preventing the fall of Kashmir's capital. The Indian soldiers then gradually drove back the Pathan tribesman, the invaders having failed to seize Srinagar when it lay defenseless, wasting their advantage on looting and pillaging. After bilateral attempts to end the fighting failed, Nehru—following

Mountbatten's counsel—took the issue to the United Nations Security Council, believing that India's legal and moral case against Pakistan was strong.[33] Quite apart from political considerations, Jawaharlal Nehru had a strong emotional attachment to Kashmir, his family's homeland. The Indian leader was a Kashmiri Pundit, a Brahmin sub-caste that ranked near the top of the Hindu social order. Nehru was also a personal friend of Sheikh Mohammed Abdullah, the charismatic leader of the nationalists in Kashmir, to whom the Maharajah turned over effective power after joining India. Politically, the Sheikh had close ties with the Indian Congress Party, supported the idea of a secular state, and opposed the concept of Pakistan.[34]

Initially, the United States was reluctant to become involved in the Kashmir problem. When British Commonwealth Secretary Noel-Baker presented detailed ideas in January 1948 for conducting a plebiscite under international control, the State Department's response was lukewarm. Near East Office Director Loy Henderson—soon to become Ambassador to India—urged Acting Secretary of State Robert Lovett to stay out of the dispute. He argued the United States was already overcommitted globally, should avoid "making a choice between giving support to the interests of India or of Pakistan," and should not through US involvement provide the Soviets an opening to mix into the affairs of South Asia. State Department officials were also skeptical the United Nations would prove effective in resolving the dispute.[35]

The United States, nonetheless, cooperated with the British when the Kashmir issue came before the UN Security Council. The initial presentations by India and Pakistan made clear the enormous gap between the two parties. As Indian political scientist Sisir Gupta wrote, "Both appeared as the aggrieved parties, both as the complainants. To India, Pakistan had committed aggression and violated her territory; to Pakistan, India was always hostile and was intent on undoing the creation of Pakistan itself."[36]

With the US and British delegations the prime movers, the Security Council on 21 April 1948 adopted a resolution setting up the UN Commission for India and Pakistan (UNCIP). The Indians reacted sourly, angry that the UN failed to condemn Pakistan as the aggressor and seemed to be treating the two countries as equal parties to the dispute. Based apparently on what Belgian Ambassador Prince de Ligne told him, Nehru saw the US stance on Kashmir as influenced less by the merits of the dispute than by US global interests in light of the tensions with the Soviets. Expressing great distress to the Viceroy Lord Mountbatten, Nehru called the American and British attitude on Kashmir, "completely wrong," warning their stance would have "far-reaching results in our relations." Writing his sister, he charged, "The U.S.A. and the U.K. have played a dirty role." Nehru told British Commonwealth Office Under Secretary Gordon Walker "the motives of the United States were to get military and economic concessions in Pakistan."[37]

During most of the summer of 1948, UNCIP shuttled back and forth between Pakistan and India trying in vain to reach agreement on arrangements for a cease-fire and a plebiscite. A major hurdle was a basic disagreement over who would control Kashmir during the plebiscite. Pakistan wanted a UN-led administration. The Indians wanted Sheikh Abdullah to remain in charge of the state, aided by UN observers. When India eventually accepted the UNCIP proposal in August, Pakistan rejected the plan.

In October 1948, as UNCIP continued its work, Secretary of State George Marshall—at the urging of British Foreign Secretary Ernest Bevin—discussed Kashmir with Prime Minister Nehru during the UN General Assembly session in Paris. According to Marshall, Nehru was touchy during their discussion, finding it difficult to remain calm while talking about Kashmir. Beyond the issue of Pakistan's aggression, Nehru asserted with much emotion that the fate of Kashmir was important for India's policy of secular democracy which he contrasted with Pakistan's idea of a state based on religion. Eventually calming down, Nehru, in the end, said he was "very conscious of this problem, was sincerely desirous of having it settled and he hoped that some solution could be worked out."[38]

1 January 1949 saw an important step forward as both countries accepted a cease-fire. Although there was no agreement on the arrangements for holding a plebiscite, the Security Council appointed Admiral Chester Nimitz, commander of the US Navy in the Pacific during World War II, as plebiscite administrator. The principal differences related to the pace of

withdrawal of Pakistani and Indian forces from Kashmir and the control of the Kashmir administration during the voting. Unlike the previous year, the Pakistanis gradually shifted their position to accept almost all UNCIP proposals. It was India that began to dig in its heels in opposition.

US pressure in support of UNCIP increasingly irked New Delhi. On 15 August 1949, reacting to charges India was not acting in good faith on Kashmir, Nehru called in Ambassador Loy Henderson—who had by then replaced Henry Grady—to complain he was "tired of receiving moral advice from the United States . . . . So far as Kashmir was concerned he would not give an inch. He would hold his ground even if Kashmir, India, and the whole world went to pieces."[39] Nor was Nehru any happier when President Truman urged him, in a 25 August message, to accept arbitration as a way to break the impasse on the plebiscite. The Indians rejected Truman's suggestion, along with a similar proposal from British Prime Minister Clement Attlee.[40]

Kashmir figured prominently in the official talks during Prime Minister Nehru's visit to the United States in October and November 1949. After President Harry Truman raised the issue during a White House meeting—and Nehru agreed on the importance of finding a solution—Secretary of State Acheson tried and failed in a subsequent talk with Nehru to pin the Indian leader down on specifics. An exasperated Acheson wrote, "I got a curious combination of a public speech and flashes of anger and deep dislike for his opponents." Nehru's main points—according to Acheson—were that the UN should not deal with the merits of the dispute until the Pakistani forces withdrew from Kashmir, that a plebiscite on the basis of a religious state would be disastrous for the stability of the subcontinent, and that the Pakistanis had no legitimate claim to Kashmir.[41]

With UNCIP stymied, the UN Security Council—to India's annoyance—did not drop the dispute. In December 1949, the Council asked its President, General McNaughton from Canada, to try to find some way to break the impasse. On 26 December, Nehru called in Ambassador Henderson to complain that "his Christmas had been spoiled by (the) message from, Bajpai (then in New York)[42] outlining McNaughton's proposals re Kashmir." Nehru's main complaint related to the details of the troop withdrawal proposals and to the fuzziness of the provision for arbitration.[43] In contrast to Nehru's frosty response, the Pakistanis adopted a positive attitude toward McNaughton's proposals.[44]

Despite Nehru's negative reaction, the United States continued to press for Indian acceptance of McNaughton's ideas. In a 9 January 1950 meeting with Mrs. Vijayalakshmi Pandit, who had become ambassador to Washington, and External Affairs Ministry Secretary General Bajpai, Dean Acheson strenuously urged India not again to refuse UN Kashmir proposals.[45]

Angry about the US démarche, Nehru sharply replied via Bajpai that Acheson's message:

> Is not only unfriendly in tone and substance but appears to us to be seeking to bring pressure on our government under threat of consequences . . . . It appears to be totally forgotten that we are not the aggressors, but that we are the victims of aggression . . . . I would like to add that it is a matter of great personal regret to me that Mr. Secretary Acheson should have sent us a message of this kind.[46]

After the failure of McNaughton's effort, the Security Council sent prominent Australian jurist Sir Owen Dixon to South Asia to try his hand. Arriving during the oven-like heat of May, Dixon toiled through the summer of 1950, working quietly with Nehru, Pakistan's Prime Minister Liaquat Ali Khan, and others. When he concluded that a statewide plebiscite was impractical, the Australian suggested an approach similar to an idea put forward earlier by Girja Bajpai—limiting the vote to the Valley while partitioning the rest of the state on religious lines. In the end, this proposal failed after Nehru rejected the idea of UN control of the Valley during the plebiscite.[47]

The Australian, who perhaps came closer to reaching a Kashmir settlement than anyone else, left disappointed at the end of the summer. In his report to the Security Council, Dixon wrote, "I have formed the opinion that if there is any chance of settling the dispute over Kashmir by agreement between India and Pakistan it now lies in partition and in some means of allocating the Valley rather than an overall plebiscite." He recommended that the UN not pursue the mediation effort on Kashmir, letting the two countries seek a political settlement on their own.[48]

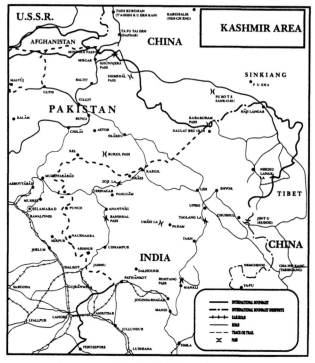

Kashmir Area

The United States—notwithstanding Dixon's recommendations—did not favor letting the issue drop. In a 17 November 1950 meeting between Secretary Acheson and Pakistan's Foreign Minister Zafrullah Khan, Acheson said, "I needed advice and guidance. We had been very discouraged by India's attitude and had been trying through our Ambassador to make India see what could be done—with what success I do not know." In the discussion that followed, Acheson was in basic agreement with Zafrullah's position that unless Indian troops were removed and a UN administration appointed for the Vale, it would not be possible to have a fair plebiscite.[49]

1951 saw a renewed effort to tackle Kashmir with Dr. Frank Graham appointed as UN mediator. A former President of the University of North Carolina and US Senator, Graham had gained an excellent reputation for his work in resolving the Dutch-Indonesia dispute. His approach was to package ideas into a series of detailed points and then seek agreement on these by both sides. By October, Graham was down to three outstanding questions: the number of Indian troops to remain in Kashmir after demilitarization, the length of the demilitarization period, and the date for the formal appointment of the plebiscite administrator. Although the assassination of Pakistan's Prime Minister Liaquat in October 1951 and India's first general elections in January 1952 delayed Graham's work, he toiled away. Graham impressed the Indians, Nehru describing him as "a sincere and earnest man anxious to do what he can to further a settlement."[50]

Chester Bowles, who replaced Loy Henderson as Ambassador in November 1951, quickly injected his own ideas on Kashmir. The contrast between the two American envoys was striking. Henderson was a veteran career diplomat, whose service in the Soviet Union helped shape a strong anti-Communist bent. Conservative in outlook, he had few hopes that Indo-American relations would be smooth. Although Henderson established a good working relationship with Secretary General Bajpai, his dealings with Nehru were often tense and blunt. Henderson's cables were down-to-earth and terse.

Bowles came to the job after losing a bid for reelection as Governor of Connecticut in the 1950 elections. A pioneer in modern advertising in the 1920s and 1930s, Bowles had gained a national reputation as the successful head of the Office of Price Administration during World War II. He became active in politics after the war as a member of the Democratic Party's liberal wing. Following the communist takeover of China, Bowles felt people would look closely at India to see if democracy could provide an alternative to communism as a path to economic development in Asia.[51]

Once he arrived in New Delhi, Bowles quickly engaged himself in recommending a less active US stance in the Kashmir dispute. In his messages, Bowles urged the United States to restrict its role to serving as a friend to both countries, willing to help in solving the dispute without taking sides. Since Bowles believed Graham's insistence on a statewide plebiscite was certain to fail, he was at a loss to understand why Graham felt unable to suggest different approaches. The State Department responded unsympathetically to Bowles' views, instructing the envoy to continue giving full and firm support to Graham's efforts.[52]

In July 1952, Bowles briefly became the man in the middle on Kashmir when, after consultations in Washington, he stopped in Karachi on the way back to Delhi. There, Pakistani Prime Minister Nazimmudin said he would be willing to make a substantial concession on the ratio of Indian to Pakistani troops to remain in Kashmir. Bowles was reasonably hopeful this proposal would be accepted since it was close to what the Indians were seeking on troop ratios.

His optimism was misplaced. When the Ambassador presented the idea to Nehru on 8 July, the Indian leader thought silently for several minutes and then rejected the proposal. Arguing ratios were not the way to deal with the problem of troop levels, Nehru refused to budge from the previous Indian position. A second meeting found Nehru still unwilling to accept the proposal. Bowles reported, "Nehru acting wholly unreasonable manner and probably will continue to do so." The Prime Minister, Bowles continued, hoped the problem would go away since he knew India had a weak position internationally.[53]

At the United Nations, the Russians generally remained silent during Kashmir debates until 1952. They abstained from voting although their propaganda portrayed the dispute as an Anglo-American imperialist plot. By not openly taking sides, they presumably hoped to avoid damage in their relations with either India or Pakistan. Soviet Delegate Jacob Malik thus caused surprise when in January 1952 he sharply criticized Dr. Frank Graham's report to the Security Council. Taken aback by Soviet support, Bajpai called in the American chargé d'affaires. Stressing that India had not asked the Soviets to intervene, Bajpai emphasized that India did not want Kashmir to become embroiled in the Cold War.[54]

Graham labored on until early 1953 before giving up. The final report, his fifth, reached the Security Council on 27 March 1953—two months after Dwight Eisenhower succeeded Harry Truman in the presidency. Combined with three UNCIP reports, those of McNaughton and Dixon, and the record of numerous Council debates, Graham's report added to an impressive library of official documentation on unsuccessful efforts to resolve the Kashmir dispute. Nothing had been achieved, in fact, since India and Pakistan agreed upon the cease fire in 1949. Although there was no progress toward a settlement, the guns at least had remained silent.[55]

Chronic friction between Washington and New Delhi over Kashmir inevitably had a negative impact on bilateral relations—as Nehru predicted. In October 1952, Nehru wrote G. L. Mehta, the Bombay businessman he appointed to succeed Mrs. Pandit as Ambassador to Washington, that India has told the State Department "in the clearest language that we consider their attitude in this matter completely wrong and unfriendly to India and that this comes in the way of the development of cordial relations between India and America, that all of us desire, more than anything else."[56]

For Indians, the Kashmir question was a central and vital foreign policy issue inevitably linked with the traumatic partition of British India and the creation of Pakistan. As Josef Korbel, onetime chairman of UNCIP, wrote:

> The struggle for Kashmir is in every sense another battle in this continuing struggle and by now irrational war of ideals. In the minds of Nehru and the Congress, Kashmir is, in miniature, another Pakistan, and if this Muslim nation can be successfully governed by India, then their philosophy of secularization is vindicated.[57]

The United States looked at Kashmir quite differently. Washington regarded the problem as a serious dispute between two countries with which the United States had friendly relations, but not as an issue involving vital US interests. Kashmir also appeared to be the type of regional dispute that the United Nations should be able to resolve, especially as India's original suggestion for a plebiscite provided a basis for settlement. The concern in Washington was that in the absence of a settlement fighting would again break out between India and Pakistan. Although at first Washington took no strong position on the merits, the United States backed the UN call for a plebiscite and gradually became exasperated by Nehru's backsliding on this question and by incremental steps New Delhi took to formally incorporate Kashmir into the Indian Union.[58] George McGhee, Assistant Secretary of State for Near Eastern and South Asian Affairs through much of this period, commented that the main

US concern was about the possible outbreak of war over Kashmir. "We wanted to avert full-scale war between India and Pakistan—this was always a threat. Our efforts failed—because of Nehru," McGhee asserted.[59]

Bilateral Relations: Mutual Misunderstanding

Quite apart from Kashmir, the United States and India found themselves at odds on many foreign policy questions unrelated to the Cold War. International control of atomic energy, Palestine, and the creation of Israel, Indonesia, and Indo-China were issues on which the two countries differed. Although Nehru's insistent independence from the West annoyed US policy makers—Ambassador Grady told him "India should get on the democratic side immediately"[60]—Washington unenthusiastically accepted India's policy not to become entangled. The overall orientation of Indian policy was not directed against the United States. In the late 1940s, India's relations with Moscow were frosty. Soviet dictator Joseph Stalin regarded Jawaharlal Nehru with suspicion as a "bourgeois democrat" and "lackey" of British imperialism. Even though Nehru sent his sister as India's first envoy to Moscow, the Soviet leader never once received Mrs. Pandit during her two years in the Soviet Union.

On 8 March 1948, when Nehru elaborated India's foreign policy before the Constituent Assembly, he made a point to have the Ministry of External Affairs inform Ambassador Grady that it would be "unthinkable" for India to be on the Russian side in the event of a world war.[61] Visiting Washington a month later, External Affairs Secretary General Girja Bajpai made the same point in meetings with Loy Henderson, then Director of the State Department's Office of Near East and South Asian Affairs, and Acting Secretary of State Robert Lovett. Bajpai stressed that people in the United States, who thought India was in the Soviet camp, were wrong. In the event of war, India would side with the forces of freedom.[62]

The desire for better relations with Washington paralleled the remarkable turnaround in relations between India and Britain after independence. Contrary to expectations and the Indian Congress Party program, independent India decided to remain in the British Commonwealth—a step which London and New

Delhi regarded at the time as of great importance.[63] After having improved ties with London, Nehru hoped in 1949 to firm up relations with the United States. The Prime Minister wrote his friend Krishna Menon, then High Commissioner in Britain, he was prepared to "align with the US somewhat" as long it was not necessary to become subservient.

Personally, Nehru had ambivalent feelings about America, a country he had never visited. The Indian leader had a considerable bias that seemed to combine the anti-American social prejudices of the British elite and the anti-American policy views of the left-wing of the British Labour Party. In foreign policy dealings, he found the United States too cocksure about the rights and wrongs of the Cold War, too insensitive to the aspirations of colonial peoples, and too patronizing in dealing with India. Despite disappointments over Kashmir and differences on anti-colonial issues, Nehru remained, nonetheless, hopeful about relations with Washington, believing the United States would be interested in friendly relations with India because "it is well recognized today all over the world that the future of Asia will be powerfully determined by the future of India."[64]

A note Nehru wrote on negotiations for a commercial treaty with the United States spelled out his ambivalent views:

> America is the most powerful and richest country in the world and can certainly help India a great deal. There is no reason why we should not get that help and remove causes of friction between us. But it is true that America represents a reactionary policy in world affairs, I think a policy which will not succeed . . . . The safest policy, therefore, appears to be friendly to America, to give them fair terms, to invite their help on such terms, and at the same time not to tie ourselves up too much with their world or their economic policy.[65]

In October and November 1949, the Indian leader paid his first visit to the United States. During the three-week trip, Nehru traveled from the Atlantic to the Pacific coasts, seeing much of America and meeting many prominent figures from a broad cross-section of US life. The Prime Minister cut an impressive figure in numerous public appearances as an eloquent advocate of India, explaining its neutralist policies and seeking friendship with the United States without becoming a political camp follower or a supplicant for economic help. The public generally accorded him a warm welcome as a leading representative of free Asia. The liberal press lauded Nehru as the hope of Asia—especially after the fall of China to the Communists.

The official side of the trip went much less well. Nehru's ambivalence toward US policy was matched by the skepticism of US leaders toward the Indian approach. The Americans found Nehru's views on foreign affairs perplexing and imprecise. They received coolly his suggestions that the West should be more reasonable in dealing with the Russians and should recognize Communist China. After a three-hour informal private meeting, Secretary of State Dean Acheson wrote:

> I was convinced that Nehru and I were not destined to have a pleasant personal relationship. He was so important to India's survival and India's survival was so important to all of us, that if he did not exist— as Voltaire said of God—he would have to be invented. Nevertheless, he was one of the most difficult men I have ever had to deal with.[66]

If the American leadership found the Indian Prime Minister stiff and vague, Nehru, in turn, found both Truman and Acheson condescending. The Prime Minister wrote Dr. S. Radhakhrishnan, the South Indian scholar-philosopher who replaced Mrs. Pandit as Indian envoy to Moscow, "They had gone all out to welcome me and I am very grateful to them for it and expressed myself so. But they expected something more than gratitude and goodwill and that more I could not supply them."[67]

The Prime Minister was taken aback by the flaunting of material wealth and what often seemed a lack of culture and good taste in the United States. In New York, for example, the hosts at a lunch with businessmen made a point of boasting that the companies represented at the table were worth more than $20 billion. Nehru also found the conversation at the White House dinner less than intellectually scintillating—a main topic of discussion between President Truman and Vice President Alben Barkley concerned the merits of Kentucky bourbon whiskey.[68]

A few months after returning to India, Nehru was annoyed by the warm welcome given Pakistan's Prime Minister Liaquat

11 October 1949, Prime Minister Jawaharlal Nehru, on arrival in Washington, DC, with Madame Vijaya Lakshmi Pandit, Indian Ambassador to the United States, and President Harry S. Truman.

Ali Khan in the United States. Writing to his sister in Washington, he carped:

> The Americans are either very naive or singularly lacking in intelligence. They go through the same routine whether it is Nehru or the Shah or Liaquat Ali . . . . It does appear that there is a concerted attempt to build up Pakistan and build down, if I may say, India. It surprises me how immature in their political thinking the Americans are! . . . In their dealings with Asia, they show a lack of understanding which is surprising.[69]

The positive public relations impact of the trip also proved short-lived. In the spring of 1950, the American Embassy in New Delhi reported about increased anti-US feelings in India. Although ostensibly directed at supposed US faults (racial prejudice, pro-colonialist policies, etc.), Ambassador Loy Henderson thought the real causes were: the lack of economic aid, the US position on Kashmir, and fears that the United States was using its economic muscle to press India to shed its socialist policies. With the Communists on the Indian political left fanning the flames, Henderson thought the upsurge was unlikely to dissipate unless the United States backed up its rhetoric about friendly relations with concrete action, especially in the area of economic aid.[70]

The State Department replied testily—reflecting growing distaste for India—that friendly relations had to be based on more than loans or gifts. The message argued the best way to win Indian friendship was to convince New Delhi that "our objectives are disinterested (and) constructive as we are confident the Inds wld [sic] wish their own to be regarded. Present Ind [sic] attitudes subj [sic] these beliefs to serious doubt."[71] When placed alongside similarly pointed comments Nehru was making about the United States in his letters to his sister and others, the exchange between the State Department and Henderson underscored the troubled nature of relations between India and America in the early months of 1950.

The Korean War: Indian Neutralism Put to the Test

The Cold War became a "hot war" after North Korean forces invaded South Korea on 25 June 1950. The initial Indian reaction to the outbreak of hostilities pleasantly surprised Washington. Sir Benegal Rau, India's UN delegate, voted for the

Security Council's condemnation of the invasion. Several days later, India voted for a second resolution calling for support to South Korea to repel the attack. Nehru delayed taking this action until the full cabinet could approve the Indian position. India appeared, thus, to be standing with the West against the Communists on a fundamental issue of war and peace. "There could be no doubt that the North Korean Government had committed aggression on a large-scale on South Korea," Nehru wrote his Chief Ministers, "to surrender to it was wrong and would have meant the collapse of the United Nations as well as led to other dangerous consequences."[72]

Prime Minister Nehru was, however, extremely uneasy. Apart from fear that events would lead to a World War, he strenuously disapproved of President Truman's linking the Korea conflict with the problems of Formosa and Indo-China. He saw US policy as threatening to enlarge the war in the defense of Western interests. Favoring Chinese incorporation of Formosa and the withdrawal of the French from Indo-China, Nehru saw both issues in terms of Asian nationalism, as part of the struggle to free the region from Western domination, rather than as a contest between pro- and anti-communist forces.

In early July, Nehru launched a vaguely coordinated peace effort with Indian envoys in Moscow (Radhakrishnan), London (Krishna Menon), New York (Sir Benegal Rau), Washington (Mrs. Pandit), and Secretary General Bajpai in New Delhi all in the act. The heart of the proposal was that in return for talks on Korea, the Soviets would return to the Security Council and the Chinese Communists would occupy the UN seat of the Chinese Nationalists. Although Stalin temporized in his reply, Dean Acheson—with Truman's blessing—turned Nehru down flatly, bruising the Indian leader's feelings. The Indian press, taking its cue from the government, blamed Washington for thwarting the peace initiative.[73]

Acheson explained in some detail in private correspondence with Nehru why the United States disagreed with the Indian approach. This extremely substantive correspondence showed that Washington took India seriously, always important for someone as sensitive as Nehru. The exchange also indicated American interest in using the Indian Ambassador in Beijing, K. M. Panikkar, as a channel to the Chinese Communists. Although

Washington regarded Panikkar with suspicion, he was the only non-Communist envoy with good access to the Chinese leadership.[74]

In September 1950, UN fortunes rose after General MacArthur's daring Inchon landing broke the back of the North Korean military. With the stage set for victory in South Korea, the question was whether UN forces should cross the 38th parallel into North Korea. India opposed a UN advance above this line from fear that the action would bring in the Chinese Communists. After the Chinese warned Ambassador Panikkar on 3 October that they would intervene if UN forces crossed the 38th parallel, Nehru pleaded for caution. The United States disregarded the Indian leader. President Truman declared that he did not take Panikkar's report "as that of an impartial observer," believing the Indian envoy played "the game of the Chinese Communists fairly regularly."[75]

Being right about the Chinese intervention won Nehru no friends in the US press or in the American leadership. The *New York Times*, once full of praise for the Indian leader, was sternly critical. "Pandit Nehru purports to speak for Asia," the *Times* wrote, "but it is the voice of abnegation, his criticism turns out to have been obstructive, his policy appeasement."[76] Mrs. Pandit reported that Truman supposedly told a Congressman that "Nehru has sold us down the Hudson. His attitude has been responsible for our losing the war in Korea."[77] At a staff meeting of the US delegation to the UN, John Foster Dulles—serving as a Republican adviser—said that since the Indians were always eager to solve someone else's problem, perhaps the United States should sit on the sidelines and let the Indians try to solve Korea. That might make them less willing to meddle in other people's affairs, the future Secretary of State commented.[78]

In early 1951, Secretary Acheson was less than enthused about a push by the Indians—supported by the British—for a Korea cease-fire resolution that collided with a US-backed drive for a UN resolution condemning the Chinese Communist military intervention. After difficult deliberations, Washington agreed to go along with the Indian proposal, which the General Assembly approved in January 1951. When the Chinese Communists rejected the resolution, the General Assembly proceeded to condemn the Chinese as aggressors by a resounding

50-7-8 majority. India and Burma were the only two countries to join the Communists in opposing this resolution. Nehru then temporarily gave up his peacemaking efforts, writing in exasperation to his friend Krishna Menon in London that we "failed in the end before the big stick of the United States."[79]

In the summer of 1951 the UN and Communists began cease-fire talks at Kaesong in Korea, but these discussions soon broke down. The war continued across the waist of the peninsula. Although neither side gained a decisive advantage, the UN gradually pressed the Chinese north of the 38th parallel where the line stabilized for the next two years. In the summer of 1952, prodding from the Americans and Chinese revived Indian interest in serving as a go-between for a cease-fire. On the US side, Eleanor Roosevelt, visiting New Delhi, and Ambassador Chester Bowles urged the Indians to tell the Chinese that the United States wanted a settlement.

At this point, a new Indian face appeared on the UN stage in New York. This was V.K. Krishna Menon, formerly Indian High Commissioner to London and an intimate foreign policy adviser to Nehru with whom he had been on close terms since the 1930s. Menon left London under a cloud after the British complained about leaks from the High Commission to the Communists and Menon's mismanagement of the Mission became a political embarrassment in New Delhi. When Nehru suggested that his friend return to Delhi or go to Moscow as Ambassador, Menon balked, having lived away from India most of his adult life. The Prime Minister finally found a solution by assigning Menon to New York to deal with the Korean issue—a subject on which India's permanent representative Sir B. N. Rau sought help.[80]

Highly strung, highly irascible, and highly intelligent, Menon was one of the few Indians Nehru accepted as his intellectual equal. The two saw eye-to-eye on the basic approach to foreign policy, although Menon stood politically to the left of Nehru. Krishna Menon's acid tongue and striking—almost diabolic—looks soon made him a media celebrity at the United Nations. Since his barbed verbal thrusts were more often than not aimed at the United States, Menon's presence added a new, and ultimately heavy, burden to Indo-American relations.

After Dwight D. Eisenhower swamped the Democrats in the November 1952 elections, the Indians and British feared that the incoming Republican administration might widen the war in Korea. They were eager to have a cease-fire in place before the new President took office in January 1953. Seizing the opportunity, Krishna Menon toiled frenetically to shape a resolution that would bridge American and Chinese and North Korean differences over the fate of the thousands of communist prisoners of war who did not want to return home. Although Nehru agreed on the basic issue of no forced repatriation, Acheson found Krishna Menon exasperatingly difficult to negotiate with. Reporting to President Truman, the Secretary commented that Menon's resolution "as they say in the strike settlement lingo, gives us the words and the other side the decision." Menon, Acheson told a staff meeting, seemed to be "a master of putting words together so that they conveyed no ideas at all." Menon's plan, the Secretary asserted, was like a room with only one door, "pointing to the north."[81]

In the end, Acheson agreed reluctantly to go along with Menon's resolution, provided amendments made the text more to Washington's liking. After Bowles intervened with Nehru, the Indians agreed to modify the draft sufficiently to gain US acceptance. Although the General Assembly adopted the resolution with an overwhelming majority, the Indian effort came to naught. Russia's Andrei Vyshinksy flatly turned down the proposal, which he attacked as a device for perpetuating the war. Ten days later the Chinese Communists followed the Soviet line, announcing their rejection. Nehru had to "confess that I was somewhat surprised at the attitude of China and the virulence of Russia," as India had remained in touch with them during the negotiations.[82]

Running parallel to Indo-American friction over the Korean war was the continuing dispute about the recognition of Communist China. Even before Indian independence, Nehru regarded good relations with China as a fundamental plank in India's foreign policy. He saw the two ancient countries and civilizations emerging from European domination to become pillars of the new Asia. When the Nationalists, with whom he had friendly relations, fell from power, Nehru believed the Communist victory was due less to the attractiveness of Marxist ideology than the shortcomings of the Chiang Kai-shek regime.

Nehru argued with American leaders during his 1949 visit that Chinese nationalism would prevent the domination of China by the Soviet Union. He believed that bringing the new China into the family of nations would accelerate this process and thought that the US desire to ostracize China would have the opposite effect, leading to strengthened Sino-Soviet ties.[83] Although India had plenty of company in its China policy— including the closest US allies, Britain and Canada, Washington's differences with New Delhi over China added to bilateral frictions, particularly after the Chinese intervened militarily in Korea.

Another bone of contention between Washington and New Delhi was the peace treaty with Japan. Negotiated by John Foster Dulles, the treaty was ready for signature in the summer of 1951. To the dismay of Washington and Dulles, Nehru decided that India would not sign. The Prime Minister believed the treaty should have included the Soviet Union and Communist China and was also unhappy about the security arrangements between Japan and the United States.[84] The US leadership, but especially treaty negotiator Dulles, was put out by India's insistence on standing apart. Apparently staggered by the final Indian turndown, Dulles told Ambassador Pandit, "I cannot accept this. Does your Prime Minister realize that I have prayed at every stage of this treaty?" The Prime Minister's sister was at a loss for words.[85] Nehru recognized that India's decision would "naturally cause resentment and some disappointment" in Washington. When the US reply "was couched in language which is not usual in correspondence between governments," the Prime Minister was annoyed but decided against using "strong language in our answer."[86]

In Kashmir, where Indian soldiers shed their blood against Pakistan, the US attitude badly upset the government of India. In Korea, where US soldiers were shedding their blood against North Korean and Chinese Communist forces, the Indian attitude badly upset the US government. India and the United States each wanted aggression punished and basic principles of international morality upheld. Fearful of expanded conflict in the Far East, the Indians urged moderation and compromise in the case of Korea. Fearful of an India-Pakistan War, the United States similarly urged moderation and compromise in the case of Kashmir. Neither Washington nor New Delhi won friends in each other's capital by playing the peacemaker.

Economic Assistance to India: A Slow Start

Although in the 1950s and 1960s, economic assistance became a major element of US policy toward India, aid was not an important issue immediately after independence. The United States had yet to initiate assistance programs for the developing world. It was only in 1948 that Washington launched Marshall Plan aid for the nations of Western Europe.

With the United States at the peak of its economic power, Nehru and other Indian leaders, nonetheless, looked to America for help. Even before the first anniversary of independence, Ministry of External Affairs Secretary General Bajpai, during an April 1948 visit to Washington, sought aid for hydroelectric projects. Bajpai's feelers led nowhere.[87] There was also limited activity on the part of the US private sector. Despite the fact that Washington encouraged investment in India, few US businesses took this advice, except for larger concerns—like the oil companies—already experienced in the international field. India's announced socialist economic policy, corporate ignorance about South Asia, and the reputation India soon acquired—not only as being a terribly poor country but as a difficult place to do business—all acted as dampeners on investment.

In India, the attitude toward foreign business was ambiguous. Although New Delhi wanted US investment, there was, at the same time, fear the United States would use its economic might to interfere with India's sovereignty or to unfairly exploit the country's resources. Nehru himself thought the concerns were overdrawn. "The question of economic domination of India by the U.S.A. is not one that frightens me," he wrote.[88] The political left in India was able, nonetheless, to exploit nationalist fears about foreign business encroachment deeply rooted in the British economic exploitation of India during the colonial period.

In his January 1949 inaugural address, President Truman announced the program of technical assistance to help poorer countries, known as Point Four. Although the idea—inserted in the speech by White House staffers without advance planning—generated much interest, little actually happened for more than a year. When the Prime Minister visited Washington in October 1949, obtaining US aid was high on Nehru's agenda, but—perhaps out of pride—in talking with US leaders, he "mentioned this, though rather casually."[89]

Just before Nehru arrived, Ambassador Henderson made the first serious proposal on aid to India, recommending a five-year $500 million program. With economic assistance, India might become a "stalwart and worthy champion of the West in Asia; without aid, Henderson argued, India "might degenerate into a vast political and economic swamp."[90] Henderson was ahead of his time in making the proposal. The Truman administration remained ambivalent about India, uncertain US interests warranted an investment on so large a scale and uncertain the US Congress would support such a program. Nehru did not help the case for economic aid when he failed to press the issue seriously during his visit. A month later, in November 1949, the State Department informed Henderson his aid proposal was rejected.[91]

India's most pressing economic need in late 1949 was for food assistance to stave off a possible famine. With this in mind, Nehru asked the President for a million tons of wheat to provide a stronger food reserve. In spite of the fact that Truman responded positively,[92] delays and misunderstandings, including an attempt to barter the wheat for strategic materials, frustrated an accord. The upshot was ill-will. The Indians thought the United States stingy, trying to use food aid as a policy lever. The Americans complained the Indians never adequately followed up after Nehru talked with Truman. As the State Department cabled stiffly to Ambassador Henderson, "(The) USG may be pardoned if it is puzzled to learn it is criticized for India's failure to obtain aid when no firm or formal request was ever made."[93]

The food situation in India failed to improve in 1950 with poor summer monsoon rains again threatening famine. This time the Government of India made clear its need, Ambassador Pandit formally requesting two million tons of wheat aid from Secretary Acheson in December.[94] Ambassador Henderson seconded the Indian request, cabling that the shortage and threat of famine were real.[95] President Truman at first held back, only giving Assistant Secretary of State George McGhee a hunting license to test the Congressional waters. In closed Senate Foreign

Relations Committee hearings in January 1951, McGhee got an earful. Committee Chairman Tom Connally of Texas stated point blank, "I want to tell you right now you are going to have one hell of a time getting this thing through the Congress."[96]

Despite the unfriendly reaction—confirmation of India's unpopularity with many in the Congress—Truman decided to proceed with food aid legislation. Enlisting the support of former Republican President Herbert Hoover—who won fame for his role in feeding Europe after World War I—Truman sent a strong message to the Congress on 12 February, urging two million tons of wheat for India on both humanitarian and national interest grounds.[97] At first, things went smoothly, but anti-Indian feelings led to procedural delays, especially in the Senate where Senator Connally refused to schedule hearings. After a plea from Truman, the Senator finally relented in mid-April. Conservatives in the House of Representative Rules Committee then raised new obstacles that threatened to block the bill. Annoyed by Congressional foot-dragging and criticism of India, Nehru hit back. "We would be unworthy of the high responsibilities with which we have been charged if we bartered away in the slightest degree our country's self-respect or freedom of action, even for something we badly need," the Indian leader stated on 1 May over All-India Radio.[98]

Nehru's comments prompted an angry response among legislators in Washington, who postponed further action on the bill until the Indian government clarified whether it, in fact, still desired the aid.[99] An additional complication was whether the wheat would be provided as a gift—the Truman administration and Senate proposal—or as a loan—the House of Representatives approach. Realizing the damage he had caused, Nehru spoke positively about food aid in Parliament on 10 May, indicating that, if given a choice, India preferred a loan rather than a gift. Nehru's statement soothed Congressional nerves. The bill approving $190 million of wheat as a long-term loan finally passed in early June.[100] On 15 June 1951, President Truman signed the measure into law, initiating the first of many US food aid shipments to India.

The arrival of US wheat ensured India could avoid famine. The extended haggling in the Congress and the outburst of anti-

15 June 1951, President Truman signs into law the bill to furnish emergency food to India, watched by Madame Pandit, Secretary of State Dean Acheson, and congressional leaders.

Indian sentiments, however, undercut any public relations benefits. Nehru commented that despite the best efforts of the US administration, "there has been a feeling of resentment in India re the long delays and obstructionist tactics of some people in the American Congress."[101] In contrast, the Soviet Union received much applause for a far smaller food shipment that arrived before US wheat.[102]

The episode made Ambassador Henderson wary of proceeding with a pending request for a regular economic aid program unless the Prime Minister personally gave "firm assurances" that India accepted the terms.[103] In late May, Nehru obliged. After spending over an hour with chargé d'affaires Lloyd Steere, he affirmed India's willingness to accept US aid conditions and stated his country was anxious to receive American economic help.[104]

After Chester Bowles replaced Loy Henderson in November 1951, the new envoy quickly made a larger bilateral aid program one of his major goals. Bowles urged a program for the coming year of $150 million, pushing this relentlessly in Washington at all levels of the administration, including directly with President Truman. In the end, the State Department agreed to support a $115 million program request from the Congress.[105] Not satisfied, Bowles asked for additional funds. When the issue was put before the President, Truman agreed with Secretary Acheson to sidetrack the proposal to the Budget Bureau. The administration thought Bowles was moving too fast, wanted to see existing aid programs launched before considering increases, and was skeptical Congress would approve an expanded effort.[106]

In the fall of 1952, Bowles renewed the campaign in lengthy letters to Dean Acheson, calling for a three-year commitment to support India's development plans, including $250 million in the coming fiscal year. Bowles' argument—one that would be repeatedly used over the next decade to justify aid to India—linked the fate of India's economic development to US security interests in Asia. The choice, Bowles declared, was between the current democratic government or, if India failed to develop, communism. After the Democrats lost the 1952 elections, Bowles' suggestions became superfluous. With one foot out the door 2 weeks before leaving office in January 1953, Acheson replied that he agreed with much of what Bowles said but would have to pass on his letters to the new Secretary of State, John Foster Dulles, and to Harold Stassen, the former Republican Governor of Minnesota, whom Eisenhower named as foreign aid chief.[107]

Although Chester Bowles' first tour as Ambassador to India lasted little more than a year, he made an enduring impression. A master at public relations, Bowles "sold" America to Indians in a way that his predecessor Loy Henderson, a superb professional diplomat but no salesman or image maker, could not do. Bowles spoke frequently with the Indian press, fielding with patience and understanding tough questions about US racial discrimination, criticism of US foreign policy, and other subjects. He traveled widely throughout India, visiting villages and impoverished urban areas as well as hobnobbing with the wealthy elite. He focussed US aid on India's community development program to help India's rural poor.

Bowles' enthusiasm and good will had a positive impact, helping to offset the policy irritants and frictions between New Delhi and Washington. He succeeded in showing Indians that America cared about them and their nation's efforts to modernize within the democratic framework. He also had an impact on informed US opinion. When India held its first democratic elections on the basis of universal suffrage in 1952, Bowles stressed the significance of India's adherence to the democratic system. He made some headway, especially among liberals, in gaining acceptance for his conviction that India deserved greater attention from American foreign policy makers. Bowles' achievement—in one short year—was substantial.[108]

Professionals in the State Department found Bowles personally warm hearted and an unusually effective salesman of the United States in India. The fact that he also acquired the reputation for becoming a salesman of India to the United States reduced the impact of his policy recommendations within the Truman administration. Bowles' cause was, however, helped by the development in Washington of what became known as the India lobby—an informal group of liberal activists who strongly urged better relations with India despite Indo-US foreign policy differences over the Cold War. Democratic Senator Hubert H. Humphrey of Minnesota was one of the earliest supporters of the

India lobby along with Supreme Court Justice William O. Douglas.[109]

US Military Supply to South Asia: The Beginnings

After 1954, the US military supply relationship with Pakistan would become a major irritant in Indo-US relations—from the Indian perspective the biggest single bar to friendlier ties. Although Pakistan first requested arms aid barely two months after independence in the fall of 1947, when it received a flat State Department turndown,[110] it was, ironically, India that first procured arms from the United States. Before the Kashmir War, modest sales of military equipment to a former World War II ally posed no difficulty for the State Department. The outbreak of fighting in Kashmir, however, led President Truman to impose an embargo on arms exports to either India or Pakistan in order to avoid fueling a conflict which the UN was trying to stop.[111]After the cease-fire agreement, in January 1949, the ban was lifted.

Pakistan's Prime Minister Liaquat Ali Khan renewed the request for US arms without success during a 1948 meeting with Secretary Marshall. Liaquat's line—similar to the approach Jinnah used when Raymond Hare called on the Muslim League leader in 1947—was to seek military aid to bolster Pakistan and other Muslim states against the Communists.[112] Liaquat continued the quest during his spring 1950 visit to the United States. In contrast to Nehru, the Pakistani leader made an excellent impression, voicing his country's support for US foreign policy at the same time he urged the United States to provide Pakistan military assistance.[113]

Even if there was no immediate payoff for the Pakistanis, the Korean War spurred American interest in containing the Soviet threat through a chain of security alliances. As Washington became more supportive of a long-standing British proposal for a Middle East Defense Organization (MEDO), Assistant Secretary McGhee strongly backed the idea of including Pakistan in a Middle East security system. US Ambassadors to South Asia, meeting in Ceylon in March 1951, endorsed the proposal although noting that until the Kashmir dispute was settled and Indo-Pakistan relations improved, the real potential could not be realized.[114] McGhee pressed the case for Pakistan in talks with the British in London and back in Washington. He told the Joint Chiefs of Staff in May, "Without Pakistan, I don't see any way to defend the Middle East."[115] When the British examined the Pakistan issue more closely, however, they decided to back off, anticipating a negative Indian reaction. Washington by the summer of 1951 appeared to come around to the same view.[116]

Henry Byroade, who replaced McGhee as the region's Assistant Secretary of State in December 1951, shared his predecessor's enthusiasm for providing arms to Pakistan. A West Point graduate, Byroade served in India during the war, building airfields in Assam. He became the Army's youngest general when General Marshall selected him as his aide for the ill-fated mission to China in 1946. After President Truman asked Marshall to serve as Secretary of State, Byroade resigned from the Army to become head of German Affairs in the State Department.

When Byroade shifted to the Near East Bureau, one of the issues on the agenda was the question of Middle East defense arrangements. It quickly became clear, according to Byroade, that the official British proposal for MEDO was going nowhere. "The British didn't seem to realize that the concept, with a British commander, belonged to the colonial age. We never said no, but just let the idea die by itself."[117]

Still as Byroade looked at the area—so close to the Soviet Union and with Persian Gulf oil so important to the West—the Assistant Secretary felt that something should be done to provide greater stability. Doubting that most Arab states would join, he gradually came to favor some sort of defense arrangement, involving Turkey, Iran, Iraq, and Pakistan, with which the United States would be associated. A student of maps, Byroade saw an alliance extending from Turkey to Pakistan as forming a natural geographic arc of Muslim states that, with help and political support from the United States, might do better economically and become more stable politically. Byroade envisaged this grouping more in political and psychological than in military terms. In Byroade's thinking, such an arrangement made much more sense than the British idea of MEDO. Two years later, with Eisenhower in the White House, the concept became a reality as the Baghdad Pact.[118]

Given India's concerns about possible US arms for Pakistan, the most significant military sales to South Asia during the Truman administration were paradoxically not to Pakistan but to India. In the summer of 1952, the Indians sought substantial numbers of tanks and aircraft to modernize their forces. The request for 200 Sherman tanks, worth at the time $19 million, received rapid approval. This action promptly drew a strong complaint from the Pakistanis who—foreshadowing later Indian complaints about arms to Pakistan—asserted that the transaction would adversely affect the military balance in the subcontinent. When the Pakistanis said menacingly they would regard the sale as an unfriendly act, Byroade asserted they were exaggerating the significance of the purchase.

A parallel Indian request to buy 200 jet aircraft costing $150 million received less sympathetic consideration. A year after the US Congress voted $190 million of food aid and at a time India was seeking substantial development aid, officials asked how India could justify spending such a large sum for arms. In the end, the Indians decided to seek a far less expensive package of 54 C-119 transport aircraft. The State Department approved this request.[119]

Shortly before the end of the Truman administration, the British decided to sound out the Pakistanis about membership in MEDO, reversing their position of the year before. In informing the US Embassy in Karachi about the planned British démarche, the State Department said the United States was ready to support the idea and take this into account in considering future Pakistani requests for arms assistance.[120] From New Delhi, Ambassador Chester Bowles shot back a strong—but uncharacteristically short—message.

The arms proposal, Bowles cabled, would be seen by the Indians as a new form of colonialism, would confirm a rumored arrangement about US bases in Pakistan, would have a bitter effect on Indo-American relations, would provide the Communists a major propaganda weapon, and would make Indo-Pakistani relations more explosive and harder to settle.[121] Bowles' message—along with a sharp response from Nehru when rumors of an arms accord started circulating—killed off the proposal. The State Department cabled New Delhi on 28 November that Washington was aware of the adverse Indian reaction and that no approach had been made to the Pakistanis.[122] In a State/Joint Chiefs of Staff meeting the same day, Byroade put the problem frankly: Pakistan would probably join an anti-Communist defense pact if the United States provided enough equipment. This would be a plus, but would run directly into the Kashmir problem and the Indians. Sooner or later, Byroade added, the United States might have to meet this question head on.[123]

During the Truman administration, arms for Pakistan thus received consideration, but nothing concrete happened despite support from senior officials, like McGhee and Byroade. Although there was some interest in the Defense Department in possible US airbases in Pakistan, South Asia did not have a high priority in the Pentagon's strategic planning. Funding for military aid was short. Needs and priorities were greater elsewhere. Washington also knew arms for Pakistan would encounter a severe Indian reaction. A comment by Secretary Dean Acheson best summed things up. The Pakistanis, Acheson recalled, "were always asking us for arms and I was always holding them off."[124] After John Foster Dulles became Republican Secretary of State in January 1953, the situation would change.

Indo-US Relations: Through The Prism of the Cold War

Once the Korean War started in June 1950, Cold War considerations became an even more dominant element in US foreign policy. Discussions between Ambassador Henderson and Prime Minister Nehru in November 1950 mirrored the sharp differences between the two countries on this basic problem—the United States stressing collective security and India following a neutralist approach as the best way to preserve the peace.

In December 1950—just after the Chinese routed UN forces in North Korea—a State Department policy review of South Asia made clear that Washington's main concern about India was that that country not be "lost" the way China was. "With China under Communist domination," the study stated, "Soviet power now encroaches along the perimeter of the Indian sub-continent. India has become the pivotal state in non-Communist Asia by virtue of its relative power, stability and influence."[125] The policy paper hoped India would agree "voluntarily to associate itself with the United States and like-minded countries opposing Communism," and supported Ambassador Henderson's recommendation that an aid program be initiated.[126]

The following month, in January 1951, after a National Security Council (NSC) review, President Truman approved NSC document 98/1, the first formal policy for South Asia. The Cold War framed the approach. Behind a fog of bureaucratic prose, NSC 98/1 stated bluntly that if India were lost to the Communists "for all practical purposes all of Asia would have been lost". The United States wanted to gain more Indian support because of the prestige of the country's leadership, and also to have continued access to strategic materials. NSC 98/1 proposed a more activist policy—closer consultations, an economic aid program, the supply of military equipment—taking into account higher priorities elsewhere—and continuing efforts to improve Indo-Pakistani relations.[127] India's importance thus rose somewhat in the eyes of the Truman administration from the relatively marginal position it had occupied in earlier years.

The continuing incompatibility of US and Indian views was, however, underscored in April 1951 discussions that Assistant Secretary McGhee and Ambassador Henderson had with Prime Minister Nehru in New Delhi. These talks confirmed a wide gap between US and Indian thinking on the major foreign policy issues of the day—handling the war in Korea, the Soviet Union, and Communist China. As Henderson put it, there remained "a fundamental difference between us about the aggressive intent of international communism."[128]

Although official Indian documents have yet to be released to the public, Nehru's public remarks and his private letters to Chief Ministers, which have been made available, provide a good picture of Indian policy views. Justifying neutralism as an effective policy to promote peace, Nehru told the Constituent Assembly on 8 March 1949:

> Our policy will continue to be not only to keep aloof from power alignments, but to try to make friendly cooperation possible . . . . If by any chance we align ourselves definitely with one power group, we may perhaps from one point of view do some good, but I have not the shadow of a doubt that from a larger point of view, not only of India, but of world peace, it will do harm . . . . Therefore, it becomes

all the more necessary that India should not be lined up with any group of powers which for various reasons are full of fear of war and preparing for war.[129]

Nehru believed firmly that the war in Korea proved that India's policy was right—just the opposite of the US view. Writing to Chief Ministers in April 1951, Nehru stated:

> I believe the policy we have pursued has been demonstrably proved to be good for India and good for world peace. I think it has averted or helped in averting the spread of the Korean War . . . . The mere fact that both our friends and critics inevitably look to India to take some step to break the present impasse in the world is significant of the virtue of India's foreign policy.[130]

The Prime Minister remained consistently critical about US policy toward Kashmir, continuing to believe this was motivated by an interest in aligning Pakistan with an Islamic bloc, under Western tutelage, against the Soviets—"Pakistan was easy to keep within their sphere of influence in regard to wider policies, while India was an uncertain and possibly not reliable quality."[131] Still, the Prime Minister doubted the United States would push too far, believing "it is thoroughly understood . . . in the U.S.A. that India counts far more than Pakistan.[132]

By the end of the Truman years, Indo-American relations had fallen into the pattern of chronic friction that has so perplexed observers over the years. Although there were positive aspects, especially with Bowles as ambassador, a sense of estrangement was only too evident. With hindsight, the reasons are not hard to find. After the Korean War made the Cold War a global struggle, US and Indian world views were bound to clash sharply—and did—on fundamental security issues. The United States saw a world-wide threat from the Soviet Union and its fellow communist states and felt peace could be secured only through a strong military posture and collective security.

India, in contrast, thought the Communist threat overstated and saw both East and West as gripped in mutual fear. Nehru's concern was that this security psychosis would end not in preserving the peace, but in provoking war. He saw peace best preserved through dialogue not force, pursuing this end as actively as the United States pursued a stronger security posture. Added to this fundamental difference of outlook was the friction over Kashmir—an issue of far greater importance to India than the United States. Stung and annoyed by India's frequent criticism of US policies, India's unwillingness to follow through with the plebiscite New Delhi itself had proposed seemed to Americans a far cry from the lofty moralism and principled views Nehru so often articulated.

Underlying the estrangement was a sense of mutual disappointment fed by unrealized expectations. Democratic and secular India expected the support of the United States on issues like Kashmir. The United States as leader of the democratic world expected that free and democratic India would back the general thrust of US policy in dealing with the Soviet threat. Washington did not welcome India's effort to follow a path between the Western democratic and Communist totalitarian camps, especially after the United States began to shed its blood in the war in Korea. And thus it was that Indo-American relations got off to a rocky start in the early years of Indian independence.

NOTES

1. Vijaya Lakshmi Pandit, *The Scope of Happiness: A Personal Memoir* (New York: Crown, 1979), pp. 195-97.
2. Gary Hess, *America Encounters India, 1941-1947,* (Baltimore: Johns Hopkins, 1971), p. 160.
3. Ibid., pp. 166-67.
4. Harold Isaacs, *Scratches on Our Mind* (White Plains, NY: M. E. Sharpe, 1980), pp. 317-19.
5. *Selected Works of Jawaharlal Nehru SWJN,* vol. 14, pp. 457-58; Nehru interview with the press, 28 October 1945.
6. *Foreign Relations of the United States FRUS,* 1946, vol. V, p. 91, dispatch from the Commissioner in India to the State Department, 10 June 1946.
7. *SWJN,* vol. 15, p. 15, message to the people of the Philippines, 5 July 1946.
8. Ibid., pp. 524-25, Nehru press interview, 15 March 1946.
9. Ibid., pp. 569-70, interview with George Jones of the *New York Times,* 30 August 1946.
10. *SWJN, Second Series,* vol. 1, p. 492, press interview, 29 September 1946.
11. *FRUS, 1946,* vol. V, pp. 92-96: memorandum from Acheson to Truman, 30 August 1946; telegram from Embassy London to State Department, 9 September 1946; and telegram to Mission New Delhi from State Department, 16 October 1946.

12. *SWJN, Second Series,* vol. 1, p. 539, Nehru to Mrs. Pandit, 14 November 1946.

13. Ibid., p. 556, Nehru letter to Asaf Ali, 21 December 1946.

14. The purpose of the initial call is to present to the Secretary a copy of the letter of accreditaton. In terms of protocol, until an envoy presents the original to the President, he or she is not formally able to function as an ambassador. The Embassy continues, on paper at least, to be run by the No. 2 as chargé d'affaires while the envoy is called "appointed ambassador."

15. *FRUS, 1947,* vol. III, pp. 147-49, memorandum of call by India's Appointed Ambassador Asaf Ali on Secretary Marshall, 26 February 1947.

16. Ibid., Nehru statement to the press, 20 January 1947.

17. Ibid., p. 138, State Department to Embassy New Delhi, 21 January 1947.

18. Kurt Stiegler, "Communism and 'Colonial Evolution': John Foster Dulles' Vision of India and Pakistan," *Journal of South Asian and Middle Eastern Studies,* 15 (Winter 1991): pp. 74-75.

19. *FRUS, 1946,* vol. V, pp. 97-98, State Department telegram to Embassy London and New Delhi, 30 November 1946.

20. Ibid., pp. 99-100, text of Acheson press statement as cabled to Embassy London, 3 December 1946.

21. Ibid.

22. Ibid., pp. 101-12: New Delhi telegram reporting talk with Sardar Patel, 11 December 1946; State Department telegram of 11 December 1946 providing guidance for talk with Nehru; London telegram of 12 December 1946 reporting discussion with Jinnah; New Delhi telegram of 14 December 1946 reporting conversation with Nehru; 27 and 29 December 1946 New Delhi telegrams reporting discussions with Liaquat Ali Khan. *FRUS, 1947,* vol. III, pp. 136-38, Embassy New Delhi instruction to Consulate Karachi, 4 January 1947, and Consulate Karachi report to State Department of interview with Jinnah, 6 January 1947.

23. Ibid., pp. 143-47, memorandum of conversation between Marshall and the British Ambassador, 20 February 1947, and British Embassy Memorandum on the Indian situation, dated 19 February 1947.

24. Ibid., pp. 155-56, Embassy London telegram to the State Department, 2 June 1947.

25. Paul Hare, "Journey to South Asia," *A Diplomatic Chronicle of the Middle East and South Asia: Biography of Ambassador Raymond A. Hare, 1924-1966* (Lanham, MD: University Press of America, 1992).

26. Ibid.

27. Ibid.

28. Nehru's activism against racial discrimination dated back to the early 1920s. Serving in his first public office, as chairman of the local government in his home city of Allahabad, Nehru in 1923 sponsored a resolution deploring the treatment of Indians in British colonies and the United States. Sarvepalli Gopal, *Jawaharlal Nehru,* vol. I, 1889-1947, (London: Jonathan Cape, 1975), p. 90.

29. William J. Barnds, *India, Pakistan and the Great Powers* (New York: Praeger, 1972), pp. 60-63.

30. *FRUS, 1947,* vol. III, pp. 160-61, Embassy New Delhi to State Department, 9 July 1947.

31. Ibid., p. 138, report of State Department Discussion on South Asia, 26 December 1947.

32. Alistair Lamb, *The Kashmir Problem* (New York: Praeger, 1967), pp. 46-47.

33. Sisir Gupta, *Kashmir, A Study in Indo-Pakistan Relations* (New Delhi: Asia Publishing House, 1966), pp. 129-39.

34. Josef Korbel, *Danger in Kashmir* (Princeton: Princeton University Press, 1954), pp. 79-80.

35. *FRUS, 1948,* vol. V, pp. 276-78, Henderson to Lovett, 9 January 1948; report of discussions between the British delegation and US officials, 10 January 1948; H. W. Brands, *The Specter of Neutralism, The United States and the Emergence of the Third World, 1947-1960* (New York: Columbia University Press, 1989), pp. 24-25.

36. Gupta, p. 148.

37. *SWJN, Second Series,* vol. 5, pp. 188-90, 203-05, 210-11, 218: letters to N. Gopalaswami Ayyangar, 17 January 1948; Gordon-Walker's record of meeting with Nehru, 30 January 1948; letter to Lord Mountbatten, 8 February 1948; and letter to Mrs. Pandit, 16 February 1948.

38. *FRUS, 1948,* vol. V, p. 431, telegram from Embassy Paris reporting Marshall-Nehru meeting, 20 October 1948.

39. *FRUS, 1949,* vol. VI, p. 1732, Embassy New Delhi to State Department, 15 August 1949.

40. Ibid., pp. 1733-34, 1736-38, State Department to New Delhi, 25 August 1949, and New Delhi to State Department, 5 September 1949.

41. Dean Acheson, *Present at the Creation* (New York: Norton & Co., 1969), pp. 334-36; *FRUS, 1949,* vol. VI, pp. 1750-51, memorandum of conversation between Nehru and Truman, 13 October 1949.

42. The former Agent General of India in Washington during World War II, Girja Shankar Bajpai stayed on briefly as No. 2 after India's first Ambassador Asaf Ali arrived in 1947. Returning to New Delhi, Bajpai sat on the sidelines for a while, but was then appointed by Nehru as Secretary General in the Ministry of External Affairs, the top civil service position in the ministry. Despite past differences in outlook

during pre-independence days, the two worked closely together until 1952 when Nehru named Bajpai governor of Bombay.

43. *FRUS, 1949,* vol. VI, pp. 1766-68, Embassy New Delhi to State Department, 26 December 1949.

44. Ibid., pp. 1763-64, 1771-72, US Mission to the UN report of talk with Zafrullah Khan of Pakistan, 20 December 1949, and US Mission telegram to State Department, 28 December 1949.

45. *FRUS, 1950,* vol. V, p. 1367, report of meeting between Acheson, Ambassador Pandit, and Secretary General Bajpai, 9 January 1950.

46. Ibid., pp. 1369-70, USUN to State Department, 16 January 1950. Bajpai delivered Nehru's response in New York during meetings at the United Nations.

47. Korbel, pp. 174-76; *FRUS, 1950,* vol. V, pp. 1415, 1422-23, cables to the State Department from Embassies New Delhi and Karachi reporting on the Dixon Mission 25 and 29 July and 15 and 21 August 1950.

48. Gupta, *Kashmir*, pp. 220-21.

49. *FRUS, 1950,* vol. V, pp. 1435-39, memorandum of Conversation by Secretary Acheson on his meeting with Sir Zafrullah Khan, 17 November 1950.

50. *Jawaharlal Nehru: Letters to Chief Ministers,* 1950-1952, vol. 2 (New Delhi: Jawaharlal Nehru Memorial Fund, 1986), pp. 432-33.

51. Chester Bowles, *Ambassador's Report* (New York: Harper & Brothers, 1954), p. 2.

52. *FRUS, 1952-4,* vol. IX, pp. 1167-70, 1183-84, 1190-91, Embassy New Delhi to State Department 10 January 1952, and State Department to Embassy New Delhi, 18 February 1952.

53. *FRUS, 1952-4,* vol. XI, pp. 1272-76, 1278-79, Embassy New Delhi to State Department, 8 and 11 July 1952.

54. *FRUS, 1952-4,* vol. IX, pp. 1172-73, USUN cable to State Department, 17 January 1952, and Embassy New Delhi cable to State Department, 18 January 1952.

55. Gupta, pp. 239-54. A good summary of Graham's patient—but ultimately unsuccessful—mediation effort.

56. Gopal, 1947-56, p. 116.

57. Korbel, p. 42.

58. The Kashmir Constituent Assembly adopted a constitution giving Kashmir a special autonomous status within the Indian Union. Pakistan complained bitterly that this action clearly ran counter to the state's future being settled by a plebiscite. The Indian response: since the people of Kashmir voted for the Assembly, this amounted to a "free choice" for India. Needless to say, the Pakistanis strenuously opposed

India's action—nor were US observers impressed with the strength of India's argument.

59. Interview with George McGhee, 14 August 1991. A Rhodes scholar, McGhee became wealthy as a young man in the oil business in Texas before entering public service through connections in the Democratic Party. After heading US aid to Greece, McGhee became the first Assistant Secretary of the new Bureau of Near East, South Asia, and Africa (NEA). He later served as Ambassador to Turkey under Truman and Under Secretary for Political Affairs and Ambassador to Germany under Kennedy and Johnson.

60. State Department Memorandum of Conversation with Henry Grady, 26 December 1947.

61. *FRUS, 1948,* vol. V, p. 498, Embassy New Delhi to State Department, 20 March 1948.

62. Ibid., pp. 502-04, 506-07, reports 2 April 1948 meetings of Bajpai first with the Office of Near Eastern Affairs and then with the Acting Secretary of State.

63. Gopal, pp. 45-46.

64. Ibid., pp. 58-59.

65. *SWJN, Second Series,* vol. 8, p. 629, note on negotiations for a Treaty of Friendship, Commerce and Navigation, 12 August 1948.

66. Acheson, p. 336.

67. 2 February 1950 letter from Nehru to Radhakrishnan, quoted by Gopal, vol. II, p. 60.

68. Pandit, pp. 252-53.

69. Letters from Nehru to Mrs. Pandit, 10 and 29 May 1950, quoted in Gopal vol. II, p. 63.

70. *FRUS, 1951,* vol. V, pp. 1461-63, Embassy New Delhi to State Department, 12 April 1950.

71. Ibid., pp. 1464-66, State Department telegram to Embassy New Delhi, April 1950. In the days when classified messages required time-consuming encoding, State Department telegrams often omitted unnecessary words and abbreviated others. Once the computer age and optical scanners arrived, cablese became a thing of the past; brevity was no longer at a premium.

72. Nehru, vol 2, p. 120, 2 July 1950.

73. Acheson, pp. 419-20; *FRUS, 1950,* vol. VII, pp. 454-55, Embassy New Delhi telegram to State Department, 23 July 1950.

74. Ibid., pp. 444-45, 447, 478-79, and 526, State Department to Embassy New Delhi, 22 July, 3 August, and Embassy New Delhi to State Department, 23 and 27 July 1950.

75. Harry S. Truman, *Memoirs, Years of Trial and Hope* (Garden City: Doubleday & Company, Inc., 1956), pp. 361-62.

76. *New York Times,* 10 October 1950.

77. Gopal, vol. II, p. 109.

78. *FRUS, 1950*, vol. VII, p. 746, Minutes of staff meeting of US Delegation to UN General Assembly, 21 September 1950.

79. Gopal, vol. II, p. 136.

80. Ibid., pp. 140-44.

81. *FRUS, 1952-54*, vol. XV, pp. 633, 653-54, Letter from Acheson to Truman and report of USUN staff meeting, 17 November 1952.

82. Nehru, vol. 2, p. 186, 4 December 1952.

83. *FRUS, 1949*, vol. VI, pp. 1750-56, memorandum of conversation between Nehru and Truman, 13 October 1949, and of meeting between Nehru and US representative to the United Nations Warren Austin, 19 October 1949.

84. Nehru, vol. 2, p. 484, letter of 15 August 1951.

85. Pandit, p. 255.

86. Nehru, vol. 2, p. 486, 31 August 1951.

87. Bimal Prasad, ed., *India's Foreign Policy: Studies in Continuity and Change* (New Delhi: Vikas, 1979), pp. 235-36; *FRUS, 1948*, vol. V, pp. 501-06, memorandum of conversation between Bajpai and Loy Henderson, Director for Near Eastern and South Asian Affairs, 2 April 1948; and Dennis Merrill, "Indo-American Relations, 1947-1950: A Missed Opportunity in Asia," *Diplomatic History* II (Summer 1987): p. 208.

88. *SWJN, Second Series*, vol. 7, p. 628, note on the Friendship, Commerce and Navigation Treaty negotiations, 12 August 1948.

89. Nehru, vol. 1, p. 483, letter of 1 December 1949.

90. Loy Henderson to Under Secretary James Webb, 3 October 1949.

91. State Department to Ambassador Henderson, 21 November 1949; Dennis Merrill, "Indo-American Relations, 1947-1950: A Missed Opportunity in Asia," *Diplomatic History* 11 (Summer 1987): pp. 220-23. The issue, of course, did not go away. Henderson continued to press the case, gradually winning support in the State Department. His successor, Chester Bowles, enthusiastically took up the cause of large-scale aid where Henderson left off.

92. *FRUS, 1949*, vol. VI, pp. 1750-52, Memorandum of conversation of the meeting between Nehru, President Truman, Secretary Acheson, and Secretary General Bajpai, 13 October 1949.

93. *FRUS, 1950*, vol. V, pp. 1461-66, Embassy New Delhi telegram to State Department, 12 April 1950, and State Department telegram to New Delhi, 21 April 1950.

94. Ibid., pp. 1481, State Department telegram reporting a meeting between Mrs. Pandit and Secretary Acheson, 30 December 1950.

95. *FRUS, 1951*, vol. VI, pp. 2087-90, 2092, Embassy New Delhi telegrams to the State Department, 20 and 28 January 1951.

96. *US Senate Executive Sessions,* vol. 3, pp. 27-46, 26 January 1951; interview with George McGhee, 14 August 1991.

97. Brands, p. 66.

98. *FRUS, 1951,* vol. VI, p. 2153, footnote 1: text of remarks from *Congressional Record,* vol. 97, pt. 4, p. 5739.

99. Ibid., pp. 2153-55, memorandum of conversation at the State Department between E.G. Mathews, South Asia Director, and B.K.Nehru, Indian Embassy Economic Minister, 2 May 1951.

100. Ibid., pp. 2155-58, New Delhi to Secstate, 4, 5, and 7 May 1951; Robert J. McMahon, "Food as a Diplomatic Weapon: The Indian Wheat Loan of 1951," *Pacific Historical Review,* LVI (August 1987): pp. 372-74.

101. Nehru, vol. 2, p. 384, 2 May 1951. Nehru also brought up the congressional delays in his letters of 18 February, 2 March, 10 and 21 April, 17 May, and 2 June 1951. (Ibid., pp. 334, 365, 370-71, 377, 395, and 409).

102. Pandit, pp. 255-56.

103. Ibid., pp. 2158-59, Embassy New Delhi to State Department, 7 May 1951.

104. *FRUS, 1951,* vol. VI, pp. 2164-66, Embassy New Delhi telegram to the State Department, 25 May 1951.

105. *FRUS, 1952-4,* vol. XI, pp. 1634-38: memorandum on India aid to Deputy Under Secretary of State Matthews, 8 February 1952; Embassy New Delhi telegram to State Department, 21 February 1952; Bowles telegram to President Truman, 21 February 1952; and State Department to Bowles, 3 March 1952.

106. Ibid., pp. 1646-48 and 1653-54, memorandum for President Truman from Secretary Acheson and Mutual Security Director Harriman, 5 June 1952, and letter to Bowles from Truman, 1 July 1952, enclosing Bureau of the Budget Memorandum.

107. Ibid., pp. 1668-77, 1679-84, letters from Bowles to Acheson, 28 October and 19 November 1952, and Acheson's reply to Bowles, 8 January 1953.

108. Bowles' book, *Ambassador's Report,* which appeared in 1954, did a good job in putting across his point of view.

109. McGhee, *Envoy to the Middle World* (New York: Harper & Row, 1983), pp. 51-52; Pandit, p. 250.

110. M.S. Venkataramani, *The American Role in Pakistan, 1947-1958* (New Delhi: Radiant, 1982). See pp. 1-31 for a discussion of the early and unsuccessful Pakistani attempt to obtain US arms aid.

111. *FRUS, 1948,* vol. v, pp. 496-97, memorandum for President Truman from Secretary Marshall, 11 March 1948.

112. Ibid., pp. 435-36, report of meeting between Liaquat and Marshall, 29 October 1948; *FRUS, 1950,* vol. V, p. 1492, "US Policy Toward Pakistan."

113. McGhee, pp. 96-97.

114. Ibid., pp. 277-83.

115. Records of the Joint Chiefs of Staff, 1951 1887/16, quoted in Robert J. McMahon, "United States Cold War Strategy in South Asia: Making a Military Commitment to Pakistan, 1947-1954," *Journal of American History 75,* no. 3, (December 1988): pp. 822-23.

116. State Department telegram to field posts, 30 June 1951, quoted in McMahon, pp. 824-25.

117. Interview with Henry Byroade, 3 May 1990. After his service as Assistant Secretary, Byroade went on to hold a series of five ambassadorships—to Egypt, South Africa, the Philippines, Afghanistan, and Pakistan—before he retired in 1981.

118. Ibid. Byroade's ideas were similar to those of former British Indian official, Sir Olaf Caroe, in his influential book, *The Wells of Power.* Although Selig Harrison, in his excellent three-part series of articles on the US decision to arm Pakistan in the August 1959 *New Republic,* reported that Caroe saw Byroade among others when he promoted his ideas during a 1951 visit to Washington, Byroade did not recall meeting Caroe or reading his book.

119. *FRUS, 1952-54,* vol. IX, pp. 1658-60, and 1678, reports of meetings between Pakistan and Indian Embassy officials and Assistant Secretary Byroade, 1 and 7 August, and 5 November 1952.

120. Ibid., pp. 315-17, State Department telegram to Karachi, New Delhi, Ankara, and London, 13 November 1952.

121. Ibid., pp. 317-19, Embassy New Delhi telegram to State Department, 20 November 1952.

122. Ibid., p. 319, fn. ii, State Department telegram to Embassy New Delhi, 28 November 1952.

123. Ibid., pp. 323-24, minutes of State/JCS meeting of 28 November 1952.

124. Selig Harrison, "Pakistan and the United States," *New Republic,* 10 August 1959, p. 14.

125. *FRUS, 1950,* vol. v, p. 1478, Department of State policy statement on India, 1 December 1950.

126. Ibid., pp. 1476-80.

127. *FRUS, 1951,* vol. VI, pp. 1650-53, draft statement proposed by the National Security Council on South Asia, 22 January 1951.

128. McGhee, pp. 293-95.

129. Jawaharlal Nehru, *Independence and After* (New York: The John Day Company, 1949), p. 241-43.

130. Nehru, vol. 2, p. 374, letter of 21 April 1951.

131. Ibid., p. 460, letter of 1 August 1951.
132. Ibid., p. 461-62, letter of 12 August 1951

Chapter III

Eisenhower I: Tougher on Communism

Dwight D. Eisenhower became President on 20 January 1953 with a mandate for change after twenty years of Democratic rule. The incoming Republicans favored a more conservative approach to the nation's problems—they wanted less government at home and a tougher policy toward Communist adversaries abroad. Above all, Eisenhower pledged an early end to the Korean War, increasingly unpopular as the conflict dragged on into its third year.

Relations with South Asia did not rank high on Eisenhower's foreign policy agenda. Prime Minister Nehru was, nonetheless, uneasy. "The new administration in the U.S.A. has not yet come out clearly with its new policy," he wrote his Chief Ministers. "All that we know is that it has a certain bent of mind which does not take us toward peace."[1] The emphasis that incoming Secretary of State John Foster Dulles placed on collective security arrangements worried the Indian leader, concerned lest US sponsored military pacts embrace India's principal antagonist and neighbor, Pakistan. The new Republican administration also appeared more tepid than the Democrats about economic assistance to developing countries, a subject of growing importance to India as food production continued to lag.

India and Korean War POW Repatriation

Soviet dictator Joseph Stalin died in March 1953 shortly after Eisenhower took office. When Stalin's successors in the Kremlin and the Chinese Communists signaled interest in ending the Korean War, stalemated roughly along the 38th parallel, armistice discussions between the United Nations and the Communists resumed. The talks inched slowly toward acceptance of arrangements for handling repatriation of prisoners of war similar to those India had proposed the previous fall. A five-nation Neutral Nations Repatriation Commission (NNRC), chaired by India with Canada, Sweden, Poland, and Czechoslovakia as members, would offer POWs an opportunity to express their wishes about returning home. Since the NNRC would take decisions by majority vote, neutral India was likely to have a key role. There was also talk of India's sending a military force to take charge of the POWs until their fate was decided.

The possible Indian role did not enthuse US officials. U. Alexis Johnson, then a senior State Department Far East expert and later Under Secretary of State for Political Affairs, told the British, "We were, of course, not dismissing India but . . . we would not be too happy over such a choice as India all too often seemed to consider it necessary to be 'more neutral' towards the Chinese Communists than the UN."[2] South Korea's President, Syngman Rhee, was more hostile. "Rhee feels very strongly," UN Commander General Mark Clark cabled Washington, "that India is not neutral and is opposed to have its (Indian) armed forces . . . on his sovereign soil."[3]

In late May 1953, with the Korean armistice talks still not settled, John Foster Dulles visited the Middle East and South Asia—the first trip to the region by a US Secretary of State. His itinerary included two days in New Delhi for talks with the Indian Prime Minister. Like Pandit Nehru, Dulles had a passion for international relations. His grandfather, John Foster, served as Secretary of State under President Benjamin Harrison in the late 1880s. His uncle, Robert Lansing, was Secretary of State under Woodrow Wilson. A prominent international lawyer and an active Republican, Dulles provided foreign policy advice to New York Governor and two-time Republican presidential candidate Thomas E. Dewey. As a sign of bipartisan foreign policy, President Truman appointed Dulles to several US delegations to the UN and named him as the negotiator of the Japanese Peace Treaty. When Eisenhower was elected President, Dulles was a natural choice to become Secretary of State.

Although Dulles had yet to declare neutralism "immoral", he was known for his hard-line views on dealing with Communists and his dislike for India's nonalignment. Given their conflicting policy approach, the meetings between Nehru and Dulles could not have been very relaxed. Korea was perhaps the subject where their views most converged, despite their differing appraisals of Communist intentions. Dulles asked India to send troops to take custody of POWs not wishing repatriation. Nehru expressed willingness, but urged a greater effort to achieve an armistice, voicing concern that otherwise the conflict would broaden. Dulles responded pointedly, "If the armistice negotiations collapsed the United States would probably make a stronger rather than a lesser military exertion and that this might well extend the area of conflict." Dulles commented in his report of the conversation, "I assumed this would be relayed (to the Chinese Communists)."[4]

The efforts to reach an armistice succeeded—on 4 June the Communists accepted UN proposals to hand over POWs to the Indians for repatriation screening. Obdurately opposed to the accord, Syngman Rhee caused an uproar when he orchestrated the mass break-out of 40,000 North Korean POWs two weeks later. Justifying this action to General Clark, Rhee stated:

> What is uppermost in my mind is the fear that if the Indian armed forces, a thousand or more, come to guard these boys to help the Communist brainwashers grill them and indoctrinate them for two or three long months, urging them to go back to the Communists, the Korean people will not let them alone.[5]

US Ambassador Ellis Briggs delivered a stiff message from President Eisenhower on 19 June, but the Korean President remained bitter about India. He declared that he would not permit "even one Indian soldier to enter ROK (Republic of Korea) territory in connection with the POWs."[6] Nehru, who regarded Rhee as an reactionary anachronism, thought the United States should have taken a tougher line with the South Korean leader instead of trying "to appease him by all kinds of assurances for the future."[7]

The Prime Minister appointed one of India's top soldiers, General K. S. Thimayya, to head the 6,000 man Indian Custodial Force. His task was to see that the POWs could freely express their personal views and that no one was sent home against his wishes. Nehru instructed Thimayya to maintain strict neutrality in both official duties and unofficial contacts. Because of Rhee's antipathy, Indian troops had to fly from the port on Inchon to the Demilitarized Zone between Communist and United Nations forces, never crossing South Korean territory.

For four months, the Indian Custodial Force had charge of 22,604 Chinese and North Korean POWs as well as 359 UN soldiers, who said they wished to remain with the Communists. The Indians did not have an easy time. The Communist observers put great psychological pressure on the prisoners during the interviews. UN supporters in the POW camp strenuously pressed fence sitters to refuse repatriation. In many instances, the POWs, especially North Koreans, refused to appear for the interviews.

Neither the Communists nor the UN had success in convincing prisoners to change their minds. Thimayya thought the heavily ideological Communist arguments went over the heads of the Chinese and North Korean soldiers, who were mostly peasants. Conversely, he found the UN explanations not sophisticated enough for the politically savvy, pro-Communist UN POWs. The Communists were terribly unhappy that 96 percent of their prisoners remained firm in refusing repatriation. None of the 359 UN POWs—22 Americans, one Briton, and 336 South Koreans—changed their minds.[8]

As the 120 days agreed upon for prisoner repatriation drew to a close, the screening process remained far from complete. The Communist insistence on lengthy explanations was one problem. Nehru also blamed the UN Command for organizing the camps politically in order to exert strong-arm pressure on POWs to refuse to appear for the interviews.[9] Rather than continue what had become a painful exercise, the Indians decided to wash their hands of the affair, handing back the remaining unrepatriated prisoners to the UN Command on 22 January 1953.

Even though the Chinese Communists were angry, Nehru refused to give ground out of concern the POWs would riot unless they were released. Thimayya told Ambassador Arthur Dean, US Korean peace negotiator, that Chou En-lai had cabled Nehru, "They are our prisoners, not yours, and you cannot release them. It would be better to let them break out on 23 January and then you must shoot them whatever happens." The Prime Minister reportedly responded to Chou that India would have no part in bloodshed and had the duty to see that the prisoners were treated in a humanitarian fashion.[10]

The POW issue had become an issue of great symbolic importance for both sides of the Cold War. The United States regarded the refusal of so many prisoners to return home as a major defeat for the Communists.[11] During the 21 January 1954 National Security Council meeting, CIA Director Allen Dulles described the POW affair as "one of the greatest psychological victories so far achieved by the free world against communism."[12]

The professional approach of General Thimayya and his troops earned respect. Ambassador Arthur Dean expressed his "tremendous admiration" for the general and his associates. He thought "the Indian troops were doing a most amazing job in extremely difficult circumstances."[13] US diplomat U. Alexis Johnson, skeptical earlier about India's role, praised Thimayya's skill in preserving "the principle that every prisoner should have the right to choose his future" and lauded Indian troops for their professional management of the POW camp.[14] The Indians, however, won few plaudits from Syngman Rhee, who remained bitterly critical. Nehru, in turn, disparaged Rhee's commitment to peace, alleging that South Korea was acting in an "utterly irresponsible" manner.[15]

In deference to Rhee, Secretary Dulles agreed to oppose India's participation in the international conference that was to deal with Korea's future. At the United Nations, US Representative Henry Cabot Lodge spoke frankly with Krishna Menon, explaining that the United States had been unable to persuade Rhee to accept India at the Korean political conference.[16] The issue split the UN camp, with the countries of the British Commonwealth—except Pakistan—supporting India's presence. In the showdown vote, a majority of the UN's Political Committee favored India, but failed to muster the two-third's vote needed to override US and Latin American opposition. Not without justification, Nehru believed that his country, having played a major role in bringing about the end to hostilities, had earned a seat at the conference. Since he regarded Rhee as an American puppet, the Indian leader found less than convincing the US explanation that Rhee would refuse to attend the Conference if India were invited.

In a frank 7 October meeting, Dulles and Indian Ambassador G. L. Mehta summed up the harmful impact of the Korean War on bilateral relations. The Secretary commented that since the United States favored "stronger methods in dealing with Communism" than New Delhi, Indian policies would "inevitably not have much popular appeal" to Americans. Acknowledging this, Mehta said the reverse was true in India where public opinion had come to believe the United States did not want peace in Korea.[17] When the Korean conference finally convened in Geneva in April 1954, the gathering soon deadlocked. After two months of futile discussion, the conference broke up in disagreement between the UN and Communist sides. Meanwhile, the armistice on the ground in Korea continued, the military conflict having given way to a hostile and tense peace.

Quite apart from the Korean War's negative repercussions for bilateral relations, the conflict had great importance for both US and Indian foreign policies. For the United States, the fact that North Korean armies invaded South Korea demonstrated to Americans that the danger of Communist aggression was real, not simply the imagination of overzealous Cold Warriors. The war firmed up the policy of containment as the chosen means of countering the Soviet Union and its Communist allies. In the wake of Korea, America was looking for allies and military pacts to contain what Washington perceived as the global Communist threat. After Eisenhower became President, the search for security partners intensified. The quest would shortly envelop South Asia, where the United States would enlist India's neighbor and foe Pakistan into the Western camp with far-reaching and baneful consequences for Indo-American relations.

For India, the Korean War was equally important, putting Nehru's concept of neutralism to the test. Staying aloof from the two major power blocs, India was able to establish itself as the country in the middle between East and West, able to serve as an honest broker and channel of communication between the Western and the Communist powers. Even though India received little praise and often much criticism from both Cold War camps, Indian diplomacy proved successful. India, in the process, gained prestige and influence far beyond its limited military or economic power. Whether one liked it or not in the mid-1950s—and usually the United States did not—India had become a factor in international affairs that could not be ignored, speaking for its four hundred million people and articulating the desires of millions of others in Asia and Africa emerging from Western colonial rule.

US Military Assistance to Pakistan

For Indo-American relations, the most important question during the May 1953 visit of John Foster Dulles to South Asia was not Korea but Pakistan's membership in a pro-Western Middle East defense grouping and American military assistance. When Nehru mentioned India's concerns about these possibilities, Secretary Dulles replied with lawyer-like precision that the Middle East Defense Organization seemed unlikely to take shape as originally projected. He made no mention of the alternative northern tier system that he would discuss in public ten days later.

Regarding arms to Pakistan, the Secretary stated that the United States "had no present plans that would bring it into a military relationship with Pakistan which could be reasonably looked upon as unneutral as regards India." Literally accurate, Dulles' statement was misleading, for the Secretary was certainly considering providing arms to Pakistan even if nothing yet had been firmly decided. The issue of reasonableness about US arms for Pakistan—on which Dulles and other American officials would place importance—was in a sense irrelevant since India regarded any US military aid to Pakistan as "unneutral." In his report of the conversation, Dulles wrote, "Nehru expressed satisfaction with this declaration."[18] One wonders.

Dulles' next stop after New Delhi was Karachi, then the capital of Pakistan. The contrast in the welcome was marked. In New Delhi, the Indians were correct, but formal, in greeting

Dulles. Nehru saw no reason to butter up visitors from Washington. In Karachi, the Pakistanis overwhelmed the Americans with the warmth of their reception. Eager to gain US military support, the Pakistanis had every reason to court Dulles and his party. Like many senior American leaders, the Secretary was flattered by Pakistani hospitality—with an individual as dour as Dulles, no mean achievement.

The Pakistani leadership, especially Army commander General Ayub Khan, forcefully urged US military aid. Ayub "reiterated the potential, both in manpower and bases that is available in Pakistan and that his country under the present government is extremely anxious to cooperate with the US." The United States, Ayub argued, should not be afraid to help those countries ready to receive help against the Communists. Ayub contended that a strengthened Pakistan would make Nehru less intransigent and more likely to agree to a Kashmir settlement.[19]

Dulles was impressed. Several days later, the Secretary cabled from Turkey that the "genuine feeling of friendship encountered in Pakistan . . . exceeded to a marked degree that encountered in any country on this trip . . . . Pakistan is one country that has moral courage to do its part resisting communism." In Dulles' opinion, "Pakistan would be a cooperative member of any defense scheme that may emerge in the Middle East and that we need not await formal defense arrangements as condition to some military assistance . . ."[20]

Dulles reiterated his positive appraisal during a 1 June NSC meeting just after returning to Washington. The Secretary declared that he was "immensely impressed by the martial and religious qualities of the Pakistanis. These qualities made him and Mr. Stassen, . . . feel that Pakistan was a potential strong point for us . . . "[21] In contrast, the Secretary's assessment of Jawaharlal Nehru was hardly flattering: Dulles described the Indian leader as "an utterly impractical statesman."[22]

The same day, the Secretary spoke about his Middle East and South Asia trip over national radio and television. After reviewing the various stops—describing Pakistan with notably more warmth than India—the final section of his remarks dealt with regional defense arrangements. Noting that the Arab States were so engrossed in their quarrels with Israel, Great Britain, or

France that they paid little heed to the menace of Soviet communism, Dulles stated:

> However, there is more concern where the Soviet Union is near. In general, the northern tier of nations shows awareness of the danger.
>
> There is a vague desire to have a collective security system. But no such system can be imposed from without. It should be designed and grown from within out of a sense of common destiny and common danger.
>
> While awaiting the formal creation of a security association, the United States can usefully help strengthen the interrelated defense of those countries which want strength, not as against each other or the West, but to resist the common threat of all free peoples.[23]

Assistant Secretary of State Henry Byroade, who drafted the speech while accompanying Dulles on the trip, said that the address provided the vehicle for getting the Secretary's agreement on the northern tier defense concept to replace the stillborn Middle East Defense Organization.[24] The idea that later became the Baghdad Pact was, thus, put on the table for public discussion with official blessing. Although Byroade, a strong supporter of the northern tier, hoped the concept would become a reality, he was unsure and in no hurry to force a decision.

Apart from the anticipated negative Indian reaction, Iran— just recovering from the radical Mossadegh era—was a questionable member, a soft spot in the middle of the defense perimeter. Iraq's participation was shaky, given its rivalry with Nasser's Egypt, which firmly opposed an alliance with the West. How the United States and Britain would associate themselves with the security arrangement remained unsettled. With resources stretched and other regions of higher priority, the Pentagon was, moreover, unenthusiastic about the nebulous northern tier concept.[25]

If the United States was in no hurry, the Pakistanis were eager to conclude the arms agreement. After the assassination of Prime Minister Liaquat Ali Khan in 1951, control of the country fell into the hands of the conservative military and civil service leadership which desperately wanted to bolster Pakistan's security against India through association with the United States.

They seized the opportunity presented by Dulles' public discussion of the northern tier concept to urge a decision by Washington on arms aid. When Karachi heard positive sounding words but saw no signs of action, General Ayub Khan came to the United States in the fall of 1953 in order to press Pakistan's case.

Tall, handsome, speaking with a clipped South Asian English accent, Ayub looked and sounded like someone central casting found for a Hollywood production of "The Lives of a Bengal Lancer." The Pakistani general lobbied hard with the State Department, the Pentagon, and the Congress, saying all the right things about the dangers of Communism and the need to stand together against the Red threat. Byroade recalled Ayub barging into his office to state bluntly: "For Christ's sake, I didn't come to the United States to look at barracks. Our army can be your army if you want us. But let's make a decision!"[26]

When Ayub met with Dulles, the Secretary assured the visiting Pakistani he supported arms aid regardless of the Indian reaction. Dulles explained to an impatient Ayub that it would take time before the issue could formally be put to President Eisenhower.[27] Byroade asked Ayub to avoid premature publicity during the time the administration was reviewing the proposal.[28] Despite the fact that Ayub agreed, he leaked what was going on to the *New York Times* correspondent shortly after returning to Karachi. The story, appearing on 3 November, provoked a loud public outcry in India. Prime Minister Nehru at first reacted only in private, warning Pakistani Prime Minister Mohammed Ali Bogra:

> If such an alliance takes place, Pakistan definitely enters into the region of cold war . . . . It must also be a matter of grave consequence to us, you will appreciate, if vast armies are built up in Pakistan with the aid of American money . . . All of our problems will have to be seen in a new light.[29]

Writing to India's Chief Ministers, Nehru roundly criticized the United States as being unable to "think of anything else but of getting bases all over the world and using their money power to get manpower elsewhere to fight for them."[30] Nehru asserted:

> A military pact between Pakistan and the U.S. changes the whole balance in this part of the world and affects India

more especially. The U.S. must realize that the reaction in India will be that this arming of Pakistan is largely against India or might be used against India, whether the U.S. wants that or not . . . . They imagine that such an alliance between Pakistan and the U.S. would bring such overwhelming pressure on India as to compel her to change her policy of nonalignment. That is a rather naive view because the effect on India will be just the opposite, that is, one of greater resentment against the U.S.[31]

Worried about being politically outflanked by rightists and Communists, Nehru soon dropped his restraint and entered the fray publicly—doubtless as Ayub hoped. Nehru warned that US arms to Pakistan would bring the Cold War to the region, and would have "very far-reaching consequences on the whole structure of things in South Asia and especially in India and Pakistan."[32]

When Indian Ambassador Mehta raised the arms issue with Dulles, the Secretary replied that, given India's military superiority over Pakistan, any possible aid would pose no "reasonable" threat to India. Dulles added that the United States could not indefinitely postpone strengthening an important region of the world just because India and Pakistan were at odds.[33] Hardly a heartening response from the Indian standpoint.

By raising a public fuss, Nehru may have avoided domestic political problems in India, but his outcry upset many opinion-makers in the United States, where India had relatively few prominent political supporters apart from former Ambassador Chester Bowles and Senator Hubert Humphrey—liberal Democrats unlikely to carry weight with the Eisenhower administration. As the American press considered the issue, the balance of opinion swung in favor of aid to Pakistan; even the *New York Times* criticized the Indian attitude. Ayub's leak thus achieved its purpose, provoking Nehru into making so much threatening noise that he backed the US administration into a corner. The question became less whether to go ahead with arms for Pakistan than whether to back down because of India's protests.

According to Byroade, the final decision was still not easy. It was tempting to back Pakistan—a country asking to become an ally—and to rebuff Nehru whose brand of neutralism few liked. Even though some hardliners, like Vice President Richard

Nixon and Senate Majority Leader William Knowland, wanted to build up Pakistan as a counterweight to India, Byroade insisted this was not the administration's purpose. The basic idea remained one of providing greater stability to the northern tier region through association with the United States, making it easier for these countries to deal with the presumed Communist threat. Because Washington saw this danger more as political and psychological than military, the Defense Department played almost no role in the decision-making process. The Pentagon undertook little serious planning for an arms aid program for Pakistan. Byroade himself was thinking of a largely symbolic program—perhaps $20 million—far less than the amount of assistance the United States later provided.[34]

In the hope of reducing the negative Indian reaction, the State Department adopted an elaborate, but transparent, scheme to suggest that Washington was responding to an initiative from the countries of the region. According to this arrangement, the Pakistanis sought and received Turkey's agreement for a bilateral defense pact and then supposedly approached Washington for arms help. It was understood that Iran would join the security arrangement when political conditions permitted.[35]

In early December, Vice President Richard Nixon—traveling on an extensive Asian tour—met in New Delhi with Nehru. The Prime Minister did most of the talking, arguing strongly against American arms assistance to Pakistan. He did not impress the Vice President. Nixon described Nehru as "the least friendly leader" he met on his seventeen nation trip.[36] The Vice President was convinced Nehru's objection to US arms for Pakistan stemmed in part from "his personal thirst for influence, if not control, over South Asia, the Middle East, and Africa."[37] After the Delhi visit, the *New York Times* reporting that Nixon supported arms aid for Pakistan, quoted an unnamed source (presumably Nixon) as saying, "The time has come to put an end to Washington's patience with Nehru. The US should take a firmer course with Nehru who has often embarrassed the US."[38]

On 4 January 1954, Secretary Dulles reviewed the issue with the President. Eisenhower gave his tentative approval, "subject, however, to our capacity to present this in a reasonable way which would allay the apprehensions of reasonable people that we were trying to help Pakistan against India."[39] Nine days later, Dulles met again with Eisenhower to get a final decision. The Secretary stressed the effect that not going ahead would have in light of Prime Minister Nehru's strong and public objections. If the United States backed down, Dulles believed this step would "do a great deal to establish Nehru as the leader of all of South and Southeast Asia and nations in that region would henceforth be reluctant to proceed on matters with the West without obtaining Nehru's support." Eisenhower gave his approval but again expressed concern about the Indian reaction. He directed that "every possible public and private means at our disposal be used to ease the effects of our action on India."[40]

On 24 February 1954, Ambassador George Allen, the career diplomat the Republicans sent to replace Bowles in New Delhi,[41] officially informed Nehru of the decision, presenting him a letter from Eisenhower supposed to allay Indian concerns. The President made two principal points: he offered military aid to India and pledged to act against any misuse by Pakistan of US military assistance against India. After reading Eisenhower's letter carefully, Nehru smiled, looking silently at his cigarette for a few moments before responding. When the Prime Minister spoke, he adopted a pleasant, almost cordial tone, commenting it was not "US motives" that disturbed him but the "possible consequences of this action," both internationally and internally on India and Pakistan. Interpreting Nehru's calm reaction as a positive sign, Allen expressed the hope the discussion of "this subject will diminish after a few days."[42]

Notwithstanding the envoy's sanguine report, the intense and emotional Indian reaction had a far more profound effect on Indo-American relations than anticipated. The US government knew the action would cause problems, but, like Allen, policy makers hoped the impact would not be too adverse or long-lasting. The revised US South Asia policy document, NSC 5409, under consideration in tandem with the decision to provide arms to Pakistan, reflected this view. NSC 5409, in typically qualified US officialese, stated, "A result may be an intensification of differences in U.S.-Indian relations and possibly more friendly Indian relations with the Soviet Union, although there would probably not be any major change in India's foreign policies."[43]

The US intelligence community also underestimated the impact. A June 1954 National Intelligence Estimate (NIE) regarding the implications of the arms decision concluded that although the northern tier security arrangements would:

> In some degree increase Indo-US tensions, it is unlikely that an open rift would develop between the US and India as a result of this factor alone . . . . Should Pakistan be materially strengthened as a result of US aid, India would also seek to build up its own forces. In any event, it is extremely unlikely that India would move significantly closer to the Soviet bloc.[44]

For Washington, the main consideration was relatively simple: through arms to Pakistan, the United States thought it was taking an important step in advancing the policy of containment of Communism by strengthening the chain of collective security arrangements around the borders of the Soviet Union. In the administration's eyes, as reflected in NSC 5409, the action strengthened the defense of the region against the Communist threat and was not intended to "make Pakistan the dominant state in South Asia."[45] The United States gained in Pakistan a new ally in the Cold War, a Muslim country with a proud military tradition and, on paper at least, a substantial number of fighting troops that would be available for the defense of the oil-rich Persian Gulf.

Although Washington recognized Pakistan's primary motivation was to strengthen itself against India, the US leadership believed Pakistan was also concerned about the threat of Communism. The Pakistanis pointedly played up their alleged worries about the danger from the Soviet bloc in talking with American officials.[46] Neither Byroade nor John Foster Dulles were concerned that US arms would upset the South Asia power balance. Because India was far stronger than its neighbor, the small amount of arms then contemplated—NSC 5409 projected only $10 million annually—could hardly enable Pakistan to present a credible military threat to India.[47] Reflecting on the decision over three decades later, Henry Byroade acknowledged having underestimated the depth of Indian and Pakistani animosity, "We knew they disliked each other. We misjudged the intensity of their feelings."[48]

Nehru reacted angrily to the US decision. Despite what Washington said, the action psychologically strengthened Pakistan in its dealings with India—this was, after all, the basic reason why Pakistan wanted the ties with the United States. Until 1954, the politically and economically weak Muslim state lacked any significant external backing. Now, Nehru told his Chief Ministers, "Behind Pakistan will stand a great and powerful country, the U.S.A. In fact, the giving of military aid to Pakistan is an unfriendly act to India."[49]

Even if John Foster Dulles claimed no "reasonable" person could construe US aid to Pakistan as threatening India, in his desire to press ahead with containing Communism, Dulles underestimated the psychological impact of the nearly six hundred years of Muslim dominance of the subcontinent before the British gained control.[50] Ingrained in the psyche of South Asians was a sense that Muslims were far more martial than Hindus. As Winston Churchill emphasized to President Roosevelt in 1942, the Muslims were the fighters, not the Hindus.[51] In 1954, many Pakistanis—heirs to the martial tradition of Muslim domination of the subcontinent—still believed, and many Indians feared, that one Muslim soldier was worth ten Hindus.

Nehru strongly opposed military alliances in Asia, but especially in South Asia. In his view, "the fact that Pakistan aligns itself completely with one of the great military blocs necessarily makes it subservient to the policy of that bloc."[52] He saw a "loss of Pakistan's freedom and that country's becoming progressively a satellite of the United States."[53] The amount of aid concerned Nehru less than the qualitative change from the arms decision. "Pakistan," he stated, "will become definitely lined up with the Western powers and a region of cold war now and shooting war perhaps later."[54]

Nehru thought that the United States, in deciding to give arms to Pakistan, was in part motivated by its opposition to Indian neutralism. Until 1954, the Indian leader hoped to develop an area of peace, a region that stood apart from the two power blocs, based loosely on the Arab-Asian group of independent states then emerging from colonialism. Burma, Indonesia, and Egypt were, in Nehru's view, leaning in this direction. By accepting US military aid, Pakistan—whose foreign policy until then was mainly concerned with the Kashmir issue—"breaks up this Arab-Asian group and enlarges the possible area of war."[55]

The public reaction in India to news of the arms decision was an irate outcry against the United States. Whatever Washington might say by way of explaining the action, the US standing in India plummeted. The ruling Indian Congress Party at its meetings at Kalyani sharply criticized the US decision. Nehru became even more disapproving of US foreign policy, stating in parliament on 1 March that US military aid amounted to intervention in South Asia that would have a direct effect on the Kashmir issue.[56] Nehru demanded the immediate removal of American members of the UN Kashmir truce observer group, asserting the United States was no longer neutral because of its new relationship with Pakistan. In the end, the Prime Minister relented somewhat, permitting the US observers to complete their tours but only on the understanding that no Americans would be sent as replacements.[57]

Allowing his animus to spill into other areas, Nehru wrote his Chief Ministers on 26 April, "We should discourage large numbers of people coming here from the United States or going to the United States from India . . . . It is not desirable for us to send out students or others to the United States for training, except for some very specialized courses."[58] In a 3 May memorandum, he stated, "I dislike more and more this business of exchange of persons between America and India. The fewer persons that go from India to America or that come from the United States to India, the better."[59]

In understanding why the United States decided to alienate much larger and more important India by entering into an arms accord with Pakistan, it is hard to ignore an emotional element in US thinking. India's neutralist approach and chronic moralizing about US foreign policy, had by 1954 thoroughly tried the patience of top levels of the State Department, the Pentagon, and many in the Congress, not to speak of Republican leaders like Richard Nixon and John Foster Dulles. The decision to provide arms to India's unfriendly neighbor, to some extent, seemed a subconscious way of hitting back at India. In analyzing the action, J. J. Singh, the longtime head of the India League in the United States, believed the US motivation was about equally divided between a desire to strengthen Western defenses against Communism and a wish to give vent to anti-Indian feelings.[60]

Whatever the cause, the consequences of the US decision to arm Pakistan were far-reaching for relations with India and for US South Asia policy. After initially trying to avoid taking sides in India-Pakistan disputes—despite the friction with India over Kashmir—Washington opted to develop a close security relationship with India's principal enemy. Pandit Nehru wrote K.M. Panikkar, then Ambassador to Egypt:

> The United States imagine that by this policy they have completely outflanked India's so-called neutralism and will thus bring India to her knees. Whatever the future may hold, this is not going to happen. The first result of all of this will be an extreme dislike of the United States in India.[61]

Kashmir Dispute: Dim Prospects for Settlement

The Kashmir dispute was deadlocked when Eisenhower took office in January 1953. Dr. Frank Graham's try at mediation on behalf of the Security Council ended in failure in March. Despite the unpromising outlook, President Eisenhower endorsed Secretary Dulles' suggestion to send Ford Foundation head Paul Hoffman, former chief of the Marshall Plan, as a private presidential emissary to South Asia. Eisenhower told Dulles, "Our world simply cannot afford an outbreak of hostilities between these two countries, and I would risk a great deal to prevent any such eventuality."[62]

When Hoffman traveled to the subcontinent in April 1953, he made some progress. Nehru, who saw little future in continuing the UN Kashmir effort, agreed to meet bilaterally with Mohammed Ali Bogra, Pakistan's new Prime Minister. "While he would not commit himself to any particular solution," Hoffman reported that Nehru "seemed confident that a satisfactory answer could be found." In Karachi, Hoffman obtained similar agreement for bilateral discussions from the Pakistanis. After returning to the United States, Hoffman wrote Secretary Dulles—with more optimism than later proved justified—that the two prime ministers, meeting to negotiate on a "neighbor to neighbor" basis, were going to persist until a settlement was reached.[63]

The Eisenhower administration initially was less fixed on the idea of a plebiscite than its predecessor. During Dulles' visit to India, the Secretary told Nehru partition of Kashmir might prove a better solution. Dulles noted that plebiscites in the interwar period stirred much emotion while failing to resolve territorial disputes. Not surprisingly, Nehru agreed that a plebiscite was not the desirable solution, commenting that he envisaged a Kashmir settlement on the basis of the cease-fire line established in 1949 with minor adjustments—a posture he would support to his death in 1964. After Dulles encountered stiff Pakistani opposition to giving up the plebiscite, he backed away from shifting US policy on the question.[64]

Nehru's initial discussions with Pakistan's Mohammed Ali Bogra were positive in tone, but produced nothing tangible. Although Nehru found the new government in Karachi inclined toward a less hostile approach toward India than its predecessor, the Prime Minister faced a problem of a different sort—rising concern in New Delhi about the attitude of Kashmiri Premier Sheikh Mohammed Abdullah. Upset by communal agitation instigated by Hindu extremists, the Sheikh began to sound less eager for the union of Kashmir with India. His talking about the possibility of an independent state greatly upset the Indians.[65] As the dominant political leader in the state, the Sheikh's opinion carried great weight and could undermine Indian control over Kashmir. To prevent this from happening, the Sheikh was ousted from power in August 1953 by his deputy, Bakshi Ghulam Mohammed, and arrested a few days later.[66]

The United States, to its dismay, found itself embroiled in Kashmir's internal political crisis. Opponents of Abdullah alleged he was conspiring with Americans, offering bases in return for US support for Kashmiri independence. A meeting in May 1953 with former Democratic presidential candidate Adlai Stevenson was cited as "proof" that Washington was encouraging the Kashmiri leader to seek independence. The Indian press reported implausibly that Eisenhower was using Stevenson, the man he had defeated in a bitter presidential election, as an envoy to Abdullah. Ambassador Allen took the criticisms sufficiently seriously that he received State Department approval to give Nehru a flat denial.[67] Despite this official disavowal, charges that the United States was up to no good in Kashmir continued to circulate. The Embassy cabled Washington, "practically every high Indian official and writer has become firmly convinced of story manufactured out of whole cloth."[68]

Even though Sheikh Abdullah's ouster caused an uproar in Pakistan, Mohammed Ali Bogra proceeded with bilateral talks, leading a large delegation to New Delhi, where, in keeping with the love-hate relationship between the two countries, he was warmly received by the populace. Surprisingly, the negotiations registered progress. In the 20 August communiqué, Nehru and his Pakistani counterpart agreed to name a new plebiscite administrator by the end of April 1954—something to which the Indians previously refused to agree.[69] Nehru reportedly told Mohammed Ali he looked to voting in 1955 "provided the atmosphere in Pakistan remains good."[70]

The improved atmospherics were short-lived. Instead of taking advantage of Nehru's more forthcoming attitude to cement plebiscite arrangements, Karachi reverted to a tougher line. Pakistan was the only member of the Commonwealth to vote against Indian participation in the Korean political conference, a move hardly likely to sit well with Nehru. The Pakistani press, contrary to an accord to tone down criticism, resumed strident attacks on India. When Nehru—annoyed by India's exclusion from the Korea peace conference and suspicious of US activities in Kashmir—balked at having an American replace Nimitz, the Pakistanis insisted on having a US citizen as the new plebiscite administrator.[71]

The final derailment came after the arms aid decision. Nehru warned the Pakistanis that they could not have it both ways: US arms would be regarded as an unfriendly act in India and the whole issue of Kashmir would change.[72] Mohammed Ali replied that a military alliance with the United States had nothing to do with India, although he told *US News and World Report* that Pakistan's enhanced military strength would improve the prospects for a Kashmir solution.[73]

Senior Indians, including Ministry of External Affairs Secretary General N. R. Pillai, who succeeded Bajpai, and Dr. S. Radhakrishnan, who became India's Vice President after serving as envoy to Moscow, urged Ambassador Allen to seek a postponement of the arms decision, arguing this step would boost the chance for progress on Kashmir and avoid entangling the two issues. Allen refused to recommend a delay to Washington, apparently unconvinced Nehru was sincere about seeking a Kashmir settlement.[74] Even though it was far from clear that Nehru was really prepared to go forward with a plebiscite—as his semi-official biographer Sarvepalli Gopal implied[75]—his intentions were unfortunately not put to the test.

Once the arms decision was firm, Nehru carried out his threat to toughen India's stance on Kashmir. The bilateral discussions collapsed. Within the year, the Indians were refusing to talk about a plebiscite as a way to settle the dispute.[76] Since then, New Delhi's position has remained that the people of Kashmir had spoken for India by electing the constituent assembly and therefore there was no need for a plebiscite to determine what Kashmiris wanted.

India Edges Closer to Moscow

Nehru was now prepared to edge India closer to the Soviet Union to offset US support for Pakistan. Post-Stalin Moscow was only too willing to reciprocate. In a sign of shifting Kremlin policy toward India, G. M. Malenkov, chairman of the Council of Ministers, in an August 1953 speech, praised India for its role in promoting peace in Korea and called for better relations.[77] If the United States disliked neutralism as contrary to Western policy goals, the new Soviet leadership viewed the Indian approach in a much more positive light. Since much of the thrust of neutralism was directed against Western colonialism, Moscow could cheerfully support the policy without risk to its interests. At a time when the West was seeking to contain the Soviets— vigorously trying to limit Moscow's contacts with the newly emergent nations—the chance to expand relations with the largest nonaligned country was an opportunity the Russians eagerly seized.

As one indication of warming relations, Nehru paid a successful official visit to the Soviet Union in June 1955. During his stay, the Indian leader became the first non-Communist leader to address the Soviet people on television. Even if Nehru remained uneasy about the totalitarian nature of the Soviet state, he was impressed—as he had been on his first visit in 1928—by signs of economic progress. He also approved of the more pragmatic foreign policy approach of the new Soviet leadership, believing their policy shift reduced the chances for global conflict.[78]

In November and December 1955, Communist Party General Secretary Nikita Khrushchev and Premier Nikolai Bulganin paid a reciprocal state visit to India. They toured the country for almost a month, receiving an enormously warm welcome wherever they went. What was popularly called "the B & K show"— because of the colorful antics of Khrushchev—reached its high point on 9 December in Srinagar, the capital of Kashmir. To the delight of his hosts, Khrushchev dropped Soviet neutrality on Kashmir to proclaim support for India's position. The Russians seconded the Indian view that the ratification of Kashmir's accession by the state's constituent assembly was proof that the people of Kashmir had already expressed their will at the ballot box. The Communist Party General Secretary declared:

> The question of Kashmir as one of the constituent states of the Indian Union has already been decided by the people of Kashmir . . . . Facts show that the population of Kashmir do not wish that Kashmir become a toy in the hands of imperialistic forces.[79]

Khrushchev's policy change boosted the Soviet Union's popularity in India. If Pakistan could count on the United States for support, India now had a powerful friend of its own. The Soviet shift also had the practical advantage of making it harder for the United Nations to reengage itself actively in efforts to settle the Kashmir dispute. India could henceforth rely on a Soviet veto to block Security Council moves which New Delhi opposed.[80]

During their visit, the Russian leaders won further friends on 28 November by calling the existence of Goa, the nearly four-century-old Portuguese colony along the Arabian Sea coast in western India, "a shame to civilization."[81] After the British granted independence, the French agreed to hand over to India Pondicherry and other small French colonial holdings. Lisbon, however, stubbornly refused to give up Goa, asserting the territory was not a colony but a province of Portugal. Soviet support on Goa contrasted with the ambivalent US position that reflected Washington's sensitivities for its NATO ally Portugal. The difference between the US and Soviet positions was further underscored when John Foster Dulles angered New Delhi by joining the Portuguese foreign minister on 2 December in criticizing Soviet statements "concerning Portuguese provinces in the Far East."[82]

Khrushchev and Bulganin offered India economic aid as well as support on Kashmir and Goa. The Soviets agreed to build a million ton public sector steel mill financed by a $112 million low-interest loan and to provide other economic assistance for industrial development during the Second Indian Five Year Plan, which was slated to commence in 1956. At the same time, Moscow and New Delhi expanded cultural and educational exchanges and increased trade with India. In deference to Nehru's complaints, Moscow ostensibly distanced itself from the Communist Party of India, the winner of more than 5 percent of the popular vote in the 1952 general elections.[83]

Even though the trend in relations pleased Nehru, he remained somewhat reserved about the Russian embrace, refusing a proposal for a nonaggression pact embodying the principles of peaceful coexistence. India similarly showed only limited interest at this point in procuring Soviet military equipment, despite the offer of easy financial terms and growing concern about the increase in Pakistan's military strength after American military aid started flowing in.[84]

Washington watched the Bulganin and Krushchev visit with uneasiness. White House adviser Nelson Rockefeller urged Eisenhower to send a personal message to Nehru pledging US support for India's development efforts. After the State Department threw cold water on the idea—since there were no additional aid funds, the gesture would be seen as a propaganda move—Eisenhower decided to take no immediate action.[85] By then, pressures were, nonetheless, building on the administration to increase foreign aid in response to what Washington perceived as a Soviet economic and diplomatic offensive in the developing world. Eisenhower and his Secretaries of State, Defense, and the Treasury discussed the possibility during an 8 December meeting at Camp David, the President's weekend retreat.[86]

Vietnam, Bandung, and *Hindi-Chini Bhai Bhai*

As if to compensate further for the diplomatic defeat India suffered when Pakistan gained US military assistance, Nehru worked hard through 1954 and 1955 to buttress Indian foreign policy, pressing for a settlement in troubled French Indo-China, playing the leading role in the first Afro-Asian summit at Bandung, and improving relations with Communist China. In a speech at Colombo on 28 April 1954, he coined the phrase "nonalignment" to describe India's policy,[87] preferring this to neutralism since it implied an active rather than a passive approach.

In Indo-China, the Vietminh victory at Dien Bien Phu signalled the end of French colonial domination. Pierre Mendès-France came to power in Paris pledging to bring peace to the region. In April 1954, Nehru proposed a six-point plan for a settlement, which the United States disliked.[88] Even though not a formal participant in the Geneva Conference on Indo-China, India was forcefully represented by the ubiquitous Krishna Menon. The unofficial Indian envoy shuttled between different delegations, with whom he had roughly 200 interviews during the three weeks of the conference. Because India was the only Asian state present, apart from Communist China, the other delegations listened to Menon's views. In the end, the Conference asked India, along with Canada and Poland, to serve on the three International Control Commissions (ICC) established to monitor the Geneva accords in the Indo-China states. Nehru felt particularly gratified India could play this role, so in keeping with his policy of nonalignment and his desire to promote peace in Asia.[89]

Lukewarm about the Geneva accords, the United States promoted an anti-Communist collective security pact for Southeast Asia that became a reality in September 1954 as the Southeast Asia Treaty Organization (SEATO). Headquartered in Bangkok, SEATO's membership underlined its narrow regional support—the only Asian countries to join were the Philippines, Thailand, and Pakistan. Geographically the oddest participant, Pakistan took the initiative to seek membership, eager to strengthen its security ties to the United States. Although Dulles recognized the problems inherent in including the Pakistanis, Washington found itself outmaneuvered by Karachi and in the end had to agree to their joining.[90] Quite apart from annoyance over Pakistan's membership, Nehru regarded SEATO as "harmful to Asia as well as the cause of peace." He commented, "The habit of the West to carry the "white man's burden" in the East still continued, even though conditions in the world and in Asia have changed greatly."[91]

Although tough on communism at home, Nehru pursued closer relations with Communist China, as well as the Soviet Union. In the summer of 1954, China's Premier Chou En-lai visited New Delhi, where he succeeded in easing Indian worries about Chinese policy toward Tibet. The upshot was a new Sino-Indian agreement, in which India relinquished the special privileges it inherited from the British in Tibet. The preamble contained the so-called Five Principles—in Hindi, *Panch Sheel.* These concepts of non-interference and mutual respect, although not in themselves new or earth-shaking, soon gained wide recognition as the articulation of the desire of Asians to shape their relationships on Asian terms rather than simply reiterating the language of Western statecraft.[92] Nehru hoped the accord would ensure peace along the Himalayan frontiers, ushering in a long period of friendship between India and China. The era of "Hindi-Chini bhai bhai" lasted, however, only five years—until the Himalayan border dispute became a matter of public knowledge in 1959.[93]

In October 1954, Nehru traveled to China where the Communist leaders arranged for a wildly enthusiastic reception. In the bilateral talks that took place Nehru raised a question of concern to the Government of India—Chinese maps showing parts of the Ladakh region in northern Kashmir and of the Northeast Frontier Agency (NEFA) that India claimed as its territory as Chinese. Chou En-lai's response—that these were old maps, which the People's Republic had yet to revise—satisfied the Prime Minister. Unfortunately, Nehru did not take up Chou's suggestion for a joint communiqué at the end of the stay. This might have dealt publicly with the map question, sparing much grief when India and China later fell out over their differing border claims.[94] On his way back to India, Nehru visited the four Indo-China states. North Vietnamese leader Ho Chi Minh made an excellent impression. "South Vietnam produced a completely opposite effect," Nehru stated.[95]

In 1955, Afro-Asian solidarity, a subject dear to Nehru's heart, received a major boost with the first gathering of the leaders of the independent nations of the two continents at

Bandung in Indonesia. Initially lukewarm about the summit for fear the gathering would become entangled with the Palestine issue,[96] Nehru gradually came around to see Bandung as a means to promote his foreign policy aims, by asserting the importance of Asian and African views in dealing with the region's problems and by stressing the importance of peace.

In the age of jet travel, multi-nation summits of the non-aligned, of the Commonwealth countries, the Communist bloc and, in recent years, of the group of seven industrial powers, have become commonplace—almost routine—events. As the first of its kind for the twenty-nine nations of Asia and Africa, many of which had just attained their independence, Bandung was novel, attracting enormous attention in the region and in the capitals of the Western and Communist blocs, anxious about Afro-Asian attitudes towards their policies.

India played a leading behind-the-scenes role in the conference, but its efforts to maintain solidarity on the communiqué were frustrated when pro-Western states, in particular, Pakistan and Ceylon, urged criticism of Communism as well as Western colonialism. Very much the father figure at Bandung, Nehru was, nonetheless, overshadowed by Chinese Premier Chou En-lai who, as Nehru himself acknowledged, attracted the most attention since he was previously "rather a mysterious figure whom people had not seen."[97] At Bandung, Nehru spoke with eloquence about nonalignment as a way to avoid the war he feared threatened humanity if the world divided into two opposing blocs. He argued for an Asian and African area of peace that eschewed military alliances, instead adopting the policies of peaceful coexistence. Well satisfied with the results, Nehru praised Bandung as "an historic process" that "opened a new chapter not only in Asia and Africa, but in the world."[98]

In the spring of 1955, Nehru stood at his political peak. He was a major figure on the world stage. His foreign policy approach of nonalignment was attracting increasing support from the new nations of Asia and Africa. Both Western and Communist powers accepted India as a peacemaker. At home, after the 1952 general elections, Indian democracy seemed well launched politically. Economically, the country was poised to adopt another of Nehru's goals—socialist planning—as a means of accelerating economic development and promoting social justice.

Even Nehru's old foe, Winston Churchill, sang the Indian leader's praise, "I hope you will think of the phrase 'Light of Asia.' It seems to me that you might be able to do what no other human being could in giving India the lead, at least in the realm of thought, throughout Asia, with the freedom and dignity of the individual as the ideal rather than the Communist Party drill book."[99]

India-US Economic Relations—Thorium Nitrate and Aid

Meanwhile in Washington, Dwight Eisenhower was unhappy about the downturn in Indo-US relations. Eisenhower was less antagonistic toward India and more concerned about relations with former colonial states than his Secretary of State. He worried that if the West failed to support decolonization and economic development, the countries of Asia and Africa would become independent anyway and find communism attractive.[100]

Concern over India's economic development was not a popular theme in the early days of the Eisenhower administration. One of Secretary Dulles' first decisions regarding India was, indeed, to slash the economic assistance request for fiscal year 1954 by 30 percent to $140 million. Refusing to sign the official letter on aid levels "as long as it carries the sum of $200 million for India," he told his deputy, Bedell Smith, "I doubt that this amount is either justified by the facts or could be justified to the Congress."[101]

The summer of 1953 saw India and the United States embroiled in an acerbic dispute over the Battle Act—a US law sponsored by Congressman Laurie C. Battle, Democrat of Alabama—barring American aid to any country that traded in strategic goods with Communist China. The trouble arose after American officials became aware the Indian Government's Rare Earths Corporation had shipped to China a strategic commodity called thorium nitrate used in the production of uranium. When Ambassador Allen raised the issue with Nehru, the Prime Minister reacted vehemently, stating flatly India would never permit the United States to tell India with whom it could trade as a price for aid.

Although Americans officials explained US legislative requirements tied their hands, the Indians refused to budge. Secretary General of the Ministry of External Affairs Pillai pleaded with Allen to "bear in mind that (the) GOI is young and perhaps supersensitive re its sovereignty."[102] Since other developing countries accepted Battle Act conditions, Americans were puzzled why India was making such a fuss. The fact that Prime Minister Nehru himself authorized the shipment—admittedly unaware that this violated US law—further complicated matters.

In the end, after much teeth gnashing in the State Department, Secretary Dulles decided not to cut off aid even though India remained unwilling to bend. Dulles agreed aid could legally continue because the thorium nitrate shipment was "not knowingly permitted" and an arrangement under which the United States bought out all Indian surplus production prevented future sales of the commodity.[103] As Dulles cabled Allen on 3 September, he feared a cut-off would hurt India's work as the Chairman of the Neutral Nations Repatriation Commission in Korea since the action would be seen as punishing India, and would provide "a great boost for Communist propaganda." Dulles also doubted that aid could be resumed easily if it were terminated, putting the United States in the awkward position of supporting India's stability and being able to do nothing about it.[104]

The lesson Ambassador Allen drew from the affair was that the United States had been too soft with the Indians on aid. Instead of insisting on a clear-cut request, Allen felt the United States allowed the Indians "to simply let us know how much aid they needed without having to ask anyone for anything . . . I believe continuation of this essentially dishonest fiction would be fraud on American people as well as continue to place US-Indian relations on false and therefore unsound basis."[105] The upper echelons of the State Department applauded Allen's tough line but shrank from his recommendations. On reviewing the record, it was also realized Allen was wrong in asserting the Indians had never asked for aid. The Ambassador was apparently unaware of Nehru's explicit request made at the insistence of Ambassador Loy Henderson in May 1951. Admitting he did not have all the facts, Allen, nonetheless, emphasized his belief that the United States should not be thrusting aid on India.[106]

Having few quarrels with Allen's views, the administration posture was to maintain—but initially not to increase—the bilateral assistance program initiated toward the end of the Truman administration. The main focus continued to be on agriculture and rural development with the Community Development Program initiated by Bowles the top priority activity. Despite the frictions in relations, the administration a year later, as part of an overall increase in economic development assistance, supported a $104 million allocation for India.[107]

In 1954, a new agricultural commodity bill—Public Law 480—also became law. PL 480, as it was soon known, permitted the US government to dispose of mounting surplus farm products in return for blocked rupees.[108] For India, struggling to raise its food production to keep pace with the mounting population, the prospect of US food in return for readily available blocked rupees instead of scarce foreign exchange was tempting. New Delhi soon sought another large food assistance package. Washington was initially slow to respond.

Although Eisenhower, and even Dulles, supported the push for increased assistance for India, the effort ran into stiff opposition. Part of the difficulty was the lack of support for foreign aid generally among Republicans, but part was the dislike for India's policies. Meeting with Congressional leaders, Dulles responded to criticism from arch-conservative Republican Senator William Knowland of California about rewarding neutralism. "We are not rewarding policies we dislike," the Secretary declared, "we are simply trying to prevent India from moving towards Communism."[109] Within the State Department, hard-line anti-Communists like Assistant Secretary of State for Far Eastern Affairs Walter Robertson also opposed helping India.[110] An internal review in November 1955, chaired by Under Secretary of State Robert Murphy, mirrored Congressional criticism.[111] The India desk (Burr Smith) urged the increase to help those supporting "sounder policies" and thwart Communist efforts to penetrate the region. Senior economic specialists (Kalijarvi and Prochnow) supported the increase "despite the often-times unfriendly or difficult statements of Mr. Nehru." Robertson strongly disagreed. Calling Nehru a Communist supporter, he charged aid to India only served to build up a government unfriendly to the United States.[112]

During 1955, George Allen left India to replace Henry Byroade as Assistant Secretary of State for Near East and South Asia. To take his place, Eisenhower selected John Sherman Cooper, a former Republican Senator from Kentucky. Concerned about poor relations with India, Eisenhower wanted Cooper to make a special effort to become friendly with Nehru, noting that the Indian leader seemed to be swayed as much "by personality as by logical argument." The President asked Secretary Dulles to try to avoid burdening the new envoy with chores that would cause problems in his developing rapport with the Prime Minister.[113]

The Cooper-Nehru relationship prospered despite the relatively short period the Kentuckian spent in New Delhi—after a year Cooper returned to US politics to win back his Senate seat. While in India, Cooper pushed strongly and successfully for a second Nehru visit to the United States. Eisenhower, at first, flirted with the possibility of making a trip to India himself but Dulles talked him out of the idea.[114] In the end, they settled on an invitation for Nehru to come to the United States. Scheduled for the summer of 1956, Nehru's visit had to be postponed until the fall after Eisenhower suffered a heart attack.

In early March 1956, during a stop in New Delhi by Secretary Dulles, Ambassador Cooper proposed a larger aid program to provide susbtantial US support for the just announced Indian Second Five Year Plan. Cooper's ideas, "A Feasible Program of US Economic Assistance for India," called for $500 million development aid and $300 million food aid over the five-year period—an annual total of $160 million. Cooper justified the boost in assistance in terms of countering the increased Soviet effort to penetrate South Asia and of supporting India's efforts to develop her economy by democratic means.[115]

Secretary Dulles set up a special study group, which agreed with some but not all of Cooper's recommendations. The result was an administration request for $80 million in development aid and approval for proceeding with a new PL 480 agreement.[116] Signed in August 1956, the food accord was the first concrete indication of the upswing in assistance. The agreement envisaged up to 5 million tons of foodgrains over three years.

More than twice the size of the 1951 wheat loan and worth $360 million, the agreement was the largest PL 480 transaction until then.[117]

Despite Cooper's friendly relations with Nehru, relations between New Delhi and Washington remained strained as Eisenhower's first term neared its end. For many Americans, Krishna Menon, now a fixture at the United Nations, had become the symbol of India—a country that preached nonalignment and high moral principles in international affairs but hypocritically favored the Communists and cold-bloodedly pursued its interests in Kashmir in disregard of UN resolutions. A typically negative reaction was that of President Eisenhower, on whom Krishna Menon called at the White House in March and June 1955 to discuss Indian efforts to help reduce tensions between the United States and Communist China. Eisenhower described the peripatetic Indian emissary as a "menace and a boor."[118]

For Indians, Menon's American counterpart was John Foster Dulles. Although hardly in Menon's league when it came to sarcasm and vituperation, the Secretary of State was given to sermonizing on the global struggle between good (the Free World) and evil (the Communist bloc). Dulles barely concealed his disdain for India's foreign policy; indeed on 9 June 1956, the Secretary spoke his mind plainly, telling an Iowa State University audience that "except under very exceptional circumstances," neutralism was "an immoral and shortsighted conception."[119] Dulles' role as the architect of Pakistan's alliance with the United States added to Indian dislike of the Secretary of State. In December 1955, Dulles further roiled the waters by appearing to support the Portuguese position on Goa.[120]

When the Secretary visited New Delhi in March 1956, he was so unpopular that special police protection was necessary to prevent unfriendly demonstrations. Not looking forward to seeing Dulles, Nehru wrote, "The most we can expect out of his visit here is that he has got some idea into his rather closed head as to what we feel about various things."[121] The talks only confirmed the wide gap between the two leaders. Nehru was optimistic on the prospect of change in the Communist world, shaken by Khrushchev's sensational attacks on Stalinism during the 20th

Party Congress in Moscow in February 1956. Dulles "broadly agreed" with Nehru's analysis but felt the pace of change would be slower than the Indian leader anticipated. Dulles believed a real transformation of the Communist system would take at least a generation.[122]

Nehru and Dulles disagreed again in their assessment of Communist China. The Indian leader also attacked Dulles' creations—SEATO and the Baghdad Pact—asserting Pakistan had not entered the alliances against the Soviets but "to get strength to use against India." Calling the Pakistanis "a martial people and a fanatical people who could readily attack India," Nehru blamed US arms aid for forcing India to increase defense spending.[123] In responding, Dulles claimed others had pressed Pakistan to join SEATO, admitting "Pakistan had no business to be there."[124] The Secretary reiterated the standard US pledge that arms assistance to Pakistan would not be used against India, and denied that US arms to Pakistan were causing an arms race.[125]

Courtesy of the Dwight D. Eisenhower Library, National Park Service photograph

14 June 1955, President Dwight D. Eisenhower, Secretary of State John Foster Dulles, UN Ambassador V. K. Krishna Menon, and Indian Ambassador G. L. Mehta meeting in the Oval Office.

Although Nehru did not know it, one important point did get through to Dulles—the extent of India's anxiety about Pakistan. Cabling President Eisenhower from Colombo a day after his talks with Nehru, Dulles stated:

> The one distinct impression that I gained is their almost pathological fear of Pakistan. I knew, of course, that they did not like our alliance with, and armament program for, Pakistan, but I never appreciated before the full depth of their feeling . . . . I do not think we can alter our Pakistan relationship which is of great value, but I do think we must try to handle it in ways which give maximum assurance to India that our military aid will be only used for purely defensive purposes.[126]

After his discussions with the Secretary, Nehru also reflected on bilateral relations with the United States—his musings very different from those of Dulles. The "singularly misconceived and harmful" US positions on Kashmir and Goa "have come in the way of better relations between India and the U.S.A. more than anything else," Nehru wrote the Chief Ministers.[127] Some believed relations depended on how much aid the United States gave, but this was "a complete misapprehension," Nehru stated.

> Whether the U.S. give us much or little or nothing at all, our relations with them will not be affected much, provided other factors are satisfactory. It is these other and political factors that are constantly coming in the way. Our general approach to the world situation differs from that of the U.S. which is based largely on military considerations. We think that there can be no solution of the major problems of the world if the approach is chiefly a military one. Indeed we have seen a progressive deterioration because of this military approach.[128]

Bilateral relations thus sank to a low point during Eisenhower's first term in the White House under the burden of policy differences between Washington and New Delhi. As in the Truman years, the frictions focused on conflicting Indian and US perceptions of the Communist threat and the differing policy responses. During Eisenhower's first term as President, however, the US response to the Communist threat—by establishing a military supply relationship with India's enemy Pakistan in 1954—directly affected South Asia, India's home teritory.

For most Indians, differences over the containment policy and nonalignment involved abstract concepts that were of interest mainly to the educated elite. Anything touching on the relationship with Pakistan, however, just seven years after the trauma of partition, was a different matter, striking a deeply emotional nerve throughout the Indian body politic. Washington knew the arms decision would upset the Indians but misjudged the extent of the response. The United States believed the gains in acquiring a new ally, Pakistan, would more than offset the losses sustained with India. Eisenhower would shortly call this judgment in question, but could not reverse history.

NOTES

1. Jawaharlal Nehru, *Letters to Chief Ministers,* vol. 3, pp. 258-59, letter of 3 March 1953.

2. *Foreign Relations of the United States (FRUS), 1952-1954,* vol. XV, pp. 831-32, memorandum of conservation between Messrs. Johnson (State Department) and Tomlinson (British Embassy), 1 April 1953.

3. Ibid., pp. 1008, General Clark's report to the Joint Chiefs of Staff of meeting with South Korean President Rhee, 12 May 1953.

4. Ibid., pp. 115-17, 119-21, Dulles' reports of his 21 and 22 May meetings with Prime Minister Nehru. Dulles later added a touch of drama, claiming in a January 1956 interview in *Life* magazine that he had threatened nuclear war during the talks. Neither Dulles' record nor Nehru's recollections supported this claim of nuclear brinkmanship. (Nehru, vol. 4, p. 339-40, letter of 16 January 1956).

5. *FRUS, 1952-1954,* vol. XV, p. 1197, letter from President Rhee to General Mark Clark, 18 June 1953.

6. Ibid., p. 1222, telegram from Embassy Seoul to the Department of State reporting Briggs' meeting with Syngman Rhee, 19 June 1953.

7. Nehru, vol. 3, p. 324, letter of 2 July 1953.

8. Humphrey Evans, *Thimayya of India: A Soldier's Life* (New York: Harcourt, Brace and Company, 1960), p. 301.

9. Nehru, vol. 3, pp. 436, 470-71, 484-85, letters of 15 November, 31 December 1953, and 18 January 1954.

10. *FRUS, 1952-1954,* vol. XV, pp. 1725-26, telegram from the Deputy Representative for the Korean Political Conference to the State Department, 15 January 1954.

11. U. Alexis Johnson with J.O. McAllister, *The Right Hand of Power* (Englewood Cliffs, NJ: Prentice-Hall, 1984), p. 170.

12. *FRUS, 1952-1954,* vol. XV, p. 1730, memorandum of discussion at the 21 January 1954 NSC meeting.

13. Ibid., pp. 1670-71, 21 December 1953, briefing at the State Department by Ambassador Dean of representatives of countries sending troops for UN forces in Korea.

14. Johnson, p. 169.

15. *FRUS, 1952-1954*, vol. XV, pp. 1529-30, Embassy New Delhi to State Department, 9 October 1953.

16. Ibid., pp. 1493-95, memorandum of conversation between Lodge and Menon, 14 August 1953.

17. *FRUS, 1952-1954*, vol. XI, *pt. 2*, pp. 1724-25, report of meeting between Dulles, Mehta, and Byroade, 7 October 1953.

18. *FRUS, 1952-1954*, vol. IX, pp. 119-21, report of 22 May 1953 meeting with Prime Minister Nehru drafted by Secretary Dulles.

19. Ibid., pp. 132-34, report of the meeting between Secretary Dulles, US Ambassador Hildreth, and General Ayub Khan, 23 May 1953.

20. Ibid., p. 147, cable from Dulles sent by Consulate General Istanbul to the State Department, 26 May 1953.

21. Ibid., pp. 379-83, minutes of 1 June 1953 NSC meeting.

22. Ibid., p. 382.

23. *Department of State Bulletin*, 15 June 1953, p. 835; text of Dulles' radio and television address, 1 June 1953.

24. Interview with Ambassador Byroade, 5 May 1990.

25. Ibid.

26. Ibid.

27. Memorandum of conversation between Secretary Dulles and General Ayub, 30 September 1953, State Department records.

28. *FRUS, 1952-1954*, vol. IX, pp. 421-22, memorandum from Assistant Secretary Byroade to the Assistant Secretary of Defense, 15 October 1953. Byroade noted the inability to reach a decision during Ayub's visit, cautioned that Ayub was not commissioned to negotiate for the Government of Pakistan, and stressed the importance of maintaining secrecy about the discussion regarding arms to Pakistan.

29. Sarvepalli Gopal, *Jawaharlal Nehru, A Biography, vol. II* (London: Jonathan Cape, 1979), p. 184.

30. Nehru, vol. 3, p. 441, letter of 15 November 1953.

31. Ibid., p. 442, letter of 15 November 1953.

32. Ibid., p. 454, Letter of 1 December 1953.

33. Gopal, vol. II, p. 186, telegram from Ambassador Mehta to Nehru, 16 November 1953; Barnds, *India, Pakistan and the Great Powers*, (New York: Praeger, 1974), pp. 95-96.

34. Interview with Ambassador Byroade, 5 May 1990.

35. *FRUS, 1952-1954*, vol. IX, pp. 433-34, 439-41, Embassy Ankara Telegram to the State Department, 30 November 1953, and State Department telegram to Embassy Ankara, 24 December 1953.

36. Richard M. Nixon, *The Memoirs of Richard Nixon* (New York: Grosset & Dunlap, 1978), p. 132.

37. Ibid.

38. *New York Times*, 9 and 10 December 1953. Selig Harrison, then Associated Press correspondent in New Delhi, told the author that Nixon, in an off-the-record press briefing after talking with Nehru, made no bones about his support for arms to Pakistan, his dislike for Nehru, and his opposition to nonalignment. See also Escott Reid, *Envoy to Nehru* (New York: Oxford University Press, 1982), pp. 100-16 for an account of events by another well-informed eye witness. Reid was then serving as Canada's High Commissioner in New Delhi.

39. *FRUS, 1952-1954*, vol. IX, pp. 443-44, memorandum of 4 January 1954 meeting with the President.

40. Ibid., pp. 453-54, memorandum of 14 January 1954 meeting with the President.

41. Prior to serving in India, Allen was Ambassador to Yugoslavia. In 1955, he replaced Byroade as Assistant Secretary for Near Eastern and South Asian Affairs, and later became the head of the United States Information Agency.

42. *FRUS, 1952-1954*, vol. IX, pp. 1717-39, Embassy Delhi telegram to the State Department, 24 February 1954.

43. *FRUS, 1952-1954*, vol. IX, pp. 1091-92, National Security Council Document 5409, "United States Policy Toward South Asia," 19 February 1954.

44. *FRUS, 1952-1954*, vol. IX, pp. 516-20, National Intelligence Estimate, "Prospects for Northern Tier and Consequences," 22 June 1954.

45. Ibid., pp. 1094-95, US Policy Towards South Asia, NSC 5409, 19 February 1954. Eisenhower formally approved the policy after it was discussed at the 4 March 1954 NSC meeting.

46. Barnds, pp. 100-02.

47. Interview with Henry Byroade, 3 May 1990; *FRUS, 1952-1954*, vol. XI, pp. 1122-23, Financial Appendix to US Policy Toward South Asia, NSC 5409. The Pakistanis were deeply upset and US Ambassador to Pakistan Horace Hildreth aghast when they learned of the small figure. Deputy Assistant Secretary John Jernagan wrote Hildreth that the Pentagon, not involved in considering the aid program, had done no thinking about assistance. He expressed confidence Pakistan would get a meaningful arms program. *FRUS, 1952-1954, vol. IX*, pp. 493, 500-02, telegram from Embassy Karachi to State Department, 9 April 1954, and 22 April 1954 letter to Hildreth from Jernagan.

48. Interview with Ambassador Byroade, 5 May 1990.

49. Nehru, vol. 3, p. 472, 31 December 1953.

50. From the end of the 12th century until the collapse of Mughal power in the 18th century, India was ruled by various Muslim dynasties.

51. W. Averell Harriman and Elie Abel, *Special Envoy to Churchill and Stalin, 1941-1946* (New York: Random House, 1975), p. 130.

52. Nehru, vol. 3, p. 476, letter of 31 December 1953.

53. Ibid., p. 187.

54. Ibid., p. 472, letter of 31 December 1953.

55. Ibid., p. 476, letter of 31 December 1953.

56. Ibid., p. 503, letter of 15 March 1954.

57. *FRUS, 1952-1954,* vol. XI, p. 1338, Embassy New Delhi telegrams to the State Department, 2 and 20 March 1954.

58. Nehru, vol. 3, pp. 530-31, letter of 26 April 1954.

59. Gopal, vol. II, p. 189.

60. M.S. Rajan, *India in World Affairs, 1954-56* (New Delhi: Asia Publishing House, 1964), p. 264.

61. Gopal, vol. II, p. 185; Nehru letter to K.M. Panikkar, 12 November 1953.

62. *FRUS, 1952-1954,* vol. XI, pp. 1314-16, memorandum from Dulles to Eisenhower, 14 March 1953, and reply from Eisenhower, 25 March 1953.

63. Ibid., pp. 1316-21, Eyes Only telegrams from Hoffman in New Delhi to Secretary Dulles, 17 and 23 April 1953, and letter from Hoffman to Secretary Dulles, 28 April 1953.

64. Ibid., pp. 119-21, report of the meeting between Dulles and Nehru, 22 May 1953.

65. Gopal, vol. II, pp. 128-29.

66. For Nehru's version of events, see *Nehru,* vol. 3, pp. 361-66, letter of 22 August 1953.

67. *FRUS,* vol. XI, 1952-1954, pp. 1323-24, Embassy New Delhi telegram to State Department, 13 July 1953, and State Department telegram to New Delhi, 15 July 1953.

68. Ibid., pp. 1325-27, Embassy New Delhi telegram of 10 August 1953 to the State Department. Not the last American ambassador to have to deal with allegations of US interference, Allen worked diligently—but in vain—to convince Indian officials the charges were false.

69. Admiral Nimitz announced his intention to resign after spending nearly four years waiting to assume his plebiscite management duties.

70. Gopal, vol. II, p. 182.

71. Ibid., p. 183. Nehru wrote Ambassador G. L. Mehta in Washington on 28 August 1953 that "With this background, I am not prepared for an instant to accept an American nominee whoever he might be.

. . . " Escott Reid, *Envoy to Nehru* (New Delhi: Oxford Press, 1981), p. 122.

72. Sisir Gupta, *Kashmir, A Study in Indo Pakistan Relations* (New Delhi: Asia Publishing House, 1966), pp. 278-79.

73. *US News and World Report*, 15 January 1954.

74. Reid, pp. 123-25.

75. Gopal, vol. II, p. 183.

76. Lamb, p. 84; Reid, pp. 124-25.

77. Robert C. Horn, *Soviet-Indian Relations: Issues and Influence* (New York: Praeger, 1982), p. 3.

78. Nehru, vol 4, pp. 195-222, 227-49. Enclosures to letters of 20 July and 2 August provided Nehru's impressions of his travels in the USSR and a number of other countries, June-July 1955.

79. Lamb, p. 88.

80. Ibid. Nehru wrote at length about the Soviet visit to his Chief Ministers in *Nehru*, vol. 4, pp. 309-25.

81. Ibid., p. 316.

82. Ibid., pp. 316-17.

83. Ibid., pp. 311-21.

84. Barnds, pp. 114-19.

85. Rockefeller to Eisenhower, 7 November 1955; Herbert Hoover, Jr. (State) to Sherman Adams, 14 November 1955, Eisenhower Library.

86. Memorandum of conversation between Eisenhower, Dulles, Humphrey, and Wilson, 9 December 1955, White House Memoranda, Eisenhower Library.

87. Richard L. Jackson, *The Non-Aligned, the UN, and the Super-powers* (New York: Praeger, 1983), p. 6.

88. Sardesai, D.R., *Indian Foreign Policy in Cambodia, Laos, and Vietnam, 1947-1964* (Berkeley, CA: University of California Press, 1968), pp. 32-46.

89. Gopal, vol. II, pp. 191-92; Sardesai, pp. 46-51; and Nehru, vol. 3, pp. 554-55, 563-65, and 574-75, letters of 3, 15, and 22 June 1954.

90. Gary Hess, "The American Search for Stability in Southeast Asia: The SEATO Structure of Containment," in *The Great Powers in East Asia, 1953-1960* (New York: Columbia University Press, 1990), pp. 283-84.

91. Nehru, vol. 4, p. 48, letter of 15 September 1954.

92. Barnds, pp. 136-37.

93. *Hindi-Chini bhai bhai* is the Hindi translation of "Indians and Chinese are brothers." The phrase came to symbolize the brief era of good feeling between New Delhi and Peking in the late 1950s.

94. Gopal, vol. II, pp. 228-30.

95. Nehru, vol. 4, p. 88. See pp. 71-89, letter of 15 November 1954, for Nehru's detailed report on the China and Indo-China trip.

96. The conference organizers solved the problem by not inviting Israel which, as an independent nation in Asia or Africa, should have been eligible to attend. Nehru went along somewhat reluctantly. "We did not decide on our invitations by our likes and dislikes . . . . In the balance one had to choose whether we would have Israel or the Arab countries. Nehru, vol. 4, p. 118, letter of 13 January 1955.

97. Ibid., p. 163.

98. Gopal, vol. II, pp. 238-41; Nehru, vol. 4, pp. 149-71. Nehru's note of 28 April 1955 provided a detailed report on the Bandung conference.

99. Letter from Winston Churchill to Nehru, 21 February 1955.

100. Stephen E. Ambrose, *Eisenhower, Volume Two, The President* (New York: Simon and Schuster, 1984), pp. 376-77.

101. *FRUS, 1952-1954,* vol. XI, p. 1692, memorandum from John Foster Dulles to Under Secretary of State Walter B. Smith, March 4, 1953. In the end, the Congress appropriated only $89 million for Fiscal Year 1954.

102. Ibid., p. 1709, Embassy New Delhi telegram to State Department, 13 August 1953.

103. The thorium nitrate export saga is related in *FRUS, 1952-1954,* vol. XI, pp. 1700-17, covering the period July to September 1953.

104. Ibid., p. 1717, telegram from Secretary Dulles to Embassy New Delhi, 3 September 1953.

105. Ibid., pp. 1710-11, telegram from Ambassador Allen to Secretary Dulles, 14 August 1953.

106. Ibid., pp. 1715-16, Embassy New Delhi to the State Department, 27 August 1953.

107. Dennis Merrill, *Bread and the Ballot: The United States and India's Economic Development, 1947-1963* (Chapel Hill: University of North Carolina Press, 1990), p. 108.

108. PL 480 legislation envisaged three types of food aid. Title I provided for the "sale" of surplus food for blocked local currencies. Title II authorized donation of food for famine and other emergencies. Title III provided for free food grants to nonprofit charitable organizations for distribution abroad. The bulk of US food aid to India came under Title I. This program ended in the 1970s with the debt settled through the rupee agreement (see chapter 8 for details). Title III programs have continued into the 1990s, running about $100 million annually.

109. Supplementary Notes: Legislative Leadership Meeting, 28 June 1955, Eisenhower Library.

110. A Virginia banker and staunch conservative, Robertson took charge of Far Eastern Affairs when Dulles became Secretary. He was known as a strong supporter of Chiang Kai-shek and Syngman Rhee, a critic of Nehru's nonalignment, and a vociferous opponent of improved relations with mainland China.

111. A career diplomat, Murphy served as Eisenhower's political adviser during the 1942 landings in North Africa. Under Dulles, he became the senior professional diplomat in the State Department.

112. *FRUS, 1955-1957,* vol. VIII, pp. 296-98, memorandum of a Meeting between Under Secretaries Murphy and Prochnow, Assistant Secretaries Kalijarvi (Economics) and Robertson (Far East), and R. Burr Smith (India Desk), 18 November 1955.

113. *FRUS, 1955-1957,* vol. VIII, p. 278, letter from Eisenhower to Secretary Dulles, 23 March 1955.

114. Memorandum of conversation between Eisenhower and Dulles, 19 July 1955, International Series, Ann Whitman File, Eisenhower Library; *FRUS, 1955-1957,* vol. 8, pp. 290-91, Allen to Dulles, 29 July 1955.

115. *FRUS, 1955-1957,* vol. VIII, pp. 311-17, letter to Dulles from Cooper, 13 March 1956.

116. Ibid., pp. 317-18, Summary Minutes of Study Group, 3 May 1956.

117. Merrill, pp. 129-130.

118. Robert H. Ferrell, ed., *The Eisenhower Diaries* (New York: W.W. Norton & Company, 1981), p. 300. Eisenhower wrote, Menon "is a boor because he conceives himself intellectually superior and rather coyly presents, to cover this, a cloak of excessive humility and modesty. He is a menace because he is a master at twisting words and meaning of others and is governed by an ambition to prove himself the master international manipulator and politician of the age."

119. *New York Times,* 10 June 1956.

120. Nehru, vol. 4, p. 317, Letter of 21 December 1955.

121. Gopal, vol. II, p. 274, letter from Nehru to Padmaja Naidu, 10 March 1956.

122. Nehru, vol. 4, p. 356, letter of 14 March 1956. History has, of course, proven Dulles correct.

123. *FRUS, 1955-1957,* vol. VIII, pp. 306-08, Memoranda of conversations between Secretary of State Dulles and Pandit Nehru, 9 and 10 March 1956; Gopal, vol. II, p. 275; Nehru's notes of his talk with Secretary Dulles, 10 March 1956.

124. Nehru, vol. 4, p. 351, letter of 14 March 1956.

125. Gopal, vol. II, p. 275, Nehru's notes of his talk with Secretary Dulles, 10 March 1956; *FRUS, 1955-1957,* vol. VIII, pp. 306-08,

Memoranda of conversations between Secretary of State Dulles and Pandit Nehru, 9 and 10 March 1956.

126. Ibid., pp. 309-11, telegram from Secretary Dulles to President Eisenhower, 11 March 1956.

127. Nehru, vol. 4, p. 350, letter of 14 March 1956.

128. Ibid., pp. 350-51.

Chapter IV

Eisenhower II: Improved Relations

In November 1956, Eisenhower easily won reelection, overwhelming Democratic candidate Adlai Stevenson for the second time. Dramatic overseas events—the simultaneous Suez and Hungary crises—almost pushed the presidential election off the front page. In the case of Suez, Nehru reacted rapidly, angrily condemning the Anglo-French-Israeli attack on Egypt as a flagrant violation of the UN Charter: "I cannot imagine a worse case of aggression," Nehru cabled Dulles, "The whole future of the relations between Europe and Asia hangs in the balance."[1] Eisenhower's insistence that the British, French, and Israelis withdraw impressed Nehru. He had not expected the United States to take such a firm stand against its allies in favor of Nasser, a neutralist with whom Washington had poor relations.

In contrast, the Indian leader was slow to react critically to Russian use of force in Hungary. In a 1 November speech in Hyderabad, Nehru pilloried Britain and France for their attack on Suez, but said nothing about the Red Army's crushing the anti-Communist revolt in Budapest. On 4 November at the United Nations, India abstained on a resolution calling for the withdrawal of Soviet troops. In a 9 November speech in Calcutta, Nehru seemed to accept Soviet explanations of their actions in Budapest, describing the crisis as an internal Hungarian affair. The same day at the United Nations, Krishna Menon voted against a resolution calling for the withdrawal of

Soviet troops from Hungary. India was the sole non-Communist country to cast a negative vote.[2]

Around the globe, reaction to India's tepid response on Hungary was loud and disapproving. The West accused Nehru of following a blatant double standard. Nehru's conduct of Indian foreign policy also came under sharp domestic criticism. Jayaprakash Narayan, onetime heir-apparent to Nehru, who had left the Congress to join the opposition Socialists, blasted the Prime Minister, characterizing his reaction on Hungary as unworthy of India. Narayan warned Nehru, "If you do not speak out you will be held guilty of abetting enslavement of a brave people by a new imperialism more dangerous than the old because it masquerades as revolutionary."[3] Bruised at home and abroad, Nehru retreated, condemning the Soviet repression in a 14 November statement with the Prime Ministers of Indonesia, Ceylon, and Burma and in a 19 November statement in the Indian parliament.[4] Nehru's about-face, somewhat weakly explained by his having received fuller information about the Hungarian situation, repaired some of the damage done to his reputation as a statesman who stood for high principle and morality in international relations.[5] The Hungary episode, nonetheless, left a bad aftertaste.

A month later, in December 1956, Nehru paid his second visit to the United States. Apart from his interest in reviewing world affairs and discussing South Asian developments with President Eisenhower, the Prime Minister was well aware that India needed more economic assistance from the United States to bolster its development efforts. In contrast to Nehru's 1949 talks with Harry Truman, the 1956 visit was a success.

Understanding that the Indian Prime Minister placed considerable emphasis on personal relationships, Eisenhower made a point of ensuring ample time for them to meet alone without aides. The two leaders spent a day and a half together at Eisenhower's farm in Gettysburg, Pennsylvania, where they were able to have fourteen hours of private talks in an informal setting.[6] The President kept India's *bête noire,* John Foster Dulles, in the background. The Indian leader, in turn, saw to it that Krishna Menon, the US *bête noire,* stayed away from Washington.

In their substantive talks, Eisenhower and Nehru broke little new ground, essentially restating the clashing policy views

17 December 1956, President Eisenhower and Prime Minister Nehru about to depart for the President's Farm at Gettysburg.

of their two governments—in particular, on the dangers of communism. In contrast to his initial soft position on Hungary, however, Nehru "described his horrified reactions" to the Soviet repression. He told Eisenhower that Hungary signalled the eventual death knell for communism—a system which had failed to take roots against nationalism. Nehru, however, refused to agree with the President that the Soviet Union was seeking world domination or represented a new form of colonialism. Not denying the logic of this view, Nehru believed that, over time, communism would defeat itself. The President observed, "It was rather cold comfort to realize that the historically inevitable doom of dictatorships often occurred only after the passage of much time, the loss of life, the postponement of peace."[7]

The two leaders continued to differ on Communist China. Nehru argued for Peking's acceptance into the family of nations. He thought it only a matter of time until Formosa fell.

Courtesy of the Dwight D. Eisenhower Library, White House album

18 December 1956, President Eisenhower and Prime Minister Nehru touring the Gettysburg farm.

Eisenhower believed the Chinese Communists needed to follow basic norms of international conduct before they joined the United Nations.[8] Regarding India's nonalignment, Nehru emphasized that this approach helped keep defense expenditures down since the policy minimized the chances of conflict on the Himalayan borders, the only logical security threat to India. In an argument that impressed Eisenhower, Nehru asserted that, given his country's economic weakness, having India as an ally would "serve to weaken rather than strengthen" the Western bloc.[9]

The Prime Minister took a tough line on Pakistan. Touching on Indian worries about US arms aid, Nehru said that many of his countrymen felt Pakistan was going to attack India, an idea fanned by "fanatics." He called partition an "egregious blunder," arguing that the Pakistanis got their independence only through the successful struggle of Indian nationalists. Nehru claimed the people of Kashmir wanted to belong to India, but he did not have to justify his opposition to a plebiscite as Eisenhower forgot to ask about this point.[10] Nehru gained the impression Eisenhower agreed that no good would be served by stirring up public interest regarding Kashmir in the near future.[11]

On economic assistance, Nehru reported that Eisenhower was enthusiastic in offering American support for India's faltering economic development plans. Eisenhower's version of the talks was different, indicating that Nehru did not directly ask for American aid but talked at length and eloquently about India's development hopes.[12] The President must have been listening to the Prime Minister; a few weeks later he was well versed about Indian economic plans during a spirited discussion in the NSC with Secretary of the Treasury George Humphrey, an opponent of aid to India. Showing far more knowledge than Humphrey, Eisenhower stoutly defended US assistance and sympathetically explained India's plans to develop public sector industries.[13]

Although the Eisenhower-Nehru talks yielded no specific agreements, both leaders came away with more respect for each other as well as a better understanding of their countries' differing positions on the major issues of the day. Eisenhower liked Nehru even though he found him "a personality of unusual contradictions." He believed the Prime Minister "sincerely wanted to help his people and lead them to higher levels of living and opportunity."[14] He was puzzled, however, by Nehru's "tolerance, relatively speaking, of Soviet attitudes"—despite his opposition to their methods. Eisenhower attributed Nehru's attitude to resentment toward the West's "condescension toward his people" and possibly a sense of identity with the Russians as a non-European people who also suffered from the West. The President thought millions in Asia and Africa probably shared Nehru's attitude.[15]

Even if Nehru disliked much about Eisenhower's policies—the emphasis on a military response to Communism and, especially, the program of arms aid to Pakistan—he respected the President for his achievements in World War II against the Nazis, for his genuine desire for world peace, for his understanding of the developing world, and for his sympathy for India. In Dwight Eisenhower—unlike Harry Truman—Nehru found an

American sincerely interested in India, its history, its aspirations, and its development efforts. The 1956 Nehru-Eisenhower meetings were perhaps an exception to the frequently ritualistic exchange of views when heads of government meet. As a result of their talks, both the President and Prime Minister seemed to have a better understanding, as well as kinder thoughts, about each other's policies. Indo-American relations began to improve.

"New Forces and New Nations Were Stirring"

In his second inaugural address in January 1957, Eisenhower signalled his concern that Communism would prove attractive to the newly emerging nations unless they enjoyed adequate economic development. "New forces and new nations were stirring across the earth . . . one-third of all mankind has entered an historic struggle for a new freedom: the freedom from grinding poverty," the President declared.[16] To counter the Soviets and their allies more effectively in the developing world, Eisenhower sought a substantial increase in foreign aid during his second term, arguing strongly that such a step was in the US national interest.[17]

As the "winds of change" signalled the demise of European colonialism, many newly independent nations followed India's lead in adopting a nonaligned policy, in trying to walk a middle road between the Western and Communist camps. With Europe and the Far East stable—despite periodic crises at flash points like Berlin and the Taiwan Straits—the Cold War focused increasingly on the uncommitted nations.[18] To a considerable extent, the East-West contest seemed to turn on how best to pursue economic development, to meet what was called at the time "the revolution of rising expectations." A group of US economists and social scientists at the Massachusetts Institute of Technology's Center for International Studies (CENIS), led by Professors Walt Rostow and Max Milliken, developed a theoretical underpinning to support the view that a substantial input of foreign aid would permit countries such as India to "take off" for self-sustaining economic growth under democracy and free enterprise.

Rostow and Milliken, in their influential *A Proposal: Key to an Effective Foreign Policy*, that appeared in 1957, offered a comprehensive argument for expanded foreign aid. Rostow, Milliken, and their colleagues asserted that more economic assistance could spur development, lead to stable societies, and thwart Communist efforts to gain the upper hand in the developing world.[19] India, because of many factors—its size and population, the use of English, Nehru's prestige, the country's economic planning (then much in vogue), and its adherence to democracy—became the model for many of the MIT theoretical studies. As Rostow wrote, "Rightly or wrongly, we believed the success or failure of India with respect to both its development and its politics would be widely influential."[20]

In 1957, India held its second democratic elections since independence. Nehru's Congress Party again won a sweeping victory, although the opposition parties on the left, the Socialists and the Communists, increased their share of the vote. The election shocker, which rang alarm bells in Washington, was the Communist victory in Kerala, a southern Indian state with India's highest level of literacy and its largest Christian population. The Kerala election marked one of the rare times a Communist government gained power in a free vote. The lesson Washington drew was that the Communists won in Kerala because the economy failed to improve rapidly enough to satisfy the population's expectations. US experts feared that if Pandit Nehru's Indian Congress Party failed to achieve adequate economic growth, Communist strength would continue to expand, presenting a real, if long-term, danger. Preventing additional Keralas became an important argument for augmenting US assistance to India.[21]

With the adoption in 1956 of "socialism" as a formal goal by the Congress Party, the emphasis of the Indian Second Five Year Plan (covering the years 1956-1961) lay on industrial development, especially for public sector industries such as steel, coal mining, and electric power. The ambitious Plan called for an expenditure of nearly $15 billion, more than double the size of the First Plan. It became evident by early 1957, however, that India lacked the foreign exchange to finance imports called for by the Plan. Unless New Delhi received fresh infusions of external financing, the centerpiece of the Congress Party's domestic platform risked failure. Nehru's bi-weekly letters to his

Chief Ministers during this period made clear his awareness of the economic straits India faced.

In contrast to other occasions, New Delhi was not diffident in seeking foreign help. In Washington, Ambassador G. L. Mehta urged Douglas Dillon, the Wall Street banker who became Under Secretary of State for Economic Affairs in 1957, to agree to an early start of talks about increased assistance, hoping to avoid a repeat of the controversy over the 1951 emergency wheat loan. Dillon was sympathetic, but emphasized the administration would not know for some time how much money it could make available.[22] India's top foreign aid official, Braj Kumar Nehru, a cousin of the Prime Minister, hurried to Washington in May to underscore the urgency of the situation. Estimating the shortfall at $700 million, B. K. Nehru stressed New Delhi's hope the United States would help fill the gap.[23] Although President Eisenhower wanted to respond positively, the administration was short of funds and reluctant to approach Congress for special legislation. There was sympathy and a recognition of India's importance on Capitol Hill, despite great resentment about Krishna Menon.[24]

In September 1957, T.T. Krishnamachari, India's Finance Minister—a prominent member of the Congress Party from South India—continued the quest for emergency assistance. TTK, as he was familiarly called, made a point with Secretary Dulles to request aid officially, stating (incorrectly) that "hitherto India has never asked for assistance from anyone." Dulles responded dryly that India should only request aid if it knows the response will be favorable. "Although the two governments might differ in their approaches to several matters," Dulles said, "it was important for India to demonstrate economic progress under freedom and democracy." When Dulles referred to past US help, the Indian Finance Minister effusively expressed "sincere appreciation" for this aid.[25]

Two weeks later, the Indian Finance Minister received a warmer reception from President Eisenhower. The Chief Executive stressed he was "sincerely interested in helping" India but warned that the US Congress would largely determine what could be done. Eisenhower emphasized he "had a substantial understanding of the Indian problem and had constantly pleaded for an understanding on the part of others."[26] In November, Ambassador Bunker summed up the argument for responding positively in a letter to Eisenhower.

> We have only to consider what our failure to act decisively and in time in the case of China has cost us in treasure and in lives, and what we would be willing to spend to reverse the process there to find the answer to what we ought to do in India. We differ with India, of course on many points of foreign policy, but it seems to me that these are not significant when viewed in the context of our overall objectives and our grand strategy in this part of the world.[27]

On 12 November 1957, President Eisenhower considered the India aid question with Vice President Nixon, Secretary of State Dulles, and Secretary of the Treasury Robert Anderson, who had replaced George Humphrey. Both Dulles and Anderson were critical of the Indians on political and economic policy grounds. They also expressed dissatisfaction that other countries, especially Germany, were not doing enough to help. In the end, the decision was, nonetheless, to agree to an additional $225 million assistance, cobbling the package together from the newly created Development Loan Fund, the Export-Import Bank, and further PL 480 food aid. The group decided not to seek a supplemental appropriation from the Congress. Because of India's unpopularity, Secretary Dulles feared there was "the danger of a spectacular defeat."[28]

Although noting that helping India would mean Pakistan and Turkey "would immediately be in for aid," Vice President Nixon argued, "If we do not, the cost will be the disintegration of India and its orientation toward the Communists."[29] Having decided to respond positively to India, the administration took the initiative in pressing America's allies to increase their help. Eisenhower sent special messages to West German and British leaders, urging that they make a special effort to provide more assistance. The US government also asked the World Bank to explore ways to boost its lending to help India out of the economic bind.[30]

By the spring of 1958, interest in doing more for India spilled over into the Congress. On 25 March, Democratic Senator John F. Kennedy of Massachusetts and Republican John

Sherman Cooper of Kentucky asked the Senate to adopt a resolution urging the United States "to join with other nations in providing support of the type, magnitude, and duration adequate to assist India to complete successfully its current program for economic development."[31] The initiative for the bipartisan resolution came from Kennedy although Cooper, as former US Ambassador to India and a supporter of increased aid, willingly joined forces. Kennedy cared about what he called the "uncommitted world," but also wanted to improve his standing with the liberal wing of the Democratic Party as he considered a run for the 1960 presidential nomination.[32] In 1957, the Massachusetts Senator spoke out in support of Algerian independence from France. Now he pressed the Eisenhower administration to do more for India's economic development—a cause in which he believed quite apart from the personal political calculations.[33]

After describing India in an October 1957 *Foreign Affairs* article as "the leading claimant for the role of a broker middle state in the larger bipolar struggle . . . and a centerpiece in a middle zone of uncommitted nations extending from Casablanca to Djakarta,"[34] Kennedy worked over the winter with Rostow, Milliken, and others at MIT to sharpen his ideas. The result was the 8,000-word speech he delivered on 25 March in support of the aid to India resolution.

Kennedy stressed the need for the West to associate itself constructively with the "uncommitted world," saw India as a critical case, described US aid as inadequate, and proposed that a team of international experts assess India's foreign exchange needs to complete the Second Plan. "India today represents as great a hope, as commanding a challenge as Western Europe did in 1947," the Senator declared, "and our people are still, I am confident, equal to the effort."[35] Although the Kennedy-Cooper resolution passed the Senate in 1958, it lacked support in the House of Representatives and died in the Joint Senate-House Conference. The resolution, nonetheless, proved a major spur to the aid India effort.

As India's short-term economic troubles continued in mid-1958, B. K. Nehru pleaded for more help from Under Secretary Dillon, who was sympathetic but underscored the reality that the US Congress would ultimately decide on appropriations. When Dillon stressed the Congress would be influenced by Indian actions and statements on world affairs, Nehru said his government would do all it could, short of changing its foreign policy, although as a democracy it could hardly gag people.[36] In looking for additional assistance funds, Dillon encouraged World Bank President Eugene Black, whom B. K. Nehru also approached, to promote a gathering of aid donors under World Bank sponsorship in an effort to raise more money. The response was positive. The donors—at the time the United States, United Kingdom, and West Germany were the main participants—agreed to provide an additional $350 million in short-term assistance. The Indians were delighted.[37] The successful August 1958 gathering became the model for the consortium technique that the World Bank has used in promoting and coordinating foreign assistance for India and numerous other developing countries during the past three decades.

In 1959, prospects for increased assistance to India substantially improved. The Democratic sweep in the November 1958 elections brought many pro-aid liberals, including former Ambassador Chester Bowles, to Congress. After Kennedy and Cooper reintroduced their resolution in February, both Houses readily adopted the measure. In order to gain backing from the Eisenhower administration, the senators agreed to broaden the resolution to speak of South Asia rather than merely India.[38]

On 4-5 May 1959, a remarkable gathering, "The Conference on India and the United States," took place in Washington. Some 88 Indian and American experts met with 724 business, political, academic, and international affairs leaders to discuss India. Sponsored by the Committee on Economic Development, the conference began with bipartisan opening remarks by Vice President Richard Nixon and Senator John Kennedy and words of welcome from Indian Ambassador Mohammed Ali Chagla[39] and B. K. Nehru, now assigned as Ambassador-at-Large and Commissioner General for Economic Affairs. Although the India lobby had no formal organization, the Conference assembled the different threads of support that, in effect, comprised the lobby—spanning the political spectrum from liberals like Bowles and Humphrey to moderates like Kennedy and Cooper. Combining humanitarian concern that the poor of India achieve a better life, political concern that India's fledgling democracy survive, and strategic concern that communism not gain ground in the developing world's largest non-Communist nation, the Conference marked a high point in generating support for additional help for India.[40]

The effort succeeded. During Eisenhower's second term, US assistance grew substantially, surging from about $400 million in 1957, to a record $822 million in 1960, Eisenhower's last year in office. In May 1960, Eisenhower and Indian Agriculture Minister S. K. Patil, the Congress Party political boss of Bombay and an outspokenly pro-American voice in the Indian cabinet, signed a mammoth $1.276 billion PL 480 food agreement. The accord called for the export of 12 million tons of US wheat over a four-year period, providing India a badly needed cushion in the face of continued slow progress in raising food production.[41]

The smooth work of B. K. Nehru, the man New Delhi sent to Washington to find additional aid funds from the United States, Western Europe, and the World Bank, greatly aided the process. Adopting a non-contentious and straight-forward approach, the Indian envoy established excellent working relations with Senator Kennedy, Under Secretary Dillon, World Bank President Black, and other key Washington figures. When Kennedy became President, the Prime Minister took advantage of his cousin's friendly ties with the new President to name him India's Ambassador to the United States.

On the US side—in addition to the interest of President Eisenhower and Senator Kennedy—another important factor was the positive attitude of Christian A. Herter, the former Republican Governor of Massachusetts. Herter became Under Secretary of State in 1956 and then the Secretary after John Foster Dulles died of cancer in 1959. Unlike his predecessor as Under Secretary of State, Herbert Hoover, Jr., or Dulles himself, Herter strongly supported foreign assistance for India and, along with Douglas Dillon, worked inside the administration to promote the large increase in the India program.[42]

In addition to boosting bilateral assistance, the United States became the major source of funding in implementing the Indus Waters Agreement, for which the World Bank succeeded in obtaining India and Pakistan's agreement in 1959.[43] US funds covered half the $1 billion worth of dams, irrigation works, and other construction projects envisaged under the accord.[44] Bank President Eugene Black worked closely with Under Secretary

4 May 1960, Indian Agriculture Minister S. K. Patil and President Eisenhower signing the 12 million ton PL 480 agreement. Indian Ambassador M. C. Chagla is seated on the President's left. Those standing include Secretary of Agriculture Ezra Taft Benson and Under Secretary of State Douglas Dillon.

Dillon, who in August 1959 got President Eisenhower to approve a $517 million US contribution. The World Bank funded about $250 million, with other donors providing the remaining $250 million.

Although Dillon correctly regarded the Indus Waters agreement as a major step in improving relations between India and Pakistan, he was overly optimistic in telling an April 1960 NSC meeting that the accord showed that the Kashmir dispute could also be settled.[45] Dillon overlooked an essential difference between the two disputes. The World Bank was able to make both India and Pakistan winners in the Indus Waters settlement, since each country received more irrigation water as a result of the agreement. In the case of Kashmir, as long as both India and Pakistan coveted Srinagar and the Valley and saw the dispute in highly emotional and ideological terms, any conceivable settlement would inevitably make one side or the other conclude itself the loser.

As the size of bilateral aid increased, US officials paid more attention to the program's impact, especially in comparison to that of Soviet economic assistance. A May 1959 Embassy New Delhi airgram reported Moscow was prepared to give New Delhi virtually everything the Indians sought on favorable repayment terms, including a pledge of up to $1 billion for India's Third Five Year Plan. The Soviet emphasis on big "show projects" and aid to Indian public sector industries was likely, in the Embassy's view, to earn the Russians much credit with Indian public opinion. To counter the Soviets, Embassy New Delhi urged US assistance to Indian public sector projects, including a million ton steel mill, to be built at Bokaro in eastern India.[46]

The question of US aid to an Indian government-owned steel mill (the Soviets, British, and West Germans were already undertaking similar steel mill projects) became a sensitive issue for a number of years. Symbolically, for many Indians, and some Americans, US willingness to fund Bokaro became a litmus test of US support for India's industrial development. Other Americans, including most Republicans, opposed using US tax dollars to pay for Bokaro. Questioning the wisdom of India's socialist economic policies, they did not think competition for favor with the Soviets provided a sufficient reason for Uncle Sam to fund a public sector steel mill. Although Bokaro received considerable high level attention in Washington during the Eisenhower administration, the Republicans reached no decision, passing the issue on to their Democratic successors.

Less in the public eye was possible US financing for an atomic power plant. After President Eisenhower proposed the Atoms for Peace program in 1955, India's Atomic Energy Chairman Homi Bhabha, a gifted scientist and energetic administrator, sought to interest Washington in building a nuclear power plant in India as a dramatic way of demonstrating US support for peaceful uses of atomic energy in the Third World. Ambassador Bunker argued in favor of the project, stressing that India needed the power and would get the plant from the Soviets should the United States refuse.[47]

The US Atomic Energy Commission, at first, doubted the economic feasibility of the project and also questioned whether India was technologically ready. The AEC agreed to consider the power plant seriously only after Prime Minister Nehru raised the subject during Eisenhower's visit to India and the State Department strongly supported sending a survey mission.[48] The team was impressed by the Indian atomic energy program, found the costs of nuclear power production in India competitive with conventional power, and concluded the project made sense. Washington agencies had the proposal under consideration when the Eisenhower administration left office in January 1961.

The aid element in the bilateral relationship, thus, radically changed during the course of a decade. In 1949, the Truman administration's Asia policy review pointedly refused to underwrite India's economic development.[49] Chester Bowles was able to expand a small technical assistance program into meaningful, but modest, support for India's rural development. The Eisenhower administration initially trod water, skeptical about foreign assistance in general and not enthusiastic about expanding the India program. As the Soviet Union increased its economic activities in the developing world, especially in India, the administration shifted gears. After 1957, expanded foreign assistance became an important foreign policy goal. Supported by a broad bipartisan coalition, the administration pushed through a major expansion of US assistance to India and energized the World Bank and US allies to increase their help. The Eisenhower administration, ironically, ended up with the type of commitment to India's development program that Chester Bowles had proposed in vain in 1952.

NSC 5701: Neutralism Not Against American Interests

By 1957, President Eisenhower concluded that India's neutralist policy was not against American interests. Quite the contrary, Eisenhower told his advisers on a number of occasions that he supported India's staying nonaligned.[50] Echoing a variation on what Pandit Nehru told him, Eisenhower stated—during a January 1957 NSC review of South Asia policy—there would not be enough money in the United States to support India should that country become an ally. Further standing US policy on its head, Eisenhower criticized "our tendency to rush out and seek allies" as "not very sensible." The President called the accord with Pakistan "perhaps the worst kind of a plan and decision we could have made. It was a terrible error, but we now seemed hopelessly involved in it."[51]

NSC 5701, a revised South Asia policy that Eisenhower approved on 10 January 1957, marked a shift in emphasis from the 1954 policy contained in NSC 5409, even if the new policy did not fully reflect the President's outburst over the consequences of arming Pakistan. NSC 5701 characterized South Asia as an important Cold War front where the Soviet Union was seeking to roll back support for the West through a vigorous diplomatic, economic, and propaganda assault. Perceiving the competition between India and China as a struggle between democratic and totalitarian development models, NSC 5701 concluded that despite India's frequent opposition to US policies:

> The risks to US security from a weak and vulnerable India would be greater than the risks of a stable and influential India . . . . A strong India would be a successful example of an alternative to Communism in an Asian context and would permit the gradual development of the means to enforce its external security interests against Communist Chinese expansion into South and Southeast Asia.[52]

On the issue of arms assistance to Pakistan, the revised policy accepted past US promises of aid—these having resulted in a "symbolic" $10 million annual program projected in NSC

5409 ballooning into a substantial $471 million by 1957—but opposed further increases in aid levels.[53] Reflecting the adjustment in policy that was then in train, NSC 5701 stressed better relations with India and placed greater emphasis on economic rather than military means in meeting the Soviet challenge.

The handling of South Asia illustrated the way Eisenhower directed the foreign policy process through the highly structured National Security Council machinery. The NSC system ran much like the military organization in which the President spent practically all his adult life. Formal policy papers, such as the ones on South Asia, NSC 5409 and 5701, tended to be comprehensive and detailed—almost akin to operational military plans—than the more general policy statements prepared during the Truman administration. The Operations Coordinating Board, a sub-group of the NSC, monitored implementation of policy papers and submitted periodic progress reports. Under Eisenhower, the NSC did not play the operational role that later developed under Kennedy and Nixon. The NSC served as a staff

Courtesy of the Dwight D. Eisenhower Library, White House album

17 January 1957, President Eisenhower and US Ambassador to India Ellsworth Bunker.

arm for the President with operations remaining the preserve of the cabinet departments.[54]

During Eisenhower's second term, the attitude toward India gradually mellowed. This process was helped along by Ellsworth Bunker, whom Eisenhower named as successor to John Sherman Cooper as Ambassador to India. A businessman and a Democrat, Bunker won praise as Harry Truman's Ambassador to Argentina and Italy and later as the President of the American Red Cross. Dulles suggested his nomination to India after Eisenhower said he would be glad to "send a Democrat to one or two diplomatic posts," a somewhat unexpected step during a period of considerable partisanship.[55] During his four years in India, Bunker, a reserved New Englander, added to his reputation as a highly effective diplomat. One measure of his skill was Bunker's ability to earn the respect of Nehru and other Indian leaders without losing credibility in Washington.

The warming in Indo-American relations even survived a testy period during and after a January 1957 UN Security Council debate on Kashmir, when Krishna Menon delivered an impassioned two-day defense of the Indian position. Nehru was annoyed the United States agreed to have Kashmir come before the Council and continued to support the idea of a plebiscite—contrary to the impression he received from Eisenhower during their talks.[56] The vitriolic UN debate provided Menon a platform to gain popularity in India and to stir even deeper antipathy among Americans. Flinging sarcasm and venom at Pakistan and acidly attacking the United States and Britain for challenging India's right to Kashmir, Menon spoke vituperatively for two days, interrupted only twice when—with theatrical flourish—he fainted.[57] After the Soviets vetoed a resolution calling for the stationing of UN troops in Kashmir, the Council agreed to send its President, Sweden's Gunnar Jarring, to the subcontinent. Jarring traveled to South Asia, talked with Indian and Pakistani leaders, and—to no one's surprise—reported back to the Council that the Kashmir dispute remained deadlocked.

Later in 1957, the Pakistanis again brought Kashmir to the Security Council. On this occasion, Nehru instructed Krishna Menon to tone down his comments after the United States complained about some of his remarks.[58] The result of the debate was Security Council approval for another mission to

South Asia by Dr. Frank Graham, who had tried unsuccessfully in the early 1950s to mediate the dispute. Graham's effort proved as fruitless as his earlier attempt at finding a settlement. In Karachi, he found the Pakistanis willing to accept any arrangement that permitted a plebiscite. In New Delhi, Graham ran into a stone wall. In so many words, the Indians told the UN representative, "The matter is settled. Kashmir is ours."[59]

After the 1954 arms pact with Pakistan, an unenthusiastic United States found itself under periodic pressure to keep the Kashmir issue alive internationally through discussion in the United Nations and by mention in SEATO and Baghdad Pact communiqués. Although this process in no way improved the chances for solving the dispute—Dulles frankly admitted as much in talking with Pakistan's Foreign Minister Feroz Khan Noon in November 1957[60]—continued attention kept the issue on the international agenda and showed the Pakistanis that their American friends, at least rhetorically, supported them. At the same time, Karachi was not unhappy that discussion of the Kashmir issue in international fora served as a chronic irritant in Indo-American relations.[61]

Despite the difficulties, Eisenhower persisted in pressing for better relations between India and Pakistan. To American observers looking at the subcontinent, one conclusion struck home: the enmity between India and Pakistan rendered South Asia vulnerable to external threats, especially from the Soviet Union or Communist China. A closing of ranks between the two antagonists seemed the logical step. Eisenhower made his views clear when India's Vice President Sarvepalli Radhakrishnan, the distinguished philosopher and former Ambassador to Moscow, met the President during a March 1958 visit to Washington.

Recalling his discussions with Prime Minister Nehru, Eisenhower said "to his mind it was incomprehensible that there had not been a settlement of the issues between India and Pakistan . . . . Nothing could be more wonderful for peace than a rapprochement." Eisenhower added that the United States was trying to be friends with both countries and not take sides between them.[62] Secretary of State Dulles had rather different sentiments. When he met Pakistan's Finance Minister Amjad Ali and General Ayub Khan in April 1958, he said that US "feelings for Pakistan were, in a sense, totally different from those for India . . . . The basic relationship with India was intellectual in contrast to its relationship with Pakistan which came from the heart."[63]

To help the process of rapprochement along, the administration launched a sincere, if ill-fated, initiative to tackle outstanding India-Pakistan differences. Originally suggested by the American Embassies in Pakistan and India, the proposal linked together in a single basket the three major areas of Indo-Pakistani friction—Kashmir, the military competition between the two nations, and their dispute over the use of the major rivers of the Indus Valley. The strategy called for using US leverage, mainly through economic assistance programs, to press for a simultaneous solution of all three problems. When Secretary Dulles put the "basket proposal" to Eisenhower, the President reacted positively: He was "all for" the initiative and ready to help personally. "There is no inconvenience at which I would balk," Eisenhower responded, "For example, I'd be ready to welcome and entertain the Prime Ministers simultaneously—I would even go out there."[64]

In April 1958, frustrated by political infighting within his Congress Party and tired after eleven years as Prime Minister, Pandit Nehru threatened to retire from office.[65] The possibility of Nehru's departure from the political stage caused shock waves not only through the body politic in India, but in Washington as well. On hearing the news, Eisenhower instructed Dulles to send a personal word urging Nehru to stay on. The President's message, apparently drafted by Dulles himself, read:

> You, if anyone, Mr. Prime Minister, deserve a long and restful vacation after all these years that you have guided your vast country toward economic, political and social progress. However I and countless others hope that you will not go too far away or for too long a time. . . . It would indeed be a misfortune, perhaps for all of us, if at what may prove to be a critical formative period, your own influence were not actively present over any really protracted period.[66]

Ambassador Bunker thought Nehru was visibly touched by Eisenhower's note, the only one of its kind received. "I am convinced," Bunker wrote the President, "it has measurably advanced the friendly atmosphere here."[67] Improved atmospherics and good personal relations with Eisenhower were, however, not enough to get Pandit Nehru to say "yes" to the US basket proposal. When Bunker presented the idea, the Indian leader questioned—probably accurately—whether the wobbly Pakistani government, then staggering from crisis to crisis[68] would be able to undertake serious negotiations. Nor did he see much hope in reaching a settlement as long as the Pakistanis continued their "attitude of hate" toward India, a stance Nehru claimed was abetted by the military alliances and the Western attitude on Kashmir.[69]

For Nehru, the underlying India-Pakistan problem was the "communal conflict and hatred and violence" rather than specific issues like Kashmir,

> I see no solution till that basic conflict in the minds of the people of Pakistan and India is resolved. . . . Great Powers like the United States and the United Kingdom talk piously of goodwill and India and Pakistan making up their quarrel. But they ignore deliberately the cause of that quarrel and the consequences of it. And so, they do not find solutions.[70]

Although disappointed by Nehru's attitude, Eisenhower continued to extend his hand in friendship. In November 1958, he wrote effusively to the Indian leader after Paul Hoffman, the former Marshall Plan administrator who served as a private emissary on Kashmir in 1953, returned from a visit to the subcontinent. "Universally," the President wrote Nehru, "You are recognized as one of the most powerful influences for peace and conciliation in the world. . . . Your influence is particularly valuable in stemming the global drift toward cynicism, mutual suspicion, materialistic opportunism and, finally, disaster."[71] During much of this period, Nehru and Eisenhower were in touch about various efforts to lower international tensions through disarmament and reduced nuclear testing, issues both regarded as of utmost importance in maintaining world peace.

Soviet tactics in Hungary shook the humanist in Nehru and made him more chary about the Soviets.[72] Although the setback to détente between the United States and the USSR depressed him greatly, Nehru tended to be somewhat less critical of Washington than before his talks with Eisenhower. India was, however, once more upset with the United States over Pakistan. After the Baghdad Pact collapsed—following the July 1958 coup in Iraq by the anti-western Abdul Karim Qasim—the northern tier defense grouping reemerged in the form of the Central Treaty Organization (CENTO), with Turkey, Iran, and Pakistan as regional members and headquarters in Ankara. In early 1959, the United States concluded a bilateral defense agreement with Pakistan to buttress the security relationship. Eisenhower was frank in telling Indian Ambassador M. C. Chagla that he found himself on the horns of dilemma between providing arms for an ally, Pakistan, and damaging US friendship with India.[73]

About this time, a development occurred that influenced US policy toward the subcontinent over the next half dozen years—Pakistan agreed to provide the United States facilities for sensitive US intelligence operations near the city of Peshawar—just a few miles from the Khyber Pass and Afghanistan. The Peshawar airfield provided the take-off point for secret overflights of the Soviet Union by CIA's U–2 aircraft, capable— the United States thought—of flying above the range of Soviet anti-aircraft defenses. In the days before satellite imagery, U–2 missions provided unique photographic intelligence about Soviet military dispositions and capabilities. The Pakistanis also permitted the United States to establish an electronic listening post, supposedly a US air force communications facility outside Peshawar. Because of its geographic location, the Peshawar base also enabled the United States to monitor electronically Soviet missile tests, the facility forming part of the chain of electronic listening posts through which the United States kept tabs on Soviet missiles. The fact of the Peshawar facility boosted Pakistan's value to US national security interests. Although CENTO and SEATO seemed of diminishing significance, the intelligence facilities were important assets that Washington was wary of losing.

Mounting Tensions Between India and Communist China

If Pakistan's willingness to provide facilities for US intelligence operations increased its importance to US national security, mounting tensions between India and Communist China

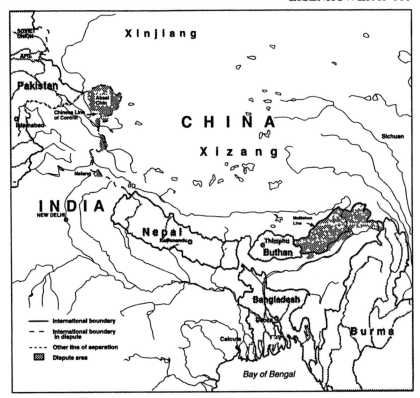

The India-China Border

added a new dimension to Washington's relations with New Delhi.[74] By 1959 it was evident—even though Nehru had managed to minimize publicity—that serious differences existed over the India-China border. The difficulties were not just a problem of outdated maps that the Communists had yet to correct as Chou-En lai suggested earlier.

In Ladakh, in the north of Kashmir, both India and China claimed a desolate and uninhabited 16,000 foot-high plateau called the Aksai Chin. The area had no intrinsic importance for India, but for China provided a valuable link between Sinkiang province and Tibet. In 1957, the Aksai Chin's significance grew after the Chinese completed a road across the plateau permitting direct communication between the two regions. The Indians only learned of the road through a report in the Chinese press. In the eastern portion of the frontier, the two countries disputed the borders between India's Northeast Frontier Agency (NEFA) and Tibet. India claimed that this frontier—the so-called Mac-Mahon Line—was fixed by the Simla convention signed in 1914. The Chinese, while implying willingness to accept the MacMahon Line, believed as a matter of principle India and China should formally negotiate the border delimitation rather than adopt a demarcation imposed by the British at a time when India was a British possession and China weak.

In December 1958, after tensions along the border mounted following the Chinese capture of an Indian military patrol in the Aksai Chin, Nehru sent a detailed letter to Chou-En lai trying to smoke out the Chinese. The Prime Minister emphasized the view that "India's boundaries were fixed and well-known." There was no question of "large parts of India being anything but India."[75] Chou's 29 January 1959 reply disagreed that the borders were fixed, stating that "the Sino-Indian boundary has never been formally delimited. Historically no treaty or agreement on the Sino-Indian boundary has ever been concluded between the Chinese Central Government and the Indian Government." Chou suggested negotiations.[76]

Two months later in March 1959, the situation became far more complicated politically after Tibet revolted against the Communists. When the Chinese military suppressed the uprising, the Dalai Lama, Tibet's spiritual and temporal leader, fled to India, and, on 31 March, received political asylum. These events caused an emotional surge of anti-Chinese sentiments in India that shattered the policy of friendship Nehru had so carefully nurtured. Although Nehru tried to temporize, following inherently conflicting goals—help for the Tibetans and continued friendship with China—his policy of *Hindi-Chini bhai bhai* was dead five years after the Nehru-Chou 1954 meetings.

For their part, the Chinese were angered by the Indian attitude toward Tibet, assuming—perhaps incorrectly—that Nehru was collaborating with the Chinese Nationalists and the US Central Intelligence Agency in providing covert assistance to the Tibetan resistance movement. The Chinese stance on the border stiffened. They reaffirmed their earlier maps which claimed the entire Northeast Frontier Agency—some 40,000 square miles—as Chinese and rejected the Indian position that the border was fixed along the MacMahon Line. A Chinese ambush of an Indian patrol killed four Indian soldiers and left five others wounded. Ten Indian soldiers were taken prisoner. This event caused an uproar in New Delhi. Under great political pressure in parliament, Nehru released the diplomatic exchanges with China over the border dispute, making plain how serious the differences were.

The result was a renewed surge of nationalist and anti-Chinese sentiments that thereafter limited Nehru's ability to maneuver in diplomatic dealings with Beijing. A compromise on the border dispute—swapping Indian desires to establish the MacMahon Line along the crest of the Assam Himalayas as the border in the east for Chinese desires to control the Aksai Chin in Ladakh—might have been possible earlier. After October 1959, Indian public opinion made such a deal politically difficult, if not impossible.

With trouble on its northern borders, as well as continued tensions with Pakistan, India began to step up its defense build-up. Responsibility for this lay in the hands of Krishna Menon, Defense Minister since 1957. Although Nehru continued his staunch support for his friend, Menon ultimately proved a disaster, politicizing and demoralizing the top ranks of the military. Those that refused to play Menon's game, like General Thimayya were, in effect, forced out and replaced by "political" generals like Lt. General B. N. Kaul, willing to bend to Menon's will. Menon minimized the significance of the troubles with China, asserting that Pakistan remained India's major security danger. Menon, to Washington's great concern, also pressed for the acquisition of Soviet military equipment to break the British and French dominance over Indian military procurement.

As the Sino-Indian rift deepened, the reaction in the West, especially of the United States, was entirely supportive of India, even though the State Department took no official position on the disputed McMahon Line border claim. Given the decade-long animosity with Communist China, Washington readily accepted the Indian version of events—a view consistent with the US perception of China as an aggressive bully. To Nehru's great satisfaction, the Soviet Union adopted a neutral stance. Nehru saw Soviet neutrality as a further vindication of his nonalignment policy as well as strategically important in India's border dispute with China. Moscow's position angered the Chinese and became an element in broader Sino-Soviet tensions then mounting between the two Communist powers.

Some in Washington regarded Sino-Indian tensions as opening the way for far closer US relations with New Delhi, with the possibility of even making India a strategic counterweight against China. When the NSC considered this idea in May 1959, President Eisenhower strongly disagreed. "India," the President stated, "had never announced any readiness to align itself with the West as an opponent of communism, as Japan for instance has. We could not talk of a counterweight if the nation in question refuses to be a counterweight." Eisenhower commented that if the United States were actually to try to make India a counterweight to Communist China, the task would be so great that America would probably bankrupt itself in the process. The President argued the US goal should be to "give India a chance to grow as a free and democratic country." Eisenhower also reiterated his felling that "the Indians were wise to adopt their attitude of non-alignment."[77]

Mounting tensions between India and China, thus, added a new dimension to Washington's relations with New Delhi, and vice versa. For once, the two countries shared a common position on an important security issue: both had bad relations with Communist China.

"My Desire to See That Country for Myself"

Dwight Eisenhower wrote in his memoirs, "During Prime Minister Nehru's visit to the United States in 1956, I had become so intrigued by the picture he painted of the region, its people, and their aspirations that my desire to see that country for myself became the stronger."[78] In December 1959, the President realized this wish, as he became the first US President to visit independent India.[79] Eisenhower told Lord Plowden, British Atomic Energy chief, he arranged his three week Europe and Middle East trip "just to get to India."[80] Air Force One, the new Boeing 707 presidential jet, which the President used for the first time on the trip, made the extensive journey feasible, enabling Eisenhower to cover far greater distances in greater comfort than had the propeller driven aircraft he had used for earlier travels.

President Eisenhower garlanded on arrival in New Delhi 10 December 1959. Left to right, Ambassador Bunker, Congress Party President UN Dhebar, Prime Minister Nehru, Vice President Radhakishnan, Indira Gandhi, President Eisenhower, and President of India Rajendra Prasad.

When the President arrived in New Delhi at dusk on 10 December 1959, he was received "with tremendous enthusiasm and emotion." In Nehru's words, "We had a expected a great welcome for the President. But even our anticipations were exceeded."[81] Millions mobbed the streets to see Eisenhower. With the largest crowds since the celebration of Indian independence, the motorcade was swallowed up in the sea of people and totally gridlocked for over an hour in downtown New Delhi.

During his four days in India, Eisenhower spoke to parliament, joined Nehru in addressing a vast throng in front of the Red Fort in Old Delhi, fulfilled a childhood dream of visiting the Taj Mahal, and held extensive discussions with the Prime Minister. Wherever Eisenhower went, he drew enormous crowds, showing that the phenomenon of "I like Ike" was as true in India as the United States. Eisenhower charmed India with his broad smile and friendly, open manner. The trip was a public relations triumph.

As in 1956, the private talks between the two leaders went well. They "had long discussions and covered almost all the current problems of Asia, Europe and even Africa."[82] In discussing the border trouble with China, Nehru explained Indian perceptions, commenting he could not understand Chinese motives. Having extended the hand of friendship, Nehru was hurt and perplexed by the hardening of the Chinese position on the Himalayan frontiers. Eisenhower did not dwell on the border dispute, saying simply that he hoped it could be resolved peacefully.[83]

On India and Pakistan problems, Eisenhower stressed how "perplexed" he was between his desire to provide military equipment for Pakistan and "an equal wish not to cause embarrassment or anxiety to India." He argued that Indian deployment of troops in Kashmir was wasteful and weakened the subcontinent's defenses. Eisenhower insisted that the United States would never permit the Pakistanis to use US equipment to attack India. The President informed Nehru that the Pakistanis, in any case, had limited amounts of ammunition since the United States provided them with only one week's supply.[84]

During the last evening in New Delhi, the President and the Prime Minister dined alone. Enthralled by Nehru's description of "India, her history, her needs, her principal problems, both domestic and foreign and of his hopes for her," Eisenhower found the Indian leader's views "palpably honest and sincere."[85] In their talk, the Prime Minister stressed his interest in some sort of declaration that India and Pakistan not use force or war to settle their differences. If Pakistan gave this assurance, Nehru said India would be less concerned about US arms to Pakistan.[86]

Eisenhower promptly followed up, instructing Ambassador William Rountree in Pakistan to raise Nehru's no-war idea with President Ayub Khan. Eisenhower wanted to make sure that Ayub understood "the great opportunity this could give him in modernization of his army."[87] As Rountree anticipated—since Nehru had proposed mutual pledges not to use force as long ago as 1949—Ayub flatly rejected the suggestion. Were he to accept, Ayub told Eisenhower, the people of Pakistan would say he had handed Kashmir on a silver platter to the Indians. Ayub asserted he was not against the "no war" declaration but wanted a

Courtesy of the Dwight D. Eisenhower Library, Collection of James C. Hagerty

President Eisenhower and Prime Minister Nehru meet with Indian Girl Scouts.

parallel agreement on principles for solving the Kashmir dispute. Without this linkage, Ayub believed the "no-war" declaration was a ploy to enable Nehru to avoid doing anything about Kashmir.[88]

Even though Eisenhower was not able to bring India and Pakistan closer together—probably no one could have succeeded in this task—his visit was a tremendous success. "We were not out to get anything from each other," Nehru wrote the Chief Ministers, "but rather to understand, and I think both of us succeeded to some extent. . . . I believe there is a greater mutual understanding between these two countries now."[89] US-Indian relations had rarely been warmer.

Sidewinder Missiles for India: Eisenhower Changes His Mind

In April 1960, Ambassador Bunker, during consultations in Washington, met with the President to review South Asian developments. Eisenhower expressed pleasure about his trip and the apparent improvement in Indo-Pakistani relations, saying he found Nehru was taking a "more realistic" view of world developments. Bunker commented that Eisenhower's strong assurance that US arms would not be used by Pakistan against India made a considerable impression on Nehru and others in the Government of India.

The discussion turned to a US decision to provide F–104 fighter aircraft to Pakistan, an action that was arousing new concerns in India. No longer questioning US motives, Bunker said the Indians worried that the F–104s would render their own air force obsolete. After Bunker observed that the Indians would find it harder to object to military aid to Pakistan if the United States offered similar equipment to India, Eisenhower responded that he saw no reason not to do so. "In fact," the President added, "we should do so." Eisenhower asked Bunker to inform the State Department of his views.[90]

Two weeks after the Bunker-Eisenhower conversation, the Indians for the first time in a number of years turned to the United States for military equipment. In early May, Defense Minister Krishna Menon approached Bunker about buying 29

Fairchild C-119 transport aircraft to help in supplying the Himalayan defenses. Bunker cabled Washington he was encouraged by the request, arguing it was "clearly in our interest to do everything possible stiffen GOI posture vis-à-vis Chinese Communists."[91] The US Government quickly approved the sale.[92]

Later in the month, during a visit to Delhi by Secretary of the Air Force Sharp, Krishna Menon asked if India could buy Sidewinder missiles, an advanced weapons system the United States promised to supply to Pakistan. Bunker urged approval, recalling that President Eisenhower was in accord with the idea of selling India the same equipment the United States was giving Pakistan.[93] After careful deliberation, the State Department's Near East Bureau, then headed by career diplomat G. Lewis Jones, recommended to Secretary Herter that the Indians be urged to purchase their missiles from Britain. Jones opposed selling Sidewinders to India because of the "present delicate state of our relations with Pakistan." Herter concurred and later discussed the question with President Eisenhower, who—reversing the position he took with Bunker—agreed to turn the Indians down.[94]

Disappointed, Ambassador Bunker argued the case again—to no avail—with Assistant Secretary Jones. In his 13 July reply, Jones defended the decision politely but firmly. His main point was that Pakistan, as an ally, deserved better treatment than nonaligned India. Jones wrote:

> In becoming our wholehearted ally, Pakistan has undertaken real responsibilities and risks, making its territory available to us for a series of projects highly important to our national security. . . . The hard fact remains that, if our mutual security system is to remain intact, we must show Pakistan . . . that substantial benefits flow from a military alignment with us against the Communist bloc.[95]

The Sidewinder episode—notwithstanding what Eisenhower told Ambassador Bunker—made clear that the United States was not willing to equate India and Pakistan in military supply matters. Washington did not want to put at risk the recently acquired intelligence facilities at Peshawar in a dispute over arms to India. The United States was also reluctant to do anything that would bolster the position of Krishna Menon, enabling the Defense Minister to claim he could obtain sophisticated weapons from Washington as well as from Moscow.

Even though the United States refused to sell Sidewinders to India, it remained uneasy about India's procuring increased quantities of military equipment from the Soviet Union. Only with great difficulty were the Americans and the British in 1957 able to dissuade Nehru from buying Soviet bombers instead of British Canberras.[96] By 1960, the combination of pro-Soviet Krishna Menon as Defense Minister, the bargain basement rupee payment terms Moscow offered, and Nehru's perception that closer ties with Moscow were helpful against China made the situation more favorable for an expanded Soviet military supply relationship.

In the summer, the possible purchase of Soviet helicopters worried Washington and the American Embassy in New Delhi. Although the Embassy saw preventing this sale as being of "paramount importance," the conclusion at an August interagency meeting in Washington was that the United States could do little to head off the transaction. Underlining US concerns, the Defense Department later changed its mind, proposing that the Air Force subsidize an offer of US helicopters to the Indians. Time ran out before the Eisenhower administration could make a decision. The proposal died in the transition to the Kennedy administration.[97]

The US attitude on arms to India was thus ambivalent. Washington did not want India to obtain more Soviet arms, fearing this would increase Soviet influence. At the same time, the United States was unwilling to sell sophisticated weaponry to India for fear of upsetting US ally Pakistan. The preferred approach was to direct the Indians toward the British, their traditional supplier, in the hope that this would suffice to keep the Soviets out. In 1957, this approach succeeded in averting the purchase of Soviet bombers. By 1960, it no longer worked.

Final Eisenhower-Nehru Meeting, September 1960

The year began with high hopes for a Big Four summit to be followed by an Eisenhower visit to the Soviet Union to reciprocate Khrushchev's 1959 trip to the United States. In May 1960, expectations for further progress toward disarmament and détente were dashed after the Soviets shot down a CIA U–2 spy plane that had taken off from Peshawar. The United States waffled at first, but eventually Eisenhower took full responsibility for the incident. Khrushchev's angry reaction was to stomp out of the Big Four meeting in Paris and cancel Eisenhower's visit. In the fall UN General Assembly session, the Soviet chief continued his theatrical performance, undiplomatically leading the Soviet delegation in pounding their shoes on the delegate desks. The Soviet leader also proposed a drastic reshuffle of the UN Secretariat to reduce the powers of the Secretary General by replacing his position with a troika or three-headed leadership.

Eisenhower and Nehru, both in New York for the UN session, met in late September for the last time. Weary from five days in Pakistan where he had signed the Indus Waters Treaty, Nehru seemed tired throughout the discussion. Eisenhower expressed astonishment at Khrushchev's conduct: Destroying the UN would be terrible, especially for smaller countries. Nehru agreed the UN's break-up would be catastrophic. He had yet to see Khrushchev but hoped the Soviet leader would calm down.

The President stressed his desire for progress on disarmament, but was pessimistic about the prospects. He reviewed at some length US-Soviet differences on verification questions, obtaining Nehru's agreement that verification was an essential part of any disarmament accord. The two leaders also talked about Africa, where the Congo was falling into chaos after the hurried grant of independence by Belgium. The UN was trying, with limited success, to prevent civil war between different factions vying for power.

Turning to India's border dispute with China, Nehru said there was unfortunately no progress toward a solution. Chou En-lai visited New Delhi in April 1960, but to little avail. The Prime Minister said that as the two sides in these talks even disagreed on the basic facts of their border claims, officials were seeking to clarify these points. Militarily, Nehru commented, the Chinese were better able to support forces in the Himalayan border areas than India because of the nature of the terrain and their superior road system.[98]

Although the two leaders did not meet again, Nehru managed to miff Eisenhower later in the UN session by failing to consult before joining other major nonaligned leaders (Nasser of Egypt, Tito of Yugoslavia, Nkrumah of Ghana, and Sukarno of

Indonesia) in publicly proposing a US-Soviet summit on disarmament. Eisenhower turned the idea down because he felt the Soviets were intransigent on arms control questions, explaining his reasons in a lengthy letter to the Prime Minister.[99]

Indo-US bilateral relations might have substantially improved, but—as the nonaligned episode showed—plenty of differences remained. Still one sensed that the edge was off Nehru's distrust of the United States during Eisenhower's second term. The good personal chemistry between the two leaders in part explained this. Eisenhower's clear concern for preserving world peace—always a critical factor in Nehru's thinking—was another element. The Soviet handling of the Hungarian revolt, especially the execution of Premier Imre Nagy, made Nehru more critical of the Russians—and perhaps less critical of the United States.

US-Indian Relations: "Increasingly Cordial"

In 1956, the NSC's Operations Coordinating Board (OCB)—charged with monitoring implementation of US policy around the world—reported gloomily that there had been little if any improvement in Indo-American relations.[100] Despite Ambassador Cooper's having established friendly relations with Prime Minister Nehru and somewhat better atmospherics, the OCB concluded that basic policy differences remained unresolved.[101]

Four years later, as the Eisenhower presidency was drawing to a close, the OCB assessment sounded much more positive notes. Indo-US relations were "increasingly cordial." The President had enjoyed an extraordinarily successful visit to New Delhi. Large-scale American aid to India had become an important positive factor in relations. Growing troubles between India and its erstwhile friend Communist China added a new element to bilateral ties. Indo-Pakistani relations, if not friendly, were at least improved as a result of the settlement of the Indus Waters dispute.[102]

When Eisenhower left office in January 1961, he could take satisfaction in his dealings with South Asia. Despite the fact that the President failed to effect a rapprochement between India and Pakistan, he was able to put bilateral relations with India on a firmer and friendlier footing. Just as India achieved good relations with both the United States and the Soviet Union, the Eisenhower administration had succeeded in maintaining friendly relations with both India and Pakistan.

On the Indian side, there was also satisfaction about the trend in relations, even if US arms for Pakistan remained a problem. US economic aid was forthcoming in increasing amounts. As trouble brewed with China, the implicit support of the United States was a comforting factor. India's nonalignment no longer seemed an anathema to the United States. Nehru could tell his Chief Ministers after the 1959 talks with Eisenhower, "He appreciated and understood our desire to keep out of military alliances; indeed he would not have it otherwise."[103]

NOTES

1. Sarvepalli Gopal, Jawaharlal *Nehru, A Biograph* vol. II, p. 285, message from Nehru to Dulles, 31 October 1956.

2. *Facts on File*, XVI, p. 377, 7-13 November 1956.

3. Gopal, vol. II, p. 292.

4. *Facts on Files*, XVI, pp. 387-88, 14-20 November 1956.

5. Gopal, vol. II, pp. 291-99.

6. Dwight D. Eisenhower, *The White House Years, Waging Peace, 1956-1961* (Garden City, NY: Doubleday, 1965), p. 108. Eisenhower devoted eight pages of his memoirs to reviewing his discussions with Nehru. The President also dictated a fourteen-page memorandum of their conversation which has been largely declassified.

7. Ibid., p. 113.

8. Ibid., pp. 112-13. Gopal, vol. III, p. 41.

9. Eisenhower, pp. 109-10.

10. Memorandum of Conversations between President Eisenhower and Prime Minister Nehru, 17-18 December 1956..

11. Gopal, vol. III, p. 41.

12. Memorandum of conversation of 17-18 December 1956 talks with Nehru, prepared by President Eisenhower; Gopal, *Nehru, vol. 3*, p. 41.

13. Foreign Relations of the United States *(FRUS), 1955-1957*, vol. VIII, *South Asia*, pp. 22-24, Minutes of the 3 January 1957 National Security Council meeting.

14. Eisenhower, p. 113.

15. Ibid., pp. 113-14.

16. Stephen E. Ambrose, *Eisenhower, The President* (New York: Simon and Schuster, 1984), pp. 367-68.

17. Ibid., pp. 377-81.

18. Walt W. Rostow, *Eisenhower, Kennedy and Foreign Aid* (Austin: University of Texas Press, 1985), pp. 14-18.

19. Ibid., pp. 44-49, provides a summary of the *Proposal*.

20. Ibid., p. 49. Rostow went on to comment that CENIS members were inclined to agree with the opening paragraph of the special supplement on India in the 22 January 1955 *Economist* by Barbara Ward: "The Indian economy today is the subject of what is, without doubt, the world's most fateful experiment."

21. *FRUS, 1955-1957,* vol. VIII, pp. 377-82, memorandum to NEA Assistant Secretary Rountree from South Asian Affairs Director Frederick Bartlett, 30 September 1957.

22. *FRUS, 1955-1957,* vol. VIII, pp. 341-44, memorandum of Mehta-Dillon meeting, 13 May 1957.

23. Ibid., pp. 344-48, report of the Dillon-Nehru meeting, 31 May 1957.

24. Ibid., pp. 348-52, letter from Ambassador Bunker to Deputy Chief of Mission Frederick Bartlett, 27 June 1957.

25. Ibid., pp. 373-77, memorandum of meeting between Indian Finance Minister Krishnamachari and Secretary of State Dulles, 25 September 1957.

26. Ibid., pp. 387-90, memorandum reporting the meeting between President Eisenhower and Indian Finance Minister Krishnamachari, 8 October 1957.

27. Ibid., pp. 403-04, letter from Ambassador Bunker to President Eisenhower, 15 November 1957.

28. Ibid., pp. 404-07, memorandum of 12 November 1957 meeting on aid to India prepared by General A. J. Goodpaster.

29. Ibid.

30. Memorandum reporting a meeting between Ambassador G.L. Mehta and Secretary of State Dulles, 17 January 1958; State Department telegrams to American embassies in Bonn and London, 25 January 1958; and Embassy Bonn telegram to the State Department, 30 January 1958.

31. *Congressional Record,* US Senate, 85th Congress, 2d sess., vol. 104, pp. 5246-55, 25 March 1958.

32. Rostow, pp. 68-69.

33. Ibid., pp. 3-6, 69.

34. John F. Kennedy, "A Democrat Looks at Foreign Policy," *Foreign Affairs* 36 (October 1957): p. 45.

35. *Congressional Record,* US Senate, 85th Congress, 2d Sess., vol. 104, pp. 5246-55, March 1958.

36. Memorandum of a meeting between B.K. Nehru and Under Secretary of State Douglas Dillon, 16 July 1958.

37. B.K. Nehru provided a personal account of the episode in Vadilal Dagli, ed., *Twenty Years of Indo-US Relations, 1947-1967* (Bombay: Vira, 1969, pp. 20-21).

38. Rostow, pp. 277-78.

39. Former Chief Justice of the Bombay High Court Chagla replaced G. L. Mehta in 1958 as the Indian ambassador to Washington.

40. For a summary of conference proceedings, see Selig Harrison, ed., *India and the United States* (New York: MacMillan), 1961.

41. As a further way to boost development assistance to India, Douglas Dillon adopted a proposal from foreign aid planner James P. Grant for so-called "islands of development," countries where the United States would put extra resources in the hope of promoting sustained growth. Dillon sold the concept to President Eisenhower, who agreed, subject to having a "Republican" country to go along with India. When the aid officials picked Taiwan—then considered a basket case—Eisenhower was delighted. (Interview with James P. Grant, 25 June 1990)

42. Interview with B.K. Nehru, 12 January 1991.

43. One of the thorniest problems caused by partition was the division of the extensive irrigation system in western India. When the Punjab was split, most of the irrigation dams remained with India, but the irrigated farmlands went to Pakistan. Since by holding back irrigation water, India could turn the West Punjab into a desert, the Indus Waters issue had enormous economic, as well as emotional, impact. During the 1950s, the World Bank worked closely with both countries to find a solution. The Bank proposed the approach—which India and Pakistan eventually accepted in 1959—of separating the two irrigation systems entirely, allotting the three eastern rivers (Ravi, Beas, and Sutlej) to India and the three western rivers (Indus, Jhelum, and Chenab) to Pakistan.

44. Gopal, vol. III, pp. 133-38, provides a good rundown of the Indus Waters settlement.

45. Meeting of the National Security Council, 30 April 1959; Memorandum of conversation between President Eisenhower and Under Secretary Dillon, 11 August 1959, Eisenhower Library.

46. Embassy New Delhi Despatch 1322 to the State Department, 12 May 1959. By this time despatches or airgrams were normally used for routine communications and only occasionally for important, but lengthy, policy analyses, such as the report on the Soviet economic offensive. In this instance, the Embassy did not expect action on its recommendations, but rather wanted the document to serve as a resource for Washington agencies as they considered the aid to India question.

47. Embassy New Delhi telegram to the State Department, 27 December 1959.

48. Embassy New Delhi telegram to the State Department, 27 December 1959; Letter from Secretary Herter to Atomic Energy Commission Chairman John McCone, 13 February 1960.

49. NSC 48/1, "The Position of the United States with Respect to Asia," discussed by the NSC 29 December 1949 and approved by Truman 30 December 1949, Harry S. Truman Library.

50. According to Ambassador Bunker, Eisenhower told him in June 1957, "We are better off with India following its policy of non-alignment than were she to join up actively on our side, with the consequent added burden on the American taxpayer and 2000 miles more of active frontier." Letter from Ambassador Bunker to Deputy Chief of Mission Frederick Bartlett, 27 June 1957, *FRUS, 1955-57,* vol. VIII, pp. 348-52.

51. Ibid., pp. 25-27, Report of the 3 January 1957 meeting of the National Security Council.

52. Ibid., p. 36, "Statement of Policy toward South Asia, NSC 5701,"10 January 1957.

53. Ibid., pp. 36-37 and 41-42.

54. One by-product of the Eisenhower system was excellent records. The minutes of NSC sessions and presidential meetings and conversations provide an enormous aid for research into the period. The detailed policy papers and periodic OCB reviews are also a great help.

55. Memorandum of Conversation with President Eisenhower and Secretary of State Dulles, 6 August 1956.

56. Gopal, vol. III, p. 46.

57. Through his impassioned defense of India's Kashmir position, Menon for the first time became a politically saleable figure in India. He won a seat in the Indian parliament in the 1957 general elections. A year later Pandit Nehru, in a controversial step, appointed his friend as India's Defense Minister.

58. Gopal, vol. III, p. 52, Nehru's telegrams to Menon, 19 and 20 November 1957.

59. Telegram from the US Mission to the UN to the State Department, 12 March 1958.

60. *FRUS, 1955-1957,* vol. VIII, pp. 156-57, memorandum of conversation between Dulles and Noon, 23 November 1957.

61. Gopal, vol. III, pp. 43-51.

62. Memorandum of a meeting at the White House between Indian Vice President Radhakrishnan and President Eisenhower, 19 March 1958.

63. Memorandum of conversation between Dulles, Amjad Ali, and Ayub Khan, 30 April 1958.

64. Memorandum to President Eisenhower from Secretary of State John Foster Dulles, "Proposal for Settlement of India-Pakistan Differences," 17 April 1958. Eisenhower conveyed his response in a handwritten "Dear Foster" note on Dulles' memorandum.

65. Nehru, vol. 5, pp. 40-41, letter of 18 May 1958.

66. Letter from President Eisenhower to Prime Minister Nehru, 30 April 1958.

67. Letter from Ambassador Bunker to President Eisenhower, 16 May 1958.

68. After the assassination of Liaquat Ali Khan in 1951, Pakistan was unable to establish a stable civilian government. As cabinets shuffled in and out of office, real power rested with the military and civil service. In November 1958, the President Iskander Mirza, a former civil servant, and Army chief Ayub Khan took over. Shortly afterwards, Ayub ousted Mirza and headed a military-backed martial law regime.

69. Embassy New Delhi telegram to Department of State, 17 May 1958; Gopal, *Nehru,* vol. III, p. 85. Nehru formally turned the proposal down in his letter of 7 June to Eisenhower. His initial reaction, reported by Bunker on 17 May, had also been negative.

70. Nehru, vol. 4, pp. 590-91. Letter of 28 October 1957.

71. Letter from President Eisenhower to Prime Minister Nehru, November 27, 1958.

72. Writing to the Chief Ministers in mid-1958, he commented, "Unfortunately, communism became too closely associated with the necessity for violence and thus the ideal which it placed before the world became a tainted one. Means distorted ends. We see here the powerful influence of wrong means and ends." (Nehru, vol. 5, pp. 82-83, letter of 13 July 1958)

73. Gopal, vol. III, pp. 87-88, Chagla telegram to Nehru, 8 December 1958.

74. A recent study of the Sino-Indian border dispute, Steven A. Hoffmann's *India and the China Crisis* (Berkeley: University of California Press), 1990—from which this section draws heavily—focused mainly on the Indian side of the dispute. Allan S. Whiting's excellent *The Chinese Calculus of Deterrence* (Ann Arbor: University of Michigan Press, 1975), looked at the problem from the Chinese vantage point. An interesting effort to view both sides of the dispute was Yaacov Y.I. Vertzberger's *Misperceptions in Foreign Policymaking: The Sino-Indian Conflict, 1959-1962* (Boulder: Westview Press, 1984). Among earlier studies, the most controversial, Neville Maxwell's *India's China War* (New York: Pantheon Books, 1970), asserted India provoked the Chinese attacks. Other helpful works consulted included Alistair Lamb, *The China-Indian Border: The Origins of the Disputed*

Boundaries (London: Oxford University Press, 1964); Dorothy Woodman, *Himalayan Frontiers* (London: Cresset Press, 1969); and W. F. Van Eekelen, *Indian Foreign Policy and the Border Dispute with China* (The Hague: Martinus Nijhoff, 1967).

75. Hoffmann, pp. 35-36.

76. Chou-En Lai to Nehru 23 January 1959, quoted in Dorothy Woodman, *Himalayan Frontiers* (London: The Cresset Press, 1969), p. 235.

77. Record of 28 May 1959 NSC meeting, Eisenhower Library.

78. Eisenhower, p. 487.

79. Before 1959, the only other President to visit India was Ulysses S. Grant, who crossed the subcontinent during his two-year around-the-world trip after leaving the White House in 1877. Visiting Bombay, Delhi, Jaipur, Agra, Benares, and Calcutta, Grant saw much more of India than Eisenhower, Nixon, or Carter, 20th century presidential visitors. William S. McFeeley, *Grant* (New York: Norton, 1974), pp. 472-73.

80. Memorandum of conversation with Lord Plowden, Chairman of the British Atomic Energy Commission, 13 November 1959.

81. Nehru, vol. 5, p. 343, letter of 15 December 1959.

82. Nehru, vol. 5, p. 343, letter of 15 December 1959.

83. Gopal, vol. III, p. 104.

84. Ibid. Memorandum of conversation between President Eisenhower, Prime Minister Nehru, Under Secretary Murphy, Secretary General Pillai, Ambassador Bunker, General Goodpaster, and Foreign Secretary Dutt, 10 December 1959.

85. Eisenhower, p. 503.

86. Memorandum of conversation between President Eisenhower and Prime Minister Nehru, 13 December 1959.

87. Telegram from President Eisenhower to Secretary Herter reporting on his talks with Ayub and Nehru, 14 December 1959. State Department records. Gopal, *Nehru, vol. III*, p. 104.

88. Telegram from Embassy Karachi to the State Department, 23 December 1959.

89. Nehru, vol. 5, p. 343, letter of 15 December 1959.

90. Memorandum of meeting between Ambassador Bunker and President Eisenhower, 25 April 1960, Eisenhower Library.

91. Embassy New Delhi telegram to the State Department, 5 May 1960.

92. The Indians were also procuring transport aircraft and helicopters from the Soviet Union, a step which greatly angered the Chinese since the equipment was used in strengthening Indian positions in the disputed border areas.

93. Embassy New Delhi telegram to State Department, 26 May 1960.

94. Memorandum for Secretary of State Herter from Assistant Secretary for Near East and South Asian Affairs G. Lewis Jones, 7 June 1960.

95. Letter to Ambassador Ellsworth Bunker from Assistant Secretary G. Lewis Jones, 13 July 1960.

96. Gopal, vol. II, pp. 273-74.

97. Memorandum of a meeting in the State Department's Office of South Asian Affairs, 17 August 1960.

98. Memorandum of meeting between President Eisenhower, Prime Minister Nehru, Foreign Secretary Dutt, Secretary of State Herter, and Assistant Secretary Lewis Jones, Waldorf Astoria Hotel, New York, 26 September 1960. Eisenhower Library.

99. Eisenhower, p. 585. Letter from President Eisenhower to Prime Minister Nehru, 2 October 1960.

100. During the Eisenhower administration, the OCB reviewed progress of South Asia policy on a semi-annual basis, first under NSC 5409 of February 1954, and later NSC 5701 of January 1957. These reviews, now largely declassified, provide an excellent—and authentic—window on official US thinking toward the subcontinent during the 1950s.

101. *FRUS, 1955-1957,* vol. VIII, p. 3, progress report by Operations Coordinating Board on NSC 5409, 30 March 1956.

102. Progress Report by Operations Coordinating Board on NSC 5701, 9 November 1960.

103. Nehru, vol. 5, p. 343, letter of 15 December 1959.

Chapter V
Kennedy: "Neither Kashmir nor India"

The 1960 presidential election race between Vice President Richard M. Nixon and Senator John F. Kennedy, one of the closest in American history, was watched closely around the globe, but especially in India and Pakistan.

Pakistan saw Nixon as a good friend.[1] India regarded the Vice President, unlike President Eisenhower, as an unrepentant Cold Warrior and a foe of Indian nonalignment. Kennedy caused uneasiness in Pakistan and stirred hopes in India. As a Senator, he co-sponsored the 1958 Senate resolution calling for increased economic aid for India and criticized the Republican policy of relying on military pacts to meet the Communist threat in the Third World. Kennedy appeared considerably more sympathetic than Nixon to the aspirations of developing nations and less antagonistic toward nonalignment. The fact that Kennedy's foreign policy adviser during the 1960 election campaign was none other than former Ambassador Chester Bowles was another big plus in India and a minus in Pakistan.

The appointment of Bowles as Under Secretary of State, the naming of Phillips Talbot, a scholar-journalist specialist on India, as Assistant Secretary of State for Near East and South Asian Affairs,[2] and the selection of Harvard Professor John

Kenneth Galbraith, a friend of President Kennedy, as the Ambassador in New Delhi, raised Indian optimism and stirred Pakistan's anxieties even more.

With Bowles' experience as Ambassador to India, Talbot's understanding of India dating back to his days as an exchange student in 1939, and Galbraith's own knowledge from extended stays in the mid-1950s, the new team gave the Kennedy administration a depth of knowledge about South Asia, and especially India, unequalled before or since. Incoming Secretary of State Dean Rusk, while no expert on South Asia, was familiar with the territory from wartime service at the China-Burma-India theater headquarters in New Delhi.

As a Senator, Kennedy took the initiative in 1958 to sponsor the resolution urging more economic aid for India, although his personal contact with Nehru was less than sparkling. The Prime Minister showed little interest in talking with the young Massachusetts Representative when he visited India in 1951.[3] Nehru's preachy neutralism put Kennedy off somewhat—it was not his style—but he respected the Prime Minister as one of the great political leaders of the 20th century and praised "the soaring idealism of Nehru" in his first State of the Union address 30 January 1961. Kennedy regarded India with its vast population, economic potential, and democratic aspirations as the centerpiece of the developing world worthy of major attention by the United States.[4]

Even if Kennedy did not accept the policy recommendations of Chester Bowles—simply to ditch Pakistan and back India to the hilt—he was willing to support the approach advocated by Galbraith, Talbot, and Robert Komer, his National Security Council staffer for South Asia,[5] of trying to develop closer and more cooperative relations with India. Well aware of intense India-Pakistan differences, Kennedy and his aides thought the United States could achieve friendlier ties with New Delhi without doing irreparable damage to relations with Pakistan. This was the administration's basic policy goal in 1961.[6]

Kennedy's policy toward South Asia marked a continuation of the shift in emphasis toward India already begun in Eisenhower's second term. While the approach may have been similar, the contrast in operating styles between the two administrations was striking. With the "New Frontier" emphasis on youth and action, Kennedy promptly disbanded the elaborate NSC machinery used by Eisenhower. Kennedy's NSC, headed by Harvard academic McGeorge Bundy, was a much smaller, informal, and collegial body. Unlike Eisenhower, Kennedy became personally engaged in the details of issues that interested him, such as India and Pakistan. According to Talbot and his deputy James P. Grant, the President frequently called them directly to discuss current problems, bypassing the formal organizational structure. NSC staffers like Robert Komer, speaking for the President, played an active and energetic role along with State, Defense, AID, and CIA representatives in shaping and implementing South Asia policy.[7]

The Congo and Laos Crises

Among the first issues confronting the new administration was the on-going Congo crisis, in which India played an important role as the source of the largest contingent of soldiers to implement the UN effort to calm the strife-ridden African nation. Kennedy modified US policy to place more emphasis than Eisenhower on using UN machinery in order to ensure genuine independence for the Congo and to keep the struggle out of the Cold War. Seeking active Indian cooperation in shaping the UN mandate, Kennedy detailed US hopes for the Congo operation in a lengthy cable he sent Nehru on 18 February 1961.

Kennedy's message ended with words Nehru himself could have written, "If we and those who share our view move forward together in the support of the United Nations in the Congo, it will succeed—and with it the opportunity for every nation, even the smallest, to work out its destiny."[8] To meet a voting deadline at the United Nations, Nehru sent a hurried response. Although he did not agree on all points about the UN mandate, Nehru's reply was positive in tone. "I need not tell you," he cabled, "how much we welcome our cooperating with the United States in order to find a solution of this difficult problem of the Congo."[9]

The Congo became even more difficult after the murder of flamboyant nationalist leader Patrice Lumumba, attempts by pro-Belgian groups to seize control of mineral-rich Katanga province, tensions between the United States and the Soviet Union, and on-the-ground friction between US Ambassador

Claire Timberlake and the UN Secretary General's representative Rajeshwar Dayal, a senior Indian civil servant. Despite these formidable difficulties, Washington and New Delhi successfully worked together in shaping and implementing a strengthened UN mandate.

India provided the backbone of the UN force in the Congo, sending a full army brigade of 5,000 soldiers—the first contingent flown from the subcontinent to Africa by the US Air Force.[10] With much patience, and also tragedy—including the death of UN Secretary General Dag Hammerskjold whose plane mysteriously crashed—Congo unity was eventually preserved. The United States deemphasized Cold War considerations. India rebuffed pressure for less measured action from Ghana and more radical nonaligned states, as well as from Moscow.[11] In keeping with his hopes for Indo-US cooperation and his informal style, Kennedy took the unusual step of calling in the Indian Embassy Deputy Chief of Mission D. N. Chatterjee, then leaving Washington to become India's envoy to the Congo. The President emphasized to Chatterjee, whom he had gotten to know as a Senator, his desires that the United States and India work together closely in trying to solve the Congo problem.[12]

Yet cooperation over the Congo was deceptive. In dealing with a problem caused in large part by former Belgian colonialists, American and Indian interests converged. On other issues, such as Southeast Asia and nuclear testing, there was less common ground. A decade of nonalignment made Nehru leery of too close a working relationship with the United States, even with an administration whose ideals he found appealing. Nonalignment itself had considerably evolved from the early 1950s when India was the dominant voice. As a host of new nations gained independence in Asia and Africa, nonaligned ranks swelled. India had to share leadership with others, with Indonesia, Egypt, Yugoslavia, and Ghana most prominently. Somewhat against Nehru's better judgment the Non-Aligned Movement began to take semi-formal shape. Although often divided among itself by conflicting regional interests and conflicts, the Non-Aligned Movement tried to achieve a consensus before taking positions, a procedure that restricted Indian room to maneuver.

The Laos crisis, which followed quickly on the heels of the Congo problem in the spring of 1961, was intrinsically more dangerous, for the dispute directly threatened Great Power confrontation. The trouble arose after the delicate balance between pro-West, pro-Communist, and neutralist factions in the small, landlocked Indo-China kingdom, appeared to collapse. The pro-Communist faction, supported by the Soviet Union, sought a monopoly of power. Although Eisenhower had considered sending in American military forces, Kennedy concluded Laos was not worth a major showdown with the Soviets. He elected instead to seek negotiations in the hopes of restoring the internal political balance.[13]

The Kennedy administration believed India could be helpful in Laos because of its good relations with the Soviet Union and its role as Chairman of the then moribund International Control Commission for Laos. Kennedy sent Secretary Rusk and Averell Harriman, who was once again active in foreign affairs at the age of 71, to see Nehru, also 71 at the time.[14] "If you can take diplomatic action to halt the fighting pending political discussions, you will perform a great service," Kennedy told the Prime Minister in a 23 March message.[15] In his reply, sent after Nehru met the US envoys, the Prime Minister confirmed he had urged Khrushchev to cooperate in seeking peace in Laos. Nehru's letter touched also in a restrained manner on the Bay of Pigs disaster. The Indians reacted with relative calm to the failed US-sponsored invasion of Cuba, reflecting the improvement in relations between New Delhi and Washington.[16]

In Laos, the Indians proved willing to be helpful—up to a point. Nehru was, however, unwilling to work in harness with the United States against the Communists in Southeast Asia. He remained wary of US intentions in the region and did not want to cross the Soviets. As Galbraith wrote Kennedy:

I am trying hard to persuade the Indians that once we accept neutrality they cannot be less concerned to protect it than we. If neutrality means that Laos goes to the Communists, the word will stink and everyone will attribute the failure to acceptance of an Indian policy.[17]

In keeping with his reluctance to become too closely identified with Washington, Nehru listened politely in late May 1961 to the entreaties of Vice President Lyndon Johnson, during his visit to New Delhi, for India to offer "counsel" and take more of a "lead" on Indo-China, but would not commit himself to a more active role. In the end, mention of Indian "counsel and leadership" in promoting peace in Southeast Asia was omitted from the communiqué issued after the Johnson visit.[18]

US Aid to India: Record Levels of Assistance

Even before entering the White House in January 1961, Kennedy appointed a task force to consider economic assistance to India. In line with the thrust of the Kennedy-Cooper resolution on aid to India, the task force set the goal of ensuring sufficient foreign financing for India's Third Five Year Plan due to start in 1962. To achieve this, the group proposed—and the Kennedy administration agreed—that the United States commit $1 billion annually for the first two years of the Third Plan on the understanding that other countries match the US contribution. The aid planners envisaged half the US share, or $500 million, in development loans or grants and the remainder in PL 480 food assistance. The Kennedy administration thus called for a tripling of US development lending from the $135 million the Eisenhower administration provided in 1960.[19]

In parallel with the ambitious Alliance for Progress launched to promote economic development in Latin America and the sending of young and idealistic Peace Corps volunteers to developing nations, the administration pressed ahead to achieve the ambitious target set for aid to India. At the April 1961 meeting of the India Aid consortium, the United States pledged a massive $1 billion in development assistance for the first two years of the Third Plan. Together with pledges from other donors, India's essential foreign exchange needs for these two years were met. India also received promises that the consortium would make available adequate financing for the Plan's final three years. On 13 May, Nehru thanked Kennedy effusively, writing:

> Our task, great as it is, has been made light by the goodwill and generous assistance that has come to us from the United States. To the people of the United States and more especially to you, Mr. President, we feel deeply grateful.[20]

On the basis of the consortium success, India closed up its Commission-General for Economic Affairs in Washington and named B. K. Nehru, the capable Commissioner-General, as its Ambassador to the United States.[21] Already friendly with the President, Nehru enjoyed easy access to the White House during the Kennedy years. Nehru's access to the President was paralleled by the unusual access Galbraith had to the Prime Minister in New Delhi.

In May 1961, the Director of the fledgling Peace Corps, Sargent Shriver, Kennedy's energetic brother-in-law, traveled to India to sell the program to Nehru. Galbraith urged caution, fearing Nehru might be touchy about having young Americans as "development missionaries" in rural India. To Galbraith's surprise, the Prime Minister responded enthusiastically.[22] By the end of 1961, the first two dozen Peace Corps volunteers reached India. The program soon grew to several hundred volunteers whose work complemented India's rural development programs in addition to proving a plus for the US image.

If quantitatively, the Kennedy administration made good on its hope for a major increase in US aid levels, qualitatively, Ambassador Galbraith remained uneasy that US assistance was

Courtesy of the John F. Kennedy Library

12 September 1961, Indian Ambassador Braja Kumar Nehru presenting his credentials to President John F. Kennedy.

being spread too thin, with public relations gains not commensurate with the $1 billion a year Washington was providing. US officials continued to worry that the Soviets, spending much less on a few highly visible public sector industrial projects, were winning more friends than the United States. Less visible US assistance was scattered around the country, often in physical and human infrastructure activities like education, agriculture, health, and transportation.

To generate more publicity, Galbraith spent two weeks in October 1962, traveling by special train, accompanied by a platoon of American and Indian newsmen, to US AID projects in the four corners of India. The trip began in Kanpur, the north Indian industrial center, where AID was funding an Indian Institute of Technology, an effort to recreate an MIT-style engineering institute, staffed with American professors. The train then chugged eastward across the Ganges plain to Bokaro in Bihar, where Galbraith hoped AID would finance the million-ton public sector steel mill, and on to the coal rich Damodar Valley to inspect a US-funded coal washery.

In central India, Galbraith visited a "package" agricultural program, under which AID was trying to increase farm output by concentrating experts, farm equipment, and agricultural inputs. At Nagarjunasagar, near the city of Hyderabad, the group observed over a hundred thousand workers building—mostly by hand labor—one of the world's largest earthen dams. USAID provided technical assistance and large grants of rupees generated by the PL 480 program. At Bombay, India's metropolis on the Arabian Sea, Galbraith saw the US AID-financed Central Training Institute, watched the unloading of 19,000 tons of PL 480 wheat, visited the site of a massive fertilizer plant, and inspected the Premier Automobile factory, an AID-assisted private sector industry. The final stop was Kotah in arid Rajasthan in western India, where US aid was helping construct an irrigation system.[23]

Galbraith continued to push hard in Washington to win approval for two major "impact" projects—the public sector steel mill at Bokaro and the nuclear power station at Tarapur near Bombay. Galbraith strongly supported Bokaro as a symbol of US commitment to Indian industrialization.[24] While many Democrats did not share the doubts of their predecessors about

US aid for Bokaro, the Kennedy administration was unable to overcome opposition to the project on Capitol Hill.

In Congress, where India remained unpopular with many members because of its foreign policy, conservative Democrats and Republicans were unenthused about spending $900 million for Bokaro, until then the largest aid project proposed. Adding to the administration's difficulties was the opposition of General Lucius Clay, whom President Kennedy asked to undertake a detailed review of economic assistance. Clay could not see why the US taxpayers should finance a steel mill in the Indian public sector. Galbraith stuck to his guns, however, gaining President Kennedy's public backing for Bokaro. "The Congress may have other views," Kennedy stated in an 8 May 1963 press conference, "but I think it would be a great mistake not to build it. India needs the steel."[25] With the President's support, Bokaro stayed alive—at least for the time being.

Galbraith had more success with the nuclear power plant to be located at Tarapur near Bombay. The size of the project— $80 million—was far more manageable. There was no ideological objection to cooperating with the Indian Atomic Energy Commission on nuclear power. US atomic energy specialists concluded the project was feasible given comparative fuel costs in India and the technical competence of the Indian AEC. The Kennedy administration gave the green light for going ahead. All that remained was for India and the United States to agree on mutually satisfactory safeguards to ensure that sensitive nuclear materials were not diverted for military purposes.[26]

The Indians proved sticky negotiators, extremely sensitive about any agreement on foreign controls and inspections that suggested any infringement on their sovereignty. After protracted negotiations, the US and Indian AECs finally worked out an arrangement under which India agreed to use only US-supplied enriched uranium in the Tarapur plant and, in return, accepted sufficient controls to satisfy Washington. It was not until May 1963—just before Galbraith left India—that the Ambassador was able to announce official approval for the project. Ironically, the Tarapur power plant—intended as a showpiece of US high technology assistance to India—became the focus for bitter controversy in the 1970s after India exploded a nuclear device.

Official Visits: Lyndon Johnson and Ayub Khan

The first senior US visitor to South Asia during the Kennedy administration was Vice President Lyndon Johnson, who swung through Southeast Asia and the subcontinent in May 1961. Because Johnson was the sort of earthy, backslapping American politician most likely to set Nehru's teeth on edge and cause one of his moody silences, Galbraith was worried how the Vice President's India visit would go. Fortunately, Nehru was on his best behavior after the announcement of the major US economic assistance pledge for the India aid consortium. The Prime Minister got the visit off to a good start, breaking protocol to greet Johnson personally at the airport. The two leaders had several friendly discussions about India's development programs. Johnson, in turn, seemed to enjoy himself, especially a day in the countryside where he made several well photographed stops in Indian villages.[27]

The Vice President's trip report to Kennedy spoke of India's being favorably inclined toward the new administration. Johnson commented:

> This, in my judgment, should be exploited not with the hope of drawing India into our sphere—which might be unnecessary as it would be improbable—but, chiefly, with the hope of cementing under Nehru an India-U.S. friendship which would endure beyond any transition of power in India.[28]

Perhaps more significant than this unexceptionable suggestion was the impression President Ayub Khan of Pakistan made on the Vice President. Like most US leaders whether Democrat or Republican, Johnson was taken with Ayub.[29] Johnson told Kennedy the Pakistani President was "the singularly most impressive and, in his way, responsible head of state encountered on the trip." The Vice President further recommended that the United States seek ways to modernize Pakistan's military, asserting Ayub "wants to resolve the Kashmir dispute to release Indian and Pakistani troops to deter the Chinese rather than each other."[30]

In mid-summer 1961, President Ayub Khan himself traveled to Washington. Nervous about the shift in emphasis of US South Asia policy, Ayub sent up warning signals in the Pakistan press and in interviews with American newsmen before leaving

Pakistan. "Can it be," Ayub asked the Associated Press correspondent, "the United States is abandoning its good friends for the people who may not prove such good friends?"[31] After arriving in Washington, Ayub maintained a bold public front. Addressing a joint session of Congress, he said bluntly Americans might not like everything Pakistan did, but his country was the best friend the United States had in Asia.[32]

During talks with Kennedy, Ayub worked hard—and successfully—to convince the President that Pakistan was, indeed, a good friend and ally of the United States, ready to help in Southeast Asia and elsewhere. Ayub discussed Kashmir, but did not belabor his country's troubles with India. His main stress lay on getting US aid to deal with the tough problem of waterlogging and salinity, then causing enormous damage to West Pakistan's richest agricultural lands in the Punjab.[33] Although Ayub failed to get Kennedy's agreement to use US economic aid as leverage to press India for a Kashmir settlement, the President agreed to support further UN discussion of Kashmir should there be no bilateral progress. Kennedy also said he would implement the Eisenhower administration's promise to provide Pakistan with F-104 fighter aircraft.[34]

Unlike the Indians, who rarely made an effort to play up to Americans, Ayub and the Pakistanis were careful—regardless of whatever they might say to the press—to cultivate close personal relations with US leaders. Ayub cleverly scored points with the Kennedys by presenting Jackie Kennedy with a magnificent stallion.[35] Capped by a glittering dinner at Mount Vernon, the Ayub visit was successful both in terms of public relations and in refurbishing Pakistan's credentials with a skeptical administration.[36]

Quite apart from the opposition of the Pakistanis and their American supporters—the unofficial Pakistan lobby was strong in the Pentagon, the intelligence community, and among conservatives in the Congress—those favoring a shift in South Asia policy toward India did not get much help from New Delhi. On 25 August 1961, Nehru hurt India's standing with Kennedy when, in the middle of a crisis over Berlin, he called Western access to the German city a "concession" rather than a right. Galbraith lamented, "This has put the skunk in the air conditioner. Washington is raving."[37] The Ambassador was able to get

Nehru—who seemed not to realize the import of his words—to "clarify" his remarks[38]; still the damage was done in Washington.

Nehru's cavalier treatment of a matter of vital importance to the United States did not sit well with senior Kennedy administration officials. The anti-American tactics of Krishna Menon, who continued to represent India at the UN while serving as Defense Minister, also remained a chronic source of trouble. During the summer of 1961, Menon infuriated Washington by misrepresenting American and Soviet nuclear disarmament policies—portraying the United States as more and the Soviet Union as less bellicose than was in fact the case.[39]

When the nonaligned, now totalling 25 nations, gathered in Belgrade for their first heads of state meeting as a "movement" in September 1961, Nehru was initially reluctant about the idea of the summit, but in the end went along. With nuclear testing a major focus of attention, the results of the Belgrade meeting disappointed the US administration. Washington found the communiqué too soft on the Soviets, especially as Moscow had, in effect, thumbed its nose at the nonaligned by resuming nuclear testing just before the gathering.[40]

The balance sheet in the fall of 1961 on Kennedy's South Asia policy seemed mixed. On the economic side, the United States dramatically increased its economic assistance for India, meeting the ambitious targets the pre-inauguration task force set and helping India harvest a foreign aid crop that met its most optimistic hopes. With Kennedy as President, India saw the United States as a friend. Senator Cooper, after a visit to New Delhi, told Kennedy "relations between India and the United States (were) the best I have ever known."[41] This did not, however, translate into broader political cooperation between the two countries. The two countries worked together in the Congo, but on most other issues, Indian and US positions continued to reflect conflicting approaches to the Cold War. Kennedy administration officials hoped the visit of Prime Minister Nehru to Washington in November 1961 would open the door to a better partnership between the two countries.

Official Visits: An Aging Nehru Disappoints the New Frontier

On 5 November 1961, the seventy-one-year-old Nehru arrived in New York for his fourth and last trip to the United States. After appearing on "Meet the Press," the television news program, he flew to Cape Cod accompanied by Ambassador B. K. Nehru for private talks with Kennedy in an informal family setting. During lunch, the President turned the conversation to Southeast Asia to seek Nehru's advice on how to deal with South Vietnam. "Here is the situation we face in Vietnam," the forty-four-year-old Kennedy said, "We have little experience in Asia. You, Mr. Prime Minister, are a great Asian statesman. Tell us what to do."[42] Ambassador Nehru recalled that the Prime Minister did not really reply. Kennedy brought the discussion back to Vietnam several times in the hope of eliciting Nehru's views. The Indian leader still gave no coherent response, instead falling "into remote silence."[43]

Things did not improve after the President and Prime Minister traveled together to Washington for the formal part of the visit. Nehru's principal business meeting at the White House with the President and senior American advisers went poorly. Kennedy did virtually all the talking, laying out in detail US policy concerns and goals. Nehru listened, saying almost nothing and leaving the President puzzled and uneasy.

Although in a private session with Kennedy the Prime Minister unbent a bit, he had little to say on the major issues confronting the superpowers: Vietnam, Berlin, and disarmament. Nehru got down to specifics only on Kashmir where he reiterated his long-standing willingness to settle the dispute on the basis of acceptance of the cease-fire line as the international boundary.[44] Kennedy at times had trouble keeping the conversation going. Nehru remained passive. The President said later, "It was like trying to grab something in your hand, only to have it turn out to be fog."[45]

A morning coffee that B.K. Nehru arranged at the Indian Embassy for the Prime Minister to meet informally with the cream of the New Frontier proved a further disappointment. Since the Indian leader usually enjoyed this sort of gathering, the

Courtesy of the John F. Kennedy Library

16 November 1961, Mrs. John F. Kennedy, Mrs. Indira Gandhi, Prime Minister Nehru, and President Kennedy during Washington arrival ceremony.

Ambassador was taken aback by Nehru's performance. He arrived about twenty minutes late, in itself unusual. When Arthur Schlesinger began by asking about the role of intellectuals in India, Nehru just waffled, talking in circles and not answering. Other questions drew similarly vague responses. "The meeting," according to Ambassador Nehru, "was a disaster."[46]Schlesinger had a similarly negative reaction, "I had the impression of an old man, his energies depleted, who heard things at a great distance and answered most questions with indifference."[47]

In his *Thousand Days*, Schlesinger quoted Kennedy as describing the Nehru visit as "the worst state visit I have had."[48] Thirty years after the fact, B. K. Nehru agreed the trip had been terrible. The ambassador knew Nehru was aging, but had not realized he was also tired and ailing. A younger and healthier Nehru would have enjoyed the busy schedule and crossing wits with the New Frontiersmen. Unfortunately, by November 1961, Nehru was no longer the man he once was.[49]

After the disappointing visit, B. K. Nehru felt that Kennedy "wrote Nehru off as finished." Although the President himself never said this, the Ambassador drew the conclusion from his excellent contacts within the administration.[50] Komer and Talbot blamed Galbraith for failing adequately to alert Washington about Nehru's condition and also overselling the prospects for political cooperation with India, especially in Southeast Asia.[51] Conversely, Galbraith, who was carrying on a running feud with Talbot and his boss, Secretary Dean Rusk, claimed Washington was unrealistic in its expectations about the help India might offer the United States.[52]

Nehru's physical decline had its direct impact on the energy level of Indian foreign policy. In earlier years, his enormous capacity for work and his extraordinarily broad background in foreign affairs enabled Nehru to carry out the trying duties of Prime Minister and at the same time serve as a hyperactive Minister for External Affairs. Using Krishna Menon as his sounding board and roving emissary to deal with the most critical problems, Nehru also worked closely with the top echelon of the Ministry of External Affairs, the Secretary General, and the Foreign Secretary. They, however, served as policy implementers not policymakers. Apart from Menon, no one had much leeway or independence.

Because Nehru kept foreign affairs as his personal, almost private, domain, he failed to develop the institutional experience in the Indian Foreign Service and Ministry of External Affairs needed to maintain the activist foreign policy India pursued in the heyday of nonalignment. As Nehru began to fade, India found itself hampered in continuing the global foreign policy that the Prime Minister successfully established in the early 1950s. Too much depended on Nehru's personal input, energy, and prestige. The upshot was that when the US foreign policy machinery was crackling with the activism and can-do spirit of Kennedy's New Frontier, India's foreign policy was beginning to creak. Nehru sadly stayed on beyond his time.

Goa, US Aid, and MiGs

Although Goa was only mentioned in passing during Nehru's visit to the United States, a crisis developed a month later. In the past, Nehru always rebuffed proposals to use force to seize the Portuguese colony, despite Lisbon's stubborn refusal to give up the territory. In December 1961, he changed his mind, apparently under pressure from Defense Minister Krishna Menon, perhaps eager to deflect attention from his handling of the Himalayan border problems with China. Galbraith, at first, doubted the Indians would mount a military action against Goa. After the press worked itself into a frenzy about Portuguese "provocations"—alleged attacks on Indian fishing vessels, internal crackdown on pro-Indian elements, and threatening Portuguese troop movements—the ambassador realized something was up.[53]

Under instructions from Washington, he made an 11th-hour effort to get Nehru to agree to a six months' delay to give diplomacy a chance to solve the problem peacefully. When the Prime Minister became evasive and sought to put off the discussion, Galbraith concluded it was too late to do anything.[54] Indian troops were, in fact, already on the move although Nehru was unaware of this since Krishna Menon kept the actual timing of the attack from the Prime Minister.[55] A day later, Indian forces completed the seizure of the territory, with the Portuguese surrendering without much of a fight.[56]

If the military action was brief and almost bloodless, this was not the case for the diplomatic encounter at the United

Nations. There the United States vociferously disapproved that India, of all countries, resorted to the use of force. US delegate Adlai Stevenson paid Krishna Menon back in kind for his many rancorous anti-American tirades. As Arthur Schlesinger wrote, "The contrast between Nehru's incessant sanctimony on the subject of non-aggression and his brisk exercise in machtpolitik was too comic not to cause comment . . . . It was almost too much to expect the targets of Nehru's past sermons not to respond in kind."[57]

The Indians were furious over Adlai Stevenson's attacks and hurt by US condemnation of their action. A testy exchange between Nehru and Kennedy followed. In a discursive seven-page letter, Nehru regretted acting against US advice, but argued inaction would have been worse. Nehru asserted the move won the approval of all India, including, "even the Cardinal Archbishop of Bombay, the highest dignitary of the Roman Catholic Church in India." Contrasting praise from Afro-Asian countries with US and British disapproval, Nehru asked:

> Why is it that something that thrills our people, should be condemned in the strongest language in the United States and some other places? . . . We could understand the difference of opinion on this Goan issue, but I confess that I have been deeply hurt by the rather extraordinary and bitter attitude of Mr. Adlai Stevenson and some others. . . . I had hoped that in the United States there would be a broad realisation of how Goa appeared to Indians.[58]

President Kennedy's briefer response was sharp and personal. Voicing his sympathy about "the colonial aspects of this issue," the President compared British rule in Ireland and India:

> And I can claim the company of most historians in saying that the colonialism to which my immediate ancestors were subject was more sterile, oppressive and even cruel than that of India. The legacy of Clive was on the whole more tolerable than that of Cromwell.[59]

Expressing regret that Nehru failed to alert him to a possible Goa action, Kennedy wrote:

> My major concern was and continues to be the effect of the action on our joint tasks, especially in terms of its impact on American opinion. Unfortunately the hard, obvious fact for our people was the resort to force—and by India. This was a shock to the majority who have admired your country's

ardent advocacy of peaceful methods, and a reinforcement to those who did not enjoy what they called "irresponsible lectures" . . . . It is not an accident that the men who are taking most advantage of the Goa matter here are the same men who are already attacking our aid programs and our support for the UN.[60]

In private, Kennedy told India's Ambassador he was annoyed less by India's action than by Nehru's not having said anything about Goa when he was in the United States. Kennedy, in fact, found the event somewhat amusing. B.K Nehru recalled the President's saying:

> My only point is why didn't you do it before, 15 years before? But Mr. Ambassador, you spent the last 15 years preaching morality to us, and then you go ahead and act the way any normal country would behave and now that you have done what you should have done long ago, people are saying, the preacher has been caught coming out of the brothel. And they are clapping. And Mr. Ambassador, I want to tell you, I am clapping too.[61]

The President may not have been very concerned, but for a couple of months Goa stirred up US public opinion against India. The episode left scars, marring Nehru's standing as the spokesman for peaceful settlement of disputes and weakening the position of those in Washington who wanted to favor India over Pakistan.[62] Because of the ruckus, the visit to the subcontinent by the President's wife, Jackie Kennedy, was postponed until March to allow tempers to subside. Her trip, when it took place, was a great success; the harsh words over Goa faded from memory.

An initiative by Kennedy to sidestep a Kashmir debate in the United Nations had a less positive outcome. In an effort to avoid having the issue surface again in New York, Kennedy on 20 January 1962 proposed that former World Bank President Eugene Black visit South Asia to see what he could do toward promoting a settlement.[63] After his success in solving the Indus Waters dispute—and his good contacts with both Nehru and Ayub—Black seemed a logical choice. Once more, the Pakistanis promptly agreed. India said, "No."

March 1962, Mrs. John F. Kennedy accompanied by Prime Minister Nehru during her visit to India.

In fact, according to B. K. Nehru, the Prime Minister initially adopted a more positive attitude, instructing him to explore the Black proposal with the State Department. Before the envoy could do so, he received new instructions from New Delhi that flatly turned down the US proposal. Puzzled, Ambassador Nehru later learned that Krishna Menon, after he found out about the original decision, talked the Prime Minister into canceling the instructions to Washington.[64] More generally, B. K. Nehru described as "unbelievable" Krishna Menon's role as a spoiler. "Whenever there was a possibility of putting a spoke in the wheel of either Indo-American or Indo-Pakistani relations, Krishna Menon did it, he came along and did something that would spoil the relationship," Nehru declared.[65]

There were no lack of spoilers in Washington as well. Throughout the Kennedy years, many in Congress and elsewhere were unhappy about expanded economic assistance for India. Some just disliked foreign aid. Others remained disenchanted with India's foreign policy and the administration's tendency to favor India over Pakistan. Reflecting this attitude, Senator Stuart Symington, a respected Missouri Democrat and former Secretary of the Air Force, tried to slash aid to India by 25 percent in May 1962. In a hard-hitting memorandum to Kennedy, Symington zeroed in on India's foreign policy:

> The policies of no other non-Communist nation have been more critical of, and therefore more embarrassing to, the United States than the policies consistently espoused by India. We cannot expect recipients of aid to always support us in international discussions and disputes. But especially because it is giving us increasing difficulties with our true friends, why should we continue to give billions to India despite the steady opposition and criticism, often bordering on contempt, which we have received from the principal leaders of that country?[66]

Kennedy was able to beat back Symington's challenge in the Senate, but only after extensive lobbying. Once more, India did not make the task easier for its friends in Washington. Just as Symington was mounting his challenge to aid levels, Defense Minister Krishna Menon gained Nehru's acceptance in principle for the procurement of MiG–21 fighter aircraft from the Soviet Union. This marked a major breakthrough by the Soviets who would displace the British as the principal supplier of fighter aircraft to the Indian Air Force. Upset by the prospect of the MiGs, Washington, in collaboration with the British, countered with a variety of proposals designed to sway New Delhi against the Soviet deal. Since Moscow was offering extremely generous terms, the Western countries could not match the Soviet offer.[67] Galbraith commented:

> The timing of the combination could hardly have been worse. The Senators thought the MiG purchase was a reaction to the cut. The Indians thought the cut was punishment for the MiG deal. Since the latter leaked out, no one could say which came first.[68]

The UN Kashmir debate that Kennedy tried to avoid took place in June 1962. When the United States supported the call for implementing earlier UN resolutions by holding a plebiscite, the Soviet Union vetoed the resolution.[69] The episode predictably added to frictions between Washington and New Delhi, especially as Nehru criticized the US stance in parliament, while also complaining about pressures on India not to buy MiGs.[70] Yet, in his private correspondence with Chief Ministers, Nehru dampened his criticism of the United States and United Kingdom, "They have helped us greatly in the past and we should be thankful for it," he wrote his colleagues on 10 July 1962, "I would earnestly hope that we . . . continue to have friendly feelings with these great countries even though they might not fall in with our wishes occasionally."[71]

The Sino-Indian Border Conflict

In his 10 July letter, Nehru also spoke about the border troubles with China:

> We have gradually been building up our position and increasing our posts in Ladakh, etc . . . . The result is that we are in a somewhat more advantageous position than we were a year or two ago . . . . The Chinese Government . . . has lately become more aggressive in tone in its statements made to us. I do not know what this signifies, and we have to be wide awake and careful.[72]

The previous year, in November 1961, India had adopted a "forward policy"—sending patrols and establishing Indian posts behind Chinese positions in the disputed Aksai Chin plateau in northern Ladakh. Nehru's strategy was to build up India's strength in the disputed border region in order to pave the way for an eventual diplomatic settlement after the two sides were on more equal military terms.[73] Although India's tactic increased the chance for border clashes, neither Washington nor New Delhi anticipated serious combat between the world's two most populous nations. Practically no one expected the Chinese would inflict so staggering a defeat on the Indian military. According to Galbraith, the US Embassy had no idea how disorganized the Indians were. "We knew the terrain was difficult," he said, "but assumed the Indians knew what they were doing. Obviously they didn't."[74] NSC staffer Komer commented, "We were flabbergasted when the Chinese wiped the floor with the Indians."[75]

When the Chinese Communists initially refrained from a military response to the "forward policy," the Indians incorrectly concluded that this meant China would not seek to turn the frontier stand-off into a test of arms in the Himalayas.[76] Despite the military advantage China possessed, Nehru doubted China would risk serious fighting in the Himalayas. He believed that such a conflict would not remain localized, but would become a broader struggle involving other powers.[77]

After July 1962, the Chinese began to stiffen their stance, threatening a forward policy of their own in the Northeast Frontier Agency, if India continued to refuse to back off in the Aksai Chin. According to Allen Whiting, then the State Department's senior China intelligence officer, the Chinese acted to "assure victory in combat should deterrence and diplomacy fail in halting the forward policy and bringing Nehru to the conference table."[78] In late summer, near the junction of India, the tiny mountain kingdom of Sikkim, and Tibet—an area where the location of the MacMahon Line was itself in dispute—Chinese troops for the first time moved south of the Indian version of the frontier to occupy Thagla ridge, a key terrain feature.

In September, the Indians countered by sending a brigade onto the disputed ridge. The Chinese, in turn, riposted by deploying superior forces around the Indian position. Nehru interpreted the Chinese move as a direct challenge: his response was to order the military to drive the Chinese off the disputed ridge. New Delhi ignored a series of Chinese warnings that trouble was brewing if India failed to pull back. Although unclear about Chinese intentions, Nehru alerted Chief Ministers a few days before the outbreak of fighting, "This situation in the North East Frontier is definitely a dangerous one, and it may lead to major conflicts."[79]

In the disputed sector, the Chinese substantially outnumbered the Indian forces, could easily resupply their troops from roads just a few miles away in Tibet, and were well equipped and acclimatized for the 15,000 foot high altitude. The Indian forces were supported by a single narrow and steep mountain road that climbed through the thickly forested Assam Himalayas. They relied mainly on inefficient air drops for resupply. The Indians had little time to become accustomed to the heights, and were poorly equipped in terms of weapons or clothing for winter combat in the mountains.

Intimidated by Defense Minister Krishna Menon and his protégé, Lt. General B. M. Kaul, Indian commanders in the eastern sector failed to tell New Delhi the truth about their untenable position in the disputed Thagla ridge sector.[80] There was, however, enough dissonance in response to the order to drive the Chinese out that General Kaul flew east for a personal reconnaissance. When he saw the terrain and the respective military dispositions, Kaul realized the impossibility of ousting the Chinese. As if to underscore the problems of acclimatization at 15,000 feet, Kaul was himself stricken with altitude sickness.

An ill Kaul flew back to New Delhi for a meeting the night of 11 October with Nehru, Menon, and the top military leadership. The upshot was confusion: the Indian attack was called off, but the brigade, although badly exposed, was left in place.[81] To make matters worse, when Nehru enplaned for Ceylon the next day, he made some offhand remarks to newsmen which the press interpreted as a call to battle. "Our instructions," Nehru was quoted as saying, "are to free our territory. I cannot fix the date, that is entirely for the Army."[82]

It was the Chinese, not the Indians, who fixed the date, striking with overwhelmingly superior forces on 20 October against the Indian brigade on Thagla ridge sector and launching attacks against Indian posts, established under the forward policy, in Ladakh. The Indian positions quickly collapsed. In Ladakh, the small isolated posts fought hard, often to the last man, but were wiped out. On Thagla ridge, despite desperate defense by some elements, poor communications and the difficulty of the terrain rendered the brigade helpless. The force disintegrated, after suffering heavy casualties. Many prisoners were taken, including the brigade commander, J. S. Dalvi.[83]

The sudden defeats in Ladakh and NEFA had a shattering effect on New Delhi. Nehru's political position was weakened and, for the time being, his policy of nonalignment undermined. Because of who he was, Nehru was able to ride out a storm that would have sunk most other political leaders. Admitting errors, the Prime Minister in oft-quoted remarks told the nation, "We were getting out of touch with reality in the modern world and we were living in an artificial atmosphere of our own creation."[84] In private, he accepted responsibility, writing Krishna Menon on 28 October, "It is not much good shifting about the blame. The fact remains we have been found lacking and there is an impression that we have approached these things in a somewhat amateurish way."[85]

Giving ground to his critics—and to the enormous satisfaction of Washington—Nehru removed Menon, who had become the principal scapegoat and target for criticism, from the Defense Ministry. He initially named his friend to a newly created post of Minister of Defense Production, but on 7 November dropped Menon entirely from the Cabinet when it became clear Nehru's own position was under threat unless he let Menon go.[86]

India's nonalignment seemed to be a thing of the past. In the face of India's glaring military weakness, Nehru reversed policy 180 degrees to seek military assistance from the United States, Great Britain, and other Western countries. President Kennedy promptly made clear American willingness to aid India: "I want to give you support as well as sympathy," he wrote Nehru on 28 October. Nehru responded the next day, "I am deeply grateful to you for what you have written and for the sympathy and the sympathy of the great nation whose head you are at a moment of difficulty and crisis for us."[87] The same day, Nehru made a formal request to Galbraith for military assistance, asking almost plaintively that the United States not insist on a military alliance as a quid pro quo.[88]

For the United States, the border conflict, which coincided with and initially was overshadowed by the Cuba missile crisis, seemed to provide an unexpected opportunity to achieve the basic goal of the Kennedy administration in South Asia—moving to better and closer relations with India without running afoul of Pakistan. Given a conflict of uncertain proportions, the administration stood ready to do what it could to help Indian defenses against Chinese incursions. By coming promptly to India's aid, the US government wanted to demonstrate to friends in Asia that Washington was ready and able to assist against Chinese Communist aggression.[89]

If Nehru was gratified by the positive response from the West, the Soviet Union's response proved disappointing. Once fighting broke out, Moscow shifted from neutrality toward the Chinese position. Presumably concerned about Beijing's attitude toward the Cuba missile crisis, the Russians advised New Delhi to accept Chinese proposals for further talks on the border. Moscow also informed the Indians MiG–21 deliveries were off—for the time being, at least. Most nonaligned countries were similarly standoffish in their reactions. Except for Nasser of Egypt and Tito of Yugoslavia, none proved very forthcoming in backing New Delhi against Beijing.[90]

Military aid to India immediately provoked grave difficulties in US relations with Pakistan although Washington hoped that India's neighbor would suspend its hostility as India battled against the Chinese incursion. Defense against the Communist threat was, after all, the supposed purpose for which the United States gave arms aid to Pakistan in 1954. Mindful of Pakistani sensitivities, Kennedy wrote Ayub Khan on 28 October, advising that any military aid would be for India's "immediate needs" and "for use against Chinese only." The President urged Ayub to take a broad, not parochial, view of the situation.[91]

Ayub spurned the President, objecting strongly to US arms shipments for India. He downplayed the seriousness of the conflict, which he described as a limited border affair rather than a broader Chinese military challenge. Ayub also complained that Washington had reneged on a promise to consult before providing arms to India. When US Ambassador Walter McConaughy tried to deliver a further presidential letter to Ayub before Washington took a final decision on military aid, the Pakistani leader chose not to be available, going off on a hunting trip. Unwilling to wait for Ayub's return, Kennedy proceeded with a positive response to the Indian arms request.[92]

Washington was careful, however, to send equipment—mostly light arms, ammunition, and communications equipment—that would be primarily useful in mountain warfare rather than against the Pakistanis.[93]

As the foreign response to the frontier crisis became clearer, the popularity of the United States and the West soared in India, that of the Soviet Union and nonaligned countries slumped. Galbraith related as typical a visit by an elderly Indian Congress Party leader who said, "They were busy reconsidering the non-alignment policy." The envoy's standard reply, taking a leaf from Eisenhower, was that "we might find alignment with India too expensive." More astonishing, but an indicator of how far things had gone, the editor of the long-time pro-Communist and fiery anti-American weekly *Blitz* advised it would be switching to a pro-American policy.[94]

For several weeks, there was a lull on the fighting front. The Chinese held their gains without trying to advance further. India regrouped its forces in the east with an eye to defensive operations during the winter snows. Emergency American and British military aid began to arrive by air, boosting Indian morale and raising Western popularity even higher although not having any immediate impact on Indian defensive capabilities.

On 14 November, the Indians launched an attack on the eastern end of the MacMahon Line near a place called Walong. The Chinese promptly counterattacked, routing the Indian forces, and also launched a full-scale attack against regrouped Indian troops at the western end of the MacMahon Line. Although the Indians had used the lull to reinforce their positions in this sector to division strength, inept military leadership triggered a retreat that soon became a rout. Some Indian units fought well, but the major force, the 4th Division, crumbled under the Chinese assault. Outflanked and bypassed, the division ceased to exist as an effective military unit. Its men fled in disorder through the forests and jungles of the Assam Himalayas. In a matter of three days, as Indian defenses collapsed, Chinese troops swept south from the mountains to the edge of the plains, gaining virtual control of the entire 40,000 square miles claimed as Chinese territory. In Ladakh, where Indian troops were better acclimatized and New Delhi let the field commanders alone, the Indians performed credibly. Even though forced back, they were not routed.[95]

In New Delhi, a state of panic reigned on 19 November 1962. The government feared the Chinese would strike against Calcutta. The loss of the province of Assam and perhaps all of eastern India was dreaded. In this mood of crisis, the Prime Minister sent off two startling letters to President Kennedy, asking that the United States intervene militarily to provide air support for the struggle against the Chinese.[96] Nehru asked for a dozen squadrons of US fighter aircraft and air defense radar and related communications equipment to protect India's major cities, thus freeing the Indian Air Force to attack Chinese forces. He also sought two squadrons of B–47 bombers to strike positions behind the front, asking that US pilots fly the B–47s until Indians could be trained to replace them.[97]

The two letters, presumably drafted by Foreign Secretary M. J. Desai, were discussed with but not shown to key cabinet members. They were sent with unusual secrecy, suggesting Nehru was aware that his action would effectively undermine his cherished policy of nonalignment. In a departure from standard procedure, the Ministry of External Affairs did not receive copies of the letters which apparently no senior official, other than Nehru and Desai, actually saw before their dispatch.[98] When Ambassador B. K. Nehru received the messages in Washington, he was embarrassed at "being the unfortunate that had to deliver" letters that ran so totally against the grain of Indian policy. He showed them to no one in the Indian Embassy, keeping the messages in his personal desk. The Ambassador believed Nehru was psychologically finished off by the mid-November military disaster and "not himself" when he signed the two letters.[99]

As Kennedy considered a response, the US Navy dispatched an aircraft carrier task force into the Bay of Bengal, a move Galbraith recommended to steady Indian nerves.[100] Ironically, the carrier was the USS *Enterprise*, the same warship that became the symbol of US hostility toward India when Nixon sent the carrier toward the Bay of Bengal during the 1971 Bangladesh crisis. Before Kennedy reached a decision, the Chinese announced a unilateral cease-fire effective 22 November and a pullback of their forces 20 kilometers north of their version of the MacMahon Line in the east and their border claim in Ladakh. The Chinese relinquished control over practically all the territory their Army gained in the east, but maintained their grip over the area of strategic importance to them, the Aksai Chin portion of Ladakh.

In what proved a political master stroke, the Chinese made clear by their actions that their aims in the border conflict were limited. Rather than occupying additional territory, the Chinese underlined their ability to impose by force of arms the compromise border settlement they proposed earlier: their acceptance of Indian claims in the east in return for Indian acceptance of Chinese control over the Aksai Chin. Because of the crushing Indian military defeat, the Chinese achieved much more than they probably expected in launching the border offensive.

The first casualty was Jawaharlal Nehru himself. The Indian leader never recovered from the staggering psychological blow. Until mid-October 1962, Nehru, although aging, was still a towering international political figure, the revered founding-father of the world's largest democracy, the spokesman for decolonization and human rights and the founder-leader of the nonaligned movement. A month later, Nehru was a beaten old man, his country seemingly dependent on the military support of the United States, his policy of nonalignment in shreds. Ambassador Galbraith wrote President Kennedy, "One of the worst problems here is that the Chinese attack strikes the country with a very tired leader whose principles and ideas also have been badly shattered by the event."[101]

A second casualty was India's international reputation. Her proud army humbled in the Himalayas, India was no longer a plausible rival to China for leadership in Asia. Indian national pride suffered a deep emotional wound from the military disaster in the Himalayas. It took many years until India could recover its national pride from the humiliating defeat in the border war. India would, henceforth, play a diminished role on the world stage.

US Arms for India and Kashmir Talks

The unilateral cease-fire left Washington—and New Delhi—unclear whether the Chinese move marked the end of the conflict or was simply a tactical pause. On 19 November, when the situation looked its bleakest, Kennedy met with Secretary of State Rusk, Secretary of Defense McNamara, CIA Director McCone, and key aides Averell Harriman, Phillips Talbot, and Robert Komer. At the urging of McNamara, Kennedy approved sending a mission to India "to find out what the real situation was." The President and his advisors also wanted more military support from the British Commonwealth, Kennedy deciding to call in the British Ambassador to press this point. Rusk thought the British should take the lead in the military mission, but the President decided to send a US team while urging the British to energize the Commonwealth.[102]

Within the week, the mission headed by Averell Harriman was off to South Asia. Because of the cease-fire, the task became as much political as military. The joint State-Defense Department group was charged with proposing US South Asia policy for the period ahead as well as assessing India's military assistance requirements against the Chinese. The British, by then more actively engaged, sent a parallel political-military team led by Commonwealth Secretary Duncan Sandys.[103]

Flying directly from Washington, with only a one-hour refueling stop in Turkey, the team met with Prime Minister Nehru almost immediately after arriving in New Delhi on 25 November. As if embarrassed to find himself beholden to the United States, Nehru "took a general attitude of extreme relaxation . . . quite at variance with the two letters he had sent to President Kennedy." When Harriman "with exquisite delicacy" hinted at the need for a Kashmir settlement and for taking joint defense measures, Nehru listened and made no comment.[104] An account of the meeting by Roger Hilsman made clear Nehru's uneasiness:

> Nehru looked tired and strained. It must have been difficult to greet Americans over the ruins of his long-pursued policy of neutralism. And the very fact that we were determined there would be from us no hint or gesture of 'I told you so' probably made it even more difficult. . . . Our welcome was not warm; it was *pro forma*, it was withdrawn, it was very limited.[105]

After shuttling between India and Pakistan, Harriman and his British counterpart Duncan Sandys achieved their immediate goal: getting Nehru and Ayub to agree for discussions on

Kashmir. After having given his blessing, Nehru then nearly scuttled the talks by stating in the Indian parliament, on 30 November, that "to upset the present arrangements in Kashmir would be very bad for the people there." Harriman was furious, telling the press Nehru had "made it quite clear" he was ready for talks "without preconditions." Sandys, who flew back to New Delhi, got Nehru to issue a "clarification," denying he was imposing any restrictions on the talks."[106]

The report Harriman submitted after his mission pointed up the dilemma the United States faced. "The U.S. has long sought to build a close relationship with India . . . The present situation provides a unique opportunity to advance this aim."[107] At the same time, there was the risk of "serious adverse repercussions" of proceeding with a major arms program since this "could lead not only to a drastic weakening of Pakistan's ties with the West, but possibly also to its closer association with China."[108] Harriman recognized that Pakistan's price for forming a joint front with India against the Communists was a Kashmir settlement "on acceptable terms." The rub, he admitted, was that terms acceptable for Pakistan were unacceptable for India.[109]

On the eve of the start of the Kashmir talks, the Pakistanis managed to upset the apple cart even more than Nehru had during Harriman's visit. Ayub's government chose this moment to announce agreement in principle with Communist China on a border delimitation. The announcement made the Indians livid. Nehru regarded Ayub's action as a contemptuous rejection of his request that the Pakistanis not cooperate with China while India was in difficulty.[110] Washington was dismayed that Pakistan thumbed its nose at US advice by continuing to improve relations with China.

The Kashmir discussions dragged on through five dreary rounds of ministerial-level talks before ending in May 1963. They achieved almost nothing. Toward the end, the United States set forth some ideas in an effort to stir some life into the talks. After Prime Minister Nehru rejected the US proposals, Ambassador Galbraith commented, "I discovered we had, indeed, brought about the first agreement in some years between India and Pakistan. Both have joined in denouncing our proposals."[111] When Secretary of State Dean Rusk visited New Delhi on 5 May, he suggested the idea of naming a Kashmir negotiator. On this occasion, Nehru's response to the suggestion was not negative, initiating a lengthy but ultimately unsuccessful effort to frame the terms of reference in a manner acceptable to both the Indians and Pakistanis.[112]

To compound the increasing difficulties the United States was having with Pakistan, the mood in India began to sour. Both in public and private, the Indians developed the view that the United States was taking advantage of their weakened position to force India to give away parts of Kashmir.[113] Although at the time Galbraith supported the Kashmir effort, with hindsight he regarded it as a blunder. The effect of leaning on Nehru was to advertise that he had become an American playing card. The Prime Minister had to compensate for his lack of strength by refusing to give on Kashmir.[114]

Disagreeing, Phillips Talbot felt that, despite failure, the effort was worthwhile. The border war had sufficiently shaken the Himalayan scene that there was at least a possibility of solving a dispute that otherwise looked as though it could continue indefinitely to cause grave tensions in South Asia, quite apart from immensely complicating US foreign policy in the region.[115] NSC staffer Robert Komer said he was skeptical about the chances for success but was convinced by Talbot to go along with the Kashmir effort.[116]

Neither India nor Pakistan, in fact, showed any real enthusiasm about the Kashmir talks, with pressure from Washington and London the only reason for their agreeing to participate. After departing from South Asia, Dean Rusk penned a gloomy assessment about the prospects for any early settlement.[117] Ted Sorenson quoted President Kennedy as saying—all too accurately—that India and Pakistan regarded the Kashmir dispute as "more important than the struggle against the Communists."[118] Reconciliation between the two foes was not in the cards.

In National Security Action Memorandum No. 209, approved on 10 December 1962, Kennedy agreed to a three-phase military aid package but specified no price tag. First came aid to reequip battered Indian forces and to make up deficiencies in Indian mountain defense capabilities. Second was help for the Indians to increase their own arms production capabilities.

Third was a review of possible US-Commonwealth help for Indian air defense.[119] On 20 December, President Kennedy and Prime Minister MacMillan, meeting at Bermuda, agreed on a $120 million short-term package split 50-50 between the United States and the Commonwealth. As the Indians were hoping for a far larger arms aid program, the Kennedy-MacMillan package was disappointing. Galbraith, sharing Indian hopes, described the talks at Bermuda as "a cheese-paring operation throughout" and asserted that a "great opportunity to bring India into much closer working association with the West" had been missed.[120]

In India, Prime Minister Nehru, although politically weakened, managed to maintain the basic thrust of Indian foreign policy despite pressure from conservatives within the Congress Party for a shift toward the West. Even though India was clearly no longer nonaligned when it came to China, the Prime Minister succeeded in blocking further change. He was willing to accept military aid from the West—with his teeth clenched, rather like a child swallowing castor oil—but he resisted a closer policy embrace. In January 1963, he wrote Sudhir Ghosh, who was urging a Western defense guarantee, that help from the United States, Britain, and others was all right, but going beyond that "will be purchased at the expense of giving up our basic policy of non-alignment. That is not merely some kind of moral issue but something which makes our people feel they have to be self-reliant and it also helps greatly in the balance of the world and our search for peace."[121]

Several factors aided Nehru's efforts. First, the fact that the Chinese maintained the cease-fire, showing no serious signs of resuming military action, reduced the pressure on Nehru for a more fundamental shift in Indian policy. Second, once the Cuba missile crisis and the Himalayan war ended, Moscow shifted policy gears. The Soviets resumed a more neutral position on the border dispute with China, agreed to proceed with the shipment of MiG–21s to India, and showed "understanding" about Indian requests for arms from the West. Pro-Soviet leftists in India, including *Blitz*, whose switching of sides proved of short duration, resumed ritual lambasting of the United States, this time claiming Washington was trying to force Kashmir concessions from a weakened India. Finally, the reluctance of the

United States to firm up a longer-term arms assistance arrangement played into Nehru's hands, undercutting arguments for a broader reorientation of Indian policy since it became unclear what a shift toward the United States would yield in security terms. Galbraith and Komer warned Kennedy, "with further foot-dragging, we will have no rpt no progress on Kashmir and no rpt no Indians either."[122]

The US administration argued internally about the size of the India military aid program for the remainder of the Kennedy presidency. In April 1963, the President met to discuss the question with his top advisers and with Chester Bowles, whom he asked to replace Galbraith. Bowles wanted $500 million spread over five years. Secretaries McNamara and Rusk argued for a smaller program, worried about the problems the United States would have with Pakistan. Bowles, supported by Komer, countered, "If we don't do this right, they (India) will go to Russia." Rusk, Talbot, and McNamara disagreed. The President remained silent throughout the meeting, not tipping his hand and not making a decision. He later asked Bowles to "see what kind of a proposition you can get out" in India and to "come back in six months, in November, and we'll see where we stand."[123]

The following month, in May 1963, T. T. Krishnamachari, the new Indian Minister for Defense Production, came to Washington to press the Indian case for a program with a price tag of $1.3 billion—over twice what even Bowles was proposing and five times as large as the Pentagon wanted. Meeting with top US government figures, including President Kennedy, the Indian cabinet minister received a positive response on the air defense concept, but no specific commitment on military aid funding levels. The Pentagon, in particular, leaned strongly toward Pakistan with whom the US military had developed many ties in the years since the arms relationship began in 1954. The future of the intelligence facilities in Peshawar was also an important factor weighing on the minds of senior American officials.[124] Since the Chinese showed no signs of resuming the conflict, Kennedy felt no great pressure to force a decision in the face of disagreements within the government. He let the arms issue simmer.

3 June 1963, President Kennedy with President of India, Dr. Sarvepalli Radhakrishnan, at the White House.

John Kenneth Galbraith departed India in June 1963, ending two busy years as Ambassador. His timing was excellent. Indians since have remembered him fondly for his role in getting emergency aid so rapidly during the border crisis in October-November 1962, and for his outspoken support for increased economic aid, including the public sector steel mill at Bokaro. Chester Bowles, whose first tour a decade earlier was extraordinarily successful, was initially reluctant to return to India when Kennedy offered him the chance. Frustrated in Washington where, after losing his post as No. 2 in the State Department, he was cut out of the policy loop, Bowles eventually decided to accept. He felt the Sino-Soviet split and Sino-Indian War had "created an unparalleled opportunity for a change in our Asian policies" and that he could aid this process from New Delhi.[125] Bowles unrealistically envisaged a de facto American-Japanese-Indian alliance, a vision that went far beyond anything Washington, New Delhi, or Tokyo was willing to consider. In any event, Bowles' influence over policy was limited. Bowles made President Kennedy uncomfortable and did not get along with Dean Rusk. Senior levels in the administration no longer took Bowles seriously and ignored his prolix messages.[126]

Not long after arriving in New Delhi, Bowles had to mop up two problems left over by Galbraith—an agreement to install a Voice of America transmitter and the Bokaro steel mill project. In early 1963, eager to bolster their radio broadcasting capability against the Chinese, the Indians agreed to locate a Voice of America transmitter in eastern India. The US government would be able to use the facility for daily VOA broadcasts at certain hours, but otherwise the Indians would control the transmitter. In effect, the agreement would have allowed the United States to use Indian territory for its propaganda broadcasts—an arrangement quite alien to the spirit of nonalignment. When opposition to the accord developed in Indian media and political circles, Nehru decided to cancel the agreement on grounds that it had not been properly staffed within the Indian government. Washington was annoyed by the Indian flip-flop, but could do little except fume.[127]

In the case of the Bokaro steel mill project, it was Washington that had to back off. Despite strong support by President Kennedy for providing US financial aid for the public sector

12 July 1963, President Kennedy greeting the Indian Parliamentary Delegation. From left to right, R.K. Khadilkar, M.N. Kaul, S.N. Dwivedi, G.S. Pathan, Dr. Thomas W. Simons, the President, Mrs. Violet Alva, Ms. Carol Laise, and Sardar Hukam Singh.

steel mill, congressional opposition to the idea refused to go away. The administration concluded by the summer of 1963 that it lacked the votes to gain approval for Bokaro without a major fight. When the situation became clear, the Indians helped Kennedy out by deciding to withdraw their request. Appreciative of US help against China and continuing large-scale economic aid, the Indians did not want to put Kennedy in a corner over Bokaro.[128] The Soviets promptly stepped in to build the mill.

A Meeting That Never Took Place

In November 1963, Ambassador Bowles returned to Washington. In line with Kennedy's instructions, he had worked with the new Indian Defense Minister Y. B. Chavan[129] and Defense Production Minister Krishnamachari to refine the Indian proposals, reducing them to a substantially more modest package of $375 million spread over five years.[130] According to Bowles, a pleased Kennedy called a meeting for 26 November, the day before Bowles was to return to India, and told the envoy he was ready to approve the arms program.[131] The meeting never took place. On 22 November 1963, an assassin's bullet ended the Kennedy presidency.

It is not possible to know what might have happened had Kennedy presided over the 26 November session. Bowles claimed that he had the President's accord for a final go-ahead. Others close to the problem—Talbot, Komer, and Grant—agreed that Kennedy would probably have approved a five-year arms aid package.[132] Since the assassination cut short the Kennedy presidency, it is difficult to evaluate definitively his handling of South Asia. In Kennedy's nearly three years in the White House, the United States placed considerable emphasis on relations with India, making a massive commitment of economic assistance. After the 1962 border conflict broke out, Kennedy rapidly responded with US military aid. Even a battered Nehru was ready to accept what one first-hand observer described as "military reliance if not military alliance."[133]

When the war ended in only a matter of weeks, the Kennedy administration failed to nail down a closer relationship because of concerns about losing Pakistan. Washington, in effect, conditioned longer-term military aid to India on progress toward settling the Kashmir dispute. Trying to solve Kashmir—still an open wound between India and Pakistan in the 1990s—was doubtless a worthy goal, but once the administration realized no agreement was possible, Kennedy can be faulted for not moving ahead more expeditiously to button up an arms agreement with India. Although Pakistan flouted US warnings not to expand its relations with Communist China, Kennedy remained reluctant to press the Pakistanis too hard. Washington continued to hope that it could somehow achieve closer ties with India without shattering the alliance links with Pakistan. In the end, however, as Galbraith and Komer warned, the United States was left with "with no progress on Kashmir and no Indians either."[134]

NOTES

1. During the Kennedy years, Nixon told then Deputy Assistant Secretary of State James Grant that his proudest achievement as Vice President was helping to forge the alliance with Pakistan. (Interview with James P. Grant, 25 June 1990).

2. The chance to become Assistant Secretary came as a total surprise to Talbot. When Rusk and Bowles decided not to fill the NEA post with a specialist in Middle East affairs, they sought someone knowledgeable about South Asia. Talbot was in New Delhi at the time, on leave from the University of Chicago and settling in for a spell as the American Field Services South Asia representative. Ambassador Ellsworth Bunker asked him to the Embassy where Bunker passed on Secretary Rusk's request that he agree to be considered for the NEA post. The surprised Talbot did not know Kennedy, had limited contact with Bowles, but had become friendly with Dean Rusk during World War II service in India.(Interview with Phillips Talbot, 26 June 1990).

3. With his brother Bobby and sister Pat, Kennedy visited India during a trip to Asia. The future President called on Nehru in his office and then was his guest at lunch. During the office call, Kennedy was less than overjoyed when Nehru began to stare at the ceiling and tap his fingers on his desk after about ten minutes. Kennedy had been forewarned Nehru did this once he became bored with a visitor. At lunch, the Prime Minister ignored the two Kennedy brothers to devote his attention to sister Pat. Arthur M. Schlesinger, Jr., *A Thousand Days, John F. Kennedy in the White House* (Boston: Houghton Miflin Company, 1965), p. 522.

4. Ibid.

5. A CIA officer, Komer served as the NSC's developing world specialist under Kennedy. He remained at the NSC under Johnson, becoming the Vietnam specialist in 1966. Johnson sent Komer as

Deputy Ambassador to Saigon and later appointed him Ambassador to Turkey. During the Carter administration, he became Under Secretary of Defense.

6. Interviews with James P. Grant, 25 June 1990; Phillips Talbot, 26 June 1990; John Kenneth Galbraith, 10 July 1990; and Robert Komer, 5 August 1990.

7. From the historian's standpoint, the Kennedy administration is harder to track than Eisenhower's. Kennedy NSC records are sparser. Although copious briefing papers are available, there are not usually minutes of NSC meetings. The general practice—in contrast to the Eisenhower administration—was to note the decisions without a record of the discussion.

8. Message from President Kennedy to Prime Minister Nehru, transmitted by State Department telegram to Embassy New Delhi, 18 February 1961.

9. Nehru's reply to Kennedy's message, transmitted by Embassy New Delhi telegram to the State Department, 20 February 1961.

10. Sarvepalli Gopal, *Jawaharlal Nehru, A Biography,* vol. III, pp. 155-59.

11. See Richard D. Mahoney, *JFK: Ordeal in Africa* (New York: Oxford University Press, 1983), pp. 64-84, for fuller account of the Congo affair.

12. Interview with Warren Unna, former correspondent for the *Washington Post* and *The Statesman* (Calcutta), who was told the story by Chatterjee.

13. For a discussion of the Laos crisis see David K. Hall, "The Laotian War of 1962 and the Indo-Pakistani War of 1971," in Barry Blechman and Stephen S. Kaplan, eds., *Force without War: U.S. Armed Forces as a Political Instrument* (Washington: The Brookings Institution, 1978), pp. 135-75.

14. Harriman, who as Roosevelt's special representative in London, talked with Churchill about Indian independence in March 1942, returned to the foreign affairs field as an adviser and roving ambassador after Kennedy became President. In the 1950s, Harriman served a term as Governor of New York and made an unsuccessful race for the Democratic presidential nomination in 1956. Kennedy later named Harriman Assistant Secretary of State for Far Eastern Affairs and Under Secretary for Political Affairs.

15. State Department telegram to Embassy New Delhi. 23 March 1960, personally drafted by Secretary Rusk.

16. Letter from Prime Minister Nehru to President Kennedy, 16 April 1961.

17. 15 August 1961 letter from Galbraith to Kennedy, quoted in John Kenneth Galbraith, *Ambassador's Journal* (Boston: Houghton Miflin Company, 1969), p. 164.

18. Embassy New Delhi telegrams to the State Department, 22 May 1961.

19. Report of the Task Force with respect to US Policy toward India, 27 December 1960, Kennedy Library.

20. Letter from Nehru to Kennedy, 13 May 19651, Kennedy Library.

21. B.K. Nehru, "The Way We Looked for Money Abroad," Vadilal Dagli, ed., *Two Decades of Indo-US Relations* (Bombay: Vora, 1969), p. 24.

22. Galbraith, pp. 83-84.

23. Ibid., pp. 354-71.

24. In a 12 July 1990 interview, Galbraith said he still thought Bokaro was a sound project.

25. *Public Papers of John F. Kennedy, 1963* (Washington: Government Printing Office, 1964), p. 377.

26. Galbraith, pp. 328-29.

27. Ibid., pp. 101-06.

28. Memorandum from Vice President Johnson to President Kennedy, 23 May 1961, "Mission to Southeast Asia, India and Pakistan."

29. Embassy Karachi telegram to the State Department, 22 May 1961.

30. Vice President's Report to President Kennedy on his Mission to Southeast Asia, India, and Pakistan, 23 May 1961.

31. Robert J. McMahon, "Choosing Sides in South Asia," in *Kennedy's Quest for Victory*, ed. Thomas J. Patterson (New York: Heath, 1989), p. 206.

32. Mohammed Ayub Khan, *Friends Not Masters* (London: Oxford University Press, 1967), p. 137.

33. Interviews with James P. Grant, 25 June 1990; Phillips Talbot, 26 June 1990, and Robert Komer, 5 August 1990.

34. McMahon, p. 208.

35. Interview with Phillips Talbot, 26 June 1990.

36. Interviews with James Grant, 25 June 1990, Phillips Talbot, 26 June 1990, and Robert Komer, 5 August 1990. Grant recalled the Pakistanis, at first, balked about the proposed Mount Vernon dinner, a first of its kind. Grant said it took much persuading to convince the Pakistanis the Mount Vernon affair would generate far more extensive publicity than the usual White House dinner for heads of state.

37. Galbraith, p. 169.

38. Ibid., p. 172.

39. The State Department briefing book, prepared for Nehru's visit to the United States in November 1961, and also the briefing paper for Menon's own meeting with President Kennedy, 23 November 1961, contained a lengthy discussion on the problems Menon caused for the United States at the United Nations. Kennedy Library.

40. Richard L. Jackson, *The Non-Aligned, the UN, and the Superpowers* (New York: Praeger, 1983), pp. 15-17.

41. Letter from Senator Cooper to President Kennedy, undated but possibly January 1961, Kennedy Library.

42. Interview with Ambassador B. K. Nehru, 12 January 1991.

43. Schlesinger, p. 524; Galbraith, p. 214; and 12 January 1991 interview with B.K. Nehru. Paradoxically, in Washington later in the visit when the Foreign Secretary M. J. Desai (no relative of Finance Minister Morarji J. Desai) asked Nehru what he should say to Dean Rusk about Vietnam, the Prime Minister came alive with a momentary flash of his old verve. "Tell them, tell them, not to go into Vietnam," Nehru recalled the Prime Minister saying with great emphasis, "They'll get bogged down. They'll never be able to get out."

44. Galbraith, p. 216.

45. Ibid.

46. Interview with B. K. Nehru, 12 January 1991.

47. Schlesinger, p. 525.

48. Ibid., p. 526.

49. Interview with B.K. Nehru, 12 January 1991.

50. Ibid.

51. Interviews with Phillips Talbot, 26 June 1990, and Robert Komer, 5 August 1990.

52. Interview with John Kenneth Galbraith, 10 July 1990.

53. Galbraith, pp. 240-46.

54. Ibid., pp. 247-48.

55. Michael Brecher, *Krishna Menon's View of the World* (New York: Praeger, 1968), pp. 131-33.

56. Ibid., pp. 128-29; Galbraith, pp. 248-50.

57. Schlesinger, p. 527.

58. Letter from Prime Minister Nehru to President Kennedy, 29 December 1961.

59. Letter from President Kennedy to Prime Minister Nehru, 18 January 1962.

60. Ibid.

61. Interview with B. K. Nehru, 12 January 1991.

62. Interview with Phillips Talbot, June 26, 1990.

63. Galbraith, p. 259.

64. Interview with B. K. Nehru, 28 February 1991.

65. Ibid.

66. Letter from Senator Stuart Symington to President Kennedy enclosing memorandum on aid to India, 11 May 1962, Kennedy Library.

67. MacMahon, p. 212; Galbraith, pp. 327-37.

68. Galbraith, p. 327.

69. MacMahon, p. 211.

70. Galbraith, pp. 336-37.

71. Nehru, vol. V, p. 507, letter of 10 July 1962.

72. Ibid., p. 510.

73. Gopal, vol. III, p. 209.

74. Interview with John Kenneth Galbraith, 12 July 1990.

75. Interview with Robert Komer, 5 August 1990.

76. Steven A. Hoffmann, *India and the China Crisis* (Berkeley: University of California Press, 1990), pp. 103-04, 114.

77. Ibid., p. 124.

78. Allan S. Whiting, *Chinese Calculus of Deterrence* (Ann Arbor: University of Michigan Press, 1975), p. 93.

79. Nehru, vol. V, p. 531-32, letter of 12 October 1962.

80. An effective bureaucrat and distant relative of Nehru, General Kaul ingratiated himself with the Prime Minister. After Menon became Defense Minister, he promoted Kaul, who had only limited field experience, to top posts jumping him over better qualified generals. Kaul retired in disgrace shortly after the military debacle.

81. Hoffmann, p. 154.

82. *The Statesman* (Calcutta), 13 October 1962.

83. Brigadier J. P. Dalvi in his account of the border struggle, *Himalayan Blunder: The Curtain Raiser to the Sino-Indian War of 1962* (Bombay: Thacker and Co., 1969), was devastating in his criticism of Gen. Kaul and others, whom Dalvi blamed for the Indian defeat.

84. Gopal, vol. III, p. 223.

85. Ibid., p. 224.

86. See Michael Brecher, "Non-Alignment Under Stress: The West and the India-China Border War," *Pacific Affairs* 52, no. 4 (Winter 1979-1980), pp. 612-30, for a detailed discussion of the internal struggle within the Congress party leadership after the border debacle.

87. Letter from President Kennedy to Prime Nehru, 29 October 1962; letter from Prime Minister Nehru to President Kennedy, 29 October 1962.

88. Galbraith, p. 387.

89. Interviews with Phillips Talbot and Robert Komer, 26 June and 5 August 1990.

90. Gopal, vol. III, p. 223.

91. Letter from President Kennedy to President Ayub Khan, 29 October 1962.

92. Interview with Phillips Talbot, 26 June 1990. Talbot said that he was never able to pin down when the United States made the pledge to "consult" with the Pakistanis over military assistance to India.

93. Interview with Robert Komer, 5 August 1990; memorandum by Robert Komer entitled, "Actions on Arms Aid to India," 12 November 1962, Kennedy Library.

94. Galbraith, pp. 394, 417. Galbraith wrote with tongue in cheek about *Blitz*, "The CIA, one gathers would henceforth be the spearhead of American-Indian friendship."

95. See Hoffmann, pp. 176-95, for a review of the second phase of the border war.

96. Gopal, vol. III, p. 228-29; Galbraith, pp. 423-24. For reasons that are unclear, the US government has yet to declassify the text of these two letters although the bulk of the extensive Kennedy-Nehru correspondence has been put into the public domain. First mention in India of Nehru's request for direct American military intervention came in 1965 when maverick journalist-politician Sudhir Ghosh told Parliament that President Kennedy had spoken to him of Nehru's letters. Although the US Embassy confirmed Ghosh's report, Prime Minister Shastri gave an evasive reply when asked for comment. (Neville Maxwell, *India's China War* (New York: Anchor Books, 1972), p. 439).

97. Hoffmann, pp. 206-08.

98. Ibid.

99. Interview with B. K. Nehru, 12 January 1991.

100. Galbraith, p. 424.

101. Letter from Ambassador Galbraith to President Kennedy, 9 November 1962, Kennedy Library.

102. Memorandum for the Record of 19 November 1962 meeting of President Kennedy and advisers, prepared by Robert Komer, Johnson Library.

103. In addition to Harriman, the high-level US team included Paul Nitze, Assistant Secretary of Defense for International Affairs, General Paul Adams, Commander of Strike Command, Carl Kaysen of the NSC staff, Roger Hilsman, Director of Intelligence and Research in the State Department, and James P. Grant, Deputy Assistant Secretary for South Asia in the State Department.

104. Roger Hilsman, *To Move a Nation* (Garden City: Doubleday & Company, 1967), p. 330. Hilsman's Memorandum for the Record on the Meeting with Prime Minister Nehru, 25 November 1962, Kennedy Library.

105. Ibid.

106. Galbraith, pp. 436-37; Hilsman, p. 336. As Galbraith put it, "Nehru gives and takes away."

107. "Report of the Harriman Mission," p. 3, Johnson Library.

108. Ibid., pp. 3-4.

109. Ibid., pp. 5, 8.

110. Gopal, vol. III, p. 256.

111. Galbraith, pp. 493-95, 497, and 509.

112. Ibid., pp. 498-500 and 503.

113. Interview with Phillips Talbot, 26 June 1990.

114. Interview with John Kenneth Galbraith, 10 July 1990.

115. Interview with Phillips Talbot, 26 June 1990.

116. Interview with Robert Komer, 5 August 1990.

117. "Notes of Karachi-New Delhi Visit," undated memorandum drafted by Dean Rusk.

118. Theodore C. Sorenson, *Kennedy* (New York: Harper & Row, 1965), p. 664.

119. National Security Action Memorandum 209, 10 December 1962, Kennedy Library. Still in shock from the defeat inflicted by the Chinese, the Indians were worried about the panic that Chinese air attacks could cause on defenseless cities like Calcutta and New Delhi. India's Foreign Secretary, M. J. Desai, suggested the idea of an "air umbrella," under which the West would supply radar and communications equipment and then, if necessary, fly in Allied aircraft to defend the cities against Chinese attacks. In September 1963, joint air defense exercises were held, but then the idea was allowed to drop.

120. Galbraith, p. 455. Galbraith claimed that only he, President Kennedy, and Assistant Secretary Talbot supported a larger program—a rare instance where Galbraith agreed with Talbot, who he otherwise pilloried in his book. Since Galbraith was also on bad terms with Talbot's boss, Secretary of State Dean Rusk, Galbraith often bypassed the State Department to approach the President and the White House directly on issues.

121. Letter from Nehru to Sudhir Ghosh, 5 January 1963. During a trip to the United States in March 1963, Ghosh argued for a de facto US-Indian alliance against China. President Kennedy met briefly with Ghosh on the recommendation of Senator Hubert Humphrey.

122. Embassy New Delhi "Eyes Only" telegram for President Kennedy and Secretary Rusk, 16 May 1963; Memorandum to the President from Robert Komer, 17 May 1962, endorsing Galbraith's position, Kennedy Library.

123. Chester Bowles, *Promises to Keep, My Years in Public Life, 1941-1969* (New York: Harper & Row, 1971), pp. 439-40; Bowles Oral History transcript, Kennedy Library, p. 68. Recalling the meeting,

NSC staffer Komer said that Bowles's story seemed basically correct. Interview with Robert Komer, 5 August 1990.

124. Interview with Phillips Talbot, 26 June 1990.

125. Bowles, p. 436.

126. Interviews with Phillips Talbot, 26 June 1990; Robert Komer, 5 August 1990.

127. The author, who was working on the India Desk at the time, recalled senior officials were particularly annoyed that the Indians went back on an agreement they had previously made.

128. Letters from Prime Minister Nehru to President Kennedy, 28 August 1963, and from President Kennedy to Prime Minister Nehru, 4 September 1963. Kennedy Library.

129. Former Chief Minister of Maharastra, Chavan at the time was highly regarded and considered a potential future prime minister.

130. Memorandum for the President from Robert Komer, 12 November 1963, Kennedy Library.

131. Bowles, pp. 476-81.

132. Interviews with Messrs. Talbot, Grant, and Komer.

133. Walter Crocker, *Nehru: A Contemporary's Estimate* (New York: Oxford University Press, 1966), p. 129.

134. Embassy New Delhi telegram for the President and Secretary Rusk, 16 May 1963, and covering note from Robert Komer, 17 May 1963.

Chapter VI

Johnson: US Pullback from South Asia

Lyndon Johnson inherited a fluid situation in terms of US relations with South Asia. Military aid for India and the deteriorating relations with Pakistan needed White House attention, even if these questions did not require action immediately after Johnson assumed the presidency. Sure-footed on domestic matters, Johnson was far less knowledgeable about foreign policy than his predecessor. An earthy, hands-on leader, the new President deeply engaged himself in substance, but often concealed his motives—a trait that would mark his dealings with South Asia, especially his handling of the 1965-1967 Indian food crisis. Kennedy's door was open to foreign envoys with B.K. Nehru a frequent caller. The new President had far less time for foreign diplomats. It was not until mid-1965 that the Indian Ambassador was able to meet privately with Lyndon Johnson.[1]

Although Johnson broadly supported the bi-partisan policy of containment of Communism and assistance to the poorer nations of the world, he was skeptical about the favored position Kennedy gave to India in US South Asia policy. President Ayub Khan of Pakistan greatly impressed Johnson during his visit to Karachi in May 1961. On the same trip he was less taken with Jawaharlal Nehru.[2] After becoming President, Johnson moved somewhat closer to the Kennedy position. NSC staffer Robert Komer, who strongly supported putting the major emphasis on

India not Pakistan, said the most persuasive argument with Johnson related to the relative population of the two countries. The President agreed that it made more sense for the United States to line up with India, a country with 400 million people, rather than to choose its enemy Pakistan, with only 100 million population.[3] The policy argument Komer advanced was vintage Cold War: Were India to founder or go Communist, US interests in Asia would suffer a major loss. "India, as the largest and potentially most powerful non-Communist Asian nation," Komer told the President, "is in fact the major prize for which we, the Soviets, and Chicoms are competing in Asia."[4]

Johnson's first meeting as President with a senior Indian came in April 1964, when he received Prime Minister Nehru's daughter, Indira Gandhi, who was traveling in the United States. She gave the President a letter from her ailing father, in which Nehru praised Johnson's efforts for a nuclear accord with the Russians, assured the President India would persist in seeking better understanding with Pakistan, and expressed appreciation for US economic and military assistance.[5] In their discussion, Johnson took friendly exception to remarks by Mrs. Gandhi to the *New York Times* that the United States favored Pakistan on the Kashmir issue. With a smile, the President said, "The Indians should realize that the Pakistanis . . . were far more unhappy about our policy toward India than India seemed to about our policy toward Pakistan."[6] During the meeting with Indira Gandhi, Johnson did not discuss military assistance—the most important item then on the Indo-American agenda.

As the session ended, the President asked Mrs. Gandhi to convey his "affectionate regards" to her sick father.[7] Three months earlier, in January 1964, Nehru had suffered a debilitating stroke from which he never fully recovered. When Assistant Secretary Talbot and Ambassador Bowles called on the Prime Minister in March, they were shocked. Nehru's condition was far worse than they expected. He hardly knew who they were and had difficulty in conversing coherently. Bowles and Talbot concluded correctly that Nehru would not remain long on the scene.[8]

Military Aid to India: Half a Loaf

The day after Johnson took office, NSC staffer Robert Komer, tried—and failed—to get the new President to consider the India arms aid proposal. "We've gotten up real momentum . . . unless we get the new President signed on now while he is still carrying out the Kennedy policy, we may lose a real opportunity," Komer urged his chief, McGeorge Bundy. The NSC chief, however, chose not to put the India issue to Johnson.[9] Instead, the new President sent General Maxwell Taylor, Chairman of the Joint Chiefs of Staff, to India (and also Pakistan) to review the situation. The policy advice received from Secretary of State Rusk was proven by later events off the mark:

> If we can move ahead, albeit somewhat jerkily in each country, . . . these proposals for military assistance to India and Pakistan will advance our strategic objective of resisting Communist pressure in the area without placing intolerable strains on our relations with either country.[10]

Following his trip to South Asia, General Taylor recommended a five-year $500 million program for India, divided between grant aid and low interest credits. Taylor urged that the Indians draw up their own defense plan, setting their own priorities, rather than having Americans do this.[11] After Secretary Rusk endorsed the proposal, President Johnson gave his blessing on 8 February 1964.[12]

In New Delhi, Defense Minister Y. B. Chavan worked closely with the newly established US military mission to shape a comprehensive five-year defense plan. The main US concerns were that India not hurt its economic development program by spending too much for defense and not seek equipment from the United States likely to create fresh trouble with Pakistan. American defense specialists were therefore not responsive to Indian interest in obtaining three squadrons of supersonic F-104 aircraft.[13] Although the United States had already given Pakistan F-104s, the Pentagon argued against India's procuring these aircraft on the grounds that supersonic fighters would be of limited utility against the Chinese and would eat up about one-third of the $500 million aid package.[14]

By May 1964, talks had advanced sufficiently that Chavan traveled to Washington to settle the final details with Secretary of Defense Robert McNamara. Except for continuing disagreement about the F–104s, the two sides agreed upon a $500 million five-year program that would help equip six Indian mountain divisions, better communications, transportation, and air defense capabilities and provide assistance to Indian defense industries. According to Komer, the Pentagon so strongly opposed including F–104s in the arms package that he did not think it necessary to put this issue to President Johnson.[15]

After an initial round of meetings in Washington, the Indian Defense Minister was visiting military facilities in the western part of the country. He was due back on 28 May to meet President Johnson and to sign the arms aid agreement with Secretary McNamara. On 27 May, Jawaharlal Nehru died in his sleep. The US Air Force sped Chavan back to Washington where he immediately enplaned with Secretary of State Dean Rusk and Ambassador Chester Bowles for the funeral ceremonies in New Delhi. Although a few days before his death, Nehru brushed off questions about a successor, his appointment of Lal Bahadur Shastri, a popular but retiring North Indian leader, to the cabinet, helped ensure a smooth transition of power.

Nehru led his nation for so long that life without Panditji, as he was affectionately called, seemed hard to imagine. His achievements as Prime Minister were striking. He set his country firmly on the democratic path, launched an ambitious economic development program, and charted a foreign policy course for India independent of the two contending power blocs. Even though after the 1962 China war, Nehru was only a shadow of his former self, his passing marked the end of an era for India.

On 3 June, Secretary McNamara picked up the threads of the military aid discussions with Chavan, who remained as Defense Minister, and quickly settled the remaining questions.[16] In announcing the accord on 6 June, their statement indicated agreement on aid to be provided during US Fiscal Year 1965 but noted—underscoring the disagreement—"the subject of air defense aircraft for India would continue under examination by both sides."[17]

After the United States refused to provide supersonics, the Indians took up a Soviet alternative. In September 1964, Chavan signed an accord in Moscow under which the Soviets agreed to provide 45 MiG–21s and to set up factories in India to assemble another 400 MiGs, making the Soviet fighter the standard Indian interceptor aircraft.[18] As Bowles warned earlier, this development gave the USSR a "much closer relationship with Indian military and particularly with Indian Air Force than they have enjoyed previously" and had a major impact on Indian public opinion.[19]

In weighing the consequences of refusing to provide India with F–104s, the Johnson administration implicitly concluded that the price it would have to pay with Pakistan—perhaps even a final rupture in the alliance relationship—was not worth the potential rewards from the Indians. Once more, US ties with Pakistan set a limit on how far Washington was willing to go with India in the military supply area—even if, as in the case of the F–104s, India was almost certain to turn to the Soviets as an alternative supplier of fighter aircraft. Despite Washington's rebuff of the request for supersonics, the military assistance agreement still seemed to represent a major development, establishing a new and presumably long-term chapter in the security relationship between the United States and India. The chapter, in fact, turned out to be very short; fifteen months later, during the 1965 Kashmir War, the United States stopped arms exports and military assistance.

India's Second Prime Minister

If Jawaharlal Nehru dominated the Indian political scene like a great banyan tree in the shade of which others grew with difficulty, Shastri, barely five foot tall, frail-looking, and already in poor health, appeared overshadowed by powerful regional Congress Party political leaders. "Diminutive, retiring and moderate" were the words the CIA used in describing the new Prime Minister.[24] Lal Bahadur was more at ease in his home-grown Indian setting and had fewer of the psychological hang-ups from which English-trained Indians, like Nehru, seemed to suffer.[25] He had never traveled outside India before he became Prime Minister and initially felt shaky in dealing with foreign policy matters.[26]

With the 1962 War fresh in mind, Shastri's preference was to define nonalignment in terms of good relations with both the Soviet Union and the United States, or as some called it, bi-alignment against the threat posed by Communist China. America's prompt help in 1962 and the continued large amounts of economic and food assistance, running $1 billion annually, impressed the Indian leadership as a sign of US friendship. Although Washington's unwillingness to sell the F–104s underscored the limits of the security relationship, Indo-US relations seemed on solid ground. They were, indeed, less troubled at the time than Washington's dealings with Pakistan.

In March 1965, with Shastri in office a little under a year, veteran diplomat Averell Harriman visited New Delhi for three and a half days of talks. The change in atmosphere from his four earlier visits during the Nehru years struck Harriman. He cabled the President and Rusk:

> I feel today quite a new attitude towards us and the world situation reflected by Indian officials and the press. I almost felt I was in a different country . . . . Discussions with Indian Ministers and officials were relaxed and frank with full agreement on such matters as aggressive intents of Red China, need to prevent Red's takeover in South Vietnam and SEA (Southeast Asia), willingness to consider objectively our policies and work with us for common objectives in other areas of world.[27]

Even though Harriman believed the Indians "remained over-hopeful of Soviet Union's good intent," and stubborn about Kashmir, "I had the feeling that I could talk freely with them without fear of being misunderstood and that we could reach understandings on a much broader area."[28]

During the fall of 1964, Ambassador Bowles urged the Prime Minister to visit the United States. Shastri was willing, but wanted to wait a year in order to gain more experience at the helm of government. To fit President Johnson's schedule, Shastri agreed to travel to Washington in early June 1965; Pakistan's Ayub Khan was due in mid-April.[29] As planning for the Shastri trip proceeded, the mood in the American Embassy in Delhi was upbeat. Then in early April, President Johnson abruptly and unexpectedly decided to put off both Ayub and Shastri.

Public criticism of US Vietnam policy by Canada's Prime Minister Lester Pearson, after he had met with Johnson, angered the President. He told the White House staff he did not want a repeat performance and further embarrassment. Worried that

Pakistan's cozying up to China and its unhelpful attitude on Vietnam could cause problems, Johnson decided to cancel Ayub Khan's trip, about to occur in two weeks. On reflection, the Chief Executive concluded he should put Shastri off as well.[30]

It was only on 14 April, after Rusk tried unsuccessfully for several days to change the President's mind, that Washington told Bowles what was up. In a telegram to New Delhi, Under Secretary of State George Ball expressed the vain hope:

> You can approach Shastri in such a way as to lead him to feel that a postponement of his visit until fall is in the interests of India. In our view it would not be useful for him to come while the aid bill is pending in spite of the fact that the Indian attitude on Vietnam has been generally helpful.[31]

A premature press leak in Washington the next day made matters worse. Bowles had no time to prepare the ground for what might have otherwise been passed off as a routine postponement. Instead, Johnson deeply offended Shastri, who was sensitive about his dignity and his lack of experience in foreign affairs. Indian officials, like Ambassador B. K. Nehru, felt insulted by Johnson's cavalier treatment of the Prime Minister and the fact that India was once again bracketed with Pakistan.[32]

The main target of US anger, Ayub Khan, perhaps more familiar with Johnson's unpredictable style, swallowed hard and contained his annoyance. As Komer wrote to McGeorge Bundy, "The Paks, who probably see the blow as directed mainly at them, are lying low and letting the Indians get themselves in trouble. The Indians are showing their injured pride in many ways. Shastri is saying nice things about the Soviets . . . We've suffered a setback here . . . "[33] Although, in time, tempers cooled, Johnson's rude treatment of the two leaders badly strained relations with India and Pakistan just as the two countries began to edge toward a second Kashmir War.

Serious clashes broke out on 9 April 1965 in a desolate and uninhabited marsh land called the Rann of Kutch. A tidal mud flat near the Arabian Sea, the Rann became a problem in 1954 when Pakistan staked a claim to half the area, asserting it was a landlocked sea. Under international law, this put the boundary in the middle of the Rann rather than at its northern edge. The Indians disputed the Pakistani position, insisting the Rann was a marsh, not a sea, and that the boundary should remain unchanged.[34]

The problem had remained quiet for ten years until early in 1965. The Pakistanis then began sending military patrols into the disputed area north of the Rann to assert their territorial claim. When the Indians countered, fighting erupted on 9 April. During the next two weeks, the clashes escalated into a brigade size battle between Indian and Pakistani forces. On 27 April, the Indians withdrew rather than risk having their troops cut off during the rainy season when the Rann flooded. New Delhi admitted suffering about 100 casualties in the fighting.[35] The impression was that the Pakistanis had the better of the affair. On the diplomatic front, the British, backed by Washington, pressed for early talks. London's efforts resulted in a formal cease-fire agreement on 27 June with India surprisingly agreeing to submit questions about the legal status of the Rann to arbitration. Shastri's flexibility contrasted with Nehru's persistent rebuff to proposals for mediation or arbitration of the Kashmir dispute.

Although the cease-fire took hold, India's pride suffered a fresh blow from the clash in the Rann of Kutch. It was one thing to be pushed around by China, quite another to be bested by Pakistan. The Shastri government came under angry criticism in the Indian parliament for its handling of the affair. Part of the ire was directed at the United States for its failure to prevent Pakistan from using US military equipment against India. This was a sensitive issue with New Delhi since the United States had given a stream of assurances that Washington would not permit the Pakistanis to use the arms to attack India. In the case of the Rann, Pakistan admitted using US-supplied equipment, but justified this on the grounds of "self-defense," claiming that India had begun the fighting.

Not eager to enter the thicket of deciding who was the aggressor, the Johnson administration stressed the importance of stopping the fighting rather than assessing blame for the misuse of US weapons.[36] In a testy exchange with Secretary Rusk on 8 May, B. K. Nehru expressed dissatisfaction with the US attitude:

While India hopes the Kutch question will be resolved, a more important question of principle is involved. US assurances to India against Pakistani misuse of arms had been the foundation of Indian defense policy. If these assurances were eroded, it would be a very serious matter . . . . as far as India was concerned, the U.S. reaction had been inadequate.[37]

The Second Kashmir War: August-September 1965

If, following the Rann of Kutch episode, India—in the words of William Barnds—became "dangerously frustrated," Pakistan became "dangerously overconfident."[38] Having ruled the country with hardly a misstep since 1958, Ayub Khan proceeded to implement Operation *Gibraltar*, a gamble to seize Kashmir, supported by Foreign Minister Zulfikar Ali Bhutto and other Pakistani hawks. The bold scheme envisaged covertly infiltrating some five thousand Pakistani trained guerrillas across the cease-fire line in order to stir an uprising in Kashmir.

Badly misreading the mood in India, Pakistan apparently did not expect Shastri to counter militarily, either from weakness or from fear that China would intervene. After the 1962 debacle and India's poor showing in the Rann of Kutch, an overconfident Ayub Khan had difficulty in taking India, and especially its leader, "little" Shastri, too seriously. The Pakistanis may have also wanted to strike in Kashmir before the military odds swung too heavily in India's favor. Although in 1965 Pakistan's armed forces could not match India's in numbers, thanks to US aid, they had gained a qualitative edge in armor and air power. The Pakistanis feared that it was only a question of time until India, having embarked on a defense build-up after the 1962 fiasco, would erase their edge.[39]

Infiltration of the guerrillas began on 5 August. The Indians quickly grasped what was going on and captured many of the intruders. Sabotage caused some damage, but the raiders failed to spark a Kashmiri uprising.[40] Contrary to Pakistani expectations, the Indians also responded militarily, crossing the Kashmir cease-fire line to capture key passes and terrain features that the Pakistanis were using as infiltration routes. Operation *Gibraltar* seemed doomed.

Rather than face defeat, the Pakistanis on 1 September escalated. Concerned about the fate of several thousand potentially stranded guerillas, Ayub Khan launched a major attack, led by US-supplied Patton tanks, across the cease-fire line in southern Kashmir. The objective was to cut the road that linked Kashmir's capital Srinagar with India.[41] "The Paks, having failed to spark off a 'war of liberation' via a Kashmiri uprising, may now feel they've got to enter the lists directly to forestall a humiliating failure," Komer told the President.[42]

After intelligence reports indicated the likelihood of the Pakistani attack, the United States pressed UN Secretary-General U Thant to urge restraint on both sides. In New Delhi, Ambassador Bowles asked Indian Foreign Minister Swaran Singh to respond calmly, warning that a military "thrust by India at some more favorable point . . . will almost certainly touch off war." The Minister's reply was to protest the use by Pakistan of US Patton tanks contrary to American assurances.[43]

Bowles followed up with an urgent plea "for direct U.S. pressure at earliest possible moment on both sides in support of SYG's appeal." Bowles asked authorization to tell Shastri that if the Indians agreed to a cease-fire and troop withdrawal, and the Pakistanis refused, the United States would cut off military aid to Pakistan.[44] Washington turned Bowles down.

President Johnson decided not to engage US influence directly in pressing for an end to the fighting, continuing to leave this to the United Nations with the United States playing a supporting role. Rusk informed Bowles:

> Highest level decision taken here not to engage in direct pressure on either Paks or Indians for time being, but to place primary reliance on UN. Given existing strains on our relations with both parties, we do not believe such further action as threats to suspend military aid along lines you suggest likely to halt fighting at this time.[45]

In Washington, Ambassador Nehru echoed Foreign Minister Swaran Singh's protests about Pakistan's use of US-supplied equipment. The Ambassador warned that unless Pakistan stopped its drive to cut off Srinagar, India would attack across the international border to the south of Kashmir. Sidestepping Indian complaints about Pakistan's misuse of American weapons, Rusk emphasized that a cease-fire was the most important thing.[46] Bowles made the same point in New Delhi, while reporting to Washington a crescendo of criticism in the media about Pakistan's use of American weapons against India.[47]

On 6 September—as Ambassador Nehru warned—the Indian Army struck across the international frontier only twenty miles east of the city of Lahore, the capital of West Pakistan.[48] Despite the threat of all-out war between India and Pakistan, the United States held back from direct diplomatic intervention, continuing to rely on the United Nations as the main vehicle to stop the fighting.[49] Key members of the Senate Foreign Relations Committee, during an 8 September breakfast, agreed with Dean Rusk that it was not "wise for us to get out in front of the UN to carry the burden of trying to force India and Pakistan to cease hostilities."[50] The United States proceeded later the same day to embargo military exports and to suspend economic assistance commitments to India and Pakistan. Personally drafted by Rusk and approved by Johnson, the administration statement aimed at averting even more drastic measures following "a volcanic reaction" by Congressmen and Senators, angry that the United States was fueling both sides of the war.[51] Washington was dismayed that India and Pakistan were battling each other, endangering their economic development programs and shredding any slim hopes of their cooperating against the Chinese.[52]

Like Washington, Moscow threw its support behind UN efforts to stop the fighting, offering its good offices for peace talks at Tashkent. After Brezhnev ousted Khrushchev as Soviet leader in 1964, the Russians had adjusted their South Asia policy to adopt a more even-handed and less pro-Indian posture. The Soviets, indeed, worked with the United States in support of the UN peace effort—a rare instance of East-West cooperation during the Cold War. The British, who had brokered the Rann of Kutch cease-fire, lost their influence with New Delhi after Prime Minister Harold Wilson imprudently charged India with aggression in crossing the international border. Notwithstanding US-UK-Soviet support, the United Nations made very slow progress. Secretary-General U Thant failed, during a 9-14 September visit to South Asia, to obtain Indian and Pakistani agreement on a cease-fire. Although Ayub Khan and Shastri tried to get Johnson to intervene directly, the President kept the focus on U Thant's peace efforts.[53]

On the battlefield, despite the fact that the Indian army made initial gains, the front stabilized at the outskirts of Lahore about 15 miles inside the border. The Pakistani drive to cut off Kashmir bogged down, falling short of its objective. Fighting was often fierce with some of the heaviest tank battles since World War II. Pakistan's armor performed poorly, suffering heavy losses. In contrast to the 1962 war against the Chinese and the fighting in the Rann of Kutch, the Indian Army gave a good account of itself.[54]

On 17 September, concern about possible Chinese Communist intervention suddenly loomed larger. Beijing issued an ultimatum that India remove construction works on the Tibet border or face the consequences. When Shastri kept his cool, and Moscow and Washington warned China against precipitate action, Beijing backed down by extending the deadline. The Chinese continued their verbal support for their Pakistani friends, but chose not to engage themselves militarily.

Finally, on 22 September, the fighting stopped. India and Pakistan accepted a "demand" by the Security Council for a cease-fire. Although both sides lost heavily in men and materiel and neither gained a decisive military advantage, India had the better of the war. New Delhi achieved its basic goal of thwarting Pakistan's attempt to seize Kashmir by force. Pakistan gained nothing from a conflict which it had instigated.

Washington breathed a sigh of relief that an all-out struggle had been averted. When the Soviets again offered to mediate, the United States supported this move—a startling reversal of policy after a decade of trying to limit Moscow's role in South Asia. Dean Rusk explained:

> We encouraged the Russians to go ahead with the Tashkent idea, because we felt we had nothing to lose. If they succeeded in bringing about any détente at Tashkent, then there would be more peace on the subcontinent between India and Pakistan, and we would gain from that fact. If the Russians failed at Tashkent, at least the Russians would have the experience of some of the frustration that we had for twenty years in trying to sort out things between India and Pakistan.[55]

In January 1966, three months after the end of fighting, Ayub and Shastri met with Kosygin in the Soviet Central Asia city of Tashkent. Shuttling between the two leaders, Kosygin proved a skilful diplomat. Eventually, on 9 January, he obtained their agreement to withdraw to positions held before the war, to exchange prisoners, and to try to solve their disputes peacefully. Given the enmity between India and Pakistan, the Tashkent agreement was a considerable achievement.[56] The conference came to a tragic end when Lal Bahadur Shastri suffered a fatal heart attack just hours after signing the accord. For the second time in a year and a half, India cremated a Prime Minister.

US policy during the 1965 war pleased neither India nor Pakistan. The Indians were angry that the United States failed to prevent the use of American arms despite repeated promises that it would do so. Washington's even-handed action in stopping military and economic assistance to both countries also irked New Delhi, for there seemed little doubt that Pakistan started the trouble by launching Operation Gibraltar. The Pakistanis were even more bitter. That Washington—their supposed ally—not only refused to help against India but even cut off the flow of military supplies seemed an act of betrayal. US-Pakistan relations plummeted. The alliance relationship appeared for all practical purposes dead.

If South Asians were indignant about Washington's reaction, the United States was dismayed that the two nations went to war with each other after a decade of heavy American investment in economic assistance and major infusions of military equipment to Pakistan and lesser amounts to India. Commenting on the 1965 war, Secretary Rusk said India and Pakistan "allowed the matter to escalate very fast, on both sides, contrary to the advice that was being given them by the United States so we in effect shrugged our shoulders and said, 'Well, if you're going to fight, go ahead and fight, but we're not going to pay for it.'"[57]

The US response marked a major turning point in South Asia policy. As Rusk's remarks suggested, Washington, in effect, walked away from the region. A decade of intense involvement in the affairs of the subcontinent, numerous attempts to solve the Kashmir dispute and to promote Indo-Pakistani rapprochement, had yielded a skimpy harvest. Supposedly a US military ally against the Communists, Pakistan entered into a close relationship with Communist China. The Indians, while seeking US support against China in the Himalayas, were unwilling to work in close harness against the Communist threat in South Vietnam.

To Washington policymakers, there appeared, in short, little justification for continuing the heavy political and security engagement in India and Pakistan. With the United States becoming increasingly absorbed in the Vietnam War, South Asia's importance in US strategic priorities declined. Washington seemed content for the Soviet Union—which the United States previously regarded as the major and sinister contender for influence—to assume the position of would-be security manager for the subcontinent.

A "Hard New Look" at Economic and PL 480 Aid

During his first year and a half in the White House, President Johnson allowed the other main element of US involvement with India—the large economic assistance and PL 480 food programs—to continue largely unchanged along the lines previously established. In September 1964, at the expiration of the four-year PL 480 program approved in 1960, Johnson agreed to a new one-year food accord to supply 4.5 million tons of wheat. In the spring of 1965, the Indians were back, seeking a two-year PL 480 program for 10 million tons. Few expected difficulties in proceeding with the new food agreement or with the annual economic assistance request.

And then, without warning, in June 1965, the President surprised his own bureaucracy and the Indians. He called a halt to routine approval of new aid commitments for India (and also for Pakistan) and demanded a "hard new look . . . before we spend a lot more money."[58] In a 9 June meeting, Johnson announced that he would personally approve new assistance for India and Pakistan until the Congress voted the Fiscal Year 1966 aid bill. Johnson also asked for early recommendations on the pending Indian PL 480 request.[59]

What caused the President to bring the Indians (and Pakistanis) up short? A number of factors appeared to explain Johnson's abrupt move. The Chief Executive's sensitive political antenna detected growing unpopularity for foreign aid with his former congressional colleagues, especially aid to South Asia which loomed large in the overall figures. Pakistan's flirtation with China made it hard to justify large-scale help on political grounds. With India's economic performance lagging, there was growing feeling in Congress that New Delhi was taking US help for granted "regardless of what they did or how effectively they used it."[60]

Johnson sensed the foreign aid program was basically "flying on automatic pilot" after the major increases of the late 1950s and early 1960s. He found little questioning of performance—whether the programs were achieving their purpose or whether the recipients were making any genuine self-help effort. There was, he believed, just the annual call for more money.[61] To make sure that India understood what was happening, Under Secretary of State Thomas Mann reviewed the problem frankly with Ambassador Nehru during a private lunch on 1 July.[62] Although the exchange—according to Mann—became somewhat heated, especially over the Indian attitude toward Vietnam, Nehru had a chance to enlist the assistance of Mann, a protégé of Johnson's, in finally getting to talk with the President. When they met, the two got along well. The door to the White House was thereafter open to a much relieved B. K. Nehru.[63]

About the same time that Johnson sensed aid weariness in the US Congress, the World Bank was encountering growing disillusionment among aid donors, disturbed by India's sluggish economic performance. Bank President George Woods decided to send economist Bernard Bell and a team of specialists to undertake a detailed review of the Indian economic situation. Bell and his team toiled through much of 1965, getting good cooperation from Indian counterparts and also keeping in close touch with the US AID Mission in New Delhi, then headed by prominent economist and former member of the Council of Economic Advisers, John P. Lewis.[64]

Sharply critical of Indian policy, Bell's Report recommended a shift of emphasis from industry to agriculture, the dismantling of the system of controls and licenses, and the devaluation of the Indian rupee. AID Director Lewis agreed with Bell's approach. Optimistic about India's long-term prospects, Lewis believed that with the necessary policy shifts—and increased foreign assistance—India could surge to self-sustaining growth, "Operation Big Push" in his words.[65]

Responding to the President's signal of caution at the 9 June meeting, AID Director David Bell proposed a one–rather than a two–year PL 480 agreement with India (to provide six million tons of wheat and 200,000 tons of rice worth $390 million). Even though Bell stressed the "urgent need" to open negotiations to prevent "an interruption in shipments," Johnson sat tight.[66] After a month had passed, the President surprised US and Indian officials by approving only a one million ton agreement—enough to provide food for two months—not the six million tons David Bell recommended. This unexpected step launched what became known as the "short tether" policy.

For several years, Orville Freeman, the Secretary of Agriculture, had been voicing his unhappiness, first to Kennedy and then to Johnson, about the sluggishness of Indian efforts to boost agricultural production. Freeman returned from a May 1964 trip to India in a gloomy frame of mind. He feared that US surpluses would one day disappear, leaving India in terrible trouble—unable to feed itself and unable to obtain food from abroad. Along with American and Indian specialists, however, Freeman was confident India could boost food production substantially if it tried seriously to do so. What was needed was higher priority on agriculture, changes in agricultural price and distribution policies, expanded irrigation, better seeds, increased use of fertilizers and other agricultural inputs.[67]

PL 480 agreements, such as the 17 million and 4.5 million ton accords of 1960 and 1964, were a political and social boon to the Government of India, ensuring adequate grain supplies at low prices for Indian cities. At the same time, the availability of US food—at little or no cost—removed the incentive for New Delhi to adopt policies encouraging farmers to produce more. As long as the wheat fields of the US Middle West stood ready to take up any slack, India was under little pressure to raise the priority for agriculture.

In 1964, Prime Minister Shastri appointed a new Agriculture Minister C. Subramaniam, who was promoted to New Delhi after a strong performance in the Madras State government. Serious about reforming agricultural policy, Subramaniam soon concluded that India should make a major push for self-sufficiency rather than continuing to rely on foreign food aid, principally from the United States.[68] Subramaniam and

Freeman broadly agreed on the policy measures needed to boost agricultural output.[69]

President Johnson also agreed on the need to address the problem. Failure to do so, Johnson wrote in his memoirs, could have spelled disaster in the future if India's population growth outran food production and the United States were no longer able to fill the gap.[70] What was unusual was not so much Johnson's support for a change in Indian farm policy as his intense, obsessive personal involvement. For the next two years, Lyndon Johnson, in effect, became the US government's "desk officer" for PL 480 food aid to India. According to Walt Rostow, "It is hard to recapture how deeply Johnson felt about getting the Indians to do a better job in producing food. The India food question went right to where he lived. It was part of Johnson's fundamental concern for human beings and his hatred of poverty."[71]

It was soon apparent that the 1965 summer monsoon rains had failed badly and, as a result, India faced the worst drought in a century. With foodgrain production plunging from 89 to 72 million tons, food supplies from the United States became the critical factor in staving off famine. Just as the US Agriculture Department was getting geared up for large-scale exports, word came down through the bureaucracy that the President would personally decide on the release of food shipments to India. Thinking there was some mistake, Freeman called Johnson, who responded abruptly, "I'll take care of the problem." He refused to give the Secretary of Agriculture any explanation. Baffled, Freeman then called Secretary of State Dean Rusk, who said he would talk with Johnson and was sure things could be worked out. A few minutes later, Rusk called back, saying simply, "The President won't talk about it." Calls elsewhere drew similar blanks.[72]

Without tipping his hand to anyone, Johnson decided to exercise maximum leverage in trying to force a change in Indian agricultural policy—and to take personal charge of the effort. At the same time that he exerted pressure by holding back exports through the "short tether" policy, he was careful to avoid a break in the food supply pipeline. Not trusting the Department of Agriculture, the President had NSC staffer Robert Komer check out details of shipping grain from the Gulf of Mexico to India.

According to Komer, the President wanted to know exactly how long he could delay shipments.[73] In late September, Johnson approved another PL 480 shipment, this time for 500,000 tons, roughly one month's supply.

The US press picked up word of the tougher approach. *The Washington Post* quoted one official, "We're using food to bargain all right, but to bargain for food—India's own productivity."[74] When the Indian press interpreted the food holdup as an effort to pressure India to make concessions on Kashmir, Bowles was instructed to issue a denial, but to state frankly the United States—dissatisfied with India's own agricultural efforts—was not ready to proceed beyond short-term agreements until the signs of Indian self-help were clearer.[75] In late October, Bundy and Rusk pressed for another short-term agreement. Although Johnson approved, he insisted Bowles tell the Indians the US government remained unhappy with their performance. The cable to Bowles stressed the view of the "highest authority" that a longer term accord "not be undertaken until such time as the USG has convincing evidence of the GOI's determination to put its food house in order."[76]

At Johnson's suggestion, Freeman and Subramaniam met privately during a Food and Agriculture Organization meeting in Rome in late November to reach agreement on the agricultural reform program. Johnson told Freeman to cable the results "Eyes Only for the President." Almost paranoid about press leaks, Johnson warned Freeman, "If anybody finds out about this, your ass will be hanging from a yardarm."[77] On 25 November, the two ministers signed what became known as the Treaty of Rome. This document—in fact a detailed statement of the specific steps India would take in order to boost food production—remained a closely held secret for a number of years to avoid the suggestion of US pressure on India.[78]

Johnson was pleased with the results. As soon as the Indian government publicly announced the new policy, the President authorized a further 1.5 million ton wheat agreement, a $50 million fertilizer commodity loan—the first economic aid commitment since the 1965 war—and set up an interdepartmental committee under Freeman to expedite wheat exports. A relieved Prime Minister Shastri, speaking in parliament on 10 December, expressed "sincere thanks to President Johnson, whose

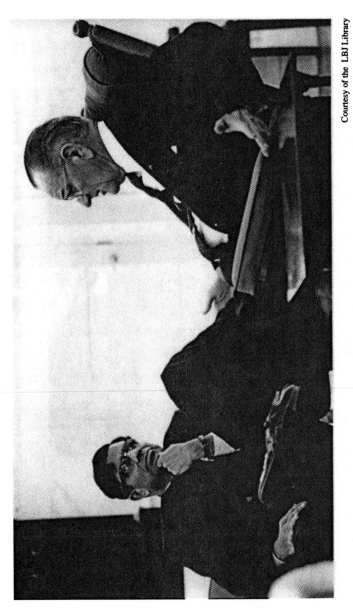

20 December 1965, President Lyndon B. Johnson with Indian Agriculture Minister C. Subramaniam.

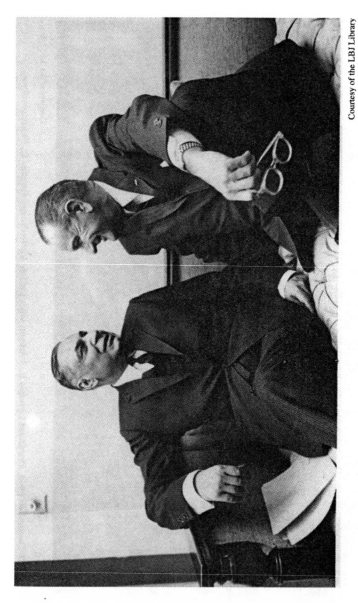

2 February 1966, President Johnson with Indian Ambassador B.K. Nehru at the White House.

decision to accelerate food aid would help substantially in tiding over the present food situation."[79]

Two weeks later, Johnson invited Subramaniam to Washington where they reviewed the situation with considerable outward cordiality. Instructing Freeman to do everything possible to help, Johnson said India's food problem "ought to be attacked as if we were at war." The President insisted he was not interested in "disciplining anyone, in becoming the master of anyone, or in dominating anyone."[80] Reflecting about Johnson a quarter of a century later, C. Subramaniam was skeptical, characterizing the President as "well-intentioned, but like the 'district nawab' wanting to be the driving force behind whatever was happening and unwilling to concede that others could also shoulder responsibility."[81]

Lyndon Johnson's short tether policy worked. India announced a far higher priority on agriculture, marking a substantial shift from the earlier policy emphasis on industry. What was surprising was that Johnson could use strong arm tactics without ruffling well-known Indian sensitivities about foreign interference. The explanation was that key Indian leaders themselves wanted to reform agricultural policy just as much as the President and, in fact, found US pressure not unhelpful in overcoming domestic political opposition.[82] In 1965—in contrast to the following year—Johnson also quickly opened up the export pipeline for large-scale wheat shipments once the Indians announced the revised agricultural policy. In 1966, the President would change his tactics.

India's Third Prime Minister—Indira Gandhi

During the fall of 1965—after the end of the India-Pakistan War—there was much discussion about rescheduling the Shastri visit to Washington. Although politically strengthened by his handling of the war, Shastri still badly needed US aid to deal with an increasingly difficult economic situation. Except for a $50 million fertilizer loan, the United States had held off making new assistance commitments. Johnson preferred to wait until Shastri came before moving ahead. Feeling the war had wiped the policy slate clean, the President wanted to build a new relationship.[83] The "central concern," Rusk cabled Bowles, "will be to develop an understanding of what constitutes a workable relationship between aid donor and recipient." Rusk warned, "Aid is not a state of nature which the US (is) bound to respect."[84]

In India, Shastri faced dissension in his cabinet about the World Bank's economic policy recommendations. Finance Minister T. T. Krishnamachari strongly opposed these, unhappy about the call for economic liberalization as well as the proposed easing of restrictions on foreign investment in fertilizer production. In the end, Shastri sided with supporters of change—Subramaniam, Planning Minister Ashok Mehta, and L. K. Jha, Secretary to the Prime Minister and Shastri's principal aide. When Krishnamachari continued to object, Shastri, who was proving that, despite his small stature, he could be a tough political leader, fired the Finance Minister.[85]

Shastri took this action just before leaving for Tashkent to meet with Pakistan's Ayub Khan and Soviet Premier Kosygin. Prior to the Prime Minister's departure, Averell Harriman came to New Delhi to discuss the Vietnam war.[86] As India under Shastri had been relatively cooperative on this issue, Washington hoped to enlist the Prime Minister's help in urging Moscow to press Hanoi to open negotiations with the United States. Shastri agreed to take up the issue with the Soviets and, after talking with Soviet Premier Kosygin, wrote Johnson from Tashkent on 6 January.[87] Four days later, the Indian leader was dead.

The man who most wanted to succeed Shastri, Morarji Desai, an ascetic conservative from Gujarat in western India and former Finance Minister, lost out to Indira Gandhi. Disliking Desai, Congress Party leaders—the so-called Syndicate—instead rallied to Nehru's daughter, who served as Minister of Information in Shastri's government. The Syndicate, particularly Congress Party president K. Kamaraj, regarded her as more pliable than the rigid and prickly Desai.[88] Then in her mid-forties, Mrs. Gandhi had yet to define her strong political personality. She appeared awkward and shy in public, unsure of her footing.

In her initial weeks in office, the new Prime Minister followed in the footsteps of her predecessor, pledging support for the Tashkent Accords, reaffirming India's adherence to the nonalignment policy established by her father, and accepting recommendations to implement the economic policy changes

28 March 1966, President Johnson with Prime Minister Indira Gandhi.

proposed by the World Bank. When President Johnson renewed the invitation extended to Shastri, Mrs. Gandhi quickly accepted. In late March, only two months after taking office, she traveled to Washington on her first foreign trip as India's Prime Minister.

Mrs. Gandhi's arrival was preceded by extensive discussions, the President himself meeting with Ambassador Nehru on 2 February to review the upcoming visit. When Nehru asked for emergency food aid, Johnson agreed to "take some interim action" but said he wanted to have a better idea of Congressional reactions and to talk with Mrs. Gandhi before making a major move.[89] A stop in New Delhi in February by Vice President Hubert Humphrey permitted another round of high level discussions and an occasion for Humphrey to announce the release of $200 million in aid funds in response to India's plea for help.[90]

Courtesy of the LBJ Library

28 March 1966, at the White House banquet, Vice President Hubert Humphrey, Prime Minister Indira Gandhi, and President Johnson.

A two-page memorandum Secretary Rusk sent the President on 26 March summed up US hopes for reaching an "economic bargain" with Mrs. Gandhi. The essence was that if India implemented economic reform, the United States would do its share with the World Bank to provide the necessary resources. As a sign of its commitment to reform, the United States wanted India promptly to "work out details with the World Bank and the International Monetary Fund."[91] Indian hopes were, in a sense, the mirror image. Although Mrs. Gandhi in public said she was going only on a goodwill visit, in private she stated frankly to journalist Inder Malhotra, "Don't publish this, but my main mission is to get both food and foreign exchange without appearing to be asking for them."[92]

The visit was a rousing success, surpassing even optimistic expectations.[93] Determined to make a good impression, Mrs. Gandhi turned on all her not inconsiderable charm. As Komer commented, "She set out to vamp LBJ and succeeded."[94] The two leaders appeared to get along famously. Johnson was sufficiently taken with India's Prime Minister that he broke protocol by staying for dinner at the Indian Embassy after an official reception. His impromptu toast at the dinner was full of friendship for India and praise for Indira.

Although their private discussions did not go into great detail, the two leaders told their advisers assembled in the White House cabinet room that they had reached a basic meeting of the minds. Johnson would send a message on food aid to Congress within the week. Mrs. Gandhi would have her advisers talk with the World Bank. They agreed on the need for peace in South Asia. Praising Johnson, Mrs. Gandhi looked to a "good working relationship" between India and the United States.[95] Johnson wrote in his memoirs, "I sympathized with the new Prime Minister in the heavy burdens she had assumed, and I tried to reinforce her considerable courage."[96]

The day after Mrs. Gandhi left Washington—on 30 March—President Johnson sent a vigorous food message to Congress, urging 3.5 million tons of food aid for India on an emergency basis—to bring the year's total to almost 7 million tons. Waxing eloquent, the President ended the message, "India is a good and deserving friend. Let it never be said that bread should be so dear and flesh and blood so cheap that we turned in indifference from her bitter need."[97] Congress responded positively, unanimously adopting a joint resolution endorsing additional food aid for India on 19 April. The contrast between the smooth sailing of the 1966 resolution and the turbulent passage of the 1951 wheat loan said much about Johnson's political savvy and the impact of Mrs. Gandhi's visit to Washington. In 1966, there were no fewer critics of India on Capitol Hill than in 1951.

Following up on US suggestions, Mrs. Gandhi sent Planning Minister Ashok Mehta to Washington where he and Bank President George Woods worked out a tentative reform package that included Indian decontrol of imports and streamlined licensing procedures with detailed sector by sector targets. In parallel talks with the IMF, the Indians agreed to a major devaluation of the rupee. For its part, the Bank said it would make a "best effort" to increase consortium lending to $1.2 billion in 1965-1966, including $900 million in so-called program loans to

29 March 1966, Prime Minister Indira Gandhi and sons Rajiv and Sanjay with President Johnson.

provide the necessary cushion from the economic jolt devaluation would cause. The following year, the Bank agreed to try for an increase in overall lending to $1.5 billion.[98]

Although Johnson was not as personally engaged in the economic reform and devaluation discussions as in food questions, he met with Mehta on 4 May.[99] A glowing President said, "The visit of Prime Minister Gandhi was as perfect as any visit could be . . . there was now a complete atmosphere of trust and confidence between India and the United States."[100] Johnson expressed appreciation for Shastri's efforts regarding Vietnam, added that he had made no specific requests of Mrs. Gandhi, "but would welcome Indian help toward a lasting peace."[101]

After Mehta returned to New Delhi, Mrs. Gandhi approved the package negotiated in Washington and instructed key civil servants to work out implementation plans in secret. Early in June—acting as if she had not yet made up her mind—Mrs. Gandhi sounded out Congress Party leaders, including K. Kamaraj, on devaluation. The response was uniformly negative. Asserting devaluation smacked too much of foreign pressure, the party seniors feared tampering with the parity rate of the rupee just six months before general elections might hurt the Congress Party at the polls. Gandhi ignored their objections and announced a large 57 percent devaluation on 6 June. For his part, President Johnson redeemed the pledge of US support by moving quickly on 11 June to approve a substantial $335 million aid commitment for the upcoming consortium meeting.[102]

In India, the announcement of devaluation triggered a hostile reaction with many from the Congress Party joining the Communists in criticizing Mrs. Gandhi's action. The attacks on her leadership were harsh. The left stridently complained she was becoming a pawn of the United States. Congress Party President Kamaraj, who stood on the moderate left, was particularly incensed about her failure to heed his judgment. When Finance Minister Sachin Chaudhuri, the Calcutta company law specialist who replaced T. T. Krishnamachari as Finance Minister, made a hash of defending the government's action in parliament, Mrs. Gandhi stood isolated. With virtually no one coming to her defense or arguing coherently that devaluation and decontrol meant a better economic future for India, the negative reaction continued to mount.[103]

Mrs. Gandhi, who never had much understanding of economics, found herself in a corner. Following the counsel of her advisers, she proceeded with devaluation without having prepared the ground politically. The attacks made the government panicky about follow-up actions, especially the license decontrol process—in itself, a key part of the economic policy shift. C. Subramaniam, a strong supporter of devaluation, blamed Finance Minister Chaudhuri for the failure. "If the doctor becomes panicky at the operating table, the patient dies. And that was what happened."[104] Ambassador Nehru believed that he and other economists supporting devaluation failed to realize that the rupee exchange rate, unchanged for many years, had assumed great symbolic importance in the public's mind. In devaluing the rupee, people thought India was somehow losing its manhood. "It was as if devaluation had castrated India," Nehru declared.[105]

In the meanwhile, the Soviet Union was growing increasingly unhappy about developments in India. The indications of improved Indian relations with the United States after Mrs. Gandhi's visit to Washington were unsettling. The adoption of more market-oriented economic policies by Mrs. Gandhi also displeased Moscow. As the Soviet Union remained a key supporter for Indian foreign policy and was becoming an increasingly important arms supplier, Mrs. Gandhi tried to mend fences during a visit to Moscow in July preceded by talks with Nasser and Tito, the two nonaligned leaders. In the talks in Egypt and Yugoslavia, Mrs. Gandhi pressed for an early reconvening of the Geneva Peace conference on Vietnam.[106]

Possibly inadvertently, possibly not, the Prime Minister made a foreign policy gesture in Moscow by agreeing to a communiqué on Vietnam that shifted India from an essentially neutral stance to one that echoed the Soviet line. In contrast to earlier Indian statements that linked reconvening the Geneva Conference and a halt to US bombing of North Vietnam, on this occasion Indira emphasized the need for the United States to take the first step. The 16 July communiqué also decried "aggressive actions of imperialist and other reactionary forces" against Vietnam.[107]

Washington was predictably unhappy about the shift in India's stance. In a 19 July memorandum to the President,

Rostow had advised that Bowles send her a "scorching personal letter" and Rusk "talked turkey" with the Indian chargé d'affaires. Rostow added that Mrs. Gandhi may have been mousetrapped by poor staff work which failed to grasp the nuances in the proposed communiqué language.[108] At a 21 July press conference, Johnson bristled in response to a question about the Indians, saying it would be helpful to see what North Vietnam would do, not just the United States.[109]

Still shaky in her first months as Prime Minister and weakened by the devaluation debacle, Mrs. Gandhi wanted to avoid the impression India was leaning toward the United States—as suggested by the rousing visit in Washington and her acceptance of devaluation. Criticism of US policy on Vietnam was a way to pacify her critics on the left—or so it may have seemed to Indira. Although American officialdom did not expect India to endorse US policy toward Vietnam, Washington was clearly annoyed by Mrs. Gandhi's less than nonaligned remarks. Ambassador Bowles wrote that when he commented Mrs. Gandhi was not saying anything more than the Pope or the UN Secretary-General, the curt response he got from Washington officials was, "The Pope and U Thant don't need our wheat."[110] The US-Indian political entente established during Indira's Washington visit proved a fragile and short-lived affair.

1966: "One More Drought"

As the summer of 1966 progressed, it became increasingly apparent that the monsoon rains were going to fail for a second year in a row. Coming on the heels of the poor 1965 monsoon, the 1966 drought proved a terrible blow, with Bihar in eastern India the worst hit area. The NSC history of the Indian food crisis stated:

> For India the prospect was one more drought, one more year of acute dependence on PL-480 imports, one more year of submission to US demands, one more year of exposure to the world as paupers. This outlook produced a sense of frustration, pessimism and fatalism.[111]

Lyndon Johnson made things much harder by following what became known as the "ship to mouth" policy—keeping the supply line so tight that foodgrains had to move directly from ships to the consumers in order to avert famine. On 23 August a recommendation from Secretaries Freeman and Rusk and AID

Administrator Bell urged the release of 2.5 million tons of wheat to prevent a break in the grain pipeline. Johnson refused to act, writing on the covering memo: "We must hold onto all the wheat we can. Send nothing unless we break an iron bound agreement by not sending."[112]

Because the United States itself suffered from drought in 1966, the crop outlook was poor. Wheat stocks were down, in part because of the large-scale PL 480 shipments to India in 1965. Johnson worried that another year of massive wheat exports to India could drive up bread prices, aggravating inflationary pressures that were already beginning to build up because of the Vietnam War.[113] The President cautioned Mrs. Gandhi in a 31 August letter, "We will do what we can to help you through the difficult food situation you face in the months ahead although the help we may be able to give may not be as much as we both would want."[114]

In September and October, Walt Rostow sent the President more memoranda warning about a break in the food pipeline early in 1967 unless he authorized wheat shipments. Johnson continued to sit tight. He kept his own counsel, but followed the India situation intensely, even receiving detailed weekly rainfall maps.[115] Johnson's knowledge of Indian agriculture impressed B. K. Nehru, despite the fact that the President's refusal to authorize more food exports frustrated the envoy.[116] In early November, the President rebuffed a plea from Secretaries Freeman and Rusk to approve an additional wheat shipment.

Disturbed by reports from the Agriculture Department that India was not fully implementing the new policies, Johnson sent a team of Agriculture Department experts to make an on-the-spot assessment. He wanted his own private appraisal of the situation and of how well India was doing in implementing the new farm policies. Because Johnson regarded Bowles as a special pleader for India, the President lacked confidence in Embassy reporting.[117]

In view of the possible need for congressional approval for another large-scale Indian food operation, Johnson also wanted to prepare the ground for sending a request forward to Capitol Hill. The President, therefore, had Freeman organize a separate bipartisan congressional group (Senators Miller and McGhee and Congressmen Poage and Dole—all agriculture specialists) to make its own assessment of India's needs and performance.[118] Both the Agriculture Department and congressional teams found the food situation grave, concluded that the Indians were fulfilling their policy reform commitments, and urged prompt action by Johnson to prevent famine in the early months of 1967.[119]

When the American press became aware of Johnson's game of hardball, the *New York Times* and the *Washington Post* roundly criticized use of pressure tactics on an India confronted with the specter of famine.[120] Stung by the media criticism and with the recommendations from the teams in hand, Johnson finally decided to release some wheat. He had Ambassador Nehru, who left Washington for New York in anger about Johnson's stonewalling tactics, called to the White House. The President personally assured the envoy he was not going to let Indians starve. Although the administration made no public announcement until the congressional group formally submitted its report, Johnson instructed Freeman to start lining up the necessary ships to move grain as rapidly as possible to India.[121]

On 22 December, four months after the initial memorandum recommending a food shipment, Johnson finally authorized Freeman to announce the allocation of 900,000 tons of PL 480 wheat. The immediate crisis was averted. For Indian officials trying to deal with the situation on the ground, Johnson's tactics were tremendously frustrating and irritating. "We were working in an emergency period then," Agriculture Minister C. Subramaniam recalled with some bitterness, "even a week's failure in supply would create grave difficulties. That, from far off, people couldn't realize. That is why I have said the United States always gives but does not give graciously."[122]

At one point during the crisis, Mrs. Gandhi telephoned Johnson to make a personal plea that he release wheat. Her press adviser, Sharada Prasad, present during the conversation, remembered the Prime Minister clenching her fingers tightly on the telephone. Talking to Johnson, she was friendly and charming, but when she hung up, she said angrily, "I don't ever want us ever to have to beg for food again."[123]

Once satisfied that India's need was genuine and the farm policy performance good, Johnson turned his attention to enlisting other countries in sharing the burden with the United States.

He agreed to send five million more tons in 1967 to India—as State, Agriculture, and AID recommended—but to release the final three million tons only when other donors provided a similar amount. At Johnson's insistence, the World Bank organized a Food for India Consortium to prod possible donors. To underscore his interest, Johnson sent Under Secretary of State Eugene Rostow (brother of the NSC's Walt Rostow) on a global sales mission. He told Rostow he wanted to raise more food for India, and also to show Congress that US allies, even if critical about Vietnam policy, were willing to cooperate with him in facing other grave problems, such as the potential Indian famine.[124]

After Rostow's return, Johnson transmitted a major message to Congress in early February urging the additional five million tons of PL 480 to help meet India's needs. Once more, Congress responded positively, approving a joint resolution endorsing food aid for India without significant opposition. The President signed the joint resolution on 1 April. Later in the month, two rounds of Food for India consortia meetings produced substantial additional supplies from other countries.[125]

The Indian general elections in February 1967—the fourth since independence—resulted in unexpectedly severe losses for the Congress Party. The party barely gained an absolute majority in parliament, winning only 283 of 520 seats. In eight of seventeen states, the Congress lost control of the state governments to opposition parties. Many Congress bosses, including the man most responsible for putting Mrs. Gandhi in office, K. Kamaraj, lost at the polls. The setback represented, in part, a vote of no-confidence about her handling of economic difficulties, the food crisis, and the unpopular devaluation of the rupee. Indira remained as Prime Minister, but agreed to accept Morarji Desai, her former rival, as Deputy Prime Minister and Finance Minister.

India somehow made it through to the 1967 monsoon without suffering famine. Fourteen million tons of American wheat, or about 20 percent of the US wheat crop, made the crucial difference, providing food for 90 million Indians. In the summer of 1967, the rains were happily plentiful. Food production jumped ahead in response to the new agriculture policies, the first sign of India's green revolution that, over the next decade, would result in self-sufficiency in food production. The crisis eased.

The whole experience, however, helped sour Mrs. Gandhi's attitude toward Washington in addition to making her determined never again to allow India to find itself in the same desperate food position.[126] A proud Mrs. Gandhi felt India's humiliating situation personally. As if to underline her country's independence from the United States, Mrs. Gandhi made a point of annoying Washington periodically by public gestures on Vietnam, such as the warm greetings she sent Ho Chi Minh on his seventy-seventh birthday.[127]

What motivated Lyndon Johnson in implementing the "ship to mouth" policy? What was he trying to achieve in putting the Indians through the wringer with his handling of food aid? Most Indian observers, and some Americans as well, including Agriculture Secretary Orville Freeman, believed he acted out of spite to punish Mrs. Gandhi for her public opposition on Vietnam.[128] Others close to Johnson, while admitting his annoyance over India's Vietnam policy, denied this lay behind his tactics. Walt Rostow and Dean Rusk stoutly maintained the President was using the leverage of food shipments to press for agricultural policy changes and then to ensure the implementation of the new policies.[129] "The whole thing gained him not a nickel politically. He offended Indian nationalism by his tactics. But he was playing a long-term game to get India to feed its people, and he succeeded," Rostow asserted.[130]

Although Agriculture Minister Subramaniam disliked Johnson's approach, he did not "connect it with Vietnam." Subramaniam stated, "Johnson thought he was driving Indian agriculture. We had already changed our policy, but implementation was important. Perhaps he thought that unless this pressure was there the policy wouldn't be properly implemented."[131] USAID Director John P. Lewis, no admirer of Johnson, also did not attribute his handling of the food crisis to Vietnam. Lewis believed the President was just following his "baseline mode" of being a bully in the way he dealt with the Indians.[132] Ambassador B. K. Nehru remained puzzled about what motivated Johnson, but commented that at no time did any American official mention India's policy on Vietnam in connection with the hold-up in food shipments.[133]

Harold Saunders, then on the NSC, thought Johnson was genuinely worried about the prospect of an India that would depend forever on the wheat fields of Kansas to feed it and was ready to exert enormous pressure to ensure full implementation of the new agricultural policies.[134] Other factors influencing Johnson's tactics, in Saunder's opinion, were the shortfall in US wheat supplies because of the US drought and 1965 shipments to India, the link between food exports to India and bread prices in US supermarkets, the impact on domestic inflation, the reaction of the Congress to the need to fund additional help for India and, presumably, Johnson's annoyance over Indira's stance on Vietnam.[135] Howard Wriggins, on the NSC staff at the time, agreed with Saunders. Although Wriggins believed Vietnam was a factor, he did not doubt Johnson's sincerity in wanting to see India able to feed itself as well as the overall complexity of food issue.[136] No one will ever know for certain what motivated President Johnson, but the author accepts Saunder's and Wriggins' views as the most plausible explanation.

The green revolution would presumably have succeeded without Johnson's pressure tactics, but, because of them, Indians from Mrs. Gandhi on down made certain that their country would become self-sufficient in foodgrain production and never again have to face the indignity suffered during the 1965 and 1966 droughts. Johnson achieved his goal—India could feed itself—but the cost was high for Indo-American relations. As Lawrence Veit, US Treasury Attaché in New Delhi in the early 1970s wrote, "The United States reaped a harvest of Indian wrath which endured for more than a decade."[137]

In addition to the affront from Johnson's tight-fisted approach to PL 480, the devaluation fiasco caused resentment in India, much of it directed against the United States. The failure of the consortium to provide the additional aid the World Bank had promised to cushion the impact of devaluation left Indian economic policy officials feeling they were badly let down.[138] Although the Aid to India Consortium redeemed the pledge of $900 million in nonproject assistance in 1966—nearly half a year after devaluation—the consortium failed to provide promised increased aid during the following two years. For 1967-

1968, when the World Bank estimated nonproject aid requirements at $750 million, the consortium offered only $295 million. To make up the difference, the Bank called for $1.275 billion in 1968-1969. At the May 1968 consortium meeting, the donors "came up miserably short," pledging only $642 million—little more than half the amount the World Bank projected.[139]

Senior Indian officials like I. G. Patel, then top economist in the Department of Economic Affairs and India's representative to the consortium meetings, were bitter. Patel told AID Director John Lewis:

> The government had entered into the 1966 transaction in good faith. At home it had sustained abuse, reverses and charges of boot-licking. Now the quid pro quo had withered . . . . Never again would India allow itself to become so vulnerably dependent on external assistance.[140]

After the electoral setback, a weakened Mrs. Gandhi began to adjust her policies and her advisers. Despite Finance Minister Morarji Desai's conservative views, economic policies began to revert to the previous system of controls. Liberalization was set back. Foreign aid advisers and like-minded Indian colleagues lost influence. Pro-market policy voices like Subramaniam and Mehta were eased out. Politically, Mrs. Gandhi was in the process of shifting to the left, strengthening her base of support for the showdown that she felt was looming for control of the Congress with the party bosses.[141]

The Non-Proliferation Treaty: India Says No

After China exploded a nuclear weapon in October 1964, one of Washington's major nonproliferation policy concerns was that New Delhi not follow suit to become the world's sixth nuclear power. And the threat was not merely theoretical. Ever since independence, India had developed a substantial civil nuclear energy program, headed by the dynamic Dr. Homi Bhabha until his death in an airplane crash in 1965. Jealous of its newly won independence, India had already proven difficult—from the US standpoint—in nonproliferation negotiations, opposing American efforts to impose international controls as an infringement on sovereignty as far back as the 1947 UN discussions regarding the Baruch Plan for international control of

Courtesy of the LBJ Library

12 September 1967, President Johnson with Morarji Desai, Deputy Prime Minister of India.

atomic energy. India and the United States, nonetheless, cooperated in the Atoms for Peace program and in the construction of the Tarapur nuclear power plant near Bombay.[142]

The initial Indian response after the Chinese explosion was encouraging. The CIA reported that the Indian cabinet would continue the country's long-standing policy of not producing nuclear weapons.[143] A secret session of Congress Party leaders endorsed Shastri's decision not to proceed with an Indian weapons program.[144] Several months later, in early 1965, Dr. Homi Bhabha reiterated this position when he met with Under Secretary of State George Ball. Bhabha stressed that India needed to show some "peaceful" nuclear achievement to offset the prestige China had gained by testing. The Indian AEC chief asserted India, if it wished to do so, could produce a nuclear device in 18 months.[145]

Prominent US scientist, Dr. Jerome Wiesner of the Massachusetts Institute of Technology, visited India in early 1965 at the urging of Washington to explore ways to offset the Chinese explosion. Writing President Johnson, Wiesner said he found no "simple technical spectacular" but urged a "determined effort to ward off the Indian nuclear decision." Wiesner believed the Indians could produce a weapon in two to three years.[146]

During this period, India tried to get a UN sponsored guarantee against the Chinese nuclear threat. Neither the Americans nor the Soviets were forthcoming. In the fall of 1965, Ambassador B. K. Nehru commented, "It is all very well to ask a person not to defend himself, but then somebody else has got to take on that defense."[147] In June 1966, the NSC considered the Indian nuclear issue. Leading off the meeting, Johnson said he was worried by pressures for India to go nuclear, expressing his view that India's "economic progress and the stability of the whole area depend on India not going nuclear." The follow-on discussion was, however, diffuse and there were no clear-cut conclusions about how to influence India to close the door on the nuclear option.[148]

In the following two years, the United States and the Soviet Union worked together to shape the Non-Proliferation Treaty in an effort to bar further proliferation. Although India came under heavy pressure from both countries to adhere to the NPT, New Delhi in the end refused. The policy debate in India focused on a number of issues, but two were primary. First was India's contention that the NPT was an "unequal" arrangement between nuclear haves and have-nots. In contrast to the 1963 Limited Test Ban Treaty, which India signed and which imposed obligations on all parties, New Delhi found the NPT a one-sided affair. Only the have-nots had to make concessions, forgoing any further prospect of developing nuclear explosions, even for peaceful purposes, and had to accept safeguards on all nuclear facilities. The Indians complained that the nuclear weapons states—the haves—neither moved toward disarmament nor placed their own nuclear facilities under international safeguards.

Second was Indian concern about the threat a nuclear China posed, especially in the hostile atmosphere that prevailed after the 1962 Sino-Indian War. New Delhi found the NPT silent on the question of security guarantees for non-nuclear powers against the threat of nuclear attack.[149] Although Indira Gandhi sent her principal aide and cabinet secretary, L. K. Jha, to Moscow, London, and Washington to explore nuclear guarantees against the Chinese threat,[150] Jha was unable to develop a formula that satisfied all concerned.[151]

After considerable debate among nuclear and foreign policy officials and in the cabinet, Mrs. Gandhi decided not to sign the NPT. India became one of the handful of holdout countries, along with Pakistan, Israel, Egypt, South Africa, Argentina, and Brazil. Given US-Soviet pressures, this was not an easy decision, but, according to then Foreign Secretary C. S. Jha, India found the negative elements of the NPT too great to agree to adherence.[152]

Despite the decision to reject the NPT, Mrs. Gandhi reiterated that India was not going to develop nuclear weapons. The Prime Minister also refused to give the go-ahead for work on a peaceful nuclear explosion. A few years later, after the Bangladesh crisis, Mrs. Gandhi would change her mind and give the Indian AEC the green light to proceed with a nuclear test. At the end of the 1960s, however, India maintained a position of ambivalence. Its refusal to sign the NPT kept open the nuclear option.

1967: Revised US Military Supply Policy

Although the bilateral focus between the United States and India shifted to economic issues after the 1965 War, the question of US arms supply to South Asia continued to nag.[153] The new American envoy to Pakistan, Eugene Locke, a Texan friend of President Johnson who replaced career diplomat Walter McConaughy, fixed on this issue as the key to rebuilding the battered relationship. Locke argued that if Washington wanted to restrain Pakistan from moving even closer to Communist China, it should ease the arms embargo, as President Ayub requested, at least to permit the Pakistanis to obtain spare parts for aircraft and other equipment the United States previously supplied.[154]

Ambassador Bowles vehemently disagreed. If $1 billion of arms aid failed to deter Pakistan from cozying up to Beijing, Bowles asked, why should $8 million in spare parts do the trick? The envoy warned that Washington should expect a "devastating" Indian reaction to a change in the arms policy, which he also thought would preclude any chance for Indo-Pakistan agreement on arms limitations.[155] The disagreement between the two ambassadors grew shriller. Not above sending private *ad hominem* arguments to Johnson via White House aide Marvin Watson, Locke charged Bowles favored India over Pakistan contrary to "the belief of President Johnson." Locke also alleged Bowles wanted to avoid the embarrassment of having personal statements that the United States would never again arm Pakistan proven wrong.[156]

After a lengthy interdepartmental review, Washington finally announced a new arms policy in April 1967 that reopened the door for Pakistan—but only a bit. Increasingly preoccupied with Vietnam and disinclined to reengage himself personally in the South Asian arms question, Johnson left the policy formulation to State and Defense.[157] The new approach called for cash sales of spare parts for weapons the United States previously supplied on a "case-by-case" basis, but continued the ban on sales of new weapons systems and barred credits or grant military assistance.[158] The basic purpose was to align US arms supply policy with the reduced US security engagement in the subcontinent.[159]

The new policy further upset Pakistan, contrary to Locke's prognosis. Still seething over Washington's treatment during the 1965 War, Pakistan judged the partial lifting of the embargo as insufficient to cause any significant warming in relations with the United States or reduction in the burgeoning arms relationship with China. The Indians were relieved that the United States had not opened the door wider for a resumption of arms supplies to Pakistan. New Delhi publicly grumbled, nonetheless, about the change which it claimed would help Pakistan.[160] The new policy, in fact, benefitted India more since New Delhi was far less reliant on US arms than Pakistan.

If Washington was pulling back from South Asia, Moscow was stepping up its engagement, pursuing better relations with Pakistan. In the face of the deepening Sino-Soviet rift, Moscow hoped to counter China's growing influence with Pakistan and to reduce even further the US role with its erstwhile ally. In the spring of 1965, the Soviets received President Ayub Khan for a well-publicized state visit to Moscow. The communiqué issued at the end of Ayub visit—and the failure to speak of Kashmir as belonging to India when Shastri came a month later—suggested a shift by the Russians toward a more neutral stance.[161] The Soviets continued the more even-handed approach through the 1965 Kashmir War and in their mediation at the Taskhent conference.

Even though the Soviets substantially increased their arms shipments to India after 1965, they crossed an important policy threshold with Pakistan in 1968 when Moscow agreed to initiate exports of sophisticated arms, including tanks, jet aircraft, armored personnel carriers, and artillery.[162] The Pakistanis, in turn, said "Thank you" to Moscow by not renewing the lease for the US base at Peshawar. Despite the fact that the development of sophisticated space satellites greatly reduced the facility's importance to US intelligence agencies, closing the Peshawar base symbolized the dramatic decline in US-Pakistani relations. Pakistan's decision to withdraw from active participation in the SEATO alliance was a further reflection of the growing strains with Washington.

The Indians were, not surprisingly, unhappy about the prospect of Soviet arms for Pakistan. Although opposition parties lost a vote in parliament to condemn the Soviets by a 200-61 count, Mrs. Gandhi made her displeasure known through private channels and spoke critically in public of the Soviet action.[163] The relative restraint in Mrs. Gandhi's response was explained by her domestic move to the left politically, by India's increased dependence on the Soviets for military equipment, and by her own assessment that private diplomacy was the best way of influencing Moscow.

For the same reasons, India reacted with relative restraint, in August 1968, after Soviet tanks crushed the liberal Communist government of Alexander Dubcek in Czechoslovakia. Despite the fact that Mrs. Gandhi strongly "deplored" the Soviet action, India refused to join in the vote to "condemn" Moscow in the United Nations, abstaining in the Security Council. As in 1956 when the Soviets crushed the Hungarian revolution, India refused to join non-Communist nations in condemning the Soviet action in Czechoslovakia.

At the end of 1968, India's relations with Moscow remained under strain. The attempt by the Soviets to pursue a more balanced policy in the subcontinent—by providing arms to both

India and Pakistan—encountered troubles not too dissimilar to those the United States experienced earlier. Soviet promises that the weapons furnished Pakistan would not be used against India met with incredulity after the experience with similar US pledges.[164]

Relations with the United States also suffered. The backlash against Johnson's PL 480 policy and devaluation were one cause. Another damaging factor was the reaction in India to revelations of widespread funding of cultural and educational groups by the Central Intelligence Agency.[165] Indian intellectuals were greatly offended to learn that prestigious organizations, like the Asia Foundation, were secretly receiving funds from the CIA. Feeling tricked and betrayed, some Indian intellectuals led an anti-US crusade, alleging academic imperialism.[166] The Soviets and their local Communist allies and fellow-travelers took full advantage of the exposures to further tarnish the US image in India.

A Summing Up: Indo-US Relations On the Decline

The five years Lyndon Johnson served in the White House saw a major shift in relations between India and the United States. For India, after the ignominious defeat by China in 1962, these were trying years, marked by sluggish economic performance and near famine. Only the 1965 war, where India thwarted Pakistan's attempt to seize Kashmir by force, buoyed morale. Pandit Nehru passed from the scene in May 1964. His successor, Lal Bahadur Shastri, was in office barely nineteen months before he died at Tashkent. Indira Gandhi, who succeeded to power in January 1966, was still struggling to consolidate her political control when Johnson's term ended in January 1969.

The United States, New Delhi thought, had treated India badly. Part of the problem related to Johnson's brusque Texan style, better designed for US Congressional arm-twisting than dealing with touchy South Asians. The rude canceling of the Shastri visit in 1965 and insensitive management of PL 480 policy left scars, whatever the President's motives. The rupee devaluation debacle and Washington's unwillingness to meet what India saw as its legitimate defense needs additionally soured New Delhi's attitude toward the United States.

Americans were also disenchanted. India seemed to be going nowhere economically. Unable to feed itself, India was hardly the model of democratic development Washington hoped other Third World countries would emulate as a rival to Communist China. Official Washington was asking what the point was of pouring hundreds of millions of dollars into a country that had performed poorly and remained at odds with much of US foreign policy? Was it worthwhile to continue to pay so much attention to South Asia, especially at a time when 500,000 American troops were fighting to save South Vietnam from a Communist takeover? All the United States had to show for more than a decade of trying to promote peace between India and Pakistan was the 1965 War. The two countries had made graphically clear that they were far more worried about each other than any external threat.

As the clock ran down on the Johnson administration, a sense of exhaustion with South Asia and its seemingly insuperable problems had taken hold even among liberal Democrats favorably inclined toward India. The glum mood of 1969 about India, contrasted strikingly with the optimism of January 1961, when John F. Kennedy became President. In the intervening eight years, because of the Vietnam war and the revised appraisal of the subcontinent's relevance to US interests, New Delhi no longer was seen as having major strategic importance. India, in Washington's eyes, had become just a big country full of poor people.

NOTES

1. Ambassador Nehru told the author the loss of access was frustrating after his easy relationship with President Kennedy. After Nehru finally met privately with Johnson in mid-1965, he was able to establish friendly personal relations and regained his access. (Interview with Ambassador B. K. Nehru, 12 January 1991).

2. Interviews with Orville Freeman, 29 October 1990; Robert Komer, 2 November 1990. According to Freeman, who worked closely with Johnson on South Asia food problems, the Indians irked Johnson by not paying him the attention he felt was due a Vice President of the United States during his May 1961 visit.

3. Interview with Robert Komer, 2 November 1990.

4. Memorandum to President Johnson from Robert Komer, 24 February 1964, Lyndon Baines Johnson (LBJ) Library.

5. Letter from Prime Minister Nehru to Lyndon Johnson, 14 April 1964. Johnson Library.

6. This was quite true at the time. Agitated by US military aid to India after the 1962 war with China, the Pakistanis continued to reject US warnings not to develop further their relationship with China. Johnson had a stormy meeting on this issue with Foreign Minister Bhutto in December 1963.

7. Memorandum reporting the meeting between President Johnson and Indira Gandhi, 15 April 1964. Johnson Library.

8. Embassy New Delhi telegram to the State Department, 20 March 1964; interview with Phillips Talbot, 26 June 1990.

9. Memorandum from Komer to Bundy, 23 November 1963.

10. Memorandum to the President from Secretary Rush on "Next Steps on Military Aid to India and Pakistan," 11 December 1963, LBJ Library.

11. Memorandum from General Taylor to the Secretary of Defense, 23 December 1963.

12. Memorandum to the President from the Secretary of State, 16 January 1964; and National Security Action Memorandum 279, 8 February 1964, LBJ Library.

13. Interview with Ambassador David Schneider, who was in charge of Indian affairs in the State Department at the time of the F–104 request, 24 October 1990.

14. *Washington Post*, 20 May 1964.

15. Interview with Robert Komer, 2 November 1990.

16. Chester Bowles, *Promises to Keep, My Years in Public Life, 1941-1969* (New York: Harper & Row, 1971), pp. 560-63, provided a puzzling and seemingly inaccurate account of the arms agreement. Bowles claimed the decision to proceed was derailed because of Nehru's death although, in fact, this event postponed the signing for only two weeks. Surprisingly, Bowles made no mention of the major policy dispute: US refusal to include F-104s in the package.

17. Telegram from Secretary McNamara to Minister of Defense Chavan, 3 June 1964; *Washington Post*, 7 June 1964.

18. Lorne Kavic, *India's Quest for Security: Defense Policies, 1947-1965* (Berkeley, CA: University of California Press, 1967), pp. 198-200.

19. Embassy New Delhi telegram to State Department, 16 July 1964.

24. Central Intelligence Agency, Office of Current Intelligence, OCI No. 1579/64, 27 May 1964.

25. According to Galbraith, Nehru once told him—only half joking—that he was the last Englishman to rule India (Interview with Ambassador Galbraith, 9 July 1990).

26. Bowles, p. 497.

27. Telegram for the President and Secretary of State from Harriman, sent from Embassy New Delhi, 7 March 1965.

28. Ibid.

29. Bowles, p. 498.

30. "National Security Council Narrative and Guide to Selected Documents on US-South Asia Relations during the Kennedy and Johnson Administrations," p. 5, LBJ Library.

31. Department of State telegram to Embassy New Delhi 2155, 14 April 1965.

32. Interview with Ambassador B. K. Nehru, 10 January 1991.

33. Memorandum from Robert Komer to McGeorge Bundy, 21 April 1965, LBJ Library.

34. *Keesing's Contemporary Archives* (Bristol, England: Keesing Publications Ltd.), 28 August-4 September 1965, p. 20927.

35. Ibid., pp. 20927-20928.

36. A study by the State Department's Bureau of Intelligence and Research reported the use of infantry weapons by the Pakistanis but not tanks, as alleged by the Indians, and found only minor Indian use of equipment—not substantial amounts as claimed by the Pakistanis. Memorandum from the Director of Intelligence and Research to the Acting Secretary of State, "Alleged Use of US-Supplied Military Equipment by India and Pakistan in the Rann of Kutch," 13 May 1965.

37. Memorandum of Conversation between Secretary Rusk, Ambassador Nehru, Deputy Assistant Secretary of State Handley, and India Country Director Schneider, 8 May 1965.

38. William J. Barnds, *India, Pakistan and the Great Powers* (New York: Praeger, 1972), p. 200.

39. Ibid., p. 201; Sivaji Ganguly, *US Policy toward South Asia* (Boulder, CO: Westview Press, 1990), pp. 120-24.

40. *Keesing's Archives*, 4-11 December 1965, p. 21103.

41. Department of State Study, "The India-Pakistan War and its Aftermath" (undated but presumably prepared in late 1968), pp. 4-6, NSC History, LBJ Library; *Keesing's Contemporary Archives*, 4-11 December 1965, p. 21104.

42. Memorandum for the President from Robert Komer, 31 August 1965.

43. Department of State telegram to US Mission to the United Nations, 31 August 1965; Embassy New Delhi telegram to Department of State, 1 September 1965.

44. Embassy New Delhi "flash" telegram to the State Department for the President and Secretary, 2 September 1965.

45. Department of State telegram to New Delhi, 2 September 1965.

46. State Department telegram to New Delhi, 3 September 1965.

47. Embassy New Delhi telegrams to State Department, 2 September and 4 September 1965.

48. As early as 1952, Jawaharlal Nehru had warned that India would respond to a Pakistan attack on Kashmir by striking elsewhere. The Pakistanis were well aware of this plan, but presumably doubted the Shastri government would risk all-out war. (Ganguly, pp. 123-24)

49. State Department telegram to Embassies New Delhi and Karachi, 6 September 1965.

50. Memorandum of breakfast meeting between Secretary Rusk, Under Secretary Thomas Mann, Assistant Secretary Douglas MacArthur, and Senators Symington, Church, Hickenlooper, and Case, 8 September 1965.

51. State Department telegrams to Embassies Karachi and New Delhi, 8 September 1965; and Memorandum for the President from Robert Komer, 7 September 1965.

52. Interview with Robert Komer, 2 November 1990.

53. State Department study, "India-Pakistan War and its Aftermath," pp. 11-13, National Security Council (NSC) Histories, LBJ Library.

54. *Keesing's Archives*, 4-11 December 1965, p. 21107.

55. Dean Rusk, Oral History, p. 36, LBJ Library. Rusk went on to say, "I once, in a semi-joking way, told the Russian Ambassador that if he wanted them we would be glad to give him all of our old memoranda on efforts we had made over the past twenty years to try to solve things between India and Pakistan . . ."

56. Interviews with Robert Komer, 5 August 1990, and David Schneider, 24 October 1990.

57. Oral history statement by Dean Rusk, p. 35, LBJ Library.

58. Memorandum for President Johnson from Robert Komer in preparation for the 9 June South Asia aid meeting, 8 June 1965, LBJ Library.

59. Memorandum from McGeorge Bundy for the Secretaries of State and Defense and the Administrator of AID, "Presidential Decisions on Aid to India/Pakistan," 9 June 1965.

60. Harold Saunders, "The History," in National Security Council (NSC) Histories, *India's Food Crisis, 1966-67*, p.1, LBJ Library. Saunders joined the NSC as Komer's assistant during the Kennedy administration. When Johnson put Komer in charge of "the other war" in Vietnam, Saunders became the senior staffer on the Near East and South Asia. In the 1970s, he shifted to the State Department, where he served as Director for Intelligence and Research and Assistant Secretary of State for Near East and South Asian Affairs.

61. Interview with Walt W. Rostow, 30 November 1990.

62. Memorandum of conversation between Ambassador Nehru and Under Secretary Thomas Mann, 1 July 1965.

63. Interview with B. K. Nehru, 12 January 1991.

64. David D.H. Denoon, *Devaluation under Pressure* (Cambridge, MA.: MIT Press, 1986), p. 32.

65. Ibid., pp. 60-61; Interview with Professor John P. Lewis, 15 April 1991.

66. Memorandum for the President from AID Administrator David Bell, 16 June 1965; NSC History; Department of State report on "India's Food Crisis, 1965-1967," pp. 5-7, LBJ Library.

67. Orville Freeman, *World Without Hunger* (New York: Frederick A. Praeger, 1968), p. 152; interview with Freeman, 29 October 1990.

68. See C. Subramaniam, *The New Strategy for Indian Agriculture* (New Delhi: Vikas, 1979). Based on a series of lectures in Australia, the book outlined how Subramaniam developed his policies that led to India's Green Revolution.

69. Interviews with Orville Freeman, 29 October 1990, and C. Subramaniam, 15 February 1991.

70. Lyndon Baines Johnson, *The Vantage Point: Perspectives of the Presidency, 1963-1969* (New York: Holt, Rhinehart and Winston, 1971), pp. 222-24.

71. Interview with Walt W. Rostow, 30 November 1990.

72. Interview with Orville Freeman, 29 October 1990.

73. Interview with Robert Komer, 5 August 1990; Johnson, pp. 225-26.

74. *Washington Post*, 12 October 1965.

75. State Department telegram 659 to Embassy New Delhi, 8 October 1965.

76. Memorandum for the record by the Secretary of State, 27 October 1965; Memorandum for the President from Under Secretary of Agriculture Schnittker, 23 October 1965; State Department telegram to New Delhi, for Bowles from the Secretary, 29 October 1965.

77. Interview with Orville Freeman, 29 October 1990. Freeman didn't recall the date of the talk in the Rose Garden but it was presumably in October or early November 1965.

78. Text of the "Treaty of Rome" was transmitted in a 26 November 1965 telegram from Embassy Rome to the Texas White House, "Eyes Only for the President from Secretary Freeman, " LBJ Library.

79. *Washington Post*, 11 December 1965.

80. Memorandum for the record of President Johnson's 20 December 1965 meeting with Indian Agriculture Minister Subramaniam. Also attending were Secretary Freeman, Ambassador Nehru, and Robert Komer. LBJ Library.

81. Interview with C. Subramaniam, 15 February 1991. In rural India, the title "nawab" was used by Muslim landed gentry and was roughly equivalent to the English or French "Count." The "district" was the basic unit of administration in India, similar to a US county. Terming someone the "district nawab" was thus about the same as calling a person the local big-shot in the United States.

82. Interview with B.K. Nehru, 12 January 1991.

83. Memorandum of conversation between Indian Finance Secretary Bhoothalingam and NSC Staffer Robert Komer, 6 October 1965.

84. Department of State Telegram to Embassy New Delhi, "NODIS For Ambassador from Secretary," 10 November 1965.

85. *Washington Post*, 2 January 1966. Ostensibly, TTK resigned after Shastri refused to squelch charges that TTK's son was engaged in corrupt practices.

86. Interview with B.K. Nehru, 11 January 1991.

87. Letter from Prime Minister Shastri to President Johnson, 6 January 1966. LBJ Library.

88. Of low caste origin, Kamaraj rose through the ranks of the Madras Congress Party to become an excellent Chief Minister in the 1950s. The fact that he spoke neither Hindi nor English probably deprived him of the chance of becoming Prime Minister; instead he had to settle for the role of kingmaker as the Congress Party president.

89. Department of State telegram 1422 to Embassy New Delhi, 7 February 1966, reporting B.K. Nehru's meeting with President Johnson.

90. State Department telegram 2342 to Saigon, 18 February 1978, provided instructions to Humphrey for the upcoming visit to New Delhi.

91. Memorandum to the President from Secretary of State Dean Rusk, 26 March 1966, LBJ Library.

92. Inder Malhotra, *Indira Gandhi: A Personal and Political Biography* (London: Hodder & Stoughton, 1989), p. 95.

93. Komer commented to the President on the eve of Mrs. Gandhi's arrival, "I think that we finally have the Indians where we've wanted them ever since last April—with the slate wiped clean of previous commitments and India coming to us asking for a new relationship on the terms we want." (Memorandum to the President from Robert Komer, 27 March 1965, LBJ Library)

94. Interview with Robert Komer, 2 November 1990.

95. Summary Record of Joint Briefing by President Johnson and Prime Minister Gandhi, 28 March 1966, LBJ Library.

96. Johnson, p. 227.

97. Ibid.

98. David D.H. Denoon, *Devaluation under Pressure* (Cambridge, MA.: MIT Press, 1986), pp. 44, 66.

99. Interview with Walt Rostow, 30 November 1990.

100. Memorandum of the President's Meeting with Indian Planning Minister Mehta, 4 May 1966. The meeting was also attended by Ambassador Nehru, AID Administrator Bell, Deputy Assistant Secretary of State William Handley, and Walt Rostow, LBJ Library.

101. Ibid.

102. Johnson approved recommendations sent by David Bell (10 June) and Walt Rostow (11 June) to pledge up to $335 million for the World Bank consortium.

103. Ibid., pp. 47-48; Shashi Tharoor, *Reasons of State* (New Delhi: Vikas, 1982), pp. 65-66, 123-24, 129. When interviewed by Tharoor in July 1977, Mrs. Gandhi denied she had acted "because the Americans said so. . . . The decision," she stated [accurately], "had been practically taken in Shastriji's time. . . . I could have stopped it then, but I'd just come in and when I consulted these people who I thought knew more about it than I did, I followed their advice. I think it was a big mistake."

104. Interview with C. Subramaniam, 15 February 1991.

105. Interview with B.K. Nehru, 12 January 1991.

106. Zareer Masini, *Indira Gandhi: A Biography* (London: Hamish Hamilton, 1975), pp. 164-65.

107. *New York Times*, 22 July 1966. Embassy New Delhi telegram to the State Department, 18 July 1966, reports on the 16 July Moscow communiqué and provides the text of Bowles' sharp letter of protest.

108. Memo to the President from Walt Rostow, "An Appropriate U.S. Reaction to Mrs. Gandhi's action in Moscow," 19 July 1966.

109. *New York Times*, 22 July 1966.

110. Bowles, p. 526.

111. National Security Council (NSC) Histories, *India's Food Crisis, 1965-67*, pp. 19-20, LBJ Library.

112. President Johnson's handwritten comments on 24 August 1966 covering memorandum from Bromley Smith attaching a memo from Howard Wriggins in support of the State-Agriculture-AID recommendations.

113. Saunders, p. 3.

114. Letter from President Johnson to Prime Minister Gandhi, 31 August 1966.

115. Copies of the weekly India rain maps can be found at the LBJ Library.

116. Interview with B.K. Nehru, 27 February 1991; Johnson in his memoirs says with apparent accuracy , "I became an expert in the ton-by-ton movement of grain from the wheat fields of Kansas to ports like

Calcutta—how many ships were required to move how many tons and how long the operation took. I described myself as a 'kind of county agricultural agent with inter-continental clients.'" (*Johnson*, p. 226)

117. Interview with Walt Rostow, 30 November 1990.

118. NSC Histories, Saunders, "The History," p. 3; letter from Howard Wriggins to Ambassador Bowles, 12 November 1966.

119. Memorandum to the President from Secretary Freeman, "India—Analysis Team Report—Recommendation," 28 November 1966; Letter to Secretary Freeman from the Congressional team, 20 December 1966.

120. *New York Times*, 29 November 1966; *Washington Post*, 11 December 1966.

121. The NSC records and B.K. Nehru's memory differed somewhat. A 9 December 1966 Memorandum by Harold Saunders reported Rostow's telling Nehru by telephone that food would be forthcoming. Nehru, who was attending the Broadway musical "Cabaret" when Rostow spoke with him, only recalled Rostow's saying that the President wanted to see him the next day. During that meeting, according to Nehru, Johnson raised the food issue indirectly. He said when his daughter Luci asked about the press stories, he assured her the reports were wrong. "I told Luci I wasn't going to let any Indians starve," the Ambassador recalled Johnson saying. Interview with B.K. Nehru 12 January 1991. See also NSC Histories, *India's Food Crisis, 1966-1967* pp. 20-24.

122. Interview with C. Subramaniam, 15 February 1991. See also *Subramaniam*, pp. 52-54.

123. Interview with Sharada Prasad, 14 January 1991.

124. Interview with Eugene Rostow, 28 March 1991.

125. *India's Food Crisis, 1966-67*, pp. 24-28; Ganguly, pp. 179-80.

126. Masani, p. 164. Based on the author's interview in 1973 with L.K. Jha.

127. Malhotra, p. 101.

128. Interview with Orville Freeman, 29 October 1990. See also James W. Bjorkman, "Public Law 480 and the Policies of Self-Help and Short-Tether: Indo-American Relations, 1965-1968," in Lloyd and Suzanne Rudolph, eds., *The Regional Imperative* (Atlantic Highlands, NJ.: Humanities Press, 1980). Bjorkman's article asserted that Johnson's "fury over Indian pronouncements on Vietnam" were the driving force behind his dribbling out the food shipments.

129. Interview with Walt Rostow, 30 November 1990; Dean Rusk Oral History, Johnson Library.

130. Interview with Walt Rostow, 30 November 1990

131. Interview with C. Subramaniam, 15 February 1991.

132. John P. Lewis, *Essays in Indian Political Economy*, unpublished manuscript, chapter 4, pp. 49, 56.

133. Interviews with B.K. Nehru, 11 January and 27 February 1991.

134. Interview with Harold Saunders, 26 April 1991.

135. Saunders believed the interplay of domestic and international issues, both short- and long-term, made the Indian food crisis among the most complex issues Johnson faced as President. Interview with Harold Saunders, 26 April 1991.

136. Interview with Harold Wriggins, 29 May 1992.

137. Lawrence Veit, *India's Second Revolution: The Dimension of Development* (New York: Council on Foreign Relations, 1976), p. 144.

138. See chapter 5, "Pro-Liberalization Leverage—and the Lessons of the 60s," in John Lewis (Princeton: Princeton University Press forthcoming), *Essays in Indian Political Economy* for a well-researched account of the devaluation episode.

139. Ibid., Chapter 5, pp. 23-24.

140. Ibid, p. 25.

141. Malhotra, *Indira Gandhi*, pp. 108-09.

142. See Ashok Kapur, *India's Nuclear Option: Atomic Diplomacy and Decision Making* (New York: Praeger, 1976), pp. 93-119 for a discussion of India's nuclear diplomacy before the Chinese test.

143. CIA report (TDCS-314/04322-64), "Indian Government Reaction to Chicom Nuclear Explosion," 19 October 1964, LBJ Library.

144. Joseph Yager, ed., *Nonproliferation and U.S. Foreign Policy* (Washington: The Brookings Institution, 1980), p. 355.

145. Memorandum of Conversation between Dr. Homi Bhabha, Ambassador Nehru, and Under Secretary Ball, 22 February 1965.

146. Letter from Professor Wiesner to President Johnson, 24 February 1965. An 18 October 1965 CIA study said the Indians could produce a test device "in about a year or so." CIA Memorandum to the NSC, "The Indian Nuclear Capability," 18 October 1965.

147. Quoted in Yager, p. 356.

148. Summary of Notes of the 558th NSC Meeting, 9 June 1965, LBJ Library.

149. C. S. Jha, *From Bandung to Tashkent: Glimpses of India's Foreign Policy* (Madras: Sangam, 1983), pp. 299-300. At the time the NPT was under consideration, Jha was serving as India's Foreign Secretary.

150. Memorandum for President Johnson on the Jha Mission, undated but possibly 19 April 1967, LBJ Library.

151. Yager, p. 356; Jha, pp. 301-02.

152. Ibid., pp. 300-06; According to Jha, the Indian political leadership was in agreement against signing the NPT. In *Nuclear Diplomacy*, (p. 196) Kapur gave a different account. Kapur asserted that after her

civil service advisers split on the question, Mrs. Gandhi took the NPT issue to the cabinet where she found strong opposition to signing, Morarji Desai being among the hostile group.

153. In 1966, Washington permitted the purchase by both countries of so-called non-lethal items, i.e. most equipment other than weapons.

154. Embassy Rawalpindi telegram to the State Department, 11 August 1966. Johnson Library.

155. Embassy Saigon telegram to the State Department of 11 August 1966 reported Bowles' views. After meeting in Saigon on 5 August, Locke and Bowles reported their differing attitude on arms supply via separate cables to Washington. They continued their disagreement in messages sent later in August.

156. Undated letter for transmittal to the President sent via Marvin Watson from Ambassador Eugene Locke, Johnson Library. Locke asked that, without the President's permission, Watson show the letter to no one except Walt Rostow, then head of the NSC staff.

157. Rudolph, p. 110.

158. *New York Times*, 13 April 1967.

159. Rudolph pp. 111-13.

160. *New York Times*, 14 August 1967.

161. Robert H. Donaldson, *Soviet Policy toward India: Ideology and Strategy* (Cambridge, MA.: Harvard University Press) 1974, p. 204.

162. Ibid., p. 212.

163. Robert C. Horn, *Soviet-Indian Relations* (New York: Praeger, 1982), pp. 24-25.

164. Ibid., p. 26.

165. Bowles, pp. 544-45.

166. Letter from Professor Stephen Cohen, 29 May 1991.

Chapter VII

Nixon: The Tilt

$\mathbf{W}$hen Richard Nixon replaced Lyndon Johnson in the White House in January 1969, his main foreign policy concern lay on winding down the unpopular war in Vietnam. The new President was content to continue the disengaged approach toward South Asia which Johnson began after the 1965 India-Pakistan War.[1] As Henry Kissinger, the Harvard international relations specialist Nixon named to head the National Security Council, wrote in his memoirs, "When the Nixon administration took office, our policy objective on the subcontinent was, quite simply, to avoid adding another complication to our agenda."[2] There was little to suggest in 1969 that US policy toward South Asia would stir great emotion and controversy.

Nixon took office unusually experienced in foreign affairs after his eight years as Vice President under Eisenhower. He continued to pursue this interest as a private citizen in the 1960s, his travels taking him to South Asia in 1964 and again in 1967. On both occasions, the Indians received him with the minimum of appropriate protocol; the Pakistanis lionized the former Vice President.[3] This treatment presumably did nothing to lessen Nixon's preference for Pakistan, the erstwhile ally of the United States, and his dislike for India and its policy of nonalignment. "Nixon, to put it mildly," Kissinger stated, "was less susceptible to Indian claims of moral leadership than some of his predecessors; indeed, he viewed what he considered their alleged obsequiousness toward India as a prime example of liberal soft-headedness."[4]

The Indian Prime Minister reciprocated Nixon's lack of enthusiasm. She told one interviewer, "I think I had excellent relations with everybody [American presidents] except Mr. Nixon. And he had made up his mind beforehand."[5] Mrs. Gandhi could scarcely conceal her boredom in receiving the former Vice President when he called on her in 1967. After about twenty minutes of desultory conversation, she asked the Ministry of External Affairs escort—speaking in Hindi so Nixon would not understand—how much longer the session would last.[6]

Despite his personal leanings, Nixon's aim at the start of his administration was to have good relations with both India and Pakistan, continuing substantial economic assistance programs, as well as a large Peace Corps program in India. Nixon had no plans to revive the close military relationship with Pakistan which he strongly supported during the Eisenhower administration.[7]

In August 1969, six months after entering the White House, Nixon became the second serving Chief Executive to visit India, stopping there and in Pakistan en route from the Far East to Europe. The public welcome in New Delhi had none of the overwhelming enthusiasm Eisenhower received ten years earlier.[8] Official meetings were low-key, almost perfunctory. Neither Mrs. Gandhi nor Nixon displayed much warmth. The substantive discussions, mainly on Vietnam, lacked spark and animation.[9]

From New Delhi, Nixon flew to Lahore in West Pakistan, where he met President Yahya Khan, who had replaced Ayub Khan five months before.[10] The reception was warmer than in India, even though relations remained strained because of continued Pakistani resentment over US arms restrictions.[11] Nixon's discussions with Yahya were also more substantive than his talks in New Delhi. Previously, Pakistan's close ties with China had caused great tension with Washington. Now Nixon took advantage of these good relations to ask Yahya Khan to convey to the Chinese leadership his interest in an opening to China.[12] Thus began two years of secret diplomatic exchanges

Courtesy of the National Archives, Nixon Presidential Materials Staff

1 August 1969, President Richard M. Nixon accompanied by Acting President of India M. Hidayatullah, on arrival in New Delhi.

through the Pakistanis that led to the stunning Kissinger trip to Beijing in July 1971.

Mrs. Gandhi Defeats the Syndicate: Shifts to the Left

At the moment Nixon was traveling through South Asia, India was swept up in political civil war between Indira Gandhi and the Congress Party bosses. In 1969, after two years of shaky coexistence, Mrs. Gandhi and the Syndicate split over who would fill the largely ceremonial post of president after Zakir Husain died in April. The contest became a fight to the death after Mrs. Gandhi refused to support the choice of the party leadership, Sanjiva Reddy, instead backing the opposition candidate, Vice President V. V. Giri, a former Congress politician and labor leader.

Pro and anti-Indira politicians were furiously lobbying the country's national and state legislators, who formed the electoral college to pick the president. The struggle was rough for each side knew the loser would be finished politically. The battle was mainly over power, but had policy overtones as well. After the Congress Party's poor showing in 1967, Indira increasingly cast herself as a populist reformer, while trying to paint the bosses as right-wing supporters of big business and conservative rural interests. When she lost out to the Syndicate over the selection of the presidential nominee, the Prime Minister struck back by firing the Finance Minister, her conservative rival Morarji Desai, and nationalizing India's major banks, moves that the left-wing of the Congress Party and the Communists warmly welcomed.[13]

Mrs. Gandhi's candidate, V. V. Giri, won by an eyelash— 420,077 to 405,427. Indira had vanquished the Syndicate. In the aftermath, a polarized Congress Party formally split in November with 222 of 284 Congress members of parliament joining Mrs. Gandhi's faction, appropriately called the Congress (I)— short for Indira. Lacking the votes for a clear parliamentary majority, she depended on the support of the Communists and other small parties to remain in power until the 1971 elections. In struggling against the Syndicate, Mrs. Gandhi consciously shifted to the left politically, toward more socialist domestic policies, positioning herself as the champion of India's poor

1 August 1969, President Nixon addressing a state banquet in the Presidential Palace in New Delhi.

masses. Although foreign policy was not a basic issue, her populist domestic shift was paralleled by strengthened relations with the Soviets—a trend hardly pleasing to the Nixon administration.[14]

As Indira moved to the left and a conservative administration took power in the United States, new frictions arose between Washington and New Delhi. Wanting to do something for his Pakistani friends, Nixon in October 1970 approved what was called the "one-time exception" to the 1967 policy of not exporting lethal weapons systems to India and Pakistan. Washington agreed to sell Pakistan 300 armored personnel carriers and same aircraft worth about $50 million, at the same time reaffirming the intention to continue the 1967 policy.[15] Although Pakistan hoped for more, Islamabad was pleased to get something from the United States. The Indians predictably were annoyed, remaining ever allergic to US arms for Pakistan and suspicious of Nixon.

Vietnam became a second cause of tension after India spoke of raising the level of its diplomatic mission in Hanoi to an Embassy. When Washington warned New Delhi that this step would mean a cutoff in US aid, Mrs. Gandhi prudently deferred action. Although assistance levels were declining, India was still receiving several hundred million dollars of American aid annually. US assistance remained an important source of foreign funds for Indian development that she did not want to lose for an act of political symbolism.[16]

A third bilateral problem had an unusual origin—the unauthorized construction of a Soviet cultural center in Trivandrum, the capital of the South India state of Kerala. After 1954, the Indians did not permit foreign governments to establish libraries or cultural centers outside New Delhi or consular cities. They did, however, allow United States Information Service (USIS) centers set up before 1954 in Lucknow, Patna, Hyderabad, Bangalore, and Trivandrum, where there were no US consular offices, to continue in operation.

The Soviets—perhaps with silent assent from friends in the Government of India—proceeded, contrary to the rules, to start building a center in Trivandrum, where the Communists were politically strong. Unfortunately, in December 1969, the building collapsed, killing nine workers. Because of the publicity the accident generated, the Indian authorities were under pressure to take some action. New Delhi's decision was to refuse to permit further work on the Soviet center in Trivandrum, but also to apply the 1954 rule to the American libraries. USIS was told to shut the five centers down.

Indignant that the United States should suffer for a Soviet misdeed, the State Department reacted angrily. In the face of the stiff reaction, New Delhi watered down the ruling, saying the USIS centers could stay open provided they were placed under the auspices of the Indian Council on Cultural Relations (ICCR). But Washington was in no mood to compromise, making it a matter of principle that the centers remain under complete US control. Neither side budged, the libraries closed, and Indo-US relations suffered.[17] The Soviets, who agreed to put the proposed Trivandrum center under the ICCR, and their friends in India doubtless concluded they had not done badly from the episode. Ever since revelations in the late 1960s about CIA funding for some groups, Indian leftists and pro-Soviet elements, charging the United States with "academic imperialism," worked hard to reduce the extent of the US intellectual presence in India.

The fourth pinprick occurred in the fall of 1970 when the United Nations celebrated its 25th anniversary. Numerous heads of government, including Prime Minister Gandhi and Pakistan's President Yahya Khan, attended the ceremonies in New York. Yahya and a number of other leaders accepted President Nixon's invitation for dinner at the White House to commemorate the UN anniversary. Perhaps reflecting her personal feelings about Nixon—Mrs. Gandhi somewhat gracelessly turned down the invitation without much of an explanation.[18] During Yahya's visit to Washington, Nixon talked further about the opening to China. He asked the Pakistani President, then planning a trip to Beijing, to tell the Chinese leaders that he regarded a Sino-American rapprochement as "essential."[19] Nixon is also said to have told Yahya, "Nobody has occupied the White House who is friendlier to Pakistan than me."[20]

Meanwhile, the Soviets in late 1969 decided to abandon their efforts to pursue balanced relations with both India and Pakistan, reverting to the previous policy of closer links with India. In March 1969, border clashes with China brought the

Sino-Soviet split to the boiling point. As the China question became uppermost for the Kremlin, Moscow must have wondered about the benefits from its even-handed approach in the subcontinent. The spirit of Tashkent proved brief, Indo-Pakistani relations soon reverting to their usual state of mutual tension and suspicion. Despite the arrival of some Soviet arms and the promise of more, the Pakistanis rebuffed Moscow's calls for looser ties with Communist China.

The leftward turn in Indira's domestic policies was highly pleasing to the Russians. The Soviet policy of balanced relations with Pakistan was, however, causing considerable strain in relations. Mrs. Gandhi and others made clear they did not like Soviet arms shipments to Pakistan; the Indians began to make noises about a rapprochement with China.[21] In late summer 1969, Kosygin stopped in India en route to and from the funeral of Ho Chi Minh. After talks on these occasions and during a September 1969 visit to Moscow by Indian Foreign Minister Dinesh Singh—regarded at the time as pro-Soviet—the Kremlin adjusted its South Asia policy. The Soviets gave up their efforts with Pakistan, deciding against further arms agreements with Islamabad, and returned to a South Asia policy anchored in close relations with India. Even though Indira Gandhi refused to agree to the anti-Chinese Asian Collective Security scheme Brezhnev proposed during 1969, Indo-Soviet tensions greatly eased and relations substantially improved.[22]

Pleased with the Kremlin's policy readjustment and decision to back off from offering additional military equipment to Pakistan, New Delhi was willing to negotiate a treaty of friendship with Moscow, similar to the agreement Moscow had with Egypt, then in its pro-Soviet period. Negotiations proceeded quietly through the Indian Embassy in Moscow under Ambassador D. P. Dhar, an outspoken supporter of closer Indo-Soviet relations. Although the two countries reached agreement, Mrs. Gandhi decided not to sign the treaty from concern that this step would cause a public stir about a change in India's nonalignment, both domestically and with the United States. Put on the shelf, the draft reemerged two years later as the basis for the 1971 Indo-Soviet Treaty.[23]

During this period, Washington, in keeping with the spirit of Nixon's underlying low-key approach to the region, stayed detached from subcontinental tensions. Relations with both India and Pakistan remained on the back burner. At the same time, the secret exchanges between Washington and Beijing through the Pakistanis, the Romanians, and others were wending their slow course.

Indira Gandhi's victory over the party bosses in 1969 underscored her evolution from the timid, stumbling "dumb doll" the Syndicate supported in 1966 rather than endure Morarji Desai. Outwitting her more experienced opponents, she had evolved into a shrewd political leader, showing unexpected skills and toughness. Once she set upon a course, she moved forcefully, exhibiting none of the tentativeness of her first year in office.[24] She differed greatly from Jawaharlal Nehru, the father she deeply loved—and knew it. She told Italian journalist Oriana Fallaci, "He was a saint who strayed into politics. . . . I am a tough politician."[25]

Although Nehru dominated the scene with his ideas, personality, and enormous prestige, he allowed provincial Congress Party leaders to rule their domains. As Mrs. Gandhi battered her way to dominance, she learned from bitter experience to trust few of her colleagues. Once Indira emerged victorious, she tightly centralized control of power. Mrs. Gandhi did not, like her father, serve as foreign minister, but none of those who held the portfolio—M. C. Chagla, Dinesh Singh, Swaran Singh, Y. B. Chavan in the 1960s and 1970s and P. V. Narasimha Rao in the 1980s—exercised independent power. It was Madame Gandhi who made the decisions. The ministers loyally implemented her wishes or ceased to be ministers.[26]

She wanted India, although poor, to be respected as a country of importance, as the dominant power in South Asia, as heir to a great civilization, and as a leader of the Non-Aligned Movement. Unlike her father, Mrs. Gandhi had no special policy formula to achieve her goals. Indira had, as Surjit Mansingh wrote, "no grand designs, no sweeping analysis of current affairs to educate her audiences, no world vision to point the way India should take . . . it was enough to accept facts, adjust to them and seek to use them to advantage."[27] Unlike her eloquent father, Mrs. Gandhi spoke in a direct, unadorned, and concise manner; like him, she was given to moody silences in private meetings that often put off visitors, who were also unsettled by her occasional flashes of sarcasm.

Despite the fact that she paid much lip service to Nehru's vision of nonalignment, the movement was in the process of transforming itself from a grouping of newly independent Afro-Asian countries seeking to stand apart from the two quarreling power blocs into a platform for the world's poorer nations, the so-called Third World, to press their economic claims against the developed world. As the Non-Aligned Movement (NAM) swelled to over a hundred countries—even implausibly embracing such aligned states as Castro's Cuba—its periodic gatherings became like UN General Assembly meetings, full of standard ritual speeches and the adoption of ritual resolutions—invariably more critical of the United States than of the Soviet Union.[28]

In the United States, Richard Nixon also centralized control over foreign policy. His chief aide, Henry Kissinger, fashioned a high-powered National Security Council staff that often operated independently of the State Department, which at times—for example, in the China initiative—was left in the dark. To occupy the bureaucracy and to develop new ideas, Kissinger commissioned a wide array of policy studies called National Security Study Memoranda or NSSMs. In keeping with South Asia's low priority, it was not until NSSM No. 109 that policy toward the subcontinent received NSC attention.[29]

Nixon broke new ground in spelling out more clearly and publicly than previous Presidents the guidelines for US foreign policy in a series of annual reports to the Congress that provided—to use the phrase popular at the time—a "conceptual framework" for US policy.[30] Looking beyond the Vietnam War and the rigidities of the Cold War, Nixon and Kissinger wanted to create a late 20th century global version of the 19th century European power balance. A key to this was bringing Communist China into the family of nations—reversing two decades of US policy to isolate Beijing.[31] Unlike the world view prevalent in the United States between 1956 and 1965, India and the Third World had little importance in the Nixon/Kissinger power equation.[32]

Reflecting South Asia's diminished role was the bland commentary in the 1970 report—a few paragraphs out of nearly 200 pages—and a low-key three pages in the 1971 report. In these passages, the President made three main points:

- US strategic concerns in South Asia were limited to seeing that neither China nor the Soviet Union gained a dominant position in the subcontinent;

- The United States accepted Pakistan's altered foreign policy and India's nonalignment. "We have no desire to press on them a closer relationship than their own interest leads them to desire," Nixon declared; and,

- The main US interests in the subcontinent were to promote economic development, to respond to humanitarian concerns and to encourage India and Pakistan to put aside their differences.[33]

But events did not allow South Asia to remain in the back waters. In 1971, the coincidence of the East Pakistan crisis and Nixon's China initiative unexpectedly placed the subcontinent at the center of US foreign policy concerns.

The East Pakistan Crisis

During the winter of 1970-1971, both India and Pakistan went to the polls—India for its fifth democratic election since independence, Pakistan for its first. The result of Pakistan's December 1970 balloting gave the pro-East Pakistan autonomy Awami League a majority in the proposed National Assembly. The Awami League swept 167 of 169 seats in the east, but won none in West Pakistan. An unhappy President Yahya Khan set about seeking a political settlement, a task for which he showed neither skill nor inclination.[34]

Four months later, in March 1971, the Indian election results were unambiguous. In what was called the "Indira wave," Mrs. Gandhi won a landslide victory after she called India's first ever mid-term general elections, a year before the end of parliament's five year term. Pledging populist economic reforms to "eradicate poverty," Mrs. Gandhi crushed her more conservative opponents to win an unchallenged political mandate. Her Congress Party faction gained 362 of 520 seats in parliament.

In Pakistan, neither President Yahya Khan, Bengali leader Mujibur Rahman, nor the election winner in West Pakistan, Zulfikar Ali Bhutto, showed much statesmanship in the period leading up to the army repression.[35] By mid-March, negotiations for a political solution stalled on the key issue—how much autonomy East Pakistan would enjoy. Yahya and Mujib seemed to be making progress in last-ditch talks in Dacca, the East Pakistan capital. However, after demonstrations on 23 March, Pakistan Day, got out of hand with widespread burning of Pakistani flags, Yahya abruptly ended the negotiations and flew back to Islamabad. During the night of 25 March, Pakistan military forces cracked down in the east. Yahya outlawed the Awami League, sought to arrest its leaders as traitors, and tried to disarm Bengali members of the armed forces.[36]

A period of confusion followed with little accurate information about the situation in East Pakistan. Only gradually, as thousands of refugees began to flee into neighboring India, did the story emerge of the Pakistan military's harsh suppression, especially of Bengali Hindus, a sizeable minority in East Pakistan. Most East Pakistani political leaders escaped to India, but Awami League leader Sheikh Mujibur Rahman, who fatalistically remained at home, was arrested and jailed in West Pakistan.

The initial foreign reaction was relatively calm, largely limited to expressions of hope that Pakistan could resolve its difficulties and return to a constitutional path. In a few weeks, the mood changed after the refugee trickle became a flood and the story of West Pakistani brutality became known. In India, there was an insistent clamor for military action to enable the people of "East Bengal," (the term adopted in India rather than "East Pakistan") to exercise their right of self-determination. Although Mrs. Gandhi strongly denounced Yahya, she resisted pressure for early Indian military intervention—her generals told her they needed six months to prepare for a campaign against East Pakistan.

At the same time, the Prime Minister took a key decision not to allow the refugees to stay permanently in India, insisting that they eventually return home. The flood of refugees, India declared, transformed an internal Pakistani problem to one between India and Pakistan.[37] Now numbering in the millions,

Bangladesh

the refugees posed an enormous economic burden on India and a potentially serious political problem in West Bengal with its tradition of leftwing radicalism.

By May, the main outlines of Indian policy were set: the goal was the undoing of Yahya's crackdown in East Pakistan, although not necessarily through the emergence of an independent Bangladesh. On the military side, the Indians increased covert help to the Bengali members of the Pakistani military who managed to escape. These became the core of the *Mukhti Bahini* or People's Brotherhood, a guerrilla force soon numbering in the thousands, which began to attack transportation, communications, and power facilities in East Pakistan. The Indian Army also started to prepare for possible action against East Pakistan in the coming winter—when dry weather would make the terrain more suitable for fighting and the snows in the Himalayas would impede Chinese help to the Pakistanis.[38]

On the political side, the Indians, together with the Bangladeshis, launched a vigorous diplomatic and public relations campaign to stir world public opinion against Pakistan. Senior Indian political leaders, like Jayaprakash Narayan and Foreign Minister Swaran Singh, roamed the globe seeking support.[39] The foreign response was not entirely to India's liking: there was much sympathy for the human suffering of the Bengali refugees, much criticism of Pakistani brutality, but little inclination to intervene.[40] The Soviet Union pressed Pakistan the hardest. To India's chagrin, however, Moscow continued its economic assistance to Pakistan and spoke of the need for restraint in solving the crisis. Although China spoke loudly in support of its Pakistani friends, Beijing provided no tangible assistance beyond verbal encouragement.[41]

In the United States, the Nixon administration urged a peaceful settlement, but both in public and private acted gingerly in its dealings with Pakistan.[42] When the US Consul General in Dacca, Archer K. Blood, forwarded a cable protesting US official silence about the human rights violations in East Pakistan, Kissinger was livid.[43] The message from Dacca was simple: since the United States had no vital interests in Pakistan, traditional concern for human rights should govern US policy, resulting in condemnation of the West Pakistanis.

Blood and his colleagues in Dacca were, of course, unaware of the role Pakistan was playing in the secret negotiations with China, which—quite apart from Nixon's liking for Pakistan—made the President disinclined to lean on Yahya. On 27 April, a month after the crackdown in East Pakistan, Agha Hilaly, the Pakistani Ambassador in Washington, delivered a key message to the White House from Chou En-lai, giving the green light for an American emissary to visit China and proposing that Pakistan serve as the channel for the arrangements.[44] With Nixon's most daring diplomatic maneuver now approaching realization, the President had even less interest in upsetting Yahya, whose country had become centrally involved in the process.

The trouble was that only a handful in the US government, not including the Secretary of State, knew either of the negotiations with China or of the role Pakistan was playing. Many in the government and the US public interpreted Nixon's reluctance to criticize Yahya as reflecting a callous attitude toward human rights and a lack of compassion for human suffering in East Pakistan. The force of opinion became so strong that, despite Nixon's pencilled note on a Kissinger memo, "To all hands. Don't squeeze Yahya at this time," the administration took some restrictive actions.[45]

Although Nixon and Kissinger tried to maintain tightly centralized control, their system broke down during the South Asia crisis. The White House failed to provide sufficiently precise guidance to enable the bureaucracy to know what Nixon wanted it to do. This was especially true during the spring months of 1971 when the China trip was the administration's most closely held secret. After State asked how to deal with the Pakistan arms question, the White House failed to respond. State acted as it thought appropriate,[46] suspending licensing military exports to Pakistan lest these be used against the people of East Pakistan. Under the 1970 "one-time exception," Nixon had agreed to provide Pakistan some $50 million in equipment; sale of spare parts was also continuing under the policy President Johnson announced in 1967.[47]

Bureaucratic confusion about the arms policy, a snafu which perhaps only someone who has worked in the US government can fully appreciate, made matters worse. The State Department thought it was embargoing all arms exports to

Pakistan, unaware the Defense Department acted only to bar new licenses. Licenses approved earlier remained valid. Equipment already in Pakistan's custody could also be exported. According to the State Department's top South Asia hand, Deputy Assistant Secretary Christopher Van Hollen, neither he nor others understood this distinction. As a result, the administration incorrectly informed visiting Indian Foreign Minister Swaran Singh that the United States had ended all arms shipments to Pakistan. Out of ignorance, US officials misled the Indians and the public.[48]

Several days later, on 22 June, *The New York Times* reported that notwithstanding the embargo, several ships were about to depart from New York carrying arms for Pakistan. The news caused an uproar in India, where an incensed Swaran Singh charged US authorities lied to him. In Washington, opposition Democrats, led by Senator Ted Kennedy, alleged duplicity, claiming that some $50 million in arms were being shipped to Pakistan at the time the embargo was supposedly in force. The US media had a field day lambasting the White House for saying one thing and doing the contrary. Although the administration shortly realized that the value of military equipment not covered by the embargo was only $5 million and not $50 million, the larger figure stuck in the public's mind.

Super-sensitive on the issue of US arms for Pakistan and distrustful of Nixon, the Indians had no trouble convincing themselves of US duplicity. They chose to ignore American explanations of what went wrong, continuing to complain about "massive" US arms shipments and to link these with Pakistan's repressive policy in the east. Speaking in parliament on 24 June, Swaran Singh charged that US arms to Pakistan, "not only amount to a condoning of these atrocities, but could be construed as an encouragement to their continuation."[49] From this point on, relations soured badly.

Kissinger Visits Beijing

Two weeks later, Henry Kissinger left Washington on a supposedly routine trip to the Far East and South Asia. Only a handful of people, including the Pakistani leadership but not the Secretary of State, knew his real mission was to slip away to China during the stay in Pakistan. After stopping for talks in

New Delhi, Kissinger flew to Islamabad, ostensibly for two days of discussions.[50] A week later, on 15 July, Nixon astonished the world by announcing the Kissinger China mission and his own upcoming trip to Beijing.

The news startled the Indians who—quite apart from a US-China rapprochement—were miffed that Kissinger's stop in New Delhi was only part of the cover for the China talks. "Here we were faced with a tremendous human problem," a high official stated, "we thought he had come to discuss it with us, and then we found we were just stepping stones on the way to China."[51] Although the Indians expected little help from Nixon in resolving the East Pakistan crisis, especially after the arms supply ruckus, closer US-Chinese relations jarred the regional power balance at the moment when South Asia faced possible war.

Before the Kissinger trip, the prospect of Soviet and per-haps US support against China provided New Delhi with an ample security blanket. That Washington's help would no longer be forthcoming was made explicit when Kissinger called Indian Ambassador L. K. Jha to the Western White House in California on 17 July to inform the envoy, "We would be unable to help you against China" if there were a Chinese military response to a war between India and Pakistan.[52]

Indira sprung her own surprise a few weeks later. On 9 August, New Delhi and Moscow signed the Indo-Soviet Friend-ship Treaty. Supporters of closer ties with Moscow, such as Foreign Secretary T. N. Kaul and Mrs. Gandhi's principal secre-tary, P. N. Haksar, convinced the Prime Minister that it would serve India's interest to cement the links with Moscow through the treaty that had been negotiated, but not signed, two years before. After the Soviets signalled their willingness to proceed, the two sides quickly agreed on the final shape of the treaty. The key articles provided for consultations in the event of crisis and pledged that neither country would support a third party against the other.[53]

Even though short of a formal alliance, the treaty forged a relationship sufficiently close that it was hard to assert—as India did—that New Delhi remained true to the cardinal princi-ple of nonalignment, independence from either major power bloc. In the summer of 1971, Nehru's daughter was willing to overlook this lapse. With India facing the prospect of war with Pakistan, the important thing was to obtain political and military reinsurance against interference from China. Despite the fact that the treaty caused modest immediate ripples in Washington, Kissinger—in an after-the-fact overstatement—described the accord in his memoirs as a "bombshell" and as "throwing a lighted match into a powder keg."[54] Although—despite the treaty—the Soviets continued to press for a peaceful settlement of the crisis,[55] Nixon regarded India as a Soviet client for the rest of the crisis.[56] It was, in fact, not until late October that the Soviets shifted to a strongly pro-Indian stance.

After the Kissinger trip, the United States and China established direct communication through their embassies in Paris. Washington no longer needed the Pakistan channel to pass messages to the Chinese. US South Asia policy no longer had to be hostage to the opening to China. The Nixon administration could have kept its head down—much as Kissinger claimed was the original intent—and let events in the subcontinent play out according to their own logic.[57] The White House chose, instead, to become more, rather than less, engaged. Operating from assumptions about South Asian events not shared by the US government's regional specialists, Nixon and Kissinger placed the crisis in a global context, but failed to communicate this rationale to the bureaucracy.[58]

Although Nixon urged Yahya to make political concessions in the East, he fell short of pressing the Pakistani leader to negotiate directly with Mujibur Rahman, the unquestioned Bengali political leader. American Consulate General officials in Calcutta also met with Awami League exiles to see what sort of compromise would satisfy them. Washington urged an expanded UN relief effort to help the refugees in India and improve economic conditions in East Pakistan. The White House hoped that, coupled with gradual political accommodation in the east, this approach would eventually ease the crisis. Even though "almost to a person, the officials working on South Asia were convinced the White House strategy would not work," Nixon and Kissinger persisted.[59] In early August, when asked at a press conference, Nixon flatly refused to put public pressure on Yahya, saying this would not be helpful in solving the crisis.[60]

To visiting Indians, like political leader Jayaprakash Narayan, Henry Kissinger stressed US interest in a peaceful solution, support for Bengali self-determination, and confidence that in time this would be achieved. Indian officials were skeptical.[61] By now thoroughly suspicious of American motives, they saw the flurry of humanitarian activity as a smoke screen designed to allow Yahya to consolidate his grip over East Pakistan without making the only concessions that Delhi believed counted—the release of Mujibur Rahman and direct negotiations with the Awami League leader. Yahya's decision in August to try Mujibur Rahman for treason hardly increased New Delhi's confidence in the likely success of US endeavors.

As the monsoon ended and the flooded rivers of East Pakistan began to subside, the terrain became more suitable for a military solution. By September, most Indians concluded that this would be the likely outcome. They did not see sufficient give on the Pakistani side to permit a peaceful settlement along lines they and the Bengalis would accept. Mrs. Gandhi pressed the Soviets hard to shift their position to a more pro-Indian stance and to supply additional military equipment needed for a cold weather campaign. Moscow hesitated. It was only on 21 October, after Yahya spurned Soviet suggestions for political concessions, that the Russians fell fully in line with India's wishes.[62]

The next day, Indira Gandhi set off on a three-week tour of Western capitals. Her message was simple: India hoped for a political solution, but this required negotiations between Yahya and Mujibur Rahman. India was patient but would not bear the refugee burden indefinitely—an implicit threat of military action. Western Europe received her warmly, especially London and Paris. Her diplomatic spade work paid off when Britain and France split with the United States in December in the UN Security Council.[63]

It was a different story in Washington where Mrs. Gandhi arrived on 4 November. As Kissinger and Nixon wrote later—and Indian participants confirmed—the discussions were a dialogue of the deaf. The visit began badly when in Nixon's welcoming remarks on the White House lawn, he offered sympathy for flood victims in the state of Bihar, but made no mention of Bengali refugees and their suffering. Untactfully, Mrs. Gandhi chided the President in her response for ignoring a "man-made

4 November 1971, President Nixon and Prime Minister Indira Gandhi during arrival ceremonies in Washington, DC.

tragedy of vast proportions."[64] The Chief Executive returned the Prime Minister's slight the next day by keeping her waiting forty-five minutes for a White House meeting.[65]

Things failed to improve in the discussions between the two leaders. Kissinger called these talks the worst and most painful in which he participated.[66] Mrs. Gandhi's longtime press adviser Sharada Prasad, who accompanied her on the trip, agreed. He recalled the White House state dinner as the most strained of the hundred or so such affairs he attended. According to Prasad, neither Nixon nor Mrs. Gandhi made much of an effort to converse with each other during dinner. Even though Mrs. Nixon tried unsuccessfully to break the tension with small talk, the atmosphere remained frosty.[67]

In the ritual after-dinner toasts, the President spoke rather aimlessly about famous statesmen who sat in the chair of honor at White House state dinners and recalled Pandit Nehru's remarks when they first met in 1953 that India needed a generation of peace. Nixon made no mention of the East Pakistan crisis. Mrs. Gandhi was blunter. "Our people," the Prime Minister declared, "cannot understand how it is that we who are the victims, we who are bearing the brunt and have restrained ourselves with such fortitude, should be equated with those whose action has caused the tragedy."[68]

Substantively, there was complete disagreement about the prospects for a political settlement. Nixon and Kissinger claimed that, if given sufficient time, the United States could get Yahya to concede self-determination for the East Pakistanis, either provincial autonomy or full independence. The Indians regarded the hope that the West Pakistanis would yield—in effect admitting that their actions since 25 March were wrong— as utterly unrealistic. US South Asia specialists shared the view that Yahya would not compromise.[69]

If Mrs. Gandhi concluded that talking with the Americans would lead nowhere,[70] Nixon, for his part, wrote in his diary of Mrs. Gandhi's "duplicitous action toward us when she actually had made up her mind to attack Pakistan at the time she saw me in Washington and assured me she would not."[71] Kissinger intoned, "Mrs. Gandhi was going to war not because she was convinced of our failure but because she feared our success."[72] Although Mrs. Gandhi's meetings with Nixon were a failure, her

4 November 1971, Prime Minister Indira Gandhi speaking during her arrival at the White House.

4 November 1971, Prime Minister Gandhi and President Nixon in the Oval Office.

5 November 1971, Prime Minister Indira Gandhi at a cabinet meeting, seated between Secretary of State William Rogers and President Nixon.

public appearances in Washington were successful. An active pro-Bangladesh lobby in Washington won the emotional support of many political activists, leading Democratic politicians, and even some Republicans. Those who criticized the Nixon administration for its handling of the Vietnam War were more than willing to fault its approach to the Bangladesh crisis. US public opinion, as measured by the Louis Harris poll, was two to one against administration policy.[73]

The Bangladesh Crisis: The December War

In November, the tempo of military action increased. The Bangladesh "freedom fighters" were becoming more aggressive in their cross-border forays, receiving artillery support from the Indian military. Late in the month, Mrs. Gandhi authorized Indian forces to enter East Pakistan to "pursue" the Pakistani forces. Tensions mounted. An all-out Indian military assault against the East seemed imminent.

Although there is dispute whether or not Indira fixed a D-Day to invade East Pakistan, Yahya resolved the problem for New Delhi.[74] On the night of 3 December, Pakistan attacked eight Indian airfields in the western part of the country, and the next day declared war on India.[75] The Indians countered, attacking in the east and mounting probing operations in the west to pin down Pakistan forces. On 6 December, India recognized the Awami League government-in-exile as the government of Bangladesh.

As tensions mounted during November, the United States perceptively hardened its stance toward India, which Kissinger and Nixon claimed was inciting the conflict. On 2 December, Washington announced a suspension of military sales to India (of which the most important was a $70 million communications system designed to improve air defense capabilities). On 6 December, the United States froze its economic assistance to India, including $87.6 million worth of aid already in the pipeline. The next day Assistant Secretary of State Joseph Sisco declared in a State Department press background briefing that India bore the major responsibility for the war. Kissinger was berating the NSC's Washington Special Action Group (WSAG) for not being more responsive to Nixon's desire to "tilt" toward Pakistan.[76]

The diplomatic scene shifted to the UN Security Council in New York. Acting under direct orders from Nixon, US Representative George Bush criticized India as responsible for the war and urged support for an immediate cease-fire. India's Soviet friends vetoed the resolution. Now that the war had started, India was bent on achieving its goal—freeing Bangladesh from Pakistani control. Participating for the first time as a Security Council member, Communist China joined the United States in supporting the resolution, but both Britain and France, the other permanent members and US allies in NATO, abstained in the Security Council vote. The United States and other supporters of Pakistan then shifted to the General Assembly where the call for a cease-fire won overwhelming support by a vote of 104-11 with 10 abstentions. Sending troops across an international border, even for a popular cause, was not an action nation-states condoned.

As badly outnumbered Pakistani forces retreated from the borders toward Dacca, the war in the east was for all intents over within a week. It was only a question of how long the Pakistanis would hold out. On 16 December, the Pakistanis ended the struggle, with some 93,000 soldiers surrendering. When, a week earlier, they discussed giving up, Yahya urged the troops in the east to fight on, apparently hoping for intervention from the United States and China.

Unlike Kissinger or Yahya, India discounted the likelihood of Beijing's intervening militarily. New Delhi reached this conclusion from an on-going assessment of the Chinese response since the crisis began in March—little or no increased military activity along the northern borders, a less negative public stance toward India than during the 1965 war, and the absence of tangible military aid to Pakistan as opposed to rhetoric. The Indians thus began the fighting assuming that the Chinese would limit their support to their Pakistani friends to verbal and moral encouragement.[77] On the basis of talks with Chou and secret discussions in New York in December with the Chinese foreign minister, Kissinger—by his own admission—reached the opposite conclusion. He incorrectly expected the Chinese to intervene militarily, possibly precipitating a Soviet military rejoinder against China.[78]

When the war ended in East Pakistan, Washington's attention turned to West Pakistan. Nixon and Kissinger—although hardly anyone else—believed that India was about to attack what was left of Pakistan.[79] A 6 December CIA report to the effect that Mrs. Gandhi was considering moving against West Pakistan greatly strengthened this worry. US South Asia specialists tended to give the intelligence report little credence, believing any further Indian military action would be limited to retaking certain strategic points in Kashmir, returned to Pakistan by the Taskhent agreement. "Virtually alone in the US Government in interpreting the report as they did," President Nixon and Kissinger were convinced they were right, making their concern to save West Pakistan the driving force behind US actions.[80]

India's capable Ambassador in Washington, L. K. Jha, assured Kissinger and the State Department that India had no designs against West Pakistan.[81] The Government of India gave similar assurances in New Delhi. Traditional Indian ambiguity about territory in disputed Kashmir sufficed to convince Nixon and Kissinger that India was lying.[82] Believing that Moscow was egging New Delhi on to humble US "ally" Pakistan, the President decided to press the Soviets to get their South Asia "client" to call off its attack.[83]

The White House made this point through a variety of channels, including a meeting with a thoroughly surprised visiting Soviet Minister of Agriculture Vladimir Matskevich. Expecting nice words about agricultural cooperation when ushered into the President's office, Matskevich was instead asked to convey to the Kremlin how seriously Nixon felt about the threat to West Pakistan.[84] In response to the flurry of messages from Nixon—including the first use of the hot line—Premier Kosygin sought assurances from visiting Indian envoy P. N. Dhar about Indian intentions in the West. Dhar promptly gave these without finding it necessary to seek instructions from New Delhi, so sure was he that India was not interested in attacking West Pakistan.[85] Based on what they heard from Dhar and from soundings in New Delhi, the Soviets passed on reassuring words about Indian intentions to Washington. These failed to satisfy Nixon.

The President decided then to escalate a step further. On 10 December, he ordered a show of US naval force, directing the aircraft carrier *Enterprise* with supporting vessels to proceed as Task Group 74 from the Far East to the Bay of Bengal. Its stated mission was to aid in the possible evacuation of US personnel in Dacca.[86] The unstated mission of the *Enterprise*, never spelled out to the US Navy, was to send a signal to the Indians and the Soviets—as Kissinger put it, "To give emphasis to our warnings about West Pakistan." The White House wanted to show the Chinese that, if they entered into a relationship with the United States they could count on US steadfastness in times of trouble.[87]

The Indians were unclear what the *Enterprise* was supposed to achieve. They failed to grasp the intended signal about West Pakistan. They did not believe the cover story about evacuating US nationals. They assumed the most likely mission was to help evacuate West Pakistanis trapped in the east.[88] Once Mrs. Gandhi achieved her goal in the east with the surrender of Pakistani forces, she quickly decided that continuing the war was not in India's interests.[89] She announced a cease-fire effective 19 December. Pakistan accepted, bringing to an end the seventeen-day conflict. Whatever its intended mission, the *Enterprise* appeared to have played no role in ending hostilities in the West. Despite Nixon's and Kissinger's later claims,[90] US actions did not seem to have been a significant factor in the decision not to move against West Pakistan.

US policy, however, deeply angered the Indians. In a scorching letter to Nixon released to the *New York Times* on 15 December, Indira Gandhi asserted that the United States paid:

> Lip service to the need for a political solution, but not a single worthwhile step was taken to bring this about. . . . We are deeply hurt by the innuendoes and insinuations that it was we who have precipitated the crisis. . . We have not received, even to this day, the barest framework of a settlement which takes into account the facts as they are.[91]

Nixon responded in a sharp but private letter to Mrs. Gandhi. He rebuked Indira for having "spurned" his efforts to find a peaceful solution to the crisis, claiming he opposed the resort to force when "statesmanship could turn the course of history away from war."[92]

A few weeks later, journalist Jack Anderson enormously embarrassed Nixon by publishing minutes of secret White House WSAG meetings dealing with the Bangladesh crisis. These documents revealed that contrary to what the administration was publicly saying about an even-handed approach, Nixon was demanding "the tilt" toward Pakistan and giving Kissinger "hell every hour" for not doing enough against India. The Anderson Papers were an appropriate postscript to a sorry chapter in US diplomacy.[93]

The US role during the crisis is reasonably clear; the rationale for the Nixon-Kissinger policy has remained less clear. Part of the difficulty has been that the President and Kissinger perceived the crisis almost entirely in terms of its global implications—as they interpreted these—and the US government's South Asia hands and most other observers considered the crisis as a regional affair with limited broader implications. For Nixon and Kissinger, the tilt was not just a means of expressing appreciation to the Pakistanis for their help in the opening to China, but, far more important, trying to impress the Chinese by the US handling of the crisis. Then NSC South Asia staffer Harold Saunders recalled Kissinger saying on several occasions:

> We are opening a relationship with China based on the proposition that we are both concerned about Soviet intentions. . . . While we are in the process of opening up our dialogue with China, we face a crisis in South Asia for Pakistan, our traditional ally. China will be looking to see how we treat that ally. . . . If the United States stands by and sees an ally dismembered what will the Chinese think about our reliability?[94]

This larger global dimension, according to Saunders, suffused the discussion of the crisis in the NSC. For Nixon and Kissinger, the human tragedy of the ten million refugees was "one of those unhappy things that happened" but not something on which one based foreign policy actions.[95] Nixon's thinking was also colored by his perception that the Soviets were egging on the Indians to "humiliate the United States" by dismembering Pakistan. The President's personal liking for Pakistan as well as his dislike of the Indians, especially Indira Gandhi, did "nothing but reinforce" the way Nixon reacted to the crisis, Saunders commented.[96]

Stung by the criticism of his South Asia policy, Nixon devoted twelve pages to presenting his version of the crisis in the 1972 Foreign Policy report. Nixon's main claims were that Indian impatience frustrated US efforts to nudge Yahya gradually toward a settlement, and that the strong US stand reduced the chance of an Indian attack on West Pakistan.[97] In their memoirs, Nixon and Kissinger were less modest, asserting that their handling of events scared the Soviets into calling off their South Asian proxy, India, from attacking West Pakistan and showed the Chinese that the United States was willing to offer steadfast help to a friend during an unpopular crisis.[98] Kissinger went so far as to claim that administration policy saved "a major American initiative of fundamental importance to the global balance of power" and that the "very structure of international order was endangered by the naked recourse to force by a Soviet partner."[99]

It is hard to agree with these assertions. Far from a diplomatic victory, the whole affair proved an unnecessary and embarrassing diplomatic setback for the United States. Through their misreading of the crisis, and their pro-Pakistan bias, Richard Nixon and Henry Kissinger succeeded in needlessly transforming a regional dispute into one which threatened to become a great power showdown.[100] The main consequences were severe and long-lasting damage to US relations with India and enhanced Soviet influence with New Delhi. In Indian eyes, US handling of the crisis, especially sending the *Enterprise* toward the Bay of Bengal, provided tangible "evidence" of US desire to thwart India's regional hopes and aspirations. Vociferous pro-Soviet and anti-US elements in India have harped on the deployment of the *Enterprise* as a symbol of US hostility for over two decades. An unintended result of the crisis was to strengthen the hand of Indians who supported proceeding with nuclear testing.[101]

After the Bangladesh Crisis: Relations At Low Ebb

The first months of 1972 saw relations between Washington and New Delhi at low ebb. Mrs. Gandhi carried through on her threat to raise the level of the Indian diplomatic mission in Hanoi from a Consulate General to an Embassy—a step she had delayed since 1969. The Prime Minister ordered the closing of the US economic assistance mission, where more than 1,200

Americans and Indians worked. She directed that the Peace Corps be reduced from over 500 to 50 volunteers.[102] The Indian government also imposed stringent restrictions on research by American academics, paradoxically, a group that had been among the vociferous opponents of Nixon's policy toward the Bangladesh crisis. American studies of India in US universities—in the 1950s and 1960s a thriving discipline—have suffered greatly ever since, weakening one of the stronger voices in the United States for improved Indo-American relations.

L. K. Jha and Kenneth Keating, the two hapless envoys during the Bangladesh crisis, ended their ambassadorial assignments in 1972. Despite a distinguished senatorial career from New York State, Keating proved himself a fusty lightweight in New Delhi. Nixon, nonetheless, named him to the sensitive post of ambassador to Israel. Jha, who won respect—even from Henry Kissinger—as a highly intelligent and effective envoy,[103] once more became a close adviser to Mrs. Gandhi after returning to India.

Following her twin triumphs at the ballot box and over Pakistan, Mrs. Gandhi stood at the peak of her power in early 1972. *The Economist* of London called her the uncrowned Empress of India.[104] She possessed unparalleled political power and a strong mandate to implement domestic social and economic reform. She managed the Bangladesh crisis flawlessly from the Indian standpoint. Pakistan was humiliated and India gained unchallengeable regional predominance. After a dismal decade, the nation could once more hold its head high.

In early July 1972, India and Pakistan concluded a peace accord at Simla, the town perched a mile high in the Himalayas that had served as the summer capital of the government of British India. Mrs. Gandhi agreed to the return of 5,000 square miles of West Pakistan territory, mostly desert, that India captured during the war. Bhutto, who replaced Yahya as the President of a shrunken Pakistan, agreed to settle all disputes, including the Kashmir issue, peacefully and bilaterally.[105]

At the time, Simla appeared to mark an important milestone in Indo-Pakistani relations, but, as in the case of the Tashkent agreement after the 1965 India-Pakistan War, the agreement unfortunately did not provide a basis for resolving bilateral antagonisms or promoting genuine rapprochement.

The Simla accord, nonetheless, led to a change in the US stance toward the Kashmir dispute. Previously, the United States stood behind relevant UN resolutions, including the call for a plebiscite. After 1972, Washington shifted ground; the US position since Simla has been to support any settlement the Indians and Pakistanis were able to work out.

Immediately after the Simla agreement, with Indo-US relations still at their nadir, Nixon made a modest gesture. He sent Secretary of the Treasury John Connally, a person whom he greatly respected, to meet Mrs. Gandhi during an around-the-world trip. Given the hostility between Indira and Nixon and the coldness of bilateral relations, Connally was apprehensive about the talks. He was relieved when these went reasonably well.[106]

In December 1972, Nixon made a further gesture toward India, selecting as Keating's replacement as ambassador, Harvard government professor Daniel Patrick Moynihan. Although a Democrat and a former Assistant Secretary of Labor in the Kennedy-Johnson years, Moynihan headed Nixon's Domestic Council and sat in the Cabinet in 1969, gaining a considerable reputation for his wit and brains. During the 1971 UN session, as a public member of the US delegation, Moynihan opposed US policy toward the Bangladesh crisis.

Nixon, with whom Moynihan remained on friendly terms, called him on several occasions about the crisis. The President said he could not spell out his reasons on the phone, but if Moynihan knew the whole story, he would understand the policy Nixon was following. Moynihan recalled his response, "We are dumb. We are going to lose, and what are we going to get for it?"[107] When Nixon called late in 1972 to ask if he would go as Ambassador to India, Moynihan was not surprised. Nixon knew—in Moynihan's opinion—that he had messed up the Bangladesh affair. His way of trying to right things was to send someone as ambassador like Moynihan, who had a White House cachet and opposed the Bangladesh policy. Even though Nixon regarded India as a stooge of the Soviets, it was a big country and a democracy, hence not a place the United States wanted to write off.[108]

The extensive section on South Asia in the 1973 Foreign Policy Report, which appeared shortly after Moynihan arrived in India, confirmed US interest in moving beyond 1971. Nixon stated:

> We want to join India in a mature relationship founded on equality, reciprocity and mutual interest, reflecting India's stature as a great free nation . . . The United States respects India as a major country. We are prepared to treat India in accordance with its new stature and responsibilities.[109]

It was not immediately evident that the Indian Prime Minister shared an interest in better relations. In an October 1972 article in *Foreign Affairs*, she lambasted "the dispatch of the warship *Enterprise* to support a ruthless military dictatorship and to intimidate a democracy." The Prime Minister went on to lecture the President, "The United States has yet to resolve the inner contradiction between the tradition of the founding fathers and of Lincoln, and the external image it gives of a superpower pursuing the cold logic of power politics."[110] In January and February 1973, she further angered Washington by charging in public that the "savage bombing" of Vietnam would not have been tolerated if the population had been European.[111]

Mrs. Gandhi's nomination of T. N. Kaul to succeed the respected Jha hardly suggested much desire for improved relations. During tours as ambassador to Moscow and as Indian Foreign Secretary, Kaul established himself as a vocal advocate of closer Indian-Soviet relations. Washington regarded Kaul as no friend of the United States. After arriving, the Indian envoy rather confounded people by establishing good relations with Henry Kissinger, who by then had become Secretary of State. At the height of his power and prestige as the Watergate scandal engulfed Nixon, Kissinger became a regular attendee at Indian functions—one of the few embassies in Washington whose invitations the Secretary would accept.[112]

If Kaul found doors open in Washington, Moynihan did not find New Delhi as hospitable. The gregarious Ambassador looked forward to visiting Indian universities, much in the manner of his Harvard colleague, John Kenneth Galbraith, a decade before. But in the wake of 1971, Moynihan was scarcely ever invited on university campuses. The envoy, in turn, kept an uncharacteristically low profile in India. Moynihan held his first and only press conference just one day prior to his departure on 6 January 1975.[113]

When Moynihan arrived in India, he faced the question of the future of US economic assistance. Formerly a central element of US relations with India, the aid program had all but vanished after Nixon froze assistance during the 1971 war. The only assistance that continued was food distributed free under Title III of PL 480 by private voluntary agencies such as CARE and Catholic Relief. Neither Moynihan nor Washington was in any rush to resume regular economic assistance—for which $75 million was placed in the budget—unless India requested this, a step Indira Gandhi was unwilling to take. Since the United States cut off aid, the Indians reasoned that it was up to the United States to take the initiative in turning on the aid tap and not for India to have to ask for Washington to do so.

As a practical matter, with the World Bank and other donors increasing the size of their programs, a resumption of US aid had less significance than it had after the 1965 War. There was, in any event, considerable ambivalence on both sides. Some Indians resented what they believed was an intrusive US aid presence and chronic US arm twisting on economic policy. They feared the United States would again try to use aid to influence Indian policies, economic or political. Some US officials, in turn, wondered about the wisdom of giving aid if the Indians felt so badly about receiving assistance from the United States.[114]

Regarding PL 480, India made it a matter of national pride—after the bitter experience with Lyndon Johnson in 1965-1967—not to resume food aid. Although food production, thanks to the green revolution, grew impressively, fluctuations in monsoons still affected harvests. When food stocks slumped after poor rains in 1972, the Indians used scarce foreign exchange to buy US wheat commercially rather than seek a resumption of PL 480 aid.

Moynihan did not basically disagree with the Indian attitude toward aid. He considered the economic assistance relationship an unequal partnership between the giver and receiver. This had perhaps been acceptable earlier, in what he called the "Age of the Demi-Raj," but had no place in the new "mature" relationship Moynihan hoped to fashion with India. A few

months after his arrival in New Delhi, the Ambassador made a
symbolic point by ensuring that the extensive complex of office
buildings built for US AID a few years before with PL 480 rupees
was handed over to the Indians. In a cable leaked to the press
after Washington floated the idea of retaining some of the buildings, Moynihan described the lavish complex as part of
America's "edifice complex."[115] Located outside New Delhi
near the 12th century Qutb Minar, the complex has since been
converted by the Indians into a luxury-class tourist hotel.

The Rupee Agreement: A Two Billion Dollar Check

Another problem worrying Moynihan was the mountain of
Indian rupees owned by the US government, repayment for
millions of tons of PL 480 foodgrain programs. Since 1954,
when the US Congress enacted Public Law 480, the Indians paid
for food aid with rupees deposited into a special interest-bearing
account with the Reserve Bank of India. The US right to spend
these deposits was limited to paying for US government ex-
penses in India plus a few other uses, such as loans to US
companies for investment in India.

Over the years, the deposits grew rapidly because of the
enormous size of PL 480 food shipments and the limited possibility for spending the rupees. Indians feared that somehow the
United States would use these huge currency claims—amounting in 1971 to over $3 billion—to destabilize the Indian econ-
omy. Even a friendly observer like Kewal Singh, then serving as
Foreign Secretary and later ambassador to Washington, commented, "It was a dangerous thing for a country to have so much
of its currency controlled by another power."[116]

Two factors stirred this anxiety which was stoked by anti-
American elements. The first was the sheer size of the rupee
deposits, amounting to as much as 20 per cent of Indian currency. The second was that, far from declining, the holdings
were likely to grow indefinitely. Expenditures for running the
Embassy and other permitted uses—under $100 million a
year—were less than the interest earned annually on the deposits. There thus seemed no end in sight to the problem.

The possibility of writing off much of the rupee debt pre-
dated Moynihan's arrival on the scene. Chester Bowles had
unsuccessfully surfaced the proposal which was also urged by

India's L. K. Jha. After becoming ambassador, Moynihan pushed the idea with vigor arguing that if left untouched the rupee problem would become a permanent psychological burden to an already shaky relationship. T. N. Kaul heartily seconded Moynihan. During the Indian envoy's presentation of credentials, Nixon asked how relations could be improved. Kaul mentioned solving the rupee problem.[117] The US bureaucracy developed a negotiating proposal that called for the US waiving future interest payments, amounting to an estimated $4 billion dollars worth of rupees, writing off a third of the holdings and keeping the remaining two-thirds for US uses. Although he did not think the Indians would agree, Moynihan let the wheels of bureaucracy grind. He then saw Nixon at the Western White House in California and won his agreement to reverse the figures—to write off $2.2 billion worth of rupees and retain $1.1 billion for US uses.[118]

Having overridden the Washington bureaucracy, Moynihan was able to negotiate the package with the Indians in fairly short order. The principal difficulty arose over efforts to tap the rupee pool for purposes other than the US government expenditures. One instance, a request for an endowment of $100 million worth of rupees for a medical school in Bangalore in South India, later proved a political bonus when the rupee agreement ran into trouble with the US Congress. The proposal's sponsor, a Catholic missionary priest named Father Bob Barrett, sought the funds to endow a center at the medical school in honor of former Speaker of the US House of Representatives John W. McCormack. Supporting the proposal as a goodwill gesture, Moynihan, after some arm-twisting, gained Indian acceptance.

Although the rupee agreement was an executive agreement not requiring approval of the Congress, there was trouble brewing on Capitol Hill. Labeling the accord a multi-billion dollar give-away, Senator Harry Byrd Jr., a conservative Virginia Democrat, succeeded in September 1973 in tacking an amendment onto the defense appropriation bill that would require congressional authorization for the rupee agreement. Since this was highly unlikely, a dejected Moynihan returned to New Delhi, fearing the rupee deal was dead.

Despite the fact that Nixon was by then deeply mired in Watergate, the President refused to accept defeat on the rupee agreement, giving the green light for administration supporters, with Moynihan in the lead, to work to overcome the Byrd amendment. In order to ensure funding for the Bangalor medical center, retired Speaker McCormack plunged actively into the fray, lining up many Democrats, including Senator Ted Kennedy and AFL-CIO Chairman George Meany, to lobby for the rupee agreement. This unusual bipartisan cooperation at the height of the Watergate scandal succeeded in killing the Byrd amendment and saving the rupee agreement.

The formal signing took place in New Delhi on 18 February 1974. Ambassador Moynihan marked the ceremony with typical flourish, presenting the Government of India a check for $2.2 billion worth of rupees, the largest check ever written until then. Moynihan deserved great credit for persevering in the effort to solve the problem. Ironically, Richard Nixon, never regarded as a friend of India, deserved part of the credit because of his willingness to back Moynihan on the issue.

With the rupee question resolved, the prospects for a resumption of bilateral assistance improved. The United States had, for some time, signalled its willingness to talk about new assistance, for which $75 million remained budgeted. In early 1974 with the Indian economy reeling after the abrupt rise in oil prices following the 1973 Arab-Israeli War and other inflationary pressures, New Delhi, at last, signalled interest.[119] Before anything was worked out, a new problem arose.

India Becomes the World's Sixth Nuclear Power

On 18 May 1974, just three months before Watergate drove Richard Nixon from office, the Indian Atomic Energy Commission exploded an underground nuclear device at Pokharan in the deserts of Rajasthan, several hundred miles west of New Delhi. The explosion made India the world's sixth nuclear power.

This reversal of Mrs. Gandhi's stance of the late 1960s may have been one of the most important, if unintended, consequences of the 1971 Bangladesh crisis.[120] The episode strengthened the hands of proponents of India's going nuclear, as well as the voice of Indian scientists who wished to demonstrate their capability to detonate a nuclear device. Mrs. Gandhi also regarded the test as a way to boost her government's lagging popularity by appealing to Indian national pride at joining the nuclear club.[121] She had failed to implement her 1971 campaign promises and, after poor harvests and the 1973 jump in oil prices, the country was suffering badly from rising unemployment and inflation.

Although American specialists were long aware India had the capability to explode a device, the act caught the US government by surprise.[122] The State Department's initial inclination was to criticize the Indian test as a damaging breach in the nonproliferation wall. Then on one of his Middle East shuttles, Secretary Kissinger disagreed, substituting milder and more neutral wording as the official reaction to the event.[123] Since the Indian explosion was an accomplished fact, Kissinger believed public scolding would not undo the event, but only add to US-Indian bilateral problems and reduce the influence Washington might have on India's future nuclear policy.[124]

Canada, which closely cooperated with India on its nuclear program, reacted in a far stronger fashion. Prime Minister Trudeau had earlier warned Mrs. Gandhi that Canada would cut off nuclear cooperation if India tested a device. He now proceeded to carry through on this threat. Canada was particularly annoyed because the plutonium used in the test was produced in a research reactor the Canadians had given India. In responding to criticism, Kissinger stated (incorrectly it turned out later) that, unlike Canada, the United States had no involvement with the Indian test.[125]

One of the immediate consequences of the test was the announcement that India's neighbor and enemy, Pakistan, was going to launch its own "peaceful" nuclear program. Mrs. Gandhi's assurances of India's peaceful intentions carried little weight in Islamabad. Prime Minister Bhutto charged that India's motives were to employ nuclear blackmail against Pakistan.[126] When Ambassador Moynihan saw Mrs. Gandhi to present the official US reaction to the test, he added some personal thoughts, telling the Prime Minister:

> India has made a huge mistake. Here you were the No. 1 hegemonic power in South Asia. Nobody was No. 2 and call Pakistan No. 3. Now in a decade's time, some Pakistani general will call you up and say I have four nuclear weapons and I want Kashmir. If not, we will drop them on you and we will all meet in heaven. And then what will you do?[127]

The Prime Minister, according to Moynihan, remained silent and offered no response.

The US nuclear nonproliferation lobby, far stronger among Democrats than Republicans, regarded the reaction of the administration—which at this point meant Kissinger since Nixon was almost sunk by Watergate—as weak and inadequate. If India, one of the world's poorest countries, could explode a device—and get away with it—the anti-nuclear proponents feared it would only be a matter of time before others followed suit. The lobby wanted the United States, like Canada, to punish India by ending nuclear cooperation.

Looking for ways to hit at India, the nonproliferation supporters found an ally in a longtime critic of India, Rep. Clarence Long, a Maryland Democrat and chairman of the foreign aid appropriations subcommittee. Shortly after the test, Long won acceptance for a bill directing the US government to vote against all loans to India in the World Bank. The action had no practical effect since the United States lacked a majority in the Bank. It was, however, a symbolic slap that made clear the force of congressional annoyance about the nuclear test.[128] Apart from nonproliferation concerns, many in Congress and elsewhere criticized India's diversion of scarce resources from economic development into the nuclear program. The retort from Mrs. Gandhi, hurt and stung by foreign criticism of the test, was to emphasize India's need for technical development such as the nuclear program and to suggest that the critics were trying to keep India down.[129]

Among the things that particularly irked the anti-nuclear lobby was Indian insistence that the explosion (or implosion as the underground blast was technically called) was in pursuit of a peaceful uses program and did not represent a shift to nuclear weapons. India, Mrs. Gandhi self-righteously maintained, was different from the five other nuclear powers; it was not interested in military uses of nuclear energy. India refused to fit into the standard equation on nuclear policy matters, trying to assert its own—and different—route.

Critics scoffed at the Indian explanation. By then, few specialists believed in the utility of peaceful nuclear explosions, which the Nonproliferation Treaty explicitly barred since it was deemed impossible to detect the difference between military and

peaceful explosions. The Pokharan test would have been a violation of the NPT, but since India had not signed the treaty, the
point was legally moot.

The attention of the US nonproliferation lobby turned to
the nuclear power plant at Tarapur outside Bombay, built as a
showpiece AID project and the major element in US-India
nuclear cooperation. Tarapur received US enriched uranium
supplied under a 30-year commercial contract in return for
which the Indians agreed to bilateral and later International
Atomic Energy inspections and safeguards designed to ensure
that sensitive material not be diverted for non-authorized uses.
For the next eight years—until alternative fuel supply arrangements were worked out in 1982—the question of licensing exports of enriched uranium for Tarapur became a major problem
between New Delhi and Washington. When Nixon resigned
from the presidency in August 1974, the issue was left
simmering.

India's going nuclear badly damaged its standing in the
United States among its traditional liberal supporters. Although
not happy about the test, Republicans like Kissinger, in effect,
shrugged their shoulders. They did not believe trying to punish
the Indians would do much good. In contrast, liberal Democrats—many of whom bitterly criticized Nixon's handling of the
Bangladesh crisis—turned their wrath on New Delhi for breach-
ing the nuclear barrier. The action in mid-1974 to absorb the
tiny protectorate of Sikkim further tarnished the Indian image.
The fact that the ruler of Sikkim was married to a former US
citizen Hope Cooke meant the Indian action received considerably more publicity than would otherwise have been the case.

Few Indian Tears Shed Over Nixon's Disgrace

In August 1974, Richard Nixon resigned from the presidency rather than face impeachment charges over the Watergate
scandals. Although many abroad regretted his departure, regarding him as one of the more skilful foreign policy practioners
among US presidents, India was one country where few shed
tears over Nixon's disgrace. Twenty-one years earlier, then Vice
President Nixon's first meeting with Jawaharlal Nehru went
badly. Nixon disliked the Prime Minister of India and found
Indira Gandhi, whom he also met at the time, "in every way

. . . her father's daughter."[130] The Vice President left South Asia, after the December 1953 visit, strongly opposed to India's policy of neutralism and strongly in favor of Pakistan. During the 1971 Bangladesh crisis, Richard Nixon's actions made it clear that his sentiments toward India and Indira had not changed.

After entering the White House in 1969, Nixon did not at first alter Johnson's policy of reduced US involvement in South Asia. Nixon's handling of the Bangladesh crisis during 1971, however, caused the US-India bilateral relationship to plunge to its nadir. Considerations of global policy—as seen by Nixon and his chief lieutenant Henry Kissinger—aligned the United States with Pakistan, supported by China, against India, backed by the Soviet Union. Disagreeing with US government South Asia specialists, Nixon saw India as a Soviet pawn and thought Mrs. Gandhi was not just out to dismember, but to destroy, Pakistan. He and Kissinger felt it important, in order to strengthen US credibility with China, that Washington continue to support Pakistan in the crisis regardless of the regional realities and costs in terms of US-India relations. The costs were high.

Once the crisis ended, the United States was willing enough to reestablish more normal relations with India, although Washington refused to take the first step in renewing economic aid. Nixon, to his credit, supported Ambassador Moynihan's effort to solve the smoldering rupee debt problem—an issue that if left unattended would have eventually caused serious trouble. Moynihan hoped to shape a "new and mature" relationship, but not enough time had elapsed for the wounds and bruises left by 1971 to heal. Probably, the goal was impossible as long as Nixon remained in the White House.

For New Delhi, the administration's policy during the Bangladesh War cast the United States as a foe of India's national aspirations. Before the fighting began, India interpreted US diplomacy as trying to assist Yahya in weathering the crisis in East Pakistan. Once the war started, Nixon went even further, pillorying India by accusing New Delhi of having designs on West Pakistan, and, in a late 20th century version of gunboat diplomacy, threatening India by sending the aircraft carrier *Enterprise* toward the Bay of Bengal. With pro-leftists fanning the flames, the prevalent Indian perception became one of US hostility, of Washington's trying to "keep India down" and prevent the country from assuming its natural place as the leading power in South Asia. Following the resentment over Lyndon Johnson's handling of the 1965-1967 food crisis and the devaluation fiasco, anger over US policy in 1971 blighted the bilateral Indo-US relationship. Moscow seemed firmly established as India's friend in times of need. It would take a long time until the legacy of Richard Nixon and the *Enterprise* would be forgotten.

NOTES

1. Thomas Perry Thornton, "US Policy in the Nixon-Ford Years," in Harold A. Gould and Sumit Ganguly, eds., *The Hope and the Reality: U.S.-Indian Relations from Roosevelt to Reagan* (Boulder, CO.: Westview Press, 1992), pp. 94-97.

2. Henry A. Kissinger, *The White House Years* (Boston: Little, Brown & Company, 1979), p. 848.

3. Henry Brandon, *The Retreat of American Power* (Garden City: Doubleday & Company, 1973), p. 252.

4. Kissinger, p. 848.

5. Shashi Tharoor, *Reasons of State* (New Delhi: Vikas, 1982), p. 112.

6. Krishnan Bhatia, *Indira Gandhi* (New York: Praeger, 1974), p. 250.

7. William J. Barnds, *India, Pakistan and the Great Powers* (New York: Praeger, 1972), p. 233.

8. *New York Times*, 1 August 1969.

9. Interviews with former Indian Foreign Secretary Rasgotra, 28 February 1991, and former Indian Ministry of External Affairs Secretary Eric Gonsalves, 10 January 1991; Kissinger, p. 848.

10. Ayub never fully recovered politically from the 1965 War and the unpopular Tashkent agreement. After a severe illness in 1968, anti-Ayub agitation mounted and in March 1969 President Ayub was replaced by the Army commander Yahya Khan.

11. *New York Times*, 2 August 1969.

12. Kissinger, pp. 180-81. Secretary of State Rogers was not informed about Nixon's discussions with Yahya. Kissinger and Pakistan's Ambassador in Washington, Agha Hilaly, became the channel for subsequent message passing between US and Chinese leaders. At this stage of the probing, Nixon also used the Romanians as a parallel channel to signal US interest in a dialogue with China.

13. Inder Malhotra, *Indira Gandhi: A Personal and Political Biography* (London: Hodder & Stoughton, 1989), pp. 115-23; Zareer Masani,

Indira Gandhi (London: Hamish Hamilton, 1975), pp. 196-201; and Bhatia, pp. 221-28.

14. Norman D. Palmer, *The United States and India, The Dimensions of Influence* (New York: Praeger, 1984), pp. 38-39.

15. Kissinger, p. 849; Richard Nixon, *U.S. Foreign Policy for the 1970's: Building for Peace* (Washington: Government Printing Office, 1973), p. 113, and Stephen P. Cohen, "South Asia and U.S. Military Policy," in Susan and Lloyd *The Regional Imperative*, Rudolph, eds., pp. 113-17.

16. Thornton, p. 96; Surjit Mansingh, *India's Search for Power: Indira Gandhi's Foreign Policy, 1966-1982* (New Delhi: Sage Publications, 1984), p. 70.

17. Palmer, p. 39; *New York Times*, 24 and 28 February 1970.

18. Kissinger described Indo-American relations at this point as having "achieved a state of exasperatedly strained cordiality, like a couple that can neither separate nor get along." Kissinger p. 848.

19. Kissinger, p. 699.

20. G. W. Choudhury, *India, Pakistan, Bangladesh, and the Major Powers* (New York: The Free Press, 1975), p. 142.

21. Robert C. Horn, *Soviet-Indian Relations* (New York: Praeger, 1982), pp. 27-34.

22. Ibid., pp. 36-40; Mansingh, pp. 138-140; and Bhatia, p. 245.

23. Horn, pp. 40-43; Richard Sisson and Leo E. Rose, *War and Secession: Pakistan, India and the Creation of Bangladesh* (Berkeley: University of California Press, 1990), pp. 196-98; and Bhatia, pp. 244-46.

24. Malhotra, pp. 123-29; Bhatia, pp. 228-36.

25. Quoted in Mansingh, p. 26.

26. Tharoor, p. 104.

27. Mansingh, p. 27.

28. Richard L. Jackson, *The Non-Aligned, the UN, and the Superpowers* (New York: Praeger, 1983), pp. 20-27.

29. Thornton, p. 94; Elmo Zumwalt, *On Watch* (New York: Quadrangle, 1976), p. 361.

30. Initiated with much fanfare, the annual editions of *U.S. Foreign Policy for the 1970's* were serious and unprecedented efforts to spell out the premises and the goals for US policy. The exercise continued through 1973. Regrettably, none of Nixon's successors has resumed the practice.

31. Paradoxically, Nixon's comments about Communist China in the 1970 annual foreign policy report could almost have been written by Pandit Nehru, who argued in 1949 with US leaders that excluding China from the international community was a grave error.

32. Thornton, p. 92-93.

33. Nixon, pp. 111-14.

34. Sisson and Rose, pp. 54-90.

35. Ibid., pp. 91-110.

36. Ibid., pp. 110-33; Robert Jackson, *South Asian Crisis: India, Pakistan and Bangladesh* (New York: Praeger, 1975), pp. 28-32; G. W. Choudhury, *The Last Days of United Pakistan* (Bloomington: Indiana University Press, 1974), pp. 161-79.

37. Sisson and Rose, pp. 138-148; Jackson, pp. 44-47.

38. Sisson and Rose, pp. 151-53, 187.

39. Ibid., pp. 186-91.

40. Jackson, p. 47.

41. Ibid., pp. 40-41.

42. Kissinger, p. 853.

43. Ibid., pp. 853-54. The State Department's reaction was immediately to upgrade the message from the routine "Limited Official Use" designation put by Blood to the highly restricted "Secret/No Distribution" category.

44. Ibid., pp. 713-14.

45. Ibid., p. 856.

46. Christopher Van Hollen, "The Tilt Revisited: Nixon-Kissinger Geopolitics and South Asia," *Asian Survey* 20 (April 1980), reprinted in Rudolph, eds., pp. 427-28.

47. Definitions became almost theological hair splitting under the arms supply policy. Although the policy barred new "lethal" equipment, it permitted the sale of ammunition since this was defined as a "spare part."

48. Interview with Ambassador Van Hollen, 5 December 1990.

49. Sisson and Rose, p. 192. Two decades after the 1971 crisis, senior Indians, such as then Foreign Secretary T. N. Kaul, Indian Embassy Minister Krishna Rasgotra, and Mrs. Gandhi's press adviser, Sharada Prasad, continued to believe that the United States played fast and loose on the question of arms to Pakistan in 1971. Interviews in New Delhi, January-February 1991.

50. Within the US Embassy in Islamabad, practically only Ambassador Joseph Farland, who worked out the details with Yahya, was aware of the China mission. Others, including the author, who was in charge of making arrangements for Kissinger's stay in Pakistan, were fooled by an elaborate cover story of Kissinger's succumbing to "Delhi belly" and agreeing, at Yahya's insistence, to "rest" in the mountain resort of Nathiagali, postponing his departure from Pakistan for a day. Instead of driving to the mountains, Kissinger, in fact, flew to Beijing in a Pakistan International Airlines jet.

51. Hersh, Seymour. *The Price of Power: Kissinger in the Nixon White House* (New York: Summit Books, 1983), p. 452.

52. Ibid.

53. Jackson, pp. 71-73; Palmer, p. 47; Malhotra, p. 135; and Horn, pp. 62-66.

54. Kissinger, pp. 867-68.

55. Horn, pp. 66-69.

56. Van Hollen, p. 432, and Raymond L. Garthoff, *Détente and Confrontation: American-Soviet Relations from Nixon to Reagan* (Washington: The Brookings Institution, 1985), pp. 266-67.

57. Van Hollen, p. 430.

58. Interviews with Harold Saunders, 26 April 1991; Christopher Van Hollen, 5 December 1990; and Thomas Thornton, 12 December 1990.

59. Van Hollen, p. 430.

60. *New York Times*, 6 August 1971.

61. According to M. K. Rasgotra, Jayaprakash Narayan was impressed with Kissinger's presentation, saying, "Our problems are solved." Narayan was rather angry when Rasgotra, then the No. 2 at the Indian Embassy, claimed Kissinger was putting on an act and not to be trusted. (Interview with K. N. Rasgotra, 27 February 1991).

62. Sisson and Rose, pp. 202, 242; Jackson, pp. 87-88; and Horn, pp. 70-71.

63. Ibid., pp. 92-93.

64. Bhatia, p. 254.

65. Hersh, p. 456.

66. Kissinger, p. 877.

67. Interviews with Sharada Prasad, 14 January and 26 February 1991. Prasad served as press adviser to Mrs. Gandhi throughout virtually all her years as prime minister.

68. Richard Nixon, *Public Papers of the President, 1971* (Washington: Government Printing Office, 1973), pp. 1079-80, 1083-84.

69. Van Hollen, p. 435.

70. January 1991 interview with an Indian source with first-hand knowledge who preferred to remain anonymous.

71. Richard Nixon, *RN: The Memoirs of Richard Nixon* (New York: Grosset & Dunlap, 1978), p. 531. Indians emphatically deny she made any such promise to Nixon.

72. Kissinger, p. 880.

73. Garthoff, p. 286.

74. In *War and Secession*, Rose and Sisson concluded that 6 December was the date set for the Indian attack on East Pakistan. Journalist Inder Malhotra, author of a recent biography of Mrs. Gandhi, understood it was 4 December. Other knowledgeable Indians, however, denied Mrs. Gandhi set a D-Day. In any event, Yahya's air attacks brought matters to a head.

75. Yahya's action reflected long-standing Pakistani doctrine that the defense of the east rested on war in the west. Then in bad disarray, the Pakistani leadership hoped the major powers, as in the two earlier Indo-Pakistani wars, would intervene to halt the fighting before India could achieve its objectives.

76. The WSAG was the National Security Council subcommittee established during the Nixon administration to deal with crises. Chaired by Kissinger, the WSAG, during the 1971 South Asia crisis, included participants from the State Department, AID, the Central Intelligence Agency, the Defense Department, and the Joint Chiefs of Staff.

77. Interview with Ambassador Eric Gonsalves, 11 January 1991. Gonsalves at the time was the Ministry of External Affairs representative on the interdepartmental group assessing Chinese intentions. See also Sisson and Rose, *War and Secession*, pp. 252-53.

78. Kissinger, pp. 906-07. This total misreading of Chinese intentions was the basis on which Nixon—according to Kissinger—decided to risk global war. Kissinger wrote that had fighting erupted between Russia and China over South Asia, Nixon would have backed the Chinese.

79. Garthoff, p. 267.

80. Van Hollen, p. 437.

81. Formerly Mrs. Gandhi's and Shastri's chief aide, Jha was a highly respected economist. He became ambassador to Washington in 1969. Despite the terrible strain in relations, Jha won high marks for his ability from Americans, including Kissinger.

82. As Van Hollen pointed out, the Indian position has been that all of Kashmir, including the Pakistan-held portion, was part of India as a result of the state's 1947 accession. "No Indian official would be likely to give such assurances—nor would any Pakistani." Van Hollen p. 437.

83. Horn, pp. 72-73.

84. Kissinger, p. 904.

85. Interview with former Indian Foreign Secretary Venkateshwaran, who participated in the Moscow talks, 24 February 1991.

86. Admiral Elmo Zumwalt, then the Chief of Naval Operations, pointed out that it was hardly credible to despatch a carrier group a distance of several thousand miles to evacuate a handful of US citizens. In any case, the Americans had left East Pakistan by the time the *Enterprise* reached the Bay of Bengal. Zumwalt, p. 367

87. Kissinger, p. 905.

88. David K. Hall, "The Laotian War of 1962 and the Indo-Pakistani War of 1971," in Blechman and Kaplan, *Force without War* (Washington: The Brookings Institution, 1978), pp. 192-94.

89. Malhotra, p. 140. Malhotra wrote that Mrs. Gandhi told her press adviser Sharada Prasad she wanted to proclaim a cease-fire in the west immediately.

90. Nixon stated, "By using diplomatic signals and behind-the-scenes pressures we had been able to save West Pakistan from the imminent threat of Indian aggression and domination." (Nixon, *Memoirs*, p. 530). Kissinger wrote, "There is no doubt in my mind that it was a reluctant decision resulting from Soviet pressure, which in turn grew out of American insistence, including the fleet movement and the willingness to risk the summit. (Kissinger, p. 913).

91. *New York Times*, 16 December 1971.

92. Bhatia, p. 260.

93. Jack Anderson with George Clifford, *The Anderson Papers* (New York: Random House, 1973).

94. Interview with Harold Saunders, 26 April 1991.

95. Ibid.

96. Ibid.

97. Nixon, *Public Papers 1973*, pp. 296-301.

98. Nixon, *Memoirs*, p. 530; Kissinger, pp. 913-15.

99. Ibid., p. 913.

100. The State Department's senior South Asia specialist, Van Hollen, convincingly makes this case in "The Tilt Revisited." See also Garthoff, p. 286.

101. Van Hollen, p. 449.

102. The Peace Corps eventually decided that it was not worthwhile to continue the effort in India on so small a scale and phased the program out.

103. Kissinger, p. 867. In perhaps the ultimate compliment, Kissinger wrote, "I was supposed to be skilful in dealing with the press. On the India-Pakistan issue Jha clearly outclassed me."

104. *The Economist*, 18 December 1971, pp. 11-12.

105. *Washington Post*, 3 and 4 July 1972. Indian participants at Simla told the author that Bhutto implied a willingness to solve the Kashmir dispute on the basis of the status quo—long the Indian objective—but that he would need time.

106. Interview with Christopher Van Hollen, 5 December 1990. Van Hollen accompanied Connally during his visit to India.

107. Interview with Ambassador Daniel Patrick Moynihan, 1 August 1991.

108. Ibid.

109. Nixon, *Public Papers, 1973*, pp. 454, 457.

110. Indira Gandhi, "India and the World," *Foreign Affairs*, 50 (October 1972): pp. 75-76.

111. *New York Times*, 26 January and 6 February 1973.

112. From 1973 until 1977, the author was in charge of Indian affairs in the State Department and thus a witness to events relating to India during the remainder of the Nixon administration as well as the Ford presidency.

113. Daniel Patrick Moynihan, *A Dangerous Place* (Boston: Little, Brown and Company, 1978), p. 16.

114. *New York Times*, 27 April 1974.

115. Ibid., 27 July 1973.

116. Interview with Kewal Singh, 1 March 1990. Since the use of the holdings was severely restricted, the deposits in fact posed no real danger to India. The impression, nonetheless, was widely held.

117. Interview with Ambassador T.N. Kaul, 12 January 1991.

118. Interview with Amb. Daniel Patrick Moynihan, 1 August 1991, and author's personal recollections.

119. *New York Times*, 5 April 1974.

120. Van Hollen, p. 449.

121. Warren Unna, Washington correspondent of the *Statesman*, said he heard this as the reason for the test from N. K. Seshan, a close collaborator of Mrs. Gandhi.

122. NSSM 202, an interagency US Government study on the Indian nuclear question, prepared in 1972, concluded that the odds were better than 50-50 that India would explode a device over the next five years. After the NSSM was sent to the NSC, nothing more was heard until after the test. The author was the principal drafter of the NSSM.

123. Department of State 19 May 1974 press statement.

124. The author drafted the initial statement in line with presumed US policy. This was cabled to Kissinger for approval; instead he sent back the milder version that was released 19 May 1974.

125. Kissinger press conference, 6 June 1974.

126. *New York Times*, 8 June 1974.

127. Interview with Amb. Daniel P. Moynihan, 1 August 1991.

128. *New York Times*, 3 July 1974.

129. Ibid., 26 May, 3 June 1974.

130. Nixon, *Memoirs*, pp. 131-32; Stephen E. Ambrose, *Nixon: The Education of a Politician, 1913-1962* (New York: Simon and Schuster, 1987), p. 325.

Chapter VIII

Ford: "Fragile and Thin"

In August 1974, Gerald Ford succeeded Richard Nixon as President after having spent over twenty years as a middle of the road Republican Congressman from Michigan and a year as Vice President. Ford seemed like an ideal replacement for Spiro Agnew when the then Vice President resigned on corruption charges, but few considered "good old Gerry" presidential timber. All the same, Ford helped restore dignity to the White House in his two years in office after the Watergate scandals.

The new President had limited experience in dealing with South Asia. As in most foreign policy matters, he took his lead from Secretary of State Kissinger, whom he greatly admired. The unsettled state of the Middle East following the 1973 war and the oil embargo, the future of détente with Moscow, and the coming apart of US policy in Indo-China all stood high on the foreign policy agenda. South Asia did not.

In October 1974, Kissinger, nonetheless, took a personal step to repair the damage with India, spending three days in New Delhi during one of his many foreign trips—sandwiching South Asia in between talks in Moscow and stops in the Middle East. Although the Secretary was never one to say "I am sorry," his trip signalled Washington's interest in patching things up.

Kissinger appeared upbeat on arrival and throughout the stay in New Delhi. At a 28 October official dinner, he spoke of past misunderstandings as removed and of a "better, more realistic relationship" between the two countries in the future.[1]

The next day, the Secretary delivered a major policy statement in a speech to the Indian Council of World Affairs. Kissinger underscored US hopes for a "mature" relationship, stressed US acceptance of India as the preeminent power in the region, and indicated Washington had no quarrel with India's policy of non-alignment. "The United States recognizes India as one of the major powers of the world and conducts its policy accordingly," Kissinger declared.[2] These were all words the Indians had long hoped to hear from the United States, especially from someone like Henry Kissinger, regarded by New Delhi as antagonistic.

At the same time, Kissinger alluded to sensitivities over US aid, commenting, "Our relationship cannot be based on dependence of one on the other." The Secretary added, "Nor can our relationship survive constant criticism of one by the other"—a reference to India's habit of sniping at US policies and Mrs. Gandhi's periodic allegations of US interference in India's internal affairs. In a press conference on 30 October, Kissinger flatly denied that the CIA was interfering in Indian affairs. He stated, "The United States is not engaged, directly or indirectly, in any attempt to influence the domestic situation in India."[3]

Although the US Embassy and much of the Indian press talked of the visit's removing bilateral bad blood and ushering in a brighter period of relations,[4] Mrs. Gandhi made it clear she still harbored resentments. The day before the Secretary of State's arrival, in an interview with the *National Herald*, a newspaper founded by the Nehru family, she complained India was regarded as "marginal" by Washington and said tartly that India was not going to beg for US aid.[5] The Prime Minister met and had lunch with Kissinger during his first day in New Delhi, but then abruptly left the capital for Kashmir in what appeared to be a calculated snub.[6]

In substantive meetings with Mrs. Gandhi and Foreign Minister Y. B. Chavan, the most important topics related to South Asia and nuclear policy. Kissinger was non-committal when the Indians pressed for a continuation of the US arms embargo toward the region. Kissinger, in turn, pressed India not to become a proliferator by exporting sensitive nuclear material to other Third World countries. Appealing to Indian pride, the Secretary did not sermonize about the nuclear test, but stressed that the United States "takes seriously India's affirmation that it has no intention to develop nuclear weapons."[7]

During the stay, Kissinger and Chavan also signed an agreement to establish an Indo-US Joint Commission. Although the Indians had wanted such a body for some time, until Kissinger agreed, US officials were unenthusiastic. They felt the approach smacked too much of the way Communist countries managed relations, placing everything under the governmental umbrella. The Indians countered that given the poor state of Indo-US bilateral ties, few cooperative activities would move forward without New Delhi's agreement.

The Joint Commission structure was simple. At the top, it consisted only of the Secretary of State and the Indian Minister of External Affairs, who would meet from time to time. Below the ministers came the heart of the structure—subcommissions dealing with science and technology, education and culture, and economics and trade.[8] Overall, in its two decades of existence, the Commission has succeeded modestly in sheltering useful joint activities from the ups and downs of the political relationship. The Science and Education Subcommissions have overseen a host of joint projects, ranging from the 1985 Year of India art exhibition to hundreds of scientific research projects. The Economic and Trade Subcommission and a parallel private sector Joint Business Council have served as convenient platforms for periodic airing of Indian and American views on current economic issues.

After the Kissinger visit, Moynihan was nearing the end of two years in India and planning to return to Harvard. He could take credit for solving the rupee debt problem and restoring the bilateral dialogue. Under the circumstances, it was not realistic to have expected more. In an interview with the *New York Times*, the envoy seemed in a "melancholy mood." Talking about relations, he said, "We've now reached a kind of plateau," less volatile and unstable than in the past, but also "fragile and thin."[9] Events would soon underscore the accuracy of Moynihan's remarks.

Arms to Pakistan: "Reopening of Old Wounds"

President Ford nominated William Saxbe, Nixon's last Attorney General and a former Republican Senator from Ohio, as the new Ambassador to India. While serving in the Senate, Saxbe gained a reputation for political independence and public frankness; during the 1971 crisis he strongly criticized US policy toward South Asia. Pleased by the nomination of a cabinet member, New Delhi granted agrément the day it was sought by Chargé d'Affaires David Schneider. As a further gesture, Foreign Secretary Kewal Singh got Mrs. Gandhi and President Fakruddin Ali Ahmed to agree that Saxbe would present his credentials the day after arriving, enabling the new envoy to avoid the usual waiting period. With Nixon no longer in the White House, the Indians wanted to make a friendly nod toward Gerald Ford's emissary.[10]

The US-Pakistan arms relationship, however, once more caused problems. Pakistan's Prime Minister Bhutto had, for some time, been urging Washington to lift the embargo on sales of new weapons systems—he would have liked military aid but recognized this was not in the cards. When Bhutto visited Washington in February 1975, Kissinger wanted to oblige. He was impressed by Bhutto and the skilful way in which he restored a sense of self-confidence after the disaster of the 1971 war.[11] Following India's crushing victory and the continued inflow of large amounts of Soviet arms, Kissinger thought New Delhi had little basis for complaint if Pakistan bought modest amounts of weapons from the United States—perhaps $100 million annually. Since the United States was not contemplating major weapon shipments, the Secretary saw no reason why ending the embargo would either undercut India's military predominance or trigger a new regional arms race.

After President Ford gave his blessing to the policy change, the State Department announced the lifting of the embargo—in effect since September 1965—on 24 February 1975, just days before Saxbe was scheduled to take up his post in New Delhi. The State Department assumed it would be better to make the announcement before Saxbe arrived so the new ambassador would not be blamed for a decision that was going to upset the Indians.

Even though Washington anticipated a strong reaction, it was even stiffer than expected. In parliament, Foreign Minister Y. B. Chavan vehemently criticized the decision, charging the resumption of US lethal arms sales to Pakistan would unsettle

19 September 1974, President Gerald R. Ford meets in the White House with Indian Foreign Minister Sardar Swaran Singh, Ambassador T.N. Kaul, Secretary of State Henry Kissinger, and National Security Adviser Brent Scowcroft.

the process of normalization between India and Pakistan. To underscore Indian ire, Chavan canceled a planned trip to the United States for the initial meeting of the new Joint Commission.[12] Two days later, Mrs. Gandhi asserted the US decision amounted "to reopening of old wounds."[13]

The shrillest reaction came not from New Delhi, but from T. N. Kaul, India's ambassador in Washington. The envoy sharply denounced Kissinger's action, declaring it would have "an adverse affect" on relations. "We do not accept or agree," Kaul told newsmen, "that the lifting of the arms embargo will not lead to an arms race or hinder the process of normalization."[14] Annoyed by public criticism from a resident ambassador—a breach of normal diplomatic conduct—the Secretary of State fired back testily, "The comments of the Indian Foreign Minister are restrained and statesmanlike, but those of the Indian ambassador are unacceptable." Kissinger went on to stress US interest in India while claiming that an arms embargo against a friendly country like Pakistan was "morally, politically and symbolically improper."[15]

The Indian envoy lost his vaunted access to Kissinger through his brash and undiplomatic outburst. The Secretary no longer appeared at Kaul's curry dinners and no longer agreed to private meetings. The ambassador's usefulness in Washington came to an end. He later defended his outspoken reaction on the grounds that Kissinger refused to delay lifting the embargo to give Foreign Minister Chavan a chance to present Indian objections directly to President Ford.[16]

With the controversy over the arms decision still swirling in the Indian media and Washington, Saxbe decided it better that he wait a few days in Bangkok before traveling to New Delhi. Meanwhile, Kewal Singh, who arranged the early presentation of credentials, found himself scoffed at by colleagues skeptical about the prospect for friendlier relations with the United States. "You see what happens when you try to be nice to the Americans," they told the embarrassed Foreign Secretary.[17]

Although Washington found the Indian response to lifting the arms embargo an overreaction, US officials could, at least, comprehend Indian concerns given the history of bitter antagonism between India and Pakistan. The State Department had much less understanding for New Delhi's chronic sniping about

27 January 1975, President Ford meeting with Ambassador Daniel Patrick Moynihan in the Oval Office.

alleged CIA interference in India. Nor did US officials appreciate the Indian government's reaction to the fall of South Vietnam and Cambodia to the Communists in April 1975—a postwar low point for US foreign policy and national pride. An almost gloating Foreign Minister Y. B. Chavan applauded these developments which he called the culmination of "the heroic struggle of the people of Indo-China to assert their independence and sovereignty and a "gratifying vindication for India's policy."[18]

Saxbe, who genuinely liked India and Indians, quickly became pessimistic about the prospects for better relations. Speaking as freely as Ambassador to India as he had as Senator from Ohio or Attorney General, Saxbe startled Indian officialdom by his frankness. To make sure the Indians got his message, Saxbe gave a number of interviews with the US press in his first months in New Delhi—a sharp contrast with Moynihan's low profile approach.

In March 1975, Saxbe told the *New York Times* that the best he could hope for with India was "grudging respect" and described US interests as limited to "humanitarian and cultural" matters.[19] Talking about lifting the arms embargo—which he had opposed—Saxbe commented to the *Washington Post* that relations did not improve whether the United States sold arms to Pakistan or not. "It's hell if you do and hell if you don't," the envoy bluntly stated.[20] Continuing his public diplomacy, Saxbe told the *New York Times*, "If India is determined to make an enemy of the United States there is not a whole lot we can do about it."[21] Expressing the annoyance many US officials felt about Indian criticisms—but rarely voiced in public—Saxbe commented:

> When I call on cabinet ministers, the President, or Governors, they all love to talk about their sons, sons-in-law and daughters in the United States and how well they are doing and how well they like things. The next day I read in the papers that the very same people are denouncing the United States . . .[22]

Saxbe adopted a novel style in other ways, refusing to make the usual diplomatic rounds of senior officials and ministers or to court the Indian media. If the Indians wanted to see him, he was available. He was not going to run after people. The point he was trying to get across was that the United States wished India well, but Mrs. Gandhi needed to decide whether she wanted better relations with Washington or not—this was something only the Indian government could determine.

Implicit in Saxbe's approach was the fact that by the mid-1970s India no longer had great strategic importance for the United States. Although Washington through its South Asia policies, its role in international financial institutions, and the US position as a major trading partner remained a major external factor for New Delhi, India cast a much reduced shadow on US interests than in the late 1950s or early 1960s. With time, Saxbe's unorthodox tactics might have had more impact, but the proclamation of the Emergency on 24 June 1975 radically altered the situation.

If Saxbe's open-mouth diplomacy upset Indians, it failed to silence Mrs. Gandhi's periodic allegations about "foreign elements trying to destabilize India." Although she did not usually specify the CIA, people knew this was what she had in mind, especially after the overthrow of Salvador Allende in Chile in 1973. Since Kissinger explicitly and publicly stated the United States was not engaging in any covert activities against India, the Prime Minister's refusal to stop her criticism galled Washington. US officials generally assumed that Indira alleged US interference as a sop to leftist supporters and also as a way to divert attention from domestic problems by raising the specter of a foreign threat.

The Emergency: The End of Indian Democracy?

By 1975, three years after Mrs. Gandhi stood at the peak of power, the Prime Minister's political position was badly eroding. Having gained an unchallengeable electoral mandate in 1971, Indira seemed unable to accomplish any of the promised reforms. Her election slogan of eradicating poverty turned out to be not much more than words. Although she shone in dealing with crises like East Pakistan, she showed little flair for implementing a coherent domestic program. Her main concern seemed to be the maintenance of her own political power.

A combination of bad harvests and the sharp rise in oil prices after the 1973 Arab-Israeli War badly weakened the Indian economy. The country began to experience an unprecedented wave of domestic unrest and trade union strikes. The disparate and fractious political opposition, although badly defeated in the 1971 general elections, revived as Mrs. Gandhi's popularity slumped. Gaining strength, the opposition united in support of the Janata (Hindi for Peoples') Party, mounting mass rallies and demonstrations against Indira's rule. In April 1975, Janata hopes for the 1976 general elections soared after the Congress lost in state balloting in Gujarat in western India—the home of Morarji Desai, who had become a Janata leader.

And then the courts delivered an unexpected blow to Mrs. Gandhi. For some time a lawsuit by Raj Narain, her opponent in the 1971 elections, sought to have Mrs. Gandhi's election to parliament set aside because of minor technical irregularities during the campaign. The judge stunned India by ruling against Mrs. Gandhi. Even though she had six months to win a parliamentary seat and could continue in office as Prime Minister during this period, the court decision sapped Mrs. Gandhi's moral and political authority. An elated opposition called for mass demonstrations in the hope of forcing Indira from office even before the 1976 general elections. Mrs. Gandhi found herself in grave political danger once more.

Her response—typical of Indira's style when cornered—was to strike back with all the force at her command. At her behest, the pliable President of India, Fakruddin Ali Ahmed, proclaimed a national emergency during the night of 24 June 1975. Imposing de facto martial law, the authorities arrested the principal opposition leaders along with thousands of their followers. Press censorship was imposed. Civil liberties were restricted. Stunned by the force of Mrs. Gandhi's action, Indian democracy seemed at an end. Once so proud of its political freedoms, India became just another Third World dictatorship.

Abroad, especially in the United States where India's biggest plus had been its adherence to democracy, the reaction was harshly negative. Already upset over the nuclear test, liberals turned against India, joining conservatives as biting critics of Mrs. Gandhi. The hero of the Bangladesh war became one of the most disliked foreign leaders for Americans. The *New York*

Times, formerly a staunch backer of US support for Indian development and a leading critic of US policy in the Bangladesh crisis, denounced Mrs. Gandhi's action.[23] Other critics were less civil, including former Ambassador Moynihan, who acidly told an interviewer from *Playboy*, "When India ceased to be a democracy, our actual interest there just plummeted. I mean, what does it export but communicable disease?"[24] Although crude, Moynihan's basic point was valid: it was India's adherence to democracy that—in the absence of other major interests—made the country of importance to the United States.[25]

The administration avoided joining in the chorus of criticism of Mrs. Gandhi, despite chiding from India's one-time liberal supporters. Secretary Kissinger believed that the United States should not base its external relations on whether or not it liked the domestic political character of foreign governments. He also did not want to provide Mrs. Gandhi ammunition to blame the United States for her country's domestic troubles or to have gratuitous US criticism serve as an impulse for an even further strengthening of Indo-Soviet relations. Because of the Emergency, President Ford, nonetheless, decided to postpone indefinitely a trip to South Asia talked about for late 1976.[26]

Through this period, Indo-Soviet relations remained cordial and close. The Russians applauded the imposition of the Emergency, labelling Mrs. Gandhi's opponents as right-wing reactionaries. Trade and cultural exchanges increased. The military supply relationship was stronger than ever. A vocal pro-Soviet lobby among intellectuals, journalists, politicians, and civil servants beat the drums to support Moscow and Marxism and to criticize the United States. The Prime Minister was, nonetheless, uncomfortable in India's appearing so reliant on one of the two superpowers. In a sense, as Kissinger wrote in his memoirs,[27] Mrs. Gandhi gave indications of wanting to maintain a certain distance from the Soviets and to seek better relations with the United States despite the scars left by 1971 and the insistent US media criticism of the Emergency.

The Prime Minister refused to agree with Brezhnev's Asian Security scheme, and, in spite of the large-scale Soviet military aid, reportedly spurned feelers from the Kremlin for naval facilities. Mrs. Gandhi's younger son, Sanjay, also began to play an important political role, even though he held no official position. Unlike his mother or grandfather, Sanjay was skeptical about Indian socialism. Like many in the younger generation of the Indian elite, Sanjay looked to the West—particularly to the United States—as an economic model, not to the Soviet Union and the Communist bloc.

At the official level, bilateral relations between Washington and New Delhi improved somewhat. In October 1975, Foreign Minister Chavan—after a delay of over a year—visited Washington for the first meeting of the Joint Commission. In early 1976, Mrs. Gandhi appeared to make a gesture toward Washington in personnel shifts. She named as Foreign Secretary, Jagat Mehta, who had long argued that friendlier Indo-US relations were in India's interests. To replace T. N. Kaul in Washington, she appointed former Foreign Secretary Kewal Singh. In contrast with the confrontational Kaul, Kewal Singh had a polite, soft-spoken style and was not regarded as pro-Soviet.

Despite these signals suggesting her interest in better relations and the Ford administration's silence about the Emergency, Mrs. Gandhi continued to talk darkly of a US threat to India. At a January 1976 Congress Party gathering at Chandrigarh in northwestern India, Mrs. Gandhi charged that the powers that destabilized Chile "nurtured similar designs against India."[28] In Washington, the State Department reacted by expressing "concern and dismay"—language that conveyed official exasperation over Indira's remarks.[29]

As if to offset her attacks at Chandrigarh, the Prime Minister unexpectedly attended Saxbe's reception to celebrate the bicentennial of the US Declaration of Independence and praised the United States for its dynamism. The Chandrigarh episode, however, exhausted Washington's patience. The State Department instructed Saxbe to inform the Indians that because of Mrs. Gandhi's unfounded allegations the United States would not proceed with a resumption of aid—for which there was $75 million in the budget.[30]

Whether Mrs. Gandhi really believed the charges about CIA was debatable. In Moynihan's book, *A Dangerous Place*, the former envoy pointed out that since Mrs. Gandhi herself—as Congress Party president—received money from CIA in the late 1950s to help oust the Communist government of Kerala, it was not surprising that she thought the CIA was helping others. After having the Embassy check on US covert activities in India, Moynihan concluded that apart from the help CIA gave the Congress Party, "We had been up to very little."[31] Some Indians who knew Mrs. Gandhi well thought that despite the fact that she was quite capable of using the United States as a political scapegoat, she was genuinely worried that she might be a CIA target, especially after events in Chile. The assassination of Mujibur Rahman in Bangladesh in the summer of 1975 added to the Prime Minister's anxieties.[32]

With the Emergency in force and Mrs. Gandhi's periodic sniping at the United States, Saxbe and the Ford administration concluded that, for the time being at least, relations would remain in the doldrums. Easing off on his statements to the press, Saxbe seemed content to spend his time improving his golf game and traveling around India.

Tarapur: To License or Not?

In 1976, the problem of shipping enriched uranium fuel for the Tarapur nuclear power plant reactor returned to center stage. Before the May 1974 test, the US AEC had routinely approved fuel exports for Tarapur—there was a legally binding supply contract between the US and Indian AECs and satisfactory safeguards were in place. After the test, however, Tarapur fuel shipments became the focus of controversy. The US AEC delayed a shipment in 1974 until Homi Sethna, the Chairman of the Indian AEC, gave written assurances to US AEC Chairperson Dixie Lee Ray that:

> Special nuclear material that has been or is hereafter made available for, or used, or produced in the Tarapur Atomic Power Station . . . will be devoted exclusively to the needs of that Station unless our two governments, hereafter specifically agree that such material be used for other purposes.[33]

In 1975, a reorganization of US nuclear activities shifted licensing authority to the newly created Nuclear Regulatory Commission (NRC). Unlike the AEC, the NRC was an independent body, not part of the Executive Branch and not subject to presidential direction. In March 1976, the NRC voted 3-1 to approve half of a pending fuel shipment or nine tons of enriched uranium and to hold public hearings regarding the export of the other nine tons in late July.

At the hearings—a first for the NRC—administration spokesman Myron Kratzer of the State Department regretted the Indian test, but said this did not bear on the shipment of enriched uranium for Tarapur. Since the United States had a legal obligation to supply the fuel, Kratzer argued that failure to do so would risk losing the safeguards on Tarapur as well as influence over the future course of India's nuclear policy. Kratzer stressed the view that non-compliance with the Tarapur contract would harm US interests by suggesting the United States was not a "reliable supplier" of nuclear fuel—then a major element in US nuclear policy.[34]

Anti-nuclear groups, such as the National Resources Defense Council, the Sierra Club, and the Union of Concerned Scientists, paraded several dozen witnesses who urged the NRC to reject the license application. The opponents wanted the United States, like Canada, to end nuclear cooperation with India because of the 1974 test. They asserted that India's using heavy water supplied by the United States in the production of the plutonium for the test was a violation of the 1956 agreement under which the heavy water was supplied. The opponents argued that if India had violated this agreement, it could violate others in the future—like the one covering Tarapur.[35] To buttress their assertion, the critics cited a 1970 unilateral US statement that any use of US-supplied nuclear material in an explosion would violate earlier Indo-US nuclear agreements. Even though the Indians refused to accept this after-the-fact interpretation, opponents claimed the presence of US heavy water in the Canadian reactor, which produced the plutonium for the Pokharan test, constituted a violation of the 1956 "peaceful uses" agreement for the heavy water. The weakness with this argument was twofold: First, in 1956, "peaceful uses" did not rule out "peaceful nuclear explosions," and, second, a unilateral US redefinition of an agreement fifteen years after signing did not bind the Indians. While politically appealing, the argument was legally weak.

The Ford administration's position, however, suffered when—because of an internal mixup—a State Department reply to a query from Senator Abraham Ribicoff (D., Conn.) stated in error that the heavy water sent to India in 1956 had evaporated and therefore could not have been involved in producing the plutonium for the nuclear device.[36] Ribicoff and others in the anti-nuclear lobby jumped on the mistake to charge the administration with trying to mislead the public—a particularly sensitive matter in the post-Watergate atmosphere. In a 2 August letter to Ribicoff, Kissinger admitted the error, but the damage was done.[37]

Even though the Indians remained silent during the NRC hearings, as a sign of their desire to maintain the Tarapur supply relationship, Homi Sethna, head of the Indian AEC, assured US officials India would not act irresponsibly in exporting sensitive nuclear materials. The Indians also offered to re-export all the used Tarapur fuel to the United States, physically ensuring the spent fuel could not be reprocessed to produce plutonium for nuclear explosions.[38]

Split down the middle, the NRC finally decided to delay a decision until after the 1976 US presidential elections. The Democratic Party candidate, Jimmy Carter, familiar with nuclear questions from his experience on US Navy nuclear submarines, was already criticizing the Indian case as an example of a flabby US nonproliferation policy. During the campaign, he made a tougher approach on nonproliferation one of his major foreign policy planks. In response to Carter's attacks, Ford announced revised and tougher nuclear export controls in October 1976, shortly before the election.

When the Democrats won a narrow victory in November, the prospects for continued nuclear cooperation with India seemed poor. On this issue—and indeed on Indo-US bilateral relations in general—traditional liberal and conservative positions had reversed themselves. US liberals, who had lambasted Nixon's Bangladesh policy and supported good US-Indian relations, were pressing to cut off nuclear cooperation and to castigate Mrs. Gandhi for the Emergency. US conservatives, formerly critics of India, were cast in the role of supporting continued nuclear cooperation and wanting to avoid further disruption of relations through US sniping at the Emergency.

1969-1977: A Summing Up

The bilateral relationship sustained grievous damage during the 1970s, first from US policy during the Bangladesh crisis and later from Indian actions—the 1974 nuclear test and the

1975 proclamation of the Emergency. Psychologically, the US approach during 1971—especially the *Enterprise* episode—etched an image of US hostility into the Indian historical memory. Nixon's termination of the economic assistance program, previously a positive offset to political frictions, removed another important element of the bilateral relationship. Even though the aid links brought their own problems, US help was a tangible sign of American interest in supporting the economic development of the world's largest democracy.

Despite there being few incentives for Washington to seek improved relations, US interests still put a limit on how bad things would get. The United States felt that it could not entirely ignore India, even if, during the two-year Ford presidency there was only a modest desire to find a modus vivendi. India remained the most populous developing nation apart from China, of limited strategic importance as the White House viewed the world in the 1970s, but of some significance because of its size and leadership role in the nonaligned movement.

Even more so, India could not ignore Washington. US South Asia policies, especially ties with Pakistan and China, could directly affect Indian security. Through the strong US voice in international financial institutions, the Americans also influenced multilateral aid flows, of growing importance as a source of external finance for Indian development. As much as US policy during 1971 offended New Delhi, it was not in India's national interest to make hostility with Washington a permanent foreign policy feature. Despite Indira Gandhi's chronic sniping at Washington, she was wary of India's becoming so closely linked to the Soviet Union that nonalignment would become a fiction. A firm nationalist, the Prime Minister wanted to maintain her country's freedom of maneuver in the international arena. To realize this goal, India needed at least the semblance of a working relationship with the United States.[39]

NOTES

1. *New York Times*, 28 October 1974.
2. Ibid., 29 October 1974.
3. Ibid., 31 October 1974.
4. Ibid., 3 November 1974.
5. Ibid., 28 October 1974.

6. According to then Foreign Secretary Kewal Singh, Mrs. Gandhi found Kissinger too full of his own importance and cleverness. Singh said she intended to put him in his place by leaving New Delhi in the middle of his stay. (Interview with the late Kewal Singh, 1 March 1991)

7. *New York Times*, 29 October 1974.

8. A subcommission on agriculture was added in 1979.

9. *New York Times*, 15 December 1974.

10. Interview with Ambassador Kewal Singh, 1 March 1991.

11. Henry A. Kissinger, *White House Years* (Boston: Little, Brown & Co, 1979), p. 907.

12. *New York Times*, 25 and 27 February 1975.

13. Ibid., 29 February 1975.

14. Ibid., 25 February 1975.

15. Ibid., 26 February 1975.

16. Interview with T. N. Kaul, 18 January 1991.

17. Interview with Kewal Singh, 1 March 1991.

18. *New York Times*, 24 April 1975.

19. Ibid., 25 March 1975.

20. *Washington Post*, 19 March 1975.

21. *New York Times*, 25 April 1975.

22. Ibid.

23. *New York Times*, 1 July 1975.

24. *Playboy*, March 1977, p. 78.

25. In retrospect, Moynihan regretted the remarks about "communicable disease," but still thought the thrust of his remarks was correct. (Interview with Senator Moynihan, 1 August 1991).

26. *New York Times*, 12 August 1976.

27. Kissinger, p. 916.

28. *Washington Post*, 1 January 1976.

29. Ibid.

30. *New York Times*, 29 February 1976; *Washington Post*, 19 February 1976.

31. Daniel Patrick Moynihan, *A Dangerous Place* (Boston: Little, Brown & Co, 1978), pp. 40-41. Moynihan revealed that India cooperated with the CIA in placing secret nuclear-powered sensoring devices in the Himalayas capable of collecting technical data on Chinese nuclear tests.

32. Interviews with Sharada Prasad, Inder Malhotra, and Kewal Singh, January-February 1991.

33. Sethna-Ray letter of 17 September 1974, quoted in N. Ram, "India's Nuclear Policy," paper prepared for the Association of Asian Studies' April 1982 annual meeting, pp. 20-21.

34. *Washington Post*, 19 and 22 July, 1976.

35. *Washington Post*, 19, 21, and 22 July 1976.

36. The author recalled that technical information on the rate of evaporation of heavy water, relayed by telephone from the nuclear specialists to the State Department, was garbled in transcription, indicating more rapid evaporation than, in fact, occurred. Based on this misinformation, the State Department wrote Ribicoff that since it had already evaporated, US heavy water could not have been present in the reactor when the material for the Indian explosive device was produced.

37. *New York Times*, 9 August 1976.

38. The author's personal recollections of discussions with the Indians.

39. This idea is developed in Thomas P. Thornton's "U.S.-India Relations in the Nixon and Ford Years," in Harold A. Gould and Sumit Ganguly, eds., *The Hope and the Reality: U.S.-Indian Relations from Roosevelt to Bush* (Boulder: Westview, 1992).

Chapter IX

Carter: Unfulfilled Hopes

As Jimmy Carter led the Democrats back to the White House, the prospects for Indo-US relations were mixed. If Ford and Kissinger were willing to look the other way about dictatorship in India on the grounds that internal political arrangements of foreign countries were not a concern of the United States, Carter felt differently. The new President pledged to make respect for human rights a cardinal principle of US foreign policy. Carter's thinking was not far from that of liberal Congressman Donald Fraser (D-Minnesota), who declared in hearings just after the inauguration, that the United States ought to avoid "endorsing implicitly or otherwise India's suspension of civil rights."[1] The new President's emphasis on human rights threatened to collide head on with the Emergency.

During the campaign, Carter stressed his desire for a tougher policy against nuclear proliferation. Within days of taking the oath of office, the new President ordered a major review of nuclear policy. Having criticized Ford's response to the Indian test as too weak, Jimmy Carter would have to decide how to deal with India—specifically, whether to continue to provide enriched uranium fuel for Tarapur.[2]

Balancing human rights and nonproliferation as issues likely to have a negative impact on relations, Carter's National Security Adviser, Columbia Professor Zbigniew Brzezinski, sketched out a foreign policy agenda that gave India a higher priority than had been the case under Nixon and Ford. The overall strategy was to deemphasize Cold War or East-West concerns and to pay more attention to North-South issues, strengthening relations with nations likely to move into positions of prominence by the end of the 20th century. Along with Saudi Arabia, Iran, Indonesia, Nigeria, Brazil, and Venezuela, Brzezinski listed India as one of the "regional influentials."[3] Carter himself was also favorably predisposed towards the Third World, in general, and India, in particular.[4]

Exactly how this policy mix would play out with regard to India was unclear when unexpectedly a major cloud over the relationship lifted. Just a week before Carter's inauguration, Indira surprised everyone by ending the Emergency, easing restrictions on democratic rights, releasing thousands from jail, and scheduling general elections for March 1977.[5] The Prime Minister explained that with India stable and the economy improved, "There seemed no reason not to have elections."[6] Even if Mrs. Gandhi vehemently denied a desire for approbation from the West,[7] her frequent interviews with Western journalists suggested the opposite—as did her comment that the elections would "uphold the fair name of India."[8]

In February, just as the campaign was getting under way, India's President, Fakhruddin Ali Ahmed, died. To represent the United States at the funeral, Carter designated his mother, "Miss Lillian," who had direct association with India from having served two years as a sixty-year old Peace Corps volunteer near Bombay during the late 1960s. Sending Miss Lillian was a nice way of showing the Indians that the Kissinger-Nixon era of realpolitik was over, and of signalling the new President's personal interest in better relations. As Thomas Thornton, the NSC staffer on South Asia during the Carter administration, wrote, "The symbolism was warm and personal."[9]

When India went to the polls in March, Mrs. Gandhi and her Congress Party suffered a stunning defeat. Running under the banner of the Janata Front, the opposition won an unexpected landslide victory, gaining 295 seats in parliament to 153 for the Congress Party. Although the Janata campaigned principally against the trampling of democracy during the Emergency, coercive birth control policies promoted by Sanjay Gandhi probably stirred as much resentment among the mass of India's rural voters. In a matter of weeks, Morarji Desai, Mrs. Gandhi's long-time opponent, moved from jail to become India's fourth prime minister. Although defeated in his run for the prime ministership after Shastri's death in 1966, and ousted in 1969 from the finance ministry by Mrs. Gandhi, the former Congress Party veteran unexpectedly emerged as India's leader at the age of 81. His Janata Front possessed a large parliamentary majority, but the numbers were deceptive. The Front comprised an unstable alliance of former Congress Party opponents of Indira, onetime socialists, and conservative Hindu nationalists from the Jan Sangh party. The glue holding the Janata together was the struggle against Mrs. Gandhi and the Emergency. After only two years in power, the glue would come unstuck, the coalition would be rent by internal rivalries, and the Janata would fall apart.

Carter and Desai: Two Moral and Moralistic Leaders

Despite their vastly different backgrounds, the onetime US Navy officer and peanut farmer from Plains, Georgia, and the austere octogenarian Gandhian from Gujarat had a good deal in common. Both owed their election to popular reaction against major domestic trauma—the Watergate scandal in the United States and the Emergency in India. Both were deeply moral and moralistic leaders. Both shared genuine concern for the principles of human rights, democracy, disarmament, and the economic growth of developing countries.

In Washington, there was a quick and enthusiastic reaction to the Indian elections. Jody Powell, White House press spokesman, called them "something that should be an inspiration." The State Department sounded equally upbeat: "This naturally is very good news that the world's second largest country has once again carried out a free and fair election."[10] With former Vice President Hubert Humphrey, again a senator from Minnesota, taking the lead, the US Congress repealed the law adopted after the 1974 nuclear test requiring the United States to vote against all World Bank loans to India.[11]

On the Indian side, the signs were similarly positive. Over the years, Morarji Desai had gained a reputation as friendly toward the United States and critical of the Soviet Union—in contrast to Washington's view of Mrs. Gandhi's as pro-Soviet and anti-American. During the campaign, Desai criticized Mrs. Gandhi's policies as leaning too closely toward Moscow and

1 January 1978, Prime Minister Morarji Desai welcomes President and Mrs. Jimmy Carter on their arrival in New Delhi.

called for "genuine" nonalignment in India's foreign policy with more balanced relations with Moscow and Washington.[12] The new Foreign Minister Atul Bihari Vajpayee of the Hindu nationalist Jan Sangh shared Desai's views about the need to bring better balance into India's ties with the two superpowers. Desai continued in office Foreign Secretary Jagat Mehta, who believed friendly ties with both Washington and Moscow were in India's interest as part of a broader policy of "beneficial bilateralism," not only with the United States and the Soviet Union, but with India's smaller neighbors in South Asia as well.[13] As the NSC's senior South Asia staffer, Brzezinski brought Thomas Thornton over from the State Department's Policy Planning Staff, so that, for the first time in a decade, the White House had a staffer with direct expertise on the subcontinent.

The selection of ambassadors similarly signalled mutual interest in better relations. Carter named former Princeton University President Robert Goheen, born in India of missionary parents. Goheen, who retained strong links with India, served as the co-chairman of the educational and cultural subcommission. Desai selected Nani Palkhivala, a respected Bombay lawyer, human rights activist, and outspoken opponent of the Emergency. A senior director of Tata's, one of India's most prestigious business enterprises, Palkhivala was an articulate booster of the free enterprise system and of close relations with the West.

When Ambassador Goheen met Carter before departing for India, the President focused on the nuclear problem, instructing Goheen to tell the Prime Minister, "If India would restrain from developing atomic weapons and agree to discuss nonproliferation, he would clear the pending Tarapur shipment."[14] A few days later when Goheen relayed Carter's message, the Prime Minister responded positively, "I will never develop a bomb and, yes, we will engage in discussions."[15] The new governments were thus off to a good start in dealing with the one serious issue that clouded an otherwise promising bilateral scene.

On 28 June, the Nuclear Regulatory Commission (NRC), under pressure from the Carter administration, approved the long-pending export license for nine tons of enriched uranium fuel. Even though opponents briefly blocked the shipment in the US District Court, the US Appellate Court, after a strong plea from the Justice Department, permitted the fuel to be exported to India. About the same time, Foreign Secretary Jagat Mehta and former Harvard Professor Joseph Nye, who became the top nuclear policymaker for the new administration, held private discussions in London after Nye visited India. The talks were positive in tone, but inconclusive.[16]

President Carter initiated a friendly and extended correspondence with the new Indian Prime Minister.[17] Confirming the exchanges in an interview with the *New York Times*, Desai commented, "From what he says, he believes in the same values that I believe in."[18] A round of high-level talks took place in July 1977 when Warren Christopher, the Deputy Secretary of State and right-hand man to Secretary Cyrus Vance, visited New Delhi. In line with the administration's desire to upgrade relations with India, Christopher pointedly did not follow the usual practice of coupling a visit to New Delhi with a stop in neighboring Pakistan—a practice that annoyed the Indians since it suggested that the United States equated relations with the two countries. On this occasion, Christopher further upset the Pakistanis by telling the press in New Delhi that the United States looked "to India as the leader in South Asia."[19]

The United States and India seemed to be coming closer together in other areas in the early months of the Carter administration. Carter and Vance made clear they cast a jaundiced eye on sales of sophisticated weapons to the subcontinent, always a subject of deep concern in New Delhi. In its last days, the Ford administration was leaning toward approving a Pakistani request to buy A-7 fighter-bomber aircraft. The outgoing administration justified such a sale as a way of inducing Pakistan not to proceed with developing its own nuclear explosive capability. The proposed A-7 sale received a chilly reaction from the new administration. Carter and Vance flatly rejected the idea.[20] When Sweden expressed interest in selling India its Viggen fighter, powered by a US General Electric engine, Washington was similarly negative. Carter sincerely believed that the United States should not be in the business of promoting sales of sophisticated weaponry to the subcontinent.

In keeping with his strong personal support for disarmament, Carter also sparked consideration of an expanded arms control agenda with the Soviets, in addition to SALT II talks on strategic nuclear arms limitations. One of the ideas was for the

2 January 1978, Prime Minister Morarji Desai meeting with President Carter in New Delhi.

total ban on nuclear testing through a Comprehensive Test Ban Treaty. Another was to explore with the Soviet Union the possible "demilitarization" of the Indian Ocean, a position positively received by the Indians, long opposed to big power naval presence in the region.[21]

After the British in the mid-1960s announced the withdrawal of most of their military forces east of Suez, Washington established a small naval communications facility on the tiny British-controlled atoll of Diego Garcia, about a thousand nautical miles south of the southern tip of India. India strongly opposed this action and supported a 1971 Sri Lankan initiative in the United Nations for an Indian Ocean Zone of Peace. In the wake of the 1973 Arab-Israeli War and the oil embargo, the facility at Diego Garcia was expanded to support a larger US naval presence near the Persian Gulf.[22]

Formal talks with the Russians on the Indian Ocean began in Moscow in June 1977. Paul Warnke, the head of the US delegation and Director of the Arms Control and Disarmament Agency (ACDA), clarified the US aim as the more modest goal of seeking to "stabilize" naval forces in the Indian Ocean rather than complete demilitarization.[23] A second and third round of negotiations in Washington and Switzerland addressed technical questions, but did not deal with the broader policy issue posed by intervention by Washington or Moscow unrelated to naval deployments. Before this larger question could be tackled, the talks stalled in early 1978 after the Soviets strengthened their position in the Horn of Africa through their own and Cuban military assistance to Ethiopia. The Indian Ocean negotiations finally collapsed following the Soviet invasion of Afghanistan in December 1979.[24]

Carter's Visit to India

In the fall of 1977 preparations were under way for Jimmy Carter to visit India. As Ambassador Goheen put it, the trip would help show "the irritants of the past have been removed, and now the groundwork for better relations, better mutual respect and trust is there."[25] In keeping with the new approach to South Asia, and unlike Eisenhower and Nixon, the two previous presidential travelers to the subcontinent, Carter did not couple his trip to India with a stop in Pakistan.

3 January 1978, President and Mrs. Carter visiting an Indian Village.

By the time the President arrived in New Delhi on New Year's Day 1978, the Janata government's version of Indian nonalignment had become clearer. A hurried visit by Soviet Foreign Minister Gromyko in April 1977, only a month after the Janata took office, and then an October trip to Moscow by Morarji Desai confirmed a basic continuity in India-Soviet relations, even though cooperation was less close than when Mrs. Gandhi was Prime Minister. The Janata emphasized to a skeptical Kremlin that it desired good Indo-Soviet relations, but did not believe these needed to be at the expense of improving New Delhi's ties with Washington.[26]

When Jimmy Carter became the third serving US President to visit India, the welcoming crowds in New Delhi were friendly and large—although nothing like the throngs that greeted Eisenhower in 1959. In a major speech before the Indian parliament, the President drew attention to the triumph of democratic values in the two countries, praised India's achievements since independence, and proposed a broad effort to develop the economic potential of the major rivers of eastern India, Bangladesh, and Nepal.[27]

To emphasize the importance attached to the Indo-US relationship, the President and Prime Minister issued a "Delhi Declaration" at the conclusion of the trip instead of the usual communiqué. Carter and Desai stressed common support for democracy and economic development, expressed their deep opposition to "the specter of war," and pledged that India and the United States "will do their utmost to resolve disputes with others amicably." In keeping with the personal convictions of the two leaders, the Delhi Declaration closed on a note of principle—"Ends can never justify evil means. Nations, like individuals, are morally responsible for their actions."[28]

Although the visit demonstrated the tangible improvement in relations and the good ties between the President and Prime Minister, bad luck made it embarrassingly clear that a tough substantive problem—the Tarapur issue—had yet to be solved. An open microphone caught some private remarks between Carter and Vance, revealing that the two sides remained far apart on the nuclear issue. The media reported the President's advising the Secretary of State, "I told him (Desai) I would authorize the transfer of fuel now . . . . It didn't seem to make an impression on him . . . . When we get back, I think we should write him another letter, just cold and very blunt."[29]

Despite the fact that the incident created much stir in the press, Morarji Desai pointedly played down the gaffe, taking the position that remarks "not intended to be heard, were not heard."[30] The remark, nonetheless, had a damaging impact in India, suggesting to many that even "friends" in the West, like Jimmy Carter, were two-faced. The open microphone incident played into the hands of the strong and active Soviet lobby which was stressing the line that only the Soviets were "true friends" of India.[31]

On the Indian side, Desai's unwillingness to pick up on the major initiative by Carter—US support for a multi-billion dollar effort to develop the Eastern Waters—revealed that the Janata government was not up to embracing this ambitious, if difficult, international development undertaking. An eastern version of the 1960 Indus waters accord, a Ganges-Brahmaputra agreement, would have led to massive financial investments in flood control, hydroelectric power, and irrigation to spur development in the subcontinent's poor and densely populated northeastern corner. The World Bank stood ready to help—as it had with the Indus project—financially and with complex negotiations on water sharing between Nepal, India, and Bangladesh.

The Indians did not, however, respond to Carter's initiative. They were politically reluctant to drop their opposition to an international, rather than a bilateral, approach to regional South Asia issues and concerned about involving the Communist government of West Bengal in such a potentially touchy problem.[32] Indian water specialists in the Ministry of Irrigation also opposed the idea of an international regime for the eastern waters, echoing their long-standing view that India had lost out to Pakistan in water-sharing arrangements under the Indus treaty.[33]

Although by mutual agreement, the President and Desai did not take up the question of economic aid, a few days later, John Gilligan, the former Ohio Governor whom Carter named to head AID, came to India to announce a resumption of US bilateral assistance after a six-year break. The Janata's Finance Minister, H. M. Patel, during a visit to Washington in October 1977, had made no bones about Indian interest in US aid. Patel said bluntly he was not going to engage in the "hypocrisy" of pretending India did not need help, or the "alphonse-gaston" routine of waiting for the other side to ask first. India, according to Patel, needed "both trade and aid."[34]

Gilligan had only $60 million in his pocket—the amount the Congress on its own initiative approved for India. The AID Administrator told the press in New Delhi that President Carter hoped for an expanded program, with $90 million in 1979 and a larger amount later, in addition to $100 million in food aid the United States was providing annually to voluntary agencies.[35] Negotiating projects to fit the revised US AID focus on "basic human needs" took a number of months. Only on 26 August 1978 were Ambassador Goheen and the Indian Finance Secretary able to sign three project agreements to use the $60 million.[36]

With memories of past frictions over aid questions, many US government specialists on India—including NSC staffer Tom Thornton and State Department Deputy Assistant Secretary Jane Coon—were at best lukewarm about the idea of resuming bilateral assistance. They worried that the economic benefits might well not outweigh the potential political disadvantages.[37] Nor did all Indians share Finance Minister Patel's enthusiasm, recalling US efforts to influence Indian economic policy as "interference" in India's internal affairs. In any case, the substantial increase in multilateral assistance to India during the 1970s, much of which the United States funded through its contributions to the World Bank's soft money loan window, IDA, ensured large assistance inflows for India and reduced the relative importance of bilateral American aid.

The Nuclear Nonproliferation Act: Trouble for Tarapur

The "cold and very blunt" message to Desai came not in the form of a letter from Carter, but in the 1978 Nuclear Nonproliferation Act (NNPA), the legislative cornerstone of the administration's nuclear policy. The US Congress adopted the NNPA with virtually no dissent, the Senate by an 88-3 margin and the House of Representatives by a unanimous 411-0 vote.[38] The heart of the new policy, as it related to India, was that the

United States could henceforth export sensitive nuclear materials, such as enriched uranium fuel, only to countries that placed all their nuclear facilities under International Atomic Energy Agency (IAEA) safeguards. Countries like India that had previously refused to accept "full scope safeguards" had 18 months to conform to the requirements of the NNPA. They would otherwise be ineligible for further exports from the United States, regardless of existing contractual arrangements.

Trouble clearly lay ahead. Unless the Indians accepted IAEA safeguards on all their nuclear facilities, not just Tarapur, the United States would have to stop supplying enriched uranium fuel. In order to get foreign assistance, the Indians agreed to safeguards on individual nuclear facilities, such as Tarapur and nuclear power reactors in Rajasthan funded by the Canadians, but stoutly refused to accept safeguards on nuclear facilities which the Indian AEC built without outside help. The Indians argued vehemently that full scope safeguards would be an unjust infringement on their sovereignty.

The Carter administration was aware that legislating unilateral requirements on existing international agreements could cause a negative reaction that "would be severely counterproductive to our nonproliferation objectives." Testifying in Congressional hearings, Carter nuclear spokesman Joseph Nye explained, "We simply do not have the leverage to exact compliance with sweeping new provisions, insistence on which could be seen by many of our nuclear partners as a breach of our supply commitments."[39] With the India case in mind, the administration tried but failed to gain acceptance for an exemption for existing contracts from the new full scope safeguard requirement.[40]

Shortly after the new law passed, the NRC made matters worse by refusing to license the next shipment for Tarapur on a split 2-2 vote—the first time the NRC had turned down an export request. Paradoxically, the two Democrats on the NRC voted against the export to Tarapur and the two Republicans supported the administration. There was no fifth or swing vote as the President had yet to fill an NRC vacancy.[41] In India, Prime Minister Desai responded sharply, warning that if the United States blocked the enriched uranium shipment, India would regard it a breach of the Tarapur contract. India would then be free, Morarji stated in parliament, "to adopt any course we like to safeguard our own interest."[42] Although aware that Carter was likely to overrule the NRC, Desai nonetheless threw down a marker that would remain the Indian position: as long as India adhered to the Tarapur contract, the United States could not unilaterally alter its terms. Legally, the Indians had a strong case, quite apart from policy considerations.

After the NRC rejected the license, the issue went to the White House. President Carter kept his promise to Desai, overturning the NRC ruling to approve the export. In a 27 April statement, Carter expressed concern that rejection of the license would "seriously undermine" ongoing efforts to negotiate on safeguards with India before the NNPA's deadline of March 1980. Carter said he wanted to use the period to "find mutually acceptable ways of meeting both India's need for the continued operation of the Tarapur atomic power station and our own need for full-scope safeguards and the attainment of other nonproliferation objectives."[43]

The Tarapur question then moved to Congress where the export could still be blocked if both Houses voted to override the President. As Morarji Desai visited Washington just at this moment, Tarapur rather than the improvement in bilateral relations became the center of attention during the Prime Minister's stay. Meeting on Capitol Hill with some fifty lawmakers, Morarji outlined his opposition to what India regarded as discriminatory safeguards, explained with sincerity why he was against developing nuclear weapons, and made clear India was not going to sign the Nonproliferation Treaty in order to get fuel for Tarapur. The Prime Minister went on to say that if the Big Powers stopped making weapons and adopted nuclear disarmament measures, India might change its mind.[44] At the National Press Club, Desai was equally forthright, asking why "must India be singled out for disfavor by a friendly country like the United States through a unilateral modification of its contractual obligations?"[45]

Overall, despite the preoccupation with the nuclear problem, the Desai visit went well. According to the White House, the two leaders ranged the globe in their talks with few areas of disagreement: Carter and Morarji looked forward to progress on disarmament, on human rights, on self-determination in southern Africa, and for continued peace and stability in South Asia. The President and Prime Minister hoped that "the significant improvement in bilateral relations over the past year . . . would be continued and deepened . . . ."[46] In a nice touch, Carter took Morarji on a private and unscheduled visit to the Lincoln Memorial after the 14 June White House dinner. According to *The Statesman*, "This gesture—unprecedented by any US President—speaks for itself when Indians back home ask how is the visit going?"[47]

Desai's straightforward approach had a positive impact in Congress. On 12 July, the House of Representatives supported the President on Tarapur. Although opponents, like liberal Democrat Richard Ottinger of New York, declared, "If we do not apply the act with respect to India, we have no reason to expect anybody to think we would apply it to anybody else,"[48] the majority agreed with the President, voting to sustain the fuel export to Tarapur, 227-181.

The two governments continued to seek a formula to solve the Tarapur issue even though the 1978 NNPA and Indian opposition to full scope safeguards gave the negotiators little leeway. Hopes that New Delhi would give ground faded after the Carter administration decided not to proceed with a Comprehensive Test Ban Treaty, one of the several conditions Desai laid down for serious Indian consideration of full scope safeguards. Side issues relating to the disposition of spent fuel rods and a reprocessing plant built at Tarapur complicated the situation.

Since the plan for the Tarapur complex developed in the early 1960s included reprocessing the spent fuel, the Indians had constructed a plant for this purpose. At the time, the United States did not regard reprocessing as a proliferation risk and interposed no objection. The only legal requirement was for a joint US-Indian determination that the reprocessing plant could be adequately safeguarded.[49] In 1969, Myron Kratzer, then head of international activities at the US Atomic Energy Commission, gave a preliminary go-ahead on this question. After the 1974 Indian test, however, US nuclear policy gradually shifted against reprocessing. In 1976, Kratzer, serving as the top State Department nuclear specialist, equivocated when the Indian AEC formally sought the joint determination.[50] By 1978, with

13 June 1978, India-US Meeting at the White House. On the US side, left to right, Peter Lande, Harold Saunders, Vice President Walter Mondale, Warren Christopher, President Carter, and David Aaron.

14 June 1978, Vice President Walter Mondale, President Carter, and Prime Minister Morarji Desai at the White House.

the Carter administration in power, US policy was firmly against reprocessing, which was now regarded as a major proliferation risk. In line with the new policy, Louis Nosenzo, Kratzer's successor, stated officially that the United States would not approve using the plant to reprocess the Tarapur spent fuel rods.[51]

If the Indians could not reprocess Tarapur spent fuel, what could be done with the nuclear waste? Because the original Tarapur concept envisaged reprocessing, the facility had limited storage capacity. After the 1974 test, the Indian AEC offered to sell the spent fuel rods back to the United States. The Indians, in effect, said: If you are worried about misuse of the fuel, buy it back. Washington said, "No, thank you," unsure how to pay for the rods or where to store them.[52] The US stance remained unchanged after the Democrats took office. In 1979, when President Jimmy Carter was asked in a press conference about taking back the fuel as a solution to the Tarapur problem, he replied, "We have no authority and no plan now for the shipment of those waste products back to our own country."[53]

In addition to the frustration over the idle reprocessing plant and the disposal of the spent fuel, the question of enriched uranium supplies remained unresolved in 1979. Passing through Delhi in March, Deputy Secretary of State Warren Christopher received a barrage of Indian complaints about the delay in shipments from Prime Minister Morarji Desai, Foreign Secretary Jagat Mehta, and others.[54] Carter had by then appointed a fifth commissioner to the NRC, John Ahearne, whose vote would decide the issue since the other four commissioners remained split two-two. After much soul searching, Ahearne finally came down in favor of issuing the license. In an explanatory statement, Ahearne said the Desai government "has acted responsibly and courageously," showing "a strong commitment towards world nonproliferation."[55]

By this time, it should have been clear that a mutually satisfactory agreement on Tarapur was not in the cards. Since India was unwilling to accept full scope safeguards, under the NNPA the United States would have to terminate fuel exports in March 1980, eighteen months after the new law went into effect, regardless of whether India continued to fulfil its obligations under the Tarapur contract. The situation argued for finding a graceful way to end the Tarapur arrangement—upholding US nonproliferation policy without doing more damage to bilateral relations. The President did not, however, want to face the problem head-on. Carter, according to Ambassador Goheen, was an optimist; even though the talks were going nowhere, he believed in dialogue and remained hopeful that somehow the Indians could be brought around.[56]

The President himself gave mixed signals in dealing with the issue. He told visiting Indian Foreign Minister Vajpayee in April 1979 that after the March 1980 NNPA cutoff date the United States would be hard put to continue the supply of Tarapur fuel.[57] At the same time, Carter publicly lamented that US actions toward nuclear disarmament and testing "have not yet been adequate to encourage other countries like India to meet those very high standards that we hope to make more stringent in the future." Carter said he found it "a little bit difficult" to talk about the nuclear question with Morarji Desai when "we ourselves have not yet restrained the spread of nuclear weapons."[58]

For the Indians, the proliferation issue became more complicated with evidence that its long-time foe Pakistan was mounting a serious covert effort to develop nuclear weapons. Former Prime Minister Bhutto's call for his country to develop nuclear weapons was proving more than mere rhetoric.[59] By early 1979, US intelligence about the Pakistan nuclear program became sufficiently hard that the Carter administration felt compelled to invoke the Symington amendment to the Foreign Assistance Act. This provision barred providing economic assistance to countries that the United States believed were moving toward a nuclear weapons capability. Predictably, after the United States suspended economic aid, US relations with Pakistan—never good during the Carter administration in view of the emphasis on improving ties with India—sharply deteriorated.

"Thin Below the Levels of Broad Principle"

The improvement in the political relationship between the United States and India was real, but somewhat deceptive. According to Ambassador Goheen, relations remained "thin below the levels of broad principles and personal diplomacy."[60]

The two governments had difficulty in moving much beyond the stage of better political atmospherics. There just was not that much going on between the United States and India.

A hoped-for expansion in the economic relationship remained largely unfulfilled. Two-way trade grew somewhat and the United States again became India's largest trading partner during the Carter-Desai years. Expectations of increased US investment were, however, stillborn. The Janata government proved as touchy and nationalistic as Mrs. Gandhi's in dealing with foreign investors. Rather surprisingly—given the Janata's pro-private sector rhetoric—George Fernandes, a vocal socialist labor leader, became Minister of Industries with responsibility for foreign investment. Far from easing controls, Fernandes insisted on strict enforcement of the restrictive Foreign Exchange Regulation Act (FERA) enacted by Mrs. Gandhi. Under the FERA, foreign investors could not own more than 40 percent of the share capital of Indian enterprises. Existing foreign owners were supposed to reduce their equity holdings to this level.

US business strongly opposed Fernandes' approach. In a meeting of the Joint Business Council, the American side made clear that it regarded the 40 percent limitation, along with high taxes and chronic red tape, as major barriers to attracting more US investment to India.[61] When Fernandes pressed ahead with rigid enforcement of the FERA, two major US companies—Coca-Cola and IBM—decided to shut down their India operations. In the case of Coca-Cola, Fernandes claimed the soft drink company was making excessively large profits—10-15 million rupees annually on an initial investment of only 600,000 rupees. Although Coca-Cola was willing to restructure its Indian subsidiary to comply with FERA regulations, the US company refused to relinquish control of its formula for coke syrup.[62] When Fernandes found the offer inadequate, Coca-Cola decided to pull out. The damage to India's image in US business circles caused by Coca-Cola's departure was considerable.[63]

The damage was even worse in the case of IBM. After Fernandes insisted IBM comply with the FERA requirements, the US company refused. Fernandes recalled IBM telling him, "General de Gaulle couldn't make us do it and we won't for India either."[64] IBM, nonetheless, wanted to remain in India and proposed a compromise. IBM would split its operations, leaving the sales and leasing operation under IBM control, but converting the service and repair division into a separate Indian registered company, in which IBM would own only 40 percent of the share capital. IBM also offered to fund joint research projects in India to promote technology development. When the offer was not good enough for Fernandes, IBM packed up and left.[65]

Unlike Coca-Cola, IBM's departure, just before the start of the personal computer revolution, proved a major technology loss for India. Nationalist sentiments against foreign business won the day, but India paid a price. The twin episodes dealt a one-two punch to India's image as a good place for US investment. Ambassador Goheen wrote, "The negative vibrations in the US business community . . . were immediate, widespread and in some quarters lasting."[66] US investment in India during the late 1970s—and in the years since then—remained small. Declining US interest in India was reflected in attendance at the 1979 Joint Business Council meetings. Twenty-eight of India's top business executives traveled to Washington; only sixteen middle-level US executives and 11 observers bothered to attend.[67]

If the private sector engagement was disappointing, renewed US economic assistance also failed to grow as much as aid supporters hoped. Instead of rising to a $300 million annual level, bilateral development assistance topped out at about $100 million annually. The revived assistance effort, while not insubstantial, remained more an expression of goodwill rather than a major policy commitment to Indian development as it had been during the Eisenhower and Kennedy years. With other issues higher on Jimmy Carter's foreign policy agenda—for example, the Panama Canal treaty, the Middle East peace negotiations, and SALT II—the President never made the personal political commitment to an expanded foreign assistance program. As a result, aid funds were simply not available to increase the India bilateral program much above the $100 million annual range.

In 1979, even though Tarapur remained a chronic problem, India-US relations were, nonetheless, better than they had been for more than a decade.[68] When Foreign Minister Vajpayee visited Washington in the spring of 1979, the US side was positively glowing about his talks with Secretary Vance and

President Carter. "It was the best exchange we have had with India for years. It had warmth, but it had more than that. Nobody was scared of disagreeing and every conceivable subject was brought up."[69]

By this time, however, two major developments negatively influenced the bilateral environment. In early 1979, the Shah of Iran, long the mainstay of US strategy in West Asia, was driven from power by virulently anti-American Shiite fundamentalists. Although Carter's achievement of the Camp David peace accord between Egypt and Israel brought far closer US-Egyptian security cooperation, the loss of Iran shook the US position in the region. After the Iranians seized hostages from the US Embassy in Tehran later in the year, this problem became the White House's major preoccupation for the rest of Carter's term.

In India, the Janata coalition, weakened by political infighting among rival leaders, finally collapsed. Morarji Desai resigned in July 1979, to be replaced by North Indian peasant leader Charan Singh. The new Prime Minister was never able to muster a parliamentary majority and served six months as a caretaker leader, the life of his government dependent on the support of Indira Gandhi and her Congress Party.

Given its weakness, the new government could do little more than mark time in foreign affairs. Although in no position to negotiate on Tarapur, Charan Singh adopted a tougher line on nuclear policy than Morarji Desai. Talking with visiting Senator Charles Percy a few weeks after taking office, the new Prime Minister said India might reconsider its approach to nuclear weapons if Pakistan persisted in trying to get a bomb. Singh stressed India would make its own decision "with nobody on the outside having any say in this."[70] The annual meeting of the International Atomic Energy Agency (IAEA) in New Delhi in December 1979 provided an opportunity to air Indian nuclear grievances. "In the name of nonproliferation," Charan Singh complained," smaller nations are forced to accept restraints and restrictions, none of which the nuclear weapons powers are prepared to accept for themselves."[71]

New general elections—India's seventh since independence—were called for the first week of January 1980. With the Emergency past history, Mrs. Gandhi campaigned vigorously against the squabbling Janata, promising a return to stable government. Although foreign policy was not an important campaign issue, Indira's Congress Party criticized Janata's handling of foreign relations, heaping scorn on the concept of "genuine non-alignment," urging closer ties with the Soviet Union, India's "true friend," and calling for Indian recognition of the Heng Samgrin regime imposed by the North Vietnamese on Kampuchea.

Afghanistan, Mrs. Gandhi, and "Peanuts"

Just a week before the elections, on 27 December 1979, the world was stunned and the superpower relationship shaken when the Soviet Union intervened militarily in Afghanistan to oust President Amin and install the more pliable Babrak Kamal regime. As a shocked President Jimmy Carter reversed course, the Cold War again became the order of the day. Disarmament talks collapsed. The President tried to prevent further erosion of the West's strategic position through stepped-up defense spending. Washington sought to punish the Soviets through measures like boycotting the 1980 Moscow Olympics and embargoing grain exports.

The impact on US policy toward South Asia was immediate. The day after the Soviet intervention, President Carter picked up the telephone to speak with Pakistan's President Zia ul-Haq to offer US support and to revive the moribund US security commitment under the 1959 bilateral agreement. Pakistan ceased to be a nuclear delinquent and became a frontline state against the threat of Soviet expansionism. The Carter administration and the Congress acted to unfreeze arms sales to Pakistan with Rep. Clement Zablocki (D., Wisconsin), Chairman of the House Foreign Affairs Committee, arguing that the Soviet threat overrode nonproliferation concerns. In the Senate, parallel moves were launched to get around Symington amendment bars to a resumption of military and economic aid to Pakistan.[72]

In India, the outgoing Charan Singh government expressed its displeasure with the Soviet action, but these were just words. Within the week, Charan Singh was on his way out as Prime Minister. After the Congress Party routed the divided Janata at the polls, Indira Gandhi was on her way back in. Three years after the electoral defeat in 1977, Mrs. Gandhi's Congress swept 350 of 542 parliamentary seats. Indira regained political power in a remarkable comeback.

At the United Nations, the United States sought Security Council condemnation of the invasion of Afghanistan, only to be blocked by the Soviet veto. The US position was unambiguous: "No state would be safe against a larger neighbor if the international community appears to condone the Soviet Union's intervention."[73] Attention shifted to the General Assembly where NATO members, virtually all Muslim states, and most of Latin America and Africa joined in censuring Moscow's action.

In New Delhi, the Ministry of External Affairs decided to clear the statement India would make on Afghanistan with the incoming Prime Minister. Besieged by the preparations for taking office, Mrs. Gandhi turned the task over to T. N. Kaul, long known for his pro-Soviet views, and G. Parthasarathy, another veteran foreign policy adviser. Ministry officials tried to soften the language, but were able only to gain acceptance for a few changes.[74] Delivered in New York by Indian UN Representative Mishra on 11 January, the statement whitewashed the Soviet action:

> We are against the presence of foreign troops and bases in any country. However, the Soviet government has assured our government that its troops went to Afghanistan first at the request of the Afghan Government on December 26, 1979 and repeated by his successor on December 28, 1979. And we have been further assured that Soviet troops will be withdrawn when requested to do so by the Afghan Government. We have no reason to doubt assurances, particularly from a friendly country like the Soviet Union with whom we have many close ties.[75]

By chance, Ambassador Goheen met with President Jimmy Carter the afternoon Mishra spoke in the UN General Assembly. On learning of the Indian statement, Carter was livid.[76] Goheen calmed him down saying, "We don't really know the circumstances. Let me go back to New Delhi and report before we do anything about this."[77] At the State Department, according to then India Country Director Howard Schaffer, "The statement hit people like a ton of bricks. When we first heard the wholesale acceptance of the Soviet line, we just couldn't believe it."[78] As in the case of Hungary in 1956 and Czechoslovakia in 1968, India chose to stand apart from the world community in not condemning the Soviet Union's use of force against another country.

On returning to New Delhi, Goheen spoke frankly with Mrs. Gandhi. He stressed, "What a devastating statement it had been from the American point of view and what a terrible backlash it had caused in the United States." When the Prime Minister responded, "Oh, it wasn't that bad," the Ambassador countered, "Oh, yes it really was."[79] Goheen made similar points with Parthasarathy, whom he had gotten to know well when they co-chaired the Indo-US education and culture subcommission. The envoy told Parthasarathy, "The terrible statement misjudged the United States and it really wasn't in India's interests in siding so openly with the Russians." Like Mrs. Gandhi, Parthasarathy tried to explain away the remarks as less serious than Goheen suggested.[80]

In Washington, where US officials were still angered about the Indian position on Afghanistan, Pakistan's Foreign Minister and Secretary General for Defense arrived for discussions with President Carter and other US leaders about a possible renewal of US military aid. Smarting from Carter administration treatment of Pakistan, President Zia played hard to get.[81] In broader strategic terms, January 1980 saw the emergence of the Carter Doctrine in the State of the Union message. In a far-reaching policy step, Carter declared on 23 January 1980 that the United States would regard any move by the Soviet Union toward the oil-rich Persian Gulf as a threat to US vital interests and would counter by all necessary means, including the use of force.[82]

In India, Mrs. Gandhi edged her public stance away from blanket acceptance of the Soviet position. After meeting with British Foreign Secretary Lord Carrington on 18 January, she commented to the press, "I don't think that any country is justified in entering another country."[83] In an interview with *Time* magazine, she said she "disapproved" of the Soviet action in Afghanistan.[84] To soften the public criticism, however, the Prime Minister often added that the Soviets intervened only after Pakistan started arming Afghan rebels against the Kabul government.[85]

At the end of January, President Carter sent two separate missions to South Asia: a high-powered group led by his National Security Adviser, Zbigniew Brzezinski, and Deputy Secretary of State Warren Christopher to Pakistan and special presidential emissary Clark Clifford to India. Although newsmen photographed Brzezinski supposedly pointing a rifle at Soviet troops across the Khyber Pass[86]—dramatizing US concern about the Soviet threat—Pakistan's cagy President Zia ul Haq disdainfully rejected the proffered $400 million as "peanuts."[87]

In New Delhi, Clark Clifford, adviser to Democratic presidents back to Harry Truman and Johnson's former Defense Secretary, sought to allay Indian concerns about renewed US arms aid to Pakistan and to urge Mrs. Gandhi to use her influence in Moscow to press for a Soviet withdrawal from Afghanistan. During Mrs. Gandhi's difficult times during the Janata period, the Americans had treated Indira politely. President Carter set the tone by sending a nice letter immediately after the March 1977 elections.[88] Ambassador Goheen had made a point of calling on Mrs. Gandhi—to the annoyance of Foreign Minister Vajpayee—and of chatting in a friendly manner when they met at diplomatic and social gatherings. Having shown Mrs. Gandhi respect, Goheen felt Mrs. Gandhi returned the courtesy after she returned to power. Even though their discussions were often substantively difficult, Goheen never received the haughty, silent treatment for which Mrs. Gandhi was well known.[89]

Clark Clifford did not change the Prime Minister's mind, but US observers believed she appreciated his visit which showed that Washington took India seriously enough to send an envoy of stature and prestige.[90] Mrs. Gandhi found Clifford a good listener as she carefully spelled out her main points: if the United States rearmed Pakistan, this would pose a threat to India, limiting India's ability to press Moscow and placing India in a situation in which it did not want to be.[91] She also suggested to Clifford that the Soviets were not entirely to blame, citing "interference" from outside in Afghan affairs. The Indians tended to equate "intervention" and "interference," then and later.[92]

After the talks, Clifford told the press: "The goal of our two governments is exactly the same—to have the Soviets withdraw their troops from Afghanistan." The Indians, however, did not believe that the US approach was the best course of action. "The Indian government," Clifford stated, "believes that negotiation, positive persuasion, might be more effective." Referring to US arms for Pakistan, Clifford said, "We understand this is not a popular move with the Indian government and yet with the gravity of the threat we believe it is a helpful policy for us to follow."[93]

Because Zia continued to play hard to get, nothing came of the Carter administration's effort to resume US arms aid to Pakistan during 1980. Events, nonetheless, underlined the strikingly different reactions in Washington and New Delhi to the Soviet intervention. For Washington, it was as if the 19th century "Great Game" for the control of Afghanistan between the British Empire and Tsarist Russia was being replayed. Opposing Moscow was the force of Afghan nationalism embodied in the tough tribal fighters. Three times, the Afghan tribesmen had thwarted British efforts to dominate their country. Battling a similar attempt by the Russians in 1980, the Afghan guerrillas were soon receiving covert military help from Saudi Arabia, Pakistan, China, and others, although not initially from the United States. Washington had, nonetheless, full sympathy and support for the Afghan cause, and for the country through which most external help flowed—Pakistan.

In New Delhi, even if few Indians were pleased by Moscow's intervention, the prevailing view was that the revival of US military aid to Pakistan posed a greater threat to Indian interests than the Soviet military presence in Afghanistan. Having bested the Pakistanis in 1965 and 1971, the Indians no longer feared their neighbor militarily. They were still viscerally opposed to the United States resuming a role as the principal arms supplier to Pakistan, thereby reestablishing itself as an important player in the subcontinent's security scene. The standard Indian Ministry of External Affairs response on arms to Pakistan made this clear—"Neither the quality nor the quantity of the arms mattered; it was the attitude that caused concern."[94]

Unlike the mid-1950s when some in Washington questioned the wisdom of providing US arms to Pakistan, Indian expressions of concern in 1980 found few sympathetic American ears. Given the dramatic change in the strategic environment after the Soviet invasion of Afghanistan, Carter administration officials listened to the Indians, but paid little attention to their complaints about US help for Pakistan.[95]

Tarapur: Next to the Last Act

And yet, the Carter administration did not write India off entirely. Washington recognized that Mrs. Gandhi might have some influence with the Soviets, and did not want to push her any closer to Moscow. Following the logic that led to the reversal of the arms supply policy toward Pakistan, Carter also changed course on supplying arms to India. Although the administration had refused permission earlier for Sweden to sell its General Electric-powered Viggen fighter to India, Washington now encouraged New Delhi to consider arms purchases from US companies. In a major departure, an Indian military procurement team visited the United States in 1980 to explore procurement of large numbers of TOW anti-tank missiles and long-range howitzers, with the package perhaps totalling $300 million. The Carter administration similarly reversed its earlier action to disapprove the use of an advanced US electronic guidance system in the Jaguar aircraft India was buying from Great Britain.[96]

In the nuclear area, despite anticipated Congressional opposition, Jimmy Carter decided to give the green light for two more enriched uranium fuel shipments for Tarapur—the last that would be legally possible under the 1978 NNPA because the transition period would have expired without India's agreeing to full scope safeguards. Mrs. Gandhi, like Desai, was adamant on the safeguards issue; unlike Desai, she refused to rule out further "peaceful nuclear experiments." In spite of this, Carter accepted State Department recommendations—over Brzezinski's objection—that he transmit two long-pending Tarapur fuel export applications to the NRC. The State Department reasoned that in light of the Afghan situation avoiding further strains with India took priority over nonproliferation objectives.[97]

That the going would be rough quickly became apparent. On 16 May, the NRC unanimously rejected the license requests by an unprecedented 5-0 vote. With the transition period over and India refusing to accept full scope safeguards, the NRC saw no basis for approving the licenses. After considerable deliberation, President Carter decided, nonetheless, to override the NRC and to authorize the shipments. This action set the stage for a major battle on Capitol Hill where the Congress could block the President's action if a majority in both Houses voted against the fuel shipment.

Carter's decision came under heavy criticism with the two most prestigious US newspapers—*The New York Times* and *The Washington Post*—attacking the administration position editorially on 22 June. The *Washington Post* called Tarapur "the ultimate test of the seriousness of U.S. nonproliferation policy."[98] *The New York Times* argued that "if the United States yields on safeguards to the only nation known to have carried out an explosion . . . it can hardly expect other suppliers and receivers of fuel to give the protective stipulations a high priority."[99]

Presenting the administration case, Ambassador Gerard Smith, veteran disarmament negotiator, argued that failure to provide the fuel would risk loss of safeguards on Tarapur and undercut the US reliability as a nuclear supplier. Smith asserted there was no question of yielding to India on safeguards since the shipments fell within the two-year grace period permitted by the law.[100] Writing in the *Washington Post*, former Kennedy aide McGeorge Bundy also supported the administration, saying the Soviet Union would probably step in to supply Tarapur if the United States backed out.[101]

In the Congress, the tide was running against Carter, especially in the House of Representatives. With Indira back in power and refusing to condemn the Soviet action in Afghanistan, there was only modest congressional concern about maintaining good relations with New Delhi. Mrs. Gandhi's recognition of the Palestine Liberation Organization and the Vietnamese-installed and dominated Kampuchea regime caused additional negative ripples. News that New Delhi was procuring $1.6 billion worth of arms from Moscow did not strengthen the administration's case.

In the House, which Carter supporters gave up as a lost cause, Tarapur opponents won an 18 September vote by a wide 298-98 margin. In the Senate, Secretary of State Edmund Muskie, the respected former Senator from Maine who had replaced

Cyrus Vance,[102] strenuously lobbied his former colleagues. Although the administration lost an 8-7 vote in the Foreign Relations Committee, the President eventually eked out a razor-thin 48-46 victory on 24 September. At the end of seven hours of debate, a two-vote majority heeded the plea of Senator Frank Church to give the President "the benefit of the doubt"—but only after Secretary Muskie agreed to hold back one of the two shipments.[103] Even though the presidential election campaign was under way, many Democrats voted against Carter, while the Republican leadership in the Senate supported the President's position.

The victory proved a Pyrrhic affair. With the two-year deadline past, and no prospect of India's accepting full scope safeguards, the Congress was clearly not going to approve any further fuel shipments for Tarapur. In India, the United States won few thanks through the exercise. New Delhi contended—not without justification—that Washington's failure to supply the fuel would amount to a breach of contract relieving India of the obligation to maintain safeguards. Because the delays in fuel shipments had caused a drop in Tarapur power production, some argued the United States was already in breach of the contract.[104]

In retrospect, one must question whether Carter's enormous effort to gain approval for the Tarapur shipment in 1980 was worthwhile. In the process, the administration weakened its overall nonproliferation posture without substantially helping relations with India or advancing a solution to the problem. It is hard to disagree with the editorial comment of *The Statesman* of Calcutta:

> It should have been clear long ago that there would be no accord on nuclear policy, and both countries should have accepted the consequences. By keeping the Tarapur issue alive, they succeeded merely in exacerbating feelings. Tarapur has been allowed to sour Indo-U.S. relations quite out of proportion to its importance.[105]

A Disappointing Four Years

Relations between the United States and India at the end of Carter's term in the White House stood about where they were at the beginning. The intervening four years saw a period of high expectations in 1977 after the end of the Emergency and the return of democracy to India, followed by a renewed slump in 1980 after the Soviet invasion of Afghanistan and Mrs. Gandhi's return to power.

When Jimmy Carter and Morarji Desai took office, there were genuine hopes that the two countries would at long last enjoy a sustained period of positive relations. As India adopted a more balanced approach toward nonalignment and Washington took its distance from Pakistan, traditional bilateral frictions lessened. The United States began to pay more attention to India as a "regional influential." Both countries stressed their common faith in democracy and human rights. Even though the Tarapur problem cast a long shadow, the two basically well-disposed governments might have been able to work out an amicable divorce over this contentious issue—as Mrs. Gandhi would do with the Reagan administration in 1982—had the Carter-Desai period lasted longer. Indian political developments and the Soviet intervention in Afghanistan, however, ensured that India and the United States were again at odds in 1980.

If the relationship soured in the final year of the Carter administration, the outlook after Ronald Reagan won the November election was for worsening relations. Highly critical of Carter's policies toward the Soviets, Reagan stated his primary foreign policy goal would be to stem rising Communist influence in Afghanistan, Africa, and Central America. The new Republican administration could be expected to address arms supply to Pakistan as a matter of top priority. Reagan was likely to be far more generous than the Democrats in providing military help to Islamabad and less concerned about India's reaction. As the Soviet Union's most prominent non-Communist friend, India could anticipate receiving even shorter shrift from the White House than during Jimmy Carter's last year as President.

NOTES

1. *The Statesman*, 2 February 1977.
2. Ibid., 31 January 1977.
3. Zbigniew Brzezinski, *Power and Principle* (New York: Farrar, Strauss and Giroux, 1983), pp. 53-56; *New York Times*, 11 February 1977.

4. Letter from Professor Thomas P. Thornton, 8 November 1991. Thornton served as senior member of the NSC staff on South Asia during the Carter administration.

5. India's sixth general elections should have been held in early 1976, but parliament voted their postponement because of the Emergency.

6. Mary Carras, *Indira Gandhi, In the Crucible of Leadership* (Boston: Beacon Press, 1979), p. 240.

7. Ibid., p. 239.

8. Myron Weiner, "Assessing the Political Impact of Foreign Assistance," in John W. Mellor, ed., *India: A Rising Middle Power* (Boulder, CO.: Westview Press, 1979), p. 60.

9. Thomas P. Thornton, "American Interest in India under Carter and Reagan," *SAIS Review* 5 (Winter-Spring 1985): p. 181.

10. *The Statesman*, 22 March 1977.

11. *Washington Post*, 3 March 1977.

12. Robert C. Horn, *Soviet-Indian Relations* (New York: Praeger, 1982), p. 147.

13. Letter from Ambassador Jagat Mehta, 14 November 1991.

14. Interview with Ambassador Robert Goheen, 15 April 1991.

15. Ibid.

16. The author, then India Country Director in the State Department, accompanied Nye for the talks with Mehta.

17. According to Dr. Thornton, Carter diplomatically also sent a friendly message to Mrs Gandhi immediately after the March 1977 elections.

18. *New York Times*, 5 July 1977.

19. *The Statesman*, 21 July 1977; *New York Times*, 2 October 1977.

20. Ibid., 24 December 1977.

21. *The Statesman*, 11 March 1977.

22. For background on US Indian Ocean policy, see Gary Sick's "The Evolution of U.S. Strategy toward the Indian Ocean and the Persian Gulf Regions," in Alvin Rubinstein, ed., *The Great Game: Rivalry in the Persian Gulf and South Asia* (New York: Praeger, 1983), pp. 52-68.

23. *The Statesman*, 27 September 1977.

24. Sick, p. 69.

25. *New York Times*, 2 October 1977.

26. Horn, pp. 148-55.

27. Text of the President's address to the Indian parliament from *New York Times*, 3 January 1978.

28. Text from *New York Times*, 4 January 1978.

29. *Facts on File*, vol. 38, 6 January 1978, p. 2; *Washington Post*, 3 January 1978.

30. Interview with Thomas Thornton, 12 December 1990. Thornton accompanied President Carter on the India trip.

31. Letter from Professor Stephen Cohen, 11 June 1991.

32. Interview with Thomas Thornton, 12 December 1990.

33. Interview with Ambassador Eric Gonsalves, 12 January 1991.

34. *The Statesman*, 2 October 1977.

35. *New York Times*, 26 January 1978.

36. *The Statesman*, 27 August 1977.

37. Interviews with Thomas Thornton and Jane Coon, December 1990. See Myron Weiner's "Assessing the Political Impact of Foreign Assistance" for an elaboration of these concerns and John P. Lewis's, "Reviving American Aid to India: Motivation, Scale, Uses, and Constraints" for the contrary view. Both articles appeared in John W. Mellor, ed., *India: A Rising Middle Power* (Boulder: Westview Press, 1979).

38. *The Statesman*, 10 February 1978.

39. Richard P. Cronin, "U.S. Uranium Fuel Exports to India: A Case Study," in *Congress and Foreign Policy—1980* (Washington: Government Printing Office, 1981), pp. 91-92.

40. Ibid., p. 91.

41. *New York Times*, 21 April 1978; *Washington Post*, 21 April 1978; and *The Statesman*, 22 April 1978.

42. *New York Times*, 25 April 1978.

43. *Washington Post*, 28 April 1978.

44. Ibid., 14 June 1978.

45. *The Statesman*, 15 June 1978.

46. Statement issued by the Office of the White House Press Secretary, 13 June 1978.

47. *The Statesman*, 15 June 1978.

48. *Facts on File*, vol. 38, 21 July 1978, p. 551.

49. N. Ram, "India's Nuclear Policy," unpublished Paper presented at the 1982 Meeting of the Association of Asian Studies, Chicago, p. 60.

50. Ibid., p. 62. Ram quotes from a letter from Kratzer to the Indian AEC dated 19 March 1976.

51. Memorandum from Louis Nosenzo, Deputy Assistant Secretary of State, to the Nuclear Regulatory Commission, 15 September 1978.

52. Author's recollection of Indo-US nuclear discussions in 1976-1977.

53. *The Statesman*, 4 April 1979.

54. Ibid., 17 March 1979.

55. Ibid., 25 March 1979.

56. Interview with Ambassador Goheen, 15 April 1991.

57. *The Statesman*, 4 May 1979.

58. Ibid., 4 April 1979.

59. Z.A. Bhutto, *The Myth of Independence* (Karachi: Oxford University Press, 1969), pp. 152-53.

60. Robert F. Goheen, "US Policy Toward India in the Carter Presidency," in Gould and Ganguly, eds., *The Hope and the Reality: U.S.-Indian Relations from Roosevelt to Bush* (Boulder, CO: Westview, 1992), p. 125.

61. *The Statesman*, 4 June 1979.

62. Interview with George Fernandes, 25 February 1991.

63. *New York Times*, 12 December 1977.

64. Interview with George Fernandes, 25 February 1991.

65. *New York Times*, 1 October 1977.

66. Goheen, p. 125.

67. *The Statesman*, 4 June 1979.

68. The then Indian Foreign Secretary, Jagat Mehta, put it, "We could never finish with the wretched thing." (Interview, 28 November 1990); the then State Department Deputy Assistant Secretary Jane Coon called Tarapur, "an albatross around our neck." (Interview, 8 December 1990).

69. *The Statesman*, 27 April 1979.

70. *The Statesman*, 18 August 1979.

71. *New York Times*, 5 December 1979.

72. *The Statesman*, 3 January 1980.

73. *Facts on File*, January 7, 1980, p. 2.

74. Interview with Eric Gonsalves, 11 January 1991.

75. Text from *India Today*, 18 January 1980.

76. Interviews with Ambassador Goheen and Thomas Thornton, both present in the meeting with President Carter.

77. Interview with Ambassador Goheen, 15 April 1991.

78. Interview with Ambassador Howard Schaffer, 17 December 1990.

79. Interview with Ambassador Goheen, 15 April 1991.

80. Ibid.

81. *The Statesman*, 12 and 14 January, 1991.

82. *New York Times*, 24 January 1980.

83. Ibid., 19 January 1980.

84. *Time*, 21 January 1980.

85. Horn, p. 183.

86. In fact, Bzrezinski wasn't pointing the gun at anything, just holding a weapon that someone handed him when the picture was taken. Letter from Thomas Thornton, a member of the Bzrezinski party, 27 May 1991.

87. Interviews with Thomas Thornton, 12 December 1990, and Ambassador Jane Coon, 5 December 1990. Both were on the trip to

Pakistan. See also Thomas Thornton, "Between Two Stools? U.S. Policy Toward Pakistan During the Carter Administration," *Asian Survey* 22, no. 10 (October 1982): pp. 959-77.

88. Interview with Thomas Thornton, 12 December 1990.

89. Interview with Ambassador Goheen, 15 April 1991.

90. Interview with Howard Schaffer, 17 December 1990. Schaffer accompanied Clifford on the India trip.

91. Interview with Ambassador Eric Gonsalves, 10 January 1980. At the time, Gonsalves was Secretary of the Ministry of External Affairs.

92. Comment from Ambassador Howard Schaffer, 17 October 1991.

93. *Washington Post*, 1 February 1980.

94. *New York Times*, 1 February 1980.

95. Interview with Thomas Thornton, 12 December 1990.

96. *New York Times*, 2 February 1980; *Washington Post*, 2 February 1980.

97. Interviews with Thomas Thornton, and Jane Coon; Bzrezinski, p. 133; *New York Times*, 8 May 1980.

98. *Washington Post*, 22 June 1980.

99. *New York Times*, 22 June 1980.

100. Ibid., 2 July 1980.

101. *Washington Post*, 13 June 1980.

102. Vance, who had opposed the Iran hostage rescue mission, resigned in protest after its failure.

103. *Washington Post*, 25 September 1980; *New York Times*, 25 September 1980.

104. Ram, pp. 64-68.

105. *The Statesman*, 12 September 1980.

Chapter X

Reagan: Gradual Warming

On 20 January 1981, Ronald Reagan took the oath of office as President of the United States. Within the hour, Iran set free the American Embassy hostages it had held for over a year, relieving Reagan from having to deal with the problem that consumed Jimmy Carter's final year in the White House. The new administration could devote full energy to its primary foreign and national security policy goal: rebuilding US military power so that the United States could counter the spread of Soviet influence in various parts of the world—in Central America, in the horn of Africa, in Angola, in Southeast Asia, and in Afghanistan.

As the Republicans assumed charge, South Asia was an area of concern principally because of the Soviet invasion of Afghanistan. The administration saw covert military assistance to the Afghan guerrillas, humanitarian aid to the refugees, and renewed military and economic assistance to Pakistan as the prime US measures. Washington wanted to act quickly and decisively to help the Afghan resistance and to revive the US-Pakistan security relationship. The Reaganites, led in the foreign policy area by Secretary of State Alexander Haig, Henry Kissinger's deputy during the Bangladesh crisis, had little interest in India—and the Third World in general—except as a battleground in the contest with the Soviet Union and its allies. The new team had scant sympathy for India, disliking above all New Delhi's close links with the Soviets and its stance on Afghanistan. Despite the fact that the Reaganites viewed Indira Gandhi as an apologist for Moscow, they had no special animus against her or India. The Republicans were back in the White House, but not Richard Nixon. Their differences with India were spawned by geopolitics, not emotional antagonism.

Although US determination to press ahead with arms for Pakistan was the major worry, New Delhi had other concerns with the incoming administration. The Tarapur problem remained unresolved. How would the Reagan administration deal with this dispute? Even if the Republican attitude on nonproliferation was less fervent than that of the Democrats, the White House had little incentive to expend political capital with the Congress for India's benefit. In terms of US law there was, in any case, no basis to continue exports of enriched uranium fuel. The new administration's attitude toward international financial institutions was another cause for anxiety. India was increasingly dependent on the World Bank and the International Monetary Fund for external financial support. If the Reagan administration insisted on tougher loan terms and stricter conditionality and opposed capital increases, India could suffer.

Despite these concerns and her reputation for being unfriendly to the United States, Mrs. Gandhi for a number of reasons wanted to narrow, not widen, the gap between New Delhi and Washington. Indira did not want India to lose its freedom of maneuver or to become a Soviet satellite or surrogate. Achieving this goal required greater distance between New Delhi and Moscow and a better relationship with the United States. Although she disparaged Morarji Desai's attempt to bring greater balance in India's nonalignment between the two superpowers, Mrs. Gandhi pursued a similar goal after settling back into office in 1980.[1] A case in point was the Soviet military presence on the Afghan/Pakistan border. Whatever the Indians may have said in their 11 January 1980 UN statement, the presence of the Red Army on the Khyber Pass was something few in New Delhi found congenial. In private discussions, the Indians made clear that they wanted the Russians to withdraw from Afghanistan. Much to India's discomfort, the Soviets showed no signs of leaving.

Indira Gandhi wanted to reduce her country's dependence on Soviet arms supplies as a way to avoid overdependence on Moscow and to have access to better technology. Despite the fact that the Soviets remained by far the largest arms supplier, offering payment terms the West could not match, India had already begun to diversify military equipment procurement. New Delhi acquired Jaguar bombers from Great Britain, submarines from West Germany, and Mirage aircraft and other equipment from France. For the first time since 1965 the Indians were talking about the possibility of arms purchases from the United States.

Realizing the limits of Soviet technology, the Indians hoped for greater access to the more advanced technologies of the West, especially the United States, not only in the defense sector but across the economic spectrum. Better ties might also, the Indians hoped, influence Washington to continue a positive attitude toward India in international financial institutions and to take greater account of India's views in US dealings with Pakistan.[2]

Whatever Indira Gandhi's tough-mindedness as a political leader, personal considerations may have been a factor in Mrs. Gandhi's seeking a less barbed relationship with Washington. During the Janata years, the Americans treated her courteously; in contrast, the Soviets maladroitly snubbed Mrs. Gandhi, virtually ignoring her when she was out of office. Ever sensitive about personal slights, Indira did not forget. On Soviet Foreign Minister Gromyko's first visit after she returned to power, he received less than the welcome an ally might expect.[3]

Indian interest in friendlier ties with the United States was influenced by the growing Indian immigrant community. Although Mrs. Gandhi's generation had strong educational and emotional ties with Great Britain, the younger generation of the elite was flocking to the United States for higher education by the thousands. So many stayed on that by 1980 the Indian immigrant community had swelled to over 300,000.[4] The immigrants, typically professionals with advanced degrees, had the highest per capita income of any ethnic group in the United States.[5] Helped by their fluency in English, the Indian immigrants fit in with relative ease; at the same time, they usually retained close ties with India. The fact that many immigrants were members of the Indian elite magnified the impact—and the attraction—of the United States.[6]

Even before Ronald Reagan took office, the Prime Minister signalled her interest in better relations. She sent her cousin, B. K. Nehru, who served as Ambassador to John Kennedy and

Lyndon Johnson in the 1960s, with a private message to the President-elect.[7] Nehru spent several hours with William Casey and Richard Allen, respectively the incoming heads of Central Intelligence and the NSC staff, but had great difficulty in getting to see Reagan. In the end, with the help of elder statesman John McCloy, the Indian envoy was able to spend a few minutes with the incoming chief executive—quite a feat as otherwise Ronald Reagan saw only West German Chancellor Helmut Schmidt among foreign dignitaries, even rebuffing the Israelis.

Arranged to convey the impression of a chance encounter, the session took place in the Capitol Hill office of Senator Paul Laxalt, a close friend of the President-elect.[8] The gist of Indira's message was that she wanted friendly relations with the United States and had no anti-American feelings. Although Nehru was not sure how much impact the words had on Reagan, the fact that Indira chose to send such a message underscored the seriousness of her desire not to return to the frosty hostility of the Nixon years.[9]

Arms to Pakistan: No Longer "Peanuts"

The Prime Minister may have thought the effort fruitless for, once in office, the Reagan administration wasted little time in implementing the new policy toward South Asia. The media reported approval of covert assistance to the Afghan freedom fighters channeled through Pakistan. Coupled with covert aid was the preparation of a far larger military and economic assistance package than the Carter administration had contemplated for Pakistan. Totalling $2.5 billion, the aid program envisaged a multi-year commitment, including 40 F–16 fighters, the most advanced US aircraft, previously supplied only to NATO allies, Egypt, and Israel. The Pakistanis, in effect, made the F–16 the test of US seriousness, the price Zia ul-Haq insisted that Washington pay to offset lingering bitterness about the way the United States treated Pakistan in the 1960s and 1970s. Islamabad pressed hard to receive these state-of-the-art aircraft, superior to anything India possessed and capable of repelling possible Soviet or Afghan air incursions.

In April 1981, Mrs. Gandhi sent two high-level envoys to lobby the administration on the arms issue: long-time foreign policy adviser G. Parthasarathy, regarded as a pro-Soviet voice, and Ministry of External Affairs Secretary Eric Gonsalves, former second-in-command of the Embassy in Washington with much experience with things American. Rejecting Indian concerns out of hand, Secretary of State Haig told Parthasarathy US help to Pakistan was in the interest of "global peace and stability."[10] Two weeks later, Haig asserted to Gonsalves, "A weak Pakistan only serves the interests of the Soviet Union. A strengthened Pakistan, in close relationship with the USA, poses no threat to India, and indeed should contribute to the overall stability of the subcontinent."[11]

On 15 June 1981, Under Secretary of State James Buckley reached agreement in Islamabad on the $2.5 billion arms and economic aid proposal, including the F–16s. The Indians reacted sourly, the Ministry of External Affairs expressing concern the F–16s might trigger an arms race, threaten Indian security, and undercut the "serious effort" under way to improve Indo-Pakistan relations.[12] The timing of the announcement upset New Delhi since Foreign Minister P. V. Narasimha Rao, in Pakistan just the week before, was hopeful that "a new and fresh relationship" was emerging. The Indians felt the Pakistanis, in effect, were thumbing their noses by announcing the resumption of the arms relationship with the United States so soon after the talks.

Unimpressed by New Delhi's complaints, Washington responded bluntly, "Our aid to Pakistan is not aimed at India. The USA is not fuelling an arms race." At the same time, the State Department called attention to a recent Indo-Soviet arms agreement,[13] and further justified the aid as "addressing those security concerns which have motivated Pakistan's nuclear program."[14] The administration argued that by providing Pakistan greater confidence about its security US arms assistance would make it easier for that country to forego nuclear weapons.

Under Secretary Buckley expressed Washington's overall exasperation with India in Congressional hearings on the Pakistan aid package. "I am not an international psychologist," Buckley declared, "I honestly don't understand the Indian reaction. But the US cannot have its actions and decisions commandeered (sic) by considerations that do not have any factual basis." The Under Secretary commented that even if Pakistan acquired the 40 F–16s, India would have a 6-1 edge in fighter aircraft.[15]

Although initially the downturn in relations after the decision to resume large-scale US arms aid to Pakistan suggested a replay of 1954, when US arms aid to Pakistan began, the situation in 1981, in fact, developed quite differently. First, in 1981, few in Washington, whether Republican or Democrat, disagreed with the decision. Bolstering Pakistan against the Soviet threat drew wide support. The aid was seen as good in itself and as a reasonable quid pro quo for Pakistan's serving as the channel for covert aid to the Afghan mujaheedin, an enormously popular cause. The main impact of Indian complaints was to damage New Delhi's credibility. As a senior State Department official put it:

> The Soviet army is standing on the marchlands of India and they are screaming about F–16s, not the Soviets in Afghanistan. People on the India desk could explain how India looked at things, the historic perspective of Pakistan, but people higher up who made policy had much greater difficulty in understanding India's response.[16]

Second, the Reagan administration avoided the trap Eisenhower fell into of offering assurances that the arms provided Pakistan would not be used against India. Although emphasizing that the United States was not giving the arms to harm India, the administration offered no guarantee Pakistan would refrain from deploying the weapons against its neighbor. Even though the Indians grumbled, the new US stance had the virtue of candor.[17] The experience of the 1960s showed that guarantees were meaningless, and only prompted recriminations in the event of India-Pakistan conflict.[18]

Third, the Pakistani attitude in the 1980s differed substantially from that of the 1950s. In return for US arms in 1954, Pakistan became a US ally and camp follower, joining two mutual security pacts and bringing its foreign policy into line with the US anti-Communist stance. As Pakistan's primary concerns in the 1950s were not the Communists, but the Indians, Washington and Karachi had different and ultimately conflicting motivations in entering the alliance relationship. In 1981, the US-Pakistan arrangement responded to the situation in Afghanistan and a shared perception of the Soviet threat. The relationship was more realistic, closer to a marriage of conve- nience than an alliance. Pakistan did not change its foreign policy, remaining a nonaligned state. Bilateral tensions contin- ued over Islamabad's quest for a nuclear capability, even though the Reagan administration obtained congressional approval to ease restrictions on aid to Pakistan in the interest of countering the Soviets in Afghanistan.

Frictions between Washington and New Delhi continued to mount during the summer of 1981. Ambassador to the United Nations Jeanne Kirkpatrick clashed with Indian leaders regard- ing US South Asia policy during a 24-27 August visit to New Delhi. When Kirkpatrick denied that Pakistan arms aid posed a problem for India, Mrs. Gandhi publicly "disagreed" with her assessment.[19]

A dispute over US diplomatic personnel made matters worse. In an unusual action, India refused to grant a visa for George Griffin, a State Department South Asia specialist, as- signed to become political counselor at the US Embassy in New Delhi. During the 1971 crisis, Griffin, then political officer in Calcutta, stirred suspicions he was a CIA operative through meetings with members of the Bangladesh government-in-exile. A decade later, while serving in Kabul, Griffin irked the Soviets by briefing Western journalists on developments in Afghanistan during visits to New Delhi to see his family.[20] After the diplomat was assigned to India, the Soviets mounted a successful dis- information campaign to discredit Griffin as a spy. Accepting Soviet fabrications—despite categorical US denials—the Gov- ernment of India refused to issue him a visa. Mrs. Gandhi herself told the press India denied the visa because Griffin was an intelligence officer. Angry that Mrs. Gandhi believed the Soviets, rather than the United States, the State Department retaliated, refusing entry for the diplomat India wished to assign as its political counselor in Washington.[21]

The Griffin incident pointed up an important fact of life in Indo-US relations: the ability of the pro-Soviet lobby to stir up trouble between Washington and New Delhi. In harness with friends in Indian government and media circles, the Soviet Embassy for many years was able to mount disinformation campaigns against US interests, such as the successful effort to discredit Griffin. No episode by itself was earthshaking, but cumulatively disinformation by the Soviets and their Indian friends added to US problems in India, in particular, strengthening suspicions that the CIA was interfering in Indian internal affairs.[22]

The most serious substantive dispute arose over India's application for a $5.8 billion loan from the International Monetary Fund (IMF)—the largest ever sought by a member country. After US Treasury Secretary Donald Regan spoke against the loan at the annual World Bank-IMF meetings, US Executive Director Richard Erb criticized the proposal as not justified by India's financial situation.[23] In the end—after President Reagan and Mrs. Gandhi met at Cancun, Mexico—the United States softened its position to abstain rather than to vote against the loan. The fact that no other major economic power joined the United States created the impression that the US position was as much politically as economically motivated.[24] As the *Economist* wrote, "It is difficult to believe that the US administration would have dealt in this way with one of its friends."[25]

Cancun and Tarapur: Back from the Brink

When President Reagan named Harry Barnes as his Ambassador to India—the first career diplomat to hold the post since George Allen in the mid-1950s—Indians interpreted the appointment as a sign of the administration's indifference. Although that judgment was probably correct, India was doubtless better off with a capable professional like Barnes than with a a non-career envoy; with a few exceptions, Reagan political appointees were poorly qualified.

Barnes, who had South Asia experience from earlier assignments in Bombay and neighboring Nepal, served as Director-General of the Foreign Service and Ambassador to Romania before coming to Delhi. Bringing a quiet but intense activism to the assignment, his game plan was to look for things that India and the United States could do together, could cooperate on, as a way to build a bilateral relationship that could eventually stand on its own feet. "Basically the thrust," Barnes said, "was to look at the whole range of the relationship and try to find those aspects that might be susceptible of some development in order to try to put the relationship with India in a broader, fuller context without so much focus on our relationship with Pakistan."[26] Barnes reviewed this approach with Robert McFarlane, Secretary Haig's right-hand man and Counselor of the State Department, who was just back from the subcontinent. McFarlane concurred with Barnes' ideas, although he was skeptical that much could be done with India.[27]

In October 1981—shortly before the new envoy arrived in New Delhi—Mrs. Gandhi, President Reagan, and other heads of government from key industrialized and developing nations held a summit at Cancun, Mexico, to consider global economic issues. The Indian and American approaches differed drastically. India pressed for concessions on debt, aid, and trade policy by the industrialized nations, vigorously supporting the call of the Non-Aligned Movement for a new world economic order that would favor the developing world. Strongly opposing these ideas, the United States stressed the importance of enlarging the scope for private enterprise and capitalism to spur economic growth for the Third World.

Reagan and Mrs. Gandhi got to know each other during the summit economic policy discussions, and, more important, also had a private meeting at Cancun. Although the two apparently discussed little of substance during this get-together, the personal chemistry between the Prime Minister and the President was positive. When word of this spread in Washington and New Delhi, the Indo-American diplomatic atmosphere began to improve.[28]

In the meanwhile, a settlement of the Tarapur problem was proving as elusive as ever. In keeping with its lower priority on nonproliferation, the Reagan administration signalled its interest in finding a quiet solution. On 2 March 1981, the US Embassy in New Delhi presented an aide mémoire on Tarapur seeking Indian views "informally and without commitment . . . on an orderly disengagement."[29] In April, Indian Atomic Energy Chairman Homi Sethna and External Affairs Secretary Eric Gonsalves traveled to Washington for talks. Even though they learned officially that the United States would no longer ship fuel for Tarapur, the Indian visitors described the Reagan team as more pragmatic than its predecessors, "who got themselves painted into a corner with President Carter's idealism over trying to stamp out nuclear proliferation."[30]

Courtesy of the National Archives: Reagan Presidential and Bush Vice Presidential Collection

21 October 1981, President Ronald Reagan and Prime Minister Indira Gandhi, Cancun, Mexico.

Two key issues remained: would India continue the safeguards after the United States pulled out, and who would replace the United States as the supplier of enriched uranium fuel? A second round of talks in New Delhi in July did not advance a solution. A third round in the fall also failed to bridge the gap. When Ambassador Barnes arrived in New Delhi, the Tarapur negotiations seemed near the breaking point. The Indians were threatening to denounce the agreement, to cancel the safeguards, and to fuel the reactors with indigenously produced mixed oxide or enriched uranium obtained from the Soviet Union.

Then, unexpectedly, the Indians stepped back from the brink, and agreed to seek a compromise solution—an event that Ambassador Barnes saw as a significant turning point.[31] Indira Gandhi—in line with her underlying desire for better relations with Washington—decided to avoid further bilateral trouble over Tarapur, overruling those pressing for a break with the United States. In December, the Prime Minister publicly ruled out unilateral action on Tarapur; she told the parliamentary consultative committee any decision to terminate the fuel supply agreement would be taken in the context of "the national interest and overall bilateral relations with the U.S."[32]

In early 1982, the Tarapur negotiations began to make progress. The main elements of a settlement took shape. The Indians dropped the idea of repudiating safeguards. The United States gave up its demands for perpetual safeguards beyond the expiration of the supply contract in 1993. France would replace the United States as the fuel supplier—a far more preferable substitute politically to Washington than the Soviets, who were the most likely alternative. Although some details remained to be ironed out, the dispute that caused rancor for nearly a decade seemed near solution.

In the spring of 1982, Barnes proposed that President Reagan invite Mrs. Gandhi to the United States. Since Indira's action on Tarapur suggested an interest on her part in better relations, Barnes believed an official visit might advance the process, especially given the indications of good personal chemistry with Reagan. When Washington approved an invitation, the Prime Minister accepted with alacrity. She had, in fact, been eager for an invitation ever since returning to office in 1980.[33] Except for a one-day stop to see a friend in Lake Placid, New York, in 1973, Mrs. Gandhi had not been to the United States for eleven years, since the ill-fated November 1971 meetings with Nixon during the Bangladesh crisis.

As if to underscore her interest in strengthening ties with Washington, Mrs. Gandhi decided she would defer paying a visit to Moscow until after she had been to the United States—a move some of her advisers opposed since it might displease the Soviets.[34] Indian rhetoric regarding US arms to Pakistan also began to taper off. In addition to wanting to create a positive atmosphere for the US visit, the Indians recognized that their protests were not going to alter US policy toward Pakistan. Although their feelings remained unchanged, according to then Foreign Minister P. V. Narasimha Rao, India tried "to be more persuasive and less rhetorical" in addressing the arms question.[35]

The Indians were in any case more confident of their ability to meet a military threat from Pakistan. The standoff in the 1965

Kashmir War and the victory in 1971 had made clear India's military superiority over its neighbor. New Delhi knew that its armed forces could, if necessary, deal with Pakistan, even a Pakistan bolstered by the latest US weaponry.[36] New Delhi knew also that the Pakistanis understood their inability to match Indian strength. Pakistan in the 1980s no longer thought that it could best India in a test of arms, as it had hoped to do in the Ayub era.

Barnes and Indian Foreign Secretary Rasgotra worked together to develop an agenda for the Prime Minister's visit that stressed those items—even if modest in scope—on which India and the United States could cooperate.[37] When Mrs. Gandhi realized the Tarapur problem was not fully solved, she sent Rasgotra ahead to Washington to work out the final details. She did not want to deal with nuclear negotiations during the visit, fearing media coverage would focus on the Tarapur dispute as it had during the 1978 Carter and Desai trips.[38]

Mrs. Gandhi's pre-departure interviews with US newsmen made clear she wanted a successful visit. "My major aim is to try to convince people that you can have friendship even if you do not agree on all matters," she told the *Washington Post.*[39] Talking with the *New York Times*, the Prime Minister stressed her desire to "correct" US misperceptions about India's relations with the Soviets. "We are friends with the Soviets and that does not prevent us from being friends with—trying to be friends with China or with the United States . . ."[40] She told journalist Tad Szulc, "We didn't join the chorus of condemnation (on Afghanistan) but we do not approve of the Soviet presence there, and we have told them privately, as we have said it publicly."[41]

Indira Gandhi Charms Washington

The Prime Minister arrived in Washington on 30 July. To greet her at Andrews Air Force Base was George Shultz, the new Secretary of State, who had just replaced Alexander Haig after the latter's stormy resignation. Landing a bit later by helicopter on the White House lawn, Mrs. Gandhi was welcomed by a smiling and relaxed Ronald Reagan—a marked contrast with Richard Nixon's tense reception eleven years before. Reagan spoke of his hope "to broaden and deepen the dialogue we began last autumn at Cancun" and of "renewed recognition of the mutual importance of strong, constructive ties between India and the United States."[42] In replying, Prime Minister Gandhi described her journey as "an adventure in search of understanding and friendship . . . . to find a common area, how so ever small, on which to build and enhance cooperation."[43]

Just as she charmed Washington during her 1966 visit, Indira, now a matronly sixty-four years old, repeated her success in 1982. Whether it was the White House, Capitol Hill, the National Press Club, or the Indian Embassy, the anti-American dragon lady of the 1970s transformed herself into a soft-spoken leader of the Third World, seeking to convince Americans that even if their two countries disagreed on issues like arms to Pakistan, they could still be friends. Only occasionally did Mrs. Gandhi bare her teeth, for example, when she compared the Soviet presence in Afghanistan to US involvement in El Salvador on "Meet the Press," the television news program.[44]

Mrs. Gandhi's friendly attitude toward the United States had a positive impact on the White House, the State Department, and elsewhere in the US Government. Official Washington was pleasantly surprised to find Indira in person different from her image as a haughty anti-American moralist.[45] The Prime Minister achieved her goal; the tensions began to lessen between Washington and New Delhi. Substantively, the visit notched up three achievements. First, the two leaders announced the Tarapur settlement, rather akin to a no-fault divorce. Under this, France was to replace the United States as the enriched uranium fuel supplier and India would continue the safeguards on the plant. Second, Reagan and Mrs. Gandhi launched an initiative for science and technology cooperation.[46] Third, they named 1985 as "the Year of India," during which a mammoth Indian art and cultural exhibition would tour the United States.[47]

In the following months, the two countries pursued the science and technology initiative seriously. In Washington, the President's science advisor, Jay Keyworth, and Allen Bromley, President of the American Association of Science (AAS), supported the effort, helping to ensure the necessary funding. On the Indian side, Mrs. Gandhi took a personal interest, meeting with the American team when it visited India to explore science projects with their Indian counterparts.[48]

Courtesy of the National Archives: Reagan Presidential and Bush Vice Presidential Collection

30 July 1982, Prime Minister Indira Gandhi being greeted on arrival in Washington by President and Mrs. Ronald Reagan.

On bilateral economic aid, the Reagan administration continued the program restarted under Carter, at first maintaining roughly the same $100 million annual level of development assistance and $100 million of food aid distributed through voluntary agencies. Under Ambassador Barnes' leadership, US AID shifted its emphasis from traditional agricultural and health programs into innovative venture capital and technology transfer areas. US bilateral aid was, however, too small to have any significant impact on Indian development or to offset the annoyance with US policy toward international financial institutions.

Running about $2 billion annually, World Bank lending dwarfed US bilateral assistance. Officials of the US AID Mission in New Delhi—major powers on the Indian economic scene in the 1950s and 1960s—became secondary players in the 1980s, treated somewhere between sufferance and disdain by Indian economic ministry civil servants. The issues that mattered for New Delhi were not the amount and nature of US bilateral aid—there was no question of any linkage to policy changes—but rather the US stance toward multilateral financial institutions and international trade issues, which were dealt with in Washington, mainly by the Treasury Department and the White House Office of the Special Trade Representative.[49]

In the year after Mrs. Gandhi's visit, the relationship became more positive as Washington responded to Indira's overtures while continuing the good ties with Pakistan. The gradual improvement in the bilateral political atmosphere eased the way for renewed talks about the sale of US arms to India, focused on 155mm howitzers and TOW anti-tank missiles. Giving official blessing to these discussions, State Department spokesman John Hughes said, "We want to help India meet its legitimate security needs and believe military sales would make a positive contribution."[50] An unexpected source of support for selling arms to India came from conservative Republican Senator Orren Hatch of Utah. Speaking on the Senate floor, Hatch raised eyebrows by asserting that "a historic shift" was under way in Indo-US relations brought about by the "strategic vision" of the Reagan administration. Urging the President to play the "India card," the Utah Senator encouraged the administration to approve any military equipment sale "India dares to request."[51]

Underlying Hatch's enthusiasm was the hope that the United States could gradually wean New Delhi away from Moscow by reducing India's dependence on Soviet weaponry. The approach was rather unrealistic given the closeness of India's foreign policy and defense links with the Soviet Union which the United States had neither the funds nor desire to displace. Support from a right-wing Republican Senator for an opening to India, nonetheless, provided a politically helpful boost to Ambassador Barnes' non-ideological approach of trying to construct an Indo-US relationship of sufficient substance that it could stand on its own.[52]

The arms talks did not lead to sales. In Washington, despite the improvement in atmospherics, many officials, especially in the Defense Department where anti-Indian and pro-Pakistani sentiments persisted, did not like the idea of selling weapons to India. Opposition focused on security issues, specifically on New Delhi's ability and willingness to prevent US-supplied equipment from falling into the hands of India's Soviet friends. This worry applied with equal force to exports of non-military items, especially civilian electronic and computer technology, that might have military application—so-called dual use items.

Military purchases from the United States raised different problems in India. Although the Indian Army wanted to procure US 155mm howitzers and TOW anti-tank missiles, their civil service masters in the Ministry of Defense had doubts about the reliability of the United States as an arms supplier. After the unilateral cutoff during the 1965 war and US reluctance to carry out the Tarapur contract, the Indians were sensitive to the terms of US government contracts. They did not like US insistence on the right to break an agreement at any time; New Delhi wanted assurances Washington would not arbitrarily cut off supplies. The Indians also disliked a standard provision that barred foreign governments from claiming refunds of prior payments in the event of a unilateral US cutoff.

In the end, India decided that with so many uncertainties, it would not proceed with the TOW and howitzer procurement. This decision seemed less motivated by politics than concern about US terms and conditions. As there had been no significant contacts since 1965, more than a decade and a half, Indian Defense Ministry civil servants—who had basic responsibility for negotiations, not the military—were on unfamiliar ground, uncomfortable with formidable US contractual requirements and suspicious about US bona fides.[53]

After the unsuccessful talks, and chronic problems encountered in exporting electronic and other dual-use technology, Washington and New Delhi realized that they needed a better means of addressing security and related concerns. This realization led to the start of negotiations on a Memorandum of Understanding on sensitive technology exports. Without an agreement that would satisfy US export control requirements, neither technology transfer nor military procurement would be feasible to any substantial extent.[54] The conclusion of an MOU thus became a key to expanding cooperation in these areas between the United States and India.

Shultz and Bush Visits: An Improvement in Relations?

In July 1983, Secretary of State George Shultz became the highest level American visitor to India since President Carter in 1978.[55] Unlike Carter, Shultz reverted to the practice of combining trips to India and Pakistan. Even though the administration sought improved relations with India, the keystone of its South Asia policy remained Pakistan, essential for continuing support for the guerrilla war in Afghanistan against the Soviets. Despite the fact that the discussions between Shultz and Mrs. Gandhi featured long pauses when neither spoke, the two appeared to get along personally. Their talks maintained the dialogue begun during the Prime Minister's 1982 visit to Washington.[56]

The most pressing substantive issue was an unresolved leftover from Tarapur: what to do about spare parts India badly needed for the nuclear power plant. In the absence of a presidential waiver, the 1978 Nuclear Nonproliferation Act prohibited the export of spares to countries like India that refused to accept safeguards on all its nuclear facilities. Shultz solved the problem by giving assurances the United States would provide the spares if India could not obtain them from other suppliers.[57] He, in effect, guaranteed a presidential waiver in extremis. This gesture drew a sharp reaction from critics of the administration's nonproliferation policy; the *New York Times*, for example, called the decision "not only a gift but a giveaway" and "appeasement" of the Indians.[58]

All was not, however, sweetness and light between New Delhi and Washington. Indian annoyance about US arms shipments to Pakistan continued; US annoyance about India's unwillingness to condemn the Soviets over Afghanistan continued. There was chronic trouble about US policy toward multilateral lending institutions, the major source of external financing for India's development plans. The World Bank, its soft-money affiliate, the International Development Authority (IDA), and the Asian Development Bank had all come under direct and indirect pressure from Washington in ways that affected India. The United States supported the membership of China in the IDA and a related drop in India's traditional 40 percent share of low interest IDA loans.

The Reagan administration was, in addition, reluctant to increase its contributions to IDA which could lead to a reduction in IDA loan levels. Washington was, at the same time, pressing India to borrow more from commercial financial markets and from the World Bank, both with higher interest rates and shorter terms than IDA loans. Finally, the United States opposed India's borrowing from the Asian Development Bank, a financial institution whose resources India had not until then tapped although it was a member of the Asian Bank.[59]

In January 1984, Prime Minister Gandhi sounded anything but upbeat in an interview with the Associated Press in New Delhi. Her good relations with Ronald Reagan were "entirely on a personal basis;" US government policy was "opposed to ours," Indira said, charging Washington played up to dictators but was indifferent to a democracy like India. She could not object to US arms to the Pakistanis, "but they are being armed to an extent that is well beyond their need" and the "guns are pointed toward us and not Afghanistan." She alleged reduced US funding for international lending agencies seemed "to be done in such a way that it hits India."[60]

The State Department review of voting records in the United Nations for 1983 provided striking confirmation that India and the United States continued to have major differences. India opposed the US position on all ten UN questions that Washington judged important in 1983. By contrast, on the same ten issues, Pakistan voted with the United States five times, Bangladesh four times, and Sri Lanka three times. Overall, India sided with the United States on only about 20 percent of votes, and with the Soviets on 80 percent.[61]

The US administration, nevertheless, continued to promote the high level dialogue, sending Vice President George Bush to India in May 1984. Relaxing protocol, the Indians invited the Bushes to stay in the Rashtrapathi Bhavan, the presidential home and palatial former residence of the British Viceroys, a courtesy not accorded Vice President Hubert Humphrey when he visited in 1966. Mrs. Gandhi devoted a whole day to discussions with the Vice President, hosting both an official State function as well as a quieter and more intimate family dinner.

Substantively, the talks broke no new ground. Although Foreign Minister Rao said flatly there was "no agreement" on arms to Pakistan, Bush was more positive with the press. The Vice President saw "no major stumbling block" between the United States and India and praised Indira Gandhi's leadership

Courtesy of the National Archives: Reagan Presidential and Bush Vice Presidential Collection

12 May 1984, Vice President Bush, Ambassador Harry Barnes, and Prime Minister Indira Gandhi.

of the Non-Aligned Movement. As if to answer her criticism of US support for dictatorships, Bush pointedly called on Pakistan to hasten its return to democracy.[62]

The Vice President's visit helped the negotiations on the high technology MOU, which were dragging because of internal differences within the Reagan administration. Together with Ambassador Harry Barnes' persistent prodding, intervention by the Vice President after he returned from India helped advance the MOU toward agreement by the end of 1984. These negotiations were not easy. Although the State and Commerce Departments took a positive attitude, Defense, Energy, and the Arms Control and Disarmament Agency (ACDA) dug in their heels, suspicious of India because of its close links with the Soviets and its nuclear policy. For its part, New Delhi was reluctant to concede anything in the way of a review procedure by US officials that could be construed as an infringement on India's sovereignty. The Indians maintained they had ample experience

Courtesy of the National Archives: Reagan Presidential and Bush Vice Presidential Collection

12 June 1985, President Reagan and Prime Minister Rajiv Gandhi on the latter's arrival in Washington.

and a good record in protecting foreign equipment from unfriendly hands. The US side, in particular the Defense Department, doubted the Indian control system was leak proof.[63]

Rajiv Gandhi Replaces His Mother

On 31 October 1984, Indira Gandhi died, assassinated by
two Sikh bodyguards in retaliation for her having ordered the
Indian Army in June 1984 to storm the Golden Temple of
Amritsar, the holy shrine of the Sikh religion. Sikh militants,
who were agitating for an independent homeland, had occupied
the temple in June as unrest mounted in the Punjab, the northwest Indian state bordering on Pakistan. The bloody army assault caused many casualties, severely damaged the temple
complex, and alienated the Sikh community still further from
the Gandhi government.

Mrs. Gandhi's violent death shocked the world; President
Reagan, who signed the condolence book at the Indian Embassy,
sent Secretary Shultz along with former US ambassadors John
Sherman Cooper, John Kenneth Galbraith, Daniel Patrick Moynihan, and Robert Goheen to participate in the funeral ceremonies.[64] In a moving meeting with Mrs. Gandhi's son and India's
new Prime Minister Rajiv Gandhi, each envoy, at Shultz's request, spoke of their personal dealings with Indira.[65]

Even though Mrs. Gandhi's associates insisted that she had
no bias against the United States, Indira made no bones over the
years about her suspicions and dislike of L S policy toward India
and US foreign policy in general. She never seemed to shed the
negative attitude about the United States developed in her student days in Britain in the 1930s, and, to some extent, passed on
from her father. This attitude was strengthened by her view of
US policy as unfriendly toward India, a perception that emerged
from her unhappy personal experience during the Johnson and
Nixon administrations. A pragmatic politician and, above all an
Indian nationalist, she was still prepared to seek better relations
in her last years with Washington when she concluded this was
in India's interest.

Whatever Mrs. Gandhi personally thought of the United
States, her impact on US attitudes toward India was on the
whole quite negative. If, in the 1950s, Krishna Menon became
the symbol of Indian antagonism to the United States, Mrs.

Gandhi assumed this role during most of her years as Prime Minister. Her often cold manner, her occasional cutting sarcasm and her frequent public criticisms alienated many Americans. Quite apart from her mannerisms, Indira succeeded in offending liberals and former India supporters through her decision to explode a nuclear device in 1974 and her imposition of the Emergency in 1975. She disenchanted conservatives by aligning India closely with the Soviet Union, a policy symbolized by her unwillingness to condemn the Soviet invasions of Czechoslovakia in 1968 and Afghanistan in 1980.

Yet over time, Indira earned grudging respect from US leaders as a major world figure. There was belated recognition that she was not a puppet of Moscow, but rather a nationalist, pressing India's interests as she saw them. Despite chronic policy differences, Washington appreciated that Indira supported a relatively moderate line in Non-Aligned Movement (NAM) deliberations—in 1983 Mrs. Gandhi hosted the NAM summit at New Delhi. Although she lacked the eloquence or vision of her father, she still articulated aspirations for a better life for hundreds of millions of Indians and others in the Third World. At the time of her death, Indira had been India's Prime Minister for fifteen years. In 1964 it was hard to think of India without Nehru; in 1984 it seemed equally hard to think that his daughter was no longer ruling India.

Stunned by Mrs. Gandhi's assassination, the ruling Congress Party swiftly chose Indira's son, Rajiv, as its leader and India's new Prime Minister. Unlike his often austere mother, or gregarious and cerebral grandfather, the third member of the Nehru dynasty was a reluctant politician. A handsome professional airline pilot, Rajiv showed little interest in political life before his mother pressed him to help in ruling India after her younger son Sanjay died in a glider accident in 1980. As Prime Minister, Rajiv got off to an impressive start, initially representing a generational change as well as a new look in Indian politics. His coming to power appeared to herald the arrival of a modern Indian leadership, one that marked the passing of a British-trained and oriented elite, often with a strong anti-American strain. Reflecting the prevailing views of the younger urban elite,

Rajiv leaned toward the private sector and had a healthy skepticism about the socialist economic dogma adopted by the Congress Party. Capitalizing on the sympathy vote and his image as representing a new younger generation, he won a record 415 seats in parliament in the general elections in January 1985—a bigger victory than either his mother or grandfather had ever achieved.

In his first year in office, the young Prime Minister pressed for solutions to the Sikh problem in the Punjab and proposed a variety of measures to modernize and reform the Indian economy. Rajiv earned the nickname of "Computerjii" (*jii* is a Hindi honorific and sign of affection added to names) because of his emphasis on using modern technology to address India's problems. His popularity stood high. The country again seemed to be on the move.

In foreign policy, Rajiv continued the policies inherited from his mother and grandfather. He accepted the Soviet Union as India's chief foreign partner and quickly made friends with its new leader, Mikhail Gorbachev. When Rajiv became Prime Minister, Washington and New Delhi were still in the early stage of groping their way out of the impasse which had made their relations largely hostage to US ties with Islamabad and India's with the Soviet Union. The immediate challenge was to overcome the obstacles to technology transfer from the United States to India by finishing up the negotiations for the technology MOU.

In December 1984, little more than a month after Rajiv succeeded his mother, US and Indian negotiators successfully reached agreement on the MOU. The two sides then tackled questions of implementation, how specifically to deal with US concerns about diversion of technology from agreed uses.[66] In May 1985, Ambassador Barnes and Foreign Secretary Romesh Bhandari, who had replaced Rasgotra, signed the MOU implementation agreement. US Commerce Secretary Malcolm Baldrige, visiting New Delhi when the accord was signed, hailed the event as providing a mechanism for speedier review of the export of controlled items. Baldrige predicted a large increase in US computer sales and cooperative technology agreements with India.[67]

Also in May, the Pentagon's Under Secretary for Policy, Dr. Fred Iklé, paid a significant visit to New Delhi. A conservative strategist, Iklé's main purpose in coming to India—in accordance with the overall approach of the Reagan administration—was to try to enlarge the scope of Indo-American security cooperation in the hope of reducing Soviet influence.[68] Iklé explored the possibility of technical cooperation in India's development of a next-generation fighter aircraft, the so-called Light Combat Aircraft (LCA). In keeping with the policy of creating indigenous defense production capabilities rather than relying on imported equipment, India hoped to produce the LCA as its Air Force mainstay in the 1990s. Iklé also discussed ways to speed up US processing of Indian applications for exports of defense-related equipment, at the same time stressing Washington's concerns that India's system of internal controls needed strengthening to prevent diversion of items to the Soviets.[69]

Iklé's talks about the LCA and follow-on discussions later in May, involving Secretary of the Air Force Vern Orr, signalled an important shift in US arms policy toward India: Washington was agreeing in principle—after a break of two decades—to cooperate with India's growing defense industry by providing technical assistance and high technology components for the production of advanced weapons systems. Although this type of cooperation was standard in India's military supply arrangements with the Soviets and West European countries, collaboration on the LCA would be a first with the United States after the limited and brief defense production arrangements twenty years earlier following the 1962 India-China war.

In his public remarks during his stay, Iklé urged US-India military cooperation to see how the two countries "can work together much as we try to work together with other major powers now to enhance our long-term security aims."[70] Looking to the 21st century, Iklé said he envisaged possible security cooperation in which India together with the United States could contribute to world stability. "And that I think," Iklé stated effusively, "is an exciting possibility and perhaps a new chapter in United States-Indian relations."[71]

Courtesy of the National Archives: Reagan Presidential and Bush Vice Presidential Collection

12 June 1985, President Reagan and Prime Minister Rajiv Gandhi meeting in the White House.

The New Prime Minister Impresses Washington

In June 1985, a month after the signing of the MOU implementation agreement and the Iklé trip, Rajiv Gandhi made an excellent impression on his American hosts during an official visit to Washington. The handsome young Prime Minister differed from the preachy, arrogant Indian stereotype. He was quiet, seemed to listen to what American leaders had to say, spoke softly but directly, and had a touch of humor.[72]

In Washington, where he opened the Festival of India exhibition agreed upon during his mother's visit in 1982, Rajiv did all the right things. He handled himself calmly and with dignity in his meetings with Ronald Reagan and senior US officials, at the National Press Club, and on Capitol Hill. There he followed in the footsteps of his grandfather in addressing the Congress, an honor not offered his mother during her three official visits to the United States. When Vice President George Bush accompanied Rajiv on a trip to the NASA space center at Houston, Texas, the two developed friendly personal ties.[73]

The Prime Minister departed from the United States having lived up to his advance billing as a "young, modern, well-informed, pragmatic" leader, someone Americans can like, understand, and deal with.[74] Rajiv's penchant for modern technology and gadgetry and his conscious adoption of an "American" management style made him appear more approachable for many Americans as did the fact that some of his closest advisers were US-trained.[75] Even though Rajiv made clear he was not going to alter the basic thrust of his country's foreign policy, pointedly visiting Moscow before Washington, his change of style from his mother's made India look different. As Ambassador Harry Barnes put it, "There was a disposition to see and hear the promise that lots of Indians saw, that this was a new start, good for India and good for the United States."[76]

After the positive visit, the challenge was to put more substance into the bilateral relationship to accompany the substantially improved atmospherics. In the State Department's view, this meant implementing the MOU in a way that demonstrated to India and also to the Washington bureaucracy that the Reagan administration was serious about making advanced technology available to India. In 1981, providing F–16s became the test of US credibility with Pakistan. With India in the mid-1980s, the test of credibility came in US willingness to provide a highly sophisticated Cray supercomputer model XMP–24 to the Indian Institute of Science to help the country's weather research program.[77]

One of the world's most advanced computers, superior to anything the Soviet Union possessed, the Cray XMP–24 which India sought had the capability of being used for nuclear weapon and ballistic missile development, for deciphering cryptographic codes, and for a host of theoretical tasks and military applications that had little to do with India's stated objective of aiding agriculture through enhanced tracking of global weather patterns. Since the United States had not sold a computer as powerful as the Cray XMP–24 outside the circle of close allies, its export to India was a difficult decision, raising security questions about the Soviets and concerns about the computer's

13 June 1985, Prime Minister Rajiv Gandhi addressing a Joint Session of Congress, applauded by Vice President Bush and Speaker Tip O'Neil.

14 June 1985, Vice President Bush with Indian Ambassador K. Shankar Bajpai aboard Air Force 2.

possible use for nuclear weapons and missile guidance development.[78] The Cray provided a genuine test of the Reagan administration's seriousness about improving relations.

Perhaps less controversial, but not less significant, were the
discussions about the transfer of military technology. In September 1985, the Science Adviser to the Defense Ministry, Dr.
Arunachalam, a key figure in India's defense industry, visited a
number of US defense plants as part of the continuing explora-
tion of possible US collaboration in the LCA. In the end, the
Indians expressed interest in procuring the General Electric 404
engine as the initial power plant for their next-generation
fighter. Used in the F–18, the GE 404 was one of the most
advanced US aircraft engines. Early approval in principle by the
Pentagon and the White House for its sale to India was a tangible
sign of the more forthcoming US stance on security cooperation
with India.[79]

About this time, Harry Barnes completed his tour in New
Delhi, where he was succeeded by another career diplomat, John
Gunther Dean. Barnes' quiet determination, energy, and bureaucratic skill, as well as his good rapport with Indians, helped
the two countries take advantage of Mrs. Gandhi's opening
toward the United States. Getting a skeptical Washington to
respond to the Indian overture, developing the science and
technology initiative, and shepherding the difficult negotiations
for the high technology MOU were substantial achievements
given the considerable residual sentiment against India in the
Washington bureaucracy. Another striking success by Barnes
was obtaining legislation to set aside $100 million from the
dwindling pool of US-owned PL 480 rupees to fund science,
technology, and education programs.[80]

During part of Harry Barnes' tenure, India had one of its
most effective envoys in Washington, K. Shankar Bajpai. The
son of the Indian Agent-General to the United States during
World War II, Bajpai had the unusual experience of returning as
ambassador to the house where he had lived as a teenager. Bajpai
was fully at home in Washington, able to represent the Indian
position forcefully without ruffling American sensitivities.[81]
During his tour, Bajpai worked to broaden Indian Embassy
contacts beyond the normal diplomatic realm of the State Department and the National Security Council. He focused, in

particular, on developing relations with the Defense Department and the Treasury, two agencies not notably well disposed toward India in the early years of the Reagan administration, but increasingly important in bilateral relations.[82]

In the fall of 1985, Rajiv returned to the United States for the UN General Assembly session. Like a number of other leaders, he met with President Ronald Reagan in New York. Although impressive in private sessions, the Prime Minister gave a lackluster reiteration of Indian foreign policy in his UN speech that compared poorly with Pakistan's Zia ul-Haq's more dramatic call for a nuclear agreement with India.[83] In New York, Rajiv also seemed to take a more pro-Soviet line than during his visit to Washington in June.[84] A hurried trip to Moscow on the way back to India raised eyebrows in Washington.

On his return to New Delhi, the Prime Minister told the press that the Americans had no cause to be upset. India had built its good relations with the Soviet Union over the past 30 years. It was not possible to build up similarly good relations with the United States in six months. The two countries, he stressed to American leaders, still were at odds on important issues like apartheid, disarmament, and Pakistan.[85] As Rajiv's comments made clear, underlying policy differences between India and the United States remained even if there were improvements in style and form since Rajiv succeeded his mother as prime minister.

In October 1986, Caspar Weinberger became the first US Secretary of Defense to visit India. His trip underscored US interest in expanding contacts and dialogue in the security area—and the lack of this in the first four decades of Indian independence. During Weinberger's four days in India, the Secretary met top Indian leaders to continue discussions about possible US cooperation in Indian defense production. Emerging from his talk with Prime Minister Gandhi, Weinberger was upbeat about the improvement in relations and the possibility of proceeding with the sale of the Cray supercomputer and the GE-404 engine.[86]

A few days later, in neighboring Pakistan, the Secretary of Defense managed to set relations back when he unexpectedly announced that the United States was in favor of providing Pakistan with the Boeing 707 Advanced Warning and Control

System (AWACS) as part of a new multi-year military and economic aid package that was being discussed with Pakistan. Despite an informal understanding with the Indians to avoid springing surprises on each other, Weinberger said nothing about the AWACS during his stay in New Delhi.[87]

Quite apart from being annoyed by being caught off guard, the Indians were genuinely upset by the prospect of Pakistan's acquiring the AWACS. The sophisticated aircraft would substantially enhance the Pakistani Air Force's capability, enabling it to track enemy aircraft at great distances. Launching a vigorous counterattack, New Delhi argued that the AWACS would be of limited use against the Soviets, were not needed against the Afghans, but would be enormously helpful against India. In Washington, Indian Ambassador P. K. Kaul, former Cabinet Secretary and successor to Shankar Bajpai, protested the AWACS in meetings with Weinberger and senior State Department officials. Adding to the chorus, visiting Indian Foreign Secretary A. P. Venkateshwaran warned Washington in January 1987 that providing the AWACS would trigger a "very destabilizing" arms race in South Asia, requiring heavy Indian expenditures to match Pakistan's new capability.[88]

Even though aid to the Afghan resistance remained tremendously popular in the United States, the idea of giving Pakistan the AWACS encountered opposition on Capitol Hill. With US-Indian relations improved, New Delhi's views carried more weight than previously. In a first, members of the Indian immigrant community staged a demonstration against sending the AWACS to Pakistan during House of Representative hearings by Representative Stephen Solarz of New York. The Democratic Congressman, who was establishing himself as an expert on Asia, opposed the AWACS because he did not believe Pakistan was sufficiently responsive to US desires that it stop its nuclear weapons program.

In the Senate, John Glenn of Ohio and others urged the Reagan administration to go slow on AWACS unless Pakistan provided firmer assurances it was halting its nuclear program. The opposition was strengthened by voices of concern from the Republican right, from Senators Orrin Hatch of Utah and Gordon Humphrey of New Hampshire, who urged that if AWACS were provided Pakistan, this should be balanced in some way acceptable to India.[89] In the face of Congressional doubts, the administration wavered about the AWACS, exploring a less expensive and less capable early warning aircraft to meet the genuine air security concerns posed by Afghan air attacks inside Pakistani territory. Islamabad, however, rebuffed US efforts to substitute a more modest system, such as the E2C, insisting on the AWACS. With the Soviets bogged down in a genuine war of national liberation in Afghanistan, the Reagan administration had a strong policy incentive to pay Pakistan's price as part of the new multi-year aid package.[90]

As if the possibility of the AWACS were not enough trouble for bilateral relations, the sale of the Cray supercomputer was encountering major obstacles within the US government. Hardliners in the Defense Department were digging in their heels against selling the computer to India. The concerns were familiar: the possible leakage of technology to the Soviets and possible use of the Cray for nuclear weapons and missile development.[91] Revelations about Soviet technology espionage in the United States heightened anxiety about sending sensitive technology to India. "If they can steal it from Silicon Valley, they can steal it from Bangalore," a Pentagon official told the *Wall Street Journal.*[92]

The debate over the Cray matched the State and Commerce Departments (which favored moving ahead with the sale) against Defense, Energy, and the National Security Agency (NSA), which disliked the proposal. An unstated, but nonetheless real, factor was the preference among some Defense Department officials for Pakistan and a related reluctance to expand security relations with India. In March 1987, the Reagan administration—after much delay—finally decided on a compromise solution: it would approve the sale to India of a Cray model XMP–14 computer which had less capability than the Cray XMP–24 India wanted. US specialists asserted the Cray XMP–14 could do sophisticated weather research work but lacked the code cracking capabilities that aroused NSA concerns.[93]

The decision disappointed the Indians. One official source alleged the Reagan administration had raised high expectations and then reneged by providing the Cray XMP–14 rather than the more powerful Cray XMP–24.[94] As India's Minister of State for External Affairs Natwar Singh put it during an April 1987 visit to Washington, US-Indian relations were like the titles of two novels of Charles Dickens, *Great Expectations* and *Hard Times*.[95] New Delhi did not, however, reject the US counter-offer out of hand. Foreign Secretary Venkateshwaran urged Prime Minister Gandhi to accept, arguing it was in India's interest to buy the XMP-14 in order to gain entry into the US high technology world. Rejecting the offer, Venkateshwaran warned, would freeze India out of high technology cooperation with the United States. In the end, Rajiv accepted this reasoning and approved the purchase of the XMP-14.[96]

Things were also not going smoothly for India in the US Congress. Michigan Republican Congressman William Broomfield led a successful initiative in the foreign aid committee to slash the bilateral assistance program for fiscal year 1988 from $50 million to $35 million. After Broomfield criticized Indian foreign policy support for the Kabul regime, for the Sandinistas in Nicaragua, and for the pro-Vietnamese Kampucheans, the members voted 18-14 in favor of the reduction.[97] Even if the vote itself was not of great consequence—given the aid program's small size—the episode was an eye opener regarding continuing resentment about India on Capitol Hill.

The Reagan administration itself had gradually reduced the level of development aid to India in the mid-1980s from $100 million down to $50 million.[98] During a period of tight development assistance budgets, AID headquarters in Washington shifted funds from India to boost development aid programs in other countries. Knowing how difficult a battle in Washington against the cuts would be, Ambassador John Gunther Dean decided not to contest the reductions. Dean doubted the benefit in terms of better relations with India would be worth the bureaucratic struggle.[99]

The administration's handling of the AWACS and the Cray—as well as congressional sniping at India over bilateral assistance—cooled off New Delhi's enthusiasm about the prospects for enhanced relations. When members of parliament, including some from Rajiv's own Congress Party, lashed out at his government for not being firm enough with Washington, the Prime Minister bent under the criticism. He adopted a tougher stance, demonstrating Indian displeasure by abruptly canceling a visit by External Affairs Minister N.D. Tiwari a week before he was due in the United States.[100]

Rajiv Gandhi: The Glow Wears Off

By 1987, when Rajiv had been prime minister for two years, the glow had begun to wear off from his political reputation. With many early expectations unrealized, he was increasingly seen as a well-intentioned but ineffective politician in handling pressing domestic matters. Although Rajiv pledged democratic reforms for the Congress Party, he failed to deliver on his promise to hold internal party elections. Reverting to his mother's style of tightly centralized control, Rajiv frequently shuffled ministers at the central and state level, more with an eye to maintaining personal political power than improving efficiency or rewarding achievement.[101]

In foreign affairs, Rajiv, like his mother and grandfather, retained effective control of policy; unlike them he lacked a sure touch in dealing with substantive issues. Shuffling foreign ministers four times during his four years as prime minister, Rajiv earned a reputation in the Ministry of External Affairs as a well-intentioned intellectual lightweight. Rajiv continued, nonetheless, to make a favorable impression abroad. His handsome presence and well-mannered approach helped retain a star quality in international gatherings and travels even though his reputation was dimming at home.

In policy terms, Rajiv continued the course Indira mapped out after returning to office in 1980. In addition to seeking better balance in India's nonalignment through improved relations with Washington, Rajiv showed increasing willingness to assert India's primacy in the subcontinent based on its size and increasing military power. In 1987, India began a major initiative by sending several thousand troops against the insurgency mounted by Tamil separatists in the neighboring island republic of Sri Lanka to India's south. Although the Sri Lanka government agreed to the intervention, the action—under which 50,000 Indian troops were eventually deployed—provided a dramatic signal of greater Indian readiness to flex its muscles regionally. Uncertain how the United States would respond, New Delhi was relieved when Washington gave its blessing to the venture. Paradoxically, in light of the accommodating US reaction, the Indo-Sri Lankan accords made gratuitous reference to "outside powers" seeking to gain a foothold on the island and to foreign radio broadcasts from Sri Lanka. Since the Voice of America had been using a transmitter in Sri Lanka for many years, the criticism of the United States was thinly veiled.

About the same time Indian troops intervened in Sri Lanka, worrisome developments regarding Pakistan's efforts to develop nuclear weapons surfaced. In late July 1987, Arshad Parvez, a Canadian national of Pakistani origin, was arrested in Philadelphia and charged with trying to bribe US customs officials to permit the export of certain prohibited material essential for Pakistan's nuclear program.[102] The incident underscored fears that the Pakistanis, despite their protestations to the contrary, were pressing ahead with their covert effort to develop a nuclear capability. The news also played into the hands of those critical of providing the AWACS aircraft to Pakistan—a proposal already under fire as a destabilizing system. After the Parvez episode, the AWACS was effectively shelved.

The administration was, in any case, having increasing difficulty in dealing with the Pakistan nuclear issue. The Congress modified the legislative approach to the Pakistan nuclear issue in 1985, adopting an amendment by Senator Larry Pressler (Republican, South Dakota), that required annual certification by the President that Pakistan did not have a nuclear device in order to continue economic and military aid. By establishing a line that Pakistan could not cross if it were to receive US aid, the amendment, in effect, gave Pakistan a choice: either hold off crossing the bomb threshold or forgo US aid. Although President Reagan continued to provide the certification, US officials were uncomfortable—caught between mounting evidence about the Pakistan nuclear program and the desire to maintain the pressure on the Soviets in Afghanistan.

In the fall of 1987, Rajiv Gandhi, after attending the United Nations session, paid his second official visit to Washington— the first time an Indian Prime Minister returned to the US capital after an interval of only two years.[103] The trip underscored Rajiv's belief that expanded dialogue was useful despite continuing policy differences. Lower key and briefer than the 1985 visit, Rajiv still touched the major bases during his stay: talks and lunch with President Reagan and meetings with Vice

President Bush, Acting Secretary of State John Whitehead, NSC chief Frank Carlucci, and Secretary of Defense Caspar Weinberger.

During the visit, Rajiv confirmed his decision that India would accept the Cray XMP–14 supercomputer. He received, in turn, an implicit US promise to provide additional computers in line with "India's need for upgraded capability and the growing mutual confidence that implementation of our agreement will provide."[104] According to the White House, the President and Rajiv also "agreed to expand defense cooperation, proceeding along the lines we have already established in working together on aspects of the Light Combat Aircraft, and in other areas."[105]

In assessing relations after his trip, the Prime Minister was upbeat, except for his comments on the Pakistan nuclear program. Rajiv asserted, "If the U.S. really exerts pressure, I have no doubt that Pakistan will change its attitude toward the nuclear weapons programme."[106] Turning to US-Indian defense cooperation, the Prime Minister stated, "We have seen progress on that confidence-building exercise. We have completed everything we had targeted to do. Now we have got to start a new phase." Overall, Rajiv declared, "We had ups and downs and our differences. But these two years have seen a very substantial improvement in our relations."[107]

By 1988, the final year of the Reagan administration, growing domestic political troubles plagued Rajiv. The taint of corruption, acknowledged to be widespread within the Congress Party, for the first time threatened to touch the Prime Minister. When former Finance and Defense Minister V. P. Singh quit the Congress Party over Rajiv's alleged failure to investigate scandals in a billion-plus dollar contract procuring Bofors howitzers from Sweden, the Prime Minister's image as a reformer suffered.

V. P. Singh started building an anti-Congress coalition—the National Front—that spanned the Indian political spectrum from right to left. Presenting himself as Mr. Clean, Singh lambasted Rajiv and his Congress Party colleagues for corruption and neglect of India's economic and social problems. Rajiv also failed to make progress in containing Sikh violence and unrest in the Punjab. The breakdown of law and order continued amidst charges that Pakistan was aiding Sikh terrorists from across the border. Restiveness in Kashmir in the north and a resurgence of disturbances in Assam in the northeast added to domestic disarray and a general sense of rising instability. Rajiv appeared to be floundering.

Regionally, with fits and starts and continued friction over alleged interference in Kashmir and the Punjab, the Prime Minister pursued more normal relations with Pakistan. This effort strengthened after the death of Zia ul-Haq in a mysterious plane crash in the summer of 1988 and the democratic election of Benazir Bhutto as Prime Minister—the first genuinely free polling in Pakistan since the December 1970 elections. To the South, in November 1988, India flexed its muscles once more as Rajiv ordered an Indian Army battalion flown to the Maldives, a thousand miles from India's southern tip, to squelch a coup attempt. Although India was responding to a request from the small island republic's legitimate government, this striking projection of power far into the Indian Ocean—in some ways more dramatic than sending troops into Sri Lanka—underlined India's growing military capability and its willingness to use this power in a big brotherly fashion.

The treatment of Nepal, nestled uncomfortably in the Himalayas between India and China, was another example of India's increased disposition to lean on its smaller neighbors. When the Nepalese irked New Delhi by procuring some arms from China, Rajiv responded by imposing the restrictions on the flow of import into the landlocked kingdom. India seemed intent on demonstrating to the Nepalese that failure to heed Indian policy sensitivities would have a cost. As Ambassador John Hubbard, whom Reagan appointed as US envoy to replace John Gunther Dean in the summer of 1988, declared, India is now "the biggest kid on the block and she's beginning to feel her oats."[108]

The United States was cautious about reacting publicly to India's increased assertion of power, a development which caused worry and suspicion among India's subcontinental neighbors. In the case of the dispute with Nepal, Washington maintained a discreet public silence. The intervention in the Maldives won Washington's approval and was closely coordinated with the United States, from whom the Maldives first sought intervention before turning to New Delhi. A US navy ship helped the Indians vector in on the escaping mercenaries and their hostages—a good example of US-Indian cooperation that did not infringe on US interests.

At the same time, Washington and New Delhi continued the expanded high level dialogue, especially in the security area. Frank Carlucci, who replaced Weinberger as Secretary of Defense, visited New Delhi and Islamabad in April 1988. Although no Secretary of Defense had traveled to India during the first 39 years of independence, two Secretaries came in less than two years. During his stay in India, Carlucci announced further agreement for cooperation in developing the Light Combat Aircraft, approving use in the LCA of a highly advanced gyroscope, something the Pentagon had previously been unwilling to permit.[109]

An important backdrop for the gradual improvement between Washington and New Delhi was the changing and less confrontational US-Soviet relationship as Gorbachev's policy of *perestroika* took hold, and increasing signs that Moscow genuinely wanted out from Afghanistan. On the margins of US-Soviet talks, Rajiv let the Russians known that India also wanted Moscow to leave and occasionally served as an unofficial channel between the United States and the Soviet Union.[110] Rajiv also continued trying to mend relations with China, especially after Gorbachev initiated an effort to reduce the frictions between Moscow and Beijing. In December 1988, Rajiv became the first Indian Prime Minister to visit China since his grandfather traveled there in 1956. Although the long-standing dispute over the Himalayan borders remained unresolved, the two Asian giants pledged to work harder to improve relations so as to negotiate a border settlement and to ensure that in the meantime the situation along the disputed frontier remained calm.[111]

1981-1989: A Gradual Warming

Just before the 1988 US elections, P. V. Narasimha Rao, whom Rajiv had reappointed as foreign minister, called on President Reagan and had a friendly breakfast with Secretary George Shultz during the UN session in New York. The amicable talks underscored the change in Indo-American relations during the eight years Ronald Reagan occupied the White House. In January 1981, prospects for friendlier relations seemed bleak, yet the two terms of the Reagan presidency saw a

27 September 1988, President Reagan meeting then Foreign Minister P. V. Narasimha Rao.

gradual warming between Washington and New Delhi. Although neither country substantially altered their basic—and often conflicting—policies, either globally or toward the subcontinent, Indo-US relations paradoxically improved.

The Reagan administration initially wrote off India as politically opposed and economically irrelevant to US interests. In South Asia, the Reagan team had its eyes on rearming Pakistan and promoting resistance against the Soviets in Afghanistan; to the extent India mattered, it was primarily as a function of New Delhi's continuing leadership role in the nonaligned world.

Gradually that view changed. After Mrs. Gandhi was all smiles during her 1982 visit, Washington perked up. When Rajiv Gandhi succeeded his mother, the United States saw new opportunities with India. Washington eased barriers to technology transfer and approved some advanced technology cooperation with India's defense industry. Although the bilateral rhetoric became more positive, adding substance to the better atmospherics was not easy. Basic policy differences continued and a legacy of mutual distrust remained. Despite skepticism about how far the improvement in relations could carry, however, neither capital gave up the effort. During Reagan's eight years in office high-level dialogue greatly increased. The Vice President, Secretary of State, two Secretaries of Defense, and three other cabinet members visited India[112]; Indira and Rajiv paid Reagan three visits to Washington. Mutual understanding increased at the top levels of government.

By 1988, both the United States and India seemed more realistic about what they could and could not expect from each other. Even though the bilateral framework remained fragile and progress toward substantive cooperation was uneven, there were smiles not frowns in New Delhi when Vice President George Bush, a friend of Prime Minister Rajiv Gandhi, defeated the Democrats in the November 1988 elections.

NOTES

1. Interviews with Ambassadors Eric Gonsalves, 12 January 1991, and Krishnan Rasgotra, 28 February 1991.

2. Interviews with Ambassadors K. R. Narayanan and P. K. Kaul, January-February 1991.

3. Interview with Inder Malhotra, journalist and biographer of Indira Gandhi, 22 February 1991.

4. Before the US immigration law changed in 1965 to permit non-discriminatory entry, the Indian immigrant community had been insignificant in size. After the more liberal 1965 law went into effect, the number of Indian immigrants grew rapidly.

5. *New York Times*, 13 September 1981.

6. A case in point was Ajit Singh, son of Charan Singh, the caretaker prime minister after the Morarji Desai government collapsed. After finishing his studies, Ajit worked in the United States as an engineer for more than a decade. When his father died, Ajit returned to India to become a prominent political leader of upper caste peasants in northern India and Minister of Industries in the National Front government that took power after the 1989 elections.

7. Interview with Ambassador B.K. Nehru, 12 January 1991.

8. The Indian press reported the meeting as a chance encounter. See *The Statesman*, 1 January 1981.

9. Interview with Ambassador Nehru, 28 February 1991.

10. *The Statesman*, 2 April 1981.

11. Ibid., 19 April 1981.

12. *New York Times*, 6 July 1981.

13. *The Statesman,* 17 June 1981.

14. *Facts on File,* 19 June 1981, p. 410.

15. *The Statesman,* 18 September 1981.

16. Interview with Ambassador Howard Schaffer, 17 December 1990. Schaffer served as India Country Director, 1979-1980, and as Deputy Assistant Secretary for South Asia, 1981-1984 and 1989-1990.

17. Interview with Ambassador K.R. Narayanan, 21 January 1991.

18. Interview with Ambassador Howard Schaffer, 17 December 1990.

19. *Facts on File,* 4 September 1981, p. 631.

20. Because of the difficult security situation in Kabul, families resided elsewhere. Since the Afghan authorities refused entry to western journalists, much of their reporting was dependent on diplomatic sources such as Griffin.

21. *New York Times,* 2 and 3 September 1981; *Washington Post,* 3 and 11 September 1981. After service as Commercial Counselor in Seoul and Lagos and a tour as Deputy Chief of Mission in Nairobi, Griffin became India Country Director in the State Department in 1990.

22. Among other examples of Soviet disinformation in India were efforts in the mid-1970s to discredit as biological warfare a US anti-malaria research program, a series of forgeries in 1981 directed against visiting USUN Ambassador Jeanne Kirkpatrick, and numerous press stories alleging that the CIA was behind domestic unrest almost anywhere in India. For fuller discussion, see Dennis Kux's "Soviet Active Measures and Disinformation," *Parameters,* Winter 1985.

23. *The Hindu,* 12 December 1981.

24. *New York Times,* 10 November 1981.

25. *Quarterly Economic Review for India and Nepal,* London: The Economist Intelligence Unit, 4th quarter 1981, p. 5.

26. Interview with Ambassador Harry Barnes, 7 May 1991.

27. Ibid.

28. Interviews with Ambassador Harry Barnes, 7 May 1991, and Eric Gonsalves, 11 January 1991.

29. Ram, "India's Nuclear Policy," unpublished Paper presented at the 1982 meeting of the Association of Asian Studies, Chicago, pp. 73-74.

30. *The Statesman,* 19 April 1981.

31. Interview with Ambassador Barnes, 7 May 1991.

32. *The Hindu,* 23 December 1981, cited in Ram, p. 91.

33. Interview with Ambassador Eric Gonsalves, 11 January 1991.

34. Interview with Ambassador K. Rasgotra, 27 February 1991. Rasgotra was then Foreign Secretary.

35. Interview with P. V. Narasimha Rao, 28 February 1991.

36. Interview with Ambassador Rasgotra, 27 February 1991.

37. Interviews with Ambassadors Rasgotra (27 February 1991) and Barnes (7 May 1991).

38. Interview with Ambassador Rasgotra, 28 February 1991.

39. *Washington Post*, 23 July 1982.

40. *New York Times*, 23 July 1982.

41. Tad Szulc, "What Indira Gandhi Wants You to Know," *Parade Magazine, Washington Post*, 25 July 1982.

42. Arrival statement by President Ronald Reagan, text from the *New York Times*, 30 July 1982.

43. Mrs. Gandhi's Arrival Statement, text from *New York Times*, 30 July 1982.

44. *New York Times*, 2 August 1982.

45. Interview with Ambassador Howard Schaffer, 17 December 1990.

46. The US side originally spoke of a "Blue Ribbon" science panel to explore possible cooperation, but later changed the name when it became clear the Indians did not understand the expression, "Blue Ribbon."

47. On the cultural side, the original idea was for parallel US and Indian exhibitions, but the US side was never able to match the Year of India exhibit. (Interviews with Ambassadors Barnes and Narayanan).

48. Interview with Ambassador Barnes, 7 May 1991.

49. Interview with Owen Cylke, US AID Director in New Delhi, 1984-1987, 25 April 1991.

50. *India Abroad*, 27 May 1983.

51. *New York Times*, 20 May 1983; *The Statesman*, 1 June 1983.

52. Interview with former Deputy Assistant Secretary of State for South Asia Robert Peck, 15 May 1991. Peck was in charge of South Asia from 1984 until 1988.

53. Interviews with former Deputy Assistant Secretaries Howard Schaffer and Robert Peck, and Indian Ambassador K. R. Narayanan.

54. Although US licensing procedures for civilian and military items differed—the Commerce Department had charge of civilian items, the State Department's Office of Munitions Control controlled arms exports—the review process was similar, generally involving State, Defense, Commerce, the Arms Control and Disarmament Agency, Energy, and relevant intelligence community agencies.

55. In late 1981, Shultz's predecessor, Secretary Alexander Haig was about to visit South Asia when the Polish government's crackdown against Solidarity caused him to postpone the trip so he could stay in Washington to deal with the Polish crisis.

56. Interview with Ambassador Schaffer, 17 December 1991. Schaffer participated in the Shultz trip.

57. *Washington Post* and *New York Times*, 1 July 1983.

58. *New York Times*, 2 and 15 July 1983.

59. *Washington Post*, 1 July 1983.

60. *The Statesman*, 23 January 1984; *India Abroad*, 2 February 1984.

61. *The Statesman*, 2 February 1984.

62. Ibid., 20 May 1984; *India Abroad*, 19 May 1984.

63. Interview with Dr. Fred Iklé, former Under Secretary of Defense for Policy, 6 June 1991; discussions with an Indian official who prefers to remain anonymous.

64. Of the former envoys still alive, Chester Bowles was too sick to travel and William Saxbe unable to make the trip.

65. Interview with Deputy Assistant Secretary Robert Peck, 17 May 1991, present during the meeting.

66. *The Statesman*, 10 March 1985.

67. *New York Times*, 17 May 1985; *The Statesman*, 18 May 1985.

68. Interview with Dr. Fred Iklé, 6 June 1991.

69. Ibid.

70. *Washington Post*, 4 May 1985.

71. Ibid., *New York Times*, 2 and 4 May 1985.

72. Interview with former Deputy Assistant Secretary Robert Peck, 17 May 1991.

73. Interviews with former Foreign Secretary Romesh Bhandari and Minister of State for External Affairs Natwar Singh, January 1991.

74. *The Statesman*, 16 June 1985.

75. Letter from Professor Stephen Cohen, 4 September 1991.

76. Interview with Ambassador Harry Barnes, 7 May 1991.

77. Interview with former Deputy Assistant Secretary Robert Peck, 19 May 1991.

78. *Washington Post*, 1 November 1986.

79. *The Statesman*, 26 September 1985.

80. After getting the blessing of Secretary George Shultz during his visit to India in 1983, Barnes won the support of Senator Daniel P. Moynihan (Dem., NY), the author of the rupee agreement when he was ambassador in New Delhi. Moynihan shepherded the necessary legislation through the Congress. Since Barnes' proposal meant the US government would have $100 million less to pay for US Embassy expenses, obtaining Congressional approval was a real achievement.

81. Interview with Deputy Assistant Secretaries Howard Schaffer, 12 December 1990; and Robert Peck, 17 May 1991.

82. Interview with Ambassador Shankar Bajpai, 30 October 1990.

83. *New York Times*, 30 October 1985.

84. *The Statesman*, 25 October and 22 November 1985.

85. Ibid., 2 November 1985.

86. *Washington Post*, 12 October 1986.

87. Interview with former Deputy Assistant Secretary Robert Peck, 19 May 1991.

88. *India Abroad*, 16 January 1987.

89. *The Statesman*, 23 February 1987.

90. Interview with former Deputy Assistant Secretary of State Robert Peck, 16 May 1991.

91. *Washington Post*, 8 July 1986, *New York Times*, 1 October 1986.

92. *Wall Street Journal*, 24 February 1987.

93. *New York Times*, 27 March 1987.

94. *Wall Street Journal*, 12 June 1987.

95. *The Statesman*, 23 April 1987.

96. Interview with former Foreign Secretary Venkateshwaran, 14 January 1991.

97. *The Statesman*, 4 April 1987.

98. The bulk of US foreign aid funds was appropriated as security assistance—aid given for political or security reasons. Israel, Egypt, Turkey, and Pakistan received their funds in this manner. A smaller portion was appropriated as development assistance—aid given purely for economic development or humanitarian purposes such as most African and South Asian programs other than Pakistan.

99. Interview with former USAID India Director Owen Cylke, 25 April 1991.

100. *India Abroad*, 15 May 1987.

101. See Bhabani Sen Gupta, *Rajiv Gandhi: A Political Study* (New Delhi: Konark, 1989), for a discussion of Rajiv's leadership in domestic affairs.

102. *The Statesman*, 13 June, 24 July 1987.

103. Previous visits by prime ministers in were 1949, 1956, 1961, 1966, 1971, 1978, 1982 and 1985. The average interval had been five years.

104. White House statement on "New Initiatives in Indo-US Relations," 20 October 1987.

105. Ibid.

106. *The Hindu*, 23 October 1987. Since one of the public rationales for substantial US military aid to Pakistan was to provide the Pakistanis a sufficient sense of assurance that they could forgo the nuclear program, Rajiv was to some extent throwing the US argument back at Washington.

107. Ibid.

108. *India Abroad*, 15 December 1989. In an embarrassing episode, President Reagan nominated Hubbard, a former University of Southern California President and political supporter, to succeed John Gunther Dean during the summer of 1988. When the Senate refused to take

up the nomination, Hubbard served without confirmation until George Bush nominated career diplomat William Clark in 1989. In the 1960s, Hubbard had worked for US AID in India as an education specialist.

109. *New York Times, Washington Post*, 7 April 1988.

110. Interview with former Foreign Secretary Romesh Bhandari, 24 January 1991.

111. *New York Times*, 19, 20, and 22 December 1988.

112. The Secretaries of Commerce and Health, Education and Welfare and the Attorney General.

Chapter XI

Bush:
End of the Cold War

President George Bush was familiar with the issues in South Asia from his eight years as Vice President, as well as from his earlier service at the United Nations, and his tenure as Director of CIA. Most others in his administration, however, had limited previous exposure to India and the subcontinent. Although Washington had at first no need to undertake initiatives in South Asia, the dramatic shifts in Soviet policy greatly affected the US stance toward the region.

In 1988, the final year of the Reagan administration, Mikhail Gorbachev signalled his intention to withdraw Soviet military forces from Afghanistan. As Moscow began to implement this step—part of the Soviet leader's unexpected decision to end the Cold War between Moscow and Washington—the United States began to look at South Asia through a different set of lenses. The departure of Soviet troops drastically reduced Washington's interest in the guerrilla conflict between the Kabul regime and its Islamic opponents. Although the United States continued to funnel arms aid through Pakistan to the Mujaheedin to parallel continuing Soviet aid to Afghan government forces, Pakistan ceased to be a "frontline" state.

Once the Red Army pullback began, support for maintaining so large a US military and economic assistance program for Pakistan declined—only partially offset by Pakistan's transition from a military dictatorship to a democratically elected government under Benazir Bhutto.[1] In congressional testimony in 1989, the Bush administration altered its justification for military aid, especially for providing Pakistan with additional F-16s. Defense and State Department witnesses no longer urged these aircraft as a way to meet a Soviet threat but justified them to help boost Pakistan's self-confidence in the transition to democracy and—doubtless the strongest argument—in order not to lose out to French competition.[2]

Beclouding Benazir Bhutto's positive political image was continuing concern about Pakistan's clandestine efforts to develop a nuclear weapons capability. In October 1989, President Bush provided the waiver required by the Pressler amendment to permit economic and military aid to continue, but as direct Soviet participation in the Afghan War was winding down, there was less reason for Bush to expend political capital with Congress for Pakistan's benefit.[3]

A year later, in October 1990, in the middle of the Persian Gulf crisis, although not directly related to it, the shoe finally fell. With the Soviet military departed from Afghanistan and mounting information regarding the scope of Pakistan's nuclear program, the administration concluded it could no longer defer taking action. The President decided he would not certify that Pakistan did not possess a nuclear weapon, and, as a consequence—in keeping with the Pressler amendment—stopped US military and economic assistance. Press reports attributed the decision to Islamabad's refusing to roll back its uranium enrichment program—a key element in its covert effort to develop a weapons capability.[4] Whatever the reason, Bush's action caused much satisfaction in India. Uneasy about Pakistan's nuclear aspirations, New Delhi had believed the United States was applying insufficient pressure against Islamabad to stop the move toward weapons. In addition to the nuclear dimension, the Indians were pleased that the flow of US arms aid to Pakistan had—for the time being at least—ended.

1989: Rajiv Gandhi Loses the Indian Elections

As the Bush administration got under way, Rajiv Gandhi was preparing to face the Indian electorate with his five-year term as Prime Minister nearing its end. His overall record was

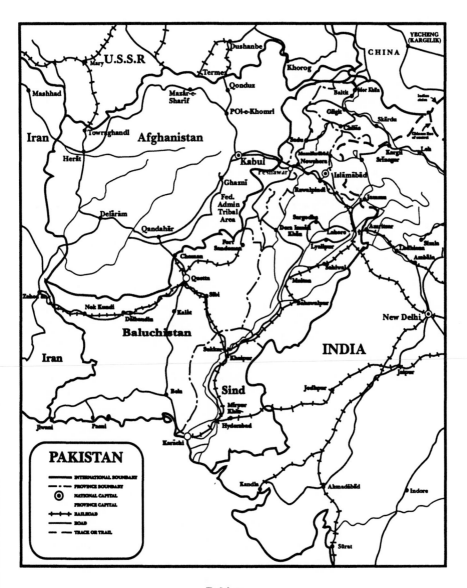

Pakistan

mixed—considerable economic progress, much less in dealing with India's domestic difficulties. The central government's heavy-handed management of Sikh separatist unrest failed to calm the Punjab where terrorist intimidation rather than law and order became the norm. As if the crisis in the Punjab and unrest in Assam in eastern India were not sufficient trouble, Rajiv began to face major turbulence in Kashmir.

Sheikh Mohammed Abdullah, the popular Kashmiri nationalist leader ousted in 1953, returned to power in the 1970s after he and Indira Gandhi reached a political accord. With the Sheikh at the helm in Srinagar, the state's position as part of India seemed secure. Although chronically poor economic conditions stirred discontent, pro-Pakistan or pro-independence elements appeared to be an unthreatening minority. After the Sheikh died in 1982, however, the situation gradually began to unravel. The blatant rigging of state elections by Abdullah's son, the then Chief Minister, and allegations of widespread corruption sparked serious disorders in Kashmir.

Reports of alleged human rights violations by India, especially in the Punjab, began to draw criticism in the US Congress. Active lobbying by supporters of the separatist movement and disapproval of harsh Indian tactics by human rights groups, such as Amnesty International and Asia Watch, stirred Congressional interest. One of the most outspoken and persistent critics was Republican Wally Herger of California, whose district included Yuba City, the home of many Sikh immigrants, including Didar Singh Bains, an outspoken supporter of Khalistan—the name of the Sikh homeland—and the largest peach grower in the United States.[5]

During 1989, Herger introduced legislation to eliminate US economic aid to India entirely because of human rights violations. Congressional perception of India as a country unfriendly to US policy helped Herger come within four votes of winning in the House of Representatives. The ban on aid to India was narrowly defeated 204–208, but only after Congressman Stephen Solarz saved the day by mounting a last minute counterattack.[6] With the assistance program already reduced to just over $20 million annually, the measure had mainly symbolic importance. That it nearly carried underscored India's lingering public relations difficulties in the US Congress despite the gradual warming in official relations that had occurred since 1982.

To help combat this chronic image problem and to improve relations with Capitol Hill, Indian Ambassador P. K. Kaul, the former cabinet secretary, whom Rajiv sent as successor to K. Shankar Bajpai, proposed that India hire a lobbyist familiar with the byways of political Washington. Despite the fact that Kaul was one of India's most senior civil servants, having served as secretary to the ministries of finance and defense, as well as cabinet secretary, he could not convince his fellow mandarins— colleagues in the prestigious Indian Administrative Service, the elite career cadre that filled India's most important civil service positions—that hiring a lobbyist was an appropriate way to spend Indian government money.[7] India's rival, Pakistan, had no such reluctance in seeking support for its cause in Washington; during most of the 1980s, Pakistan was represented by Denis Neill, regarded as one of the more skilled Washington lobbyists.[8]

In 1989, the impetus for better bilateral relations through an enhanced dialogue seemed to slacken. Bush and Secretary of State Baker had nothing against better US-Indian relations, but their attention turned elsewhere, especially toward the startling whirl of events in Eastern Europe as Gorbachev allowed the Soviet Union's former satellite states freedom to discard communism and to end their security ties with Moscow. With the Soviet Union disengaging itself around the globe from former battlegrounds with the United States—Angola, Ethiopia, and Nicaragua, as well as eastern Europe and Afghanistan—the Cold War wound down. The goal of trying to wean India away from the Soviet Union thus had a much reduced strategic relevance in Washington.

In terms of defense and security cooperation, Defense Minister K. C. Pant paid a friendly official visit to the United States in July 1989—the first time an Indian defense minister had come to Washington since Y. B. Chavan's trip in May 1964. In September, senior Indian official and non-official security specialists also held informal talks with their counterparts at Fort McNair in Washington. This discussions were organized by the National Defense University's Institute of National Strategic Studies (NDU/INSS) and India's Institute of Defense Analysis

(IDA), a think tank affiliated with the Indian Ministry of Defense. Although the United States had informal exchanges of this sort with many countries, the fall 1989 meetings were the first ever with India. A year later, the US group traveled to India for similar discussions in Pune (Poona), establishing what Washington and New Delhi hoped would develop into an ongoing dialogue on security matters.

The most significant item of defense cooperation remained the US Air Force collaboration on the Light Combat Aircraft. Progress on the LCA was slow, but continuing. No new projects came to fruition, however, nor did there appear to be any serious consideration about major military procurement initiatives. In the absence of a push from the political level, the Pentagon's traditional reluctance to expand high technology sales to India again became apparent. Even though the MOU was supposed to facilitate technology transfer, the export review process began to drag once more.

Congressional concerns focusing on India's space program added to the problem. The fact that in April 1989 India was on the verge of launching an intermediate-range rocket, the Agni, prompted Senator Jeff Bingaman, a Democrat from New Mexico, to call the development "profoundly disturbing to the countries of the region and indeed to the world community" and to urge the US government to end "cooperation with their space program."[9]

The licensing for export of a $1.2 million Combined Acceleration Vibration Climatic Test System (CAVTS), a sophisticated rocket testing device that simulated the heat and vibration of reentry into the earth's atmosphere, became an issue. Although Washington initially leaned toward approval, after India successfully tested the Agni in June, the Bush administration reversed field. The United States refused to approve the export on the grounds that CAVTS could aid in developing a nuclear missile system.[10]

The export of a second supercomputer, discussed during Rajiv Gandhi's 1987 visit, also encountered serious delays. When India asked for a Cray XMP-22, twice as powerful as XMP-14, US export review authorities reargued the pros and cons of selling a supercomputer to India. Defense, ACDA, and Energy expressed unhappiness about proceeding because the

Cray XMP–22 could help develop a nuclear weapons capability; State and Commerce urged approval of the license for the $50 million sale.[11] It was only in December 1990, over two years after the Indians broached the subject, that President Bush finally ruled in principle in favor of the export license. Opponents of the sale gained some satisfaction, however, when Bush required the negotiation of supplementary controls to guard against the computer's use in nuclear weapons development.[12]

As the general elections drew nearer, Rajiv Gandhi had little time to worry about bilateral relations with Washington. Rajiv's once lustrous image as a bright young reformer was replaced by that of a bumbling successor to his mother, equally autocratic but politically less astute or effective. His standing was further tarnished by continued refusal to investigate corruption charges surrounding the purchase of Bofors guns from Sweden. The Congress Party appeared to be in considerable difficulty at the polls.

The opposition, led by Rajiv's former finance and defense minister, V. P. Singh, forged an unlikely electoral alliance. Its components were the right-wing Hindu fundamentalist Bharatiya Janata Party (BJP), Singh's centrist National Front, comprising his Janata Dal and several regional parties, and the left-wing Communists. Hurt by Rajiv Gandhi's flagging popularity, the public's growing discontent with corruption in the Congress Party, and V. P. Singh's image as a "Mr. Clean," the Congress lost more than half its seats in the December 1989 election. Although Congress still emerged as the largest party with 195 seats, Rajiv lacked sufficient allies to form a new government.

V. P. Singh Forms a Minority Government

The National Front, which came through with 145 seats, formed a minority government headed by V. P. Singh, with support from the BJP on the right and the Communists on the left. Rajiv became the Leader of the Opposition in parliament. Like the Janata in 1977, the National Front and its allies agreed on opposing the Congress, but on little else. Personal rivalries and animosities among National Front leaders, as well as policy contradictions with the BJP and the Communist supporters, suggested V. P. Singh was going to have a difficult time staying in power.

India's seventh prime minister hailed from the landed aristocracy of Uttar Pradesh, India's most populous state in the Ganges heartland and the home of all previous prime ministers, except Morarji Desai. A relative loner in politics, Singh had progressed up the Congress Party ladder as a loyal supporter of Indira Gandhi. After a term as Chief Minister of Uttar Pradesh, Singh established his reputation as Rajiv's reform-minded finance minister. His 1985 budget marked a sharp turn away from traditional Congress socialism and toward a more market-oriented economy. Shifted later to the Defense Ministry, Singh ran afoul of Rajiv over the Bofors scandal. Dismayed by the Prime Minister's unwillingness to investigate—believed by many to cover up his own involvement or that of people close to him—Singh quit the government and was subsequently kicked out of the Congress Party.

In foreign policy, V. P. Singh made few overall changes except to adopt a less domineering approach toward India's smaller neighbors, with the exception of Pakistan. In a sense, the National Front government followed a "good neighbor policy" rather like that of the 1977-1979 Janata government. Singh accelerated the withdrawal of Indian troops from the anti-insurgency struggle in Sri Lanka, a costly and largely unsuccessful venture instituted by Rajiv Gandhi. The National Front government also settled the trade dispute with India's small northern neighbor, Nepal, in a relatively amicable fashion. Even though neither of these developments drew much reaction from Washington, this was not the case when the Kashmir dispute flared up early in 1990, threatening war between India and Pakistan.

The internal situation in Kashmir came to a head in December 1989 as the Kashmiri dissidents switched to terrorist tactics, kidnapping the daughter of the Home Minister in V. P. Singh's newly installed government. With the dissidents, allegedly aided by Pakistan, stirring mass disturbances, the Kashmir government collapsed and New Delhi imposed direct rule. As violence swept the state, Indian security forces responded harshly, triggering further alienation among Kashmiris and radicalizing the insurgency. Support for joining Pakistan or for an independent Islamic Kashmir grew. As in the case of the Sikh separatist revolt in the Punjab, New Delhi met violence with violence. Angered by its inability either to quash the trouble or to find a political solution to its liking, India blamed neighboring Pakistan for arming the dissidents in Kashmir and in the Punjab.

A frustrated New Delhi strengthened its military forces and increased their readiness along the de facto Kashmir border. Pakistan, in turn, responded. Cross border firing, chronic in Kashmir, became more intense. India-Pakistan tensions rose to the highest level in years. In New Delhi, Prime Minister Singh warned the country to prepare itself for possible war with Pakistan.

In Washington, with anxiety about an India-Pakistan conflict growing, Under Secretary of State for Political Affairs Robert Kimmett publicly called on the two countries to avoid steps "which could lead events to spin dangerously out of control."[13] The United States was worried not just about a possible fourth conventional arms war between India and Pakistan, but about the possibility that the conflict might escalate into a nuclear confrontation. Although India had tested its nuclear capability only once, it was assumed that, in the intervening fifteen years since the 1974 implosion, New Delhi had developed a weapons capability. Similarly, observers believed that Pakistan's secret nuclear development program had advanced to the point where Islamabad could assemble a nuclear device for use against India.

As tensions continued to increase, President Bush sent his deputy National Security adviser, Robert Gates, and Assistant Secretary of State John Kelly to South Asia to urge caution on India and Pakistan. Arguing against resort to force and proposing confidence-building measures, Gates warned leaders of both countries that relations with the United States would suffer badly if they went to war.[14] After Gates visited New Delhi and Islamabad—and Moscow and Beijing also urged caution—the threat of a third India-Pakistan conflict over Kashmir receded. The two countries lowered their guards and agreed to initiate talks regarding confidence-building measures, hot lines, advanced warning on troop movements, and other ways of averting conflict through mutual misperceptions.

Despite skepticism within the US government about its ability to resolve the underlying India-Pakistan conflict, the risk of nuclear confrontation impelled Washington to involve itself more directly in subcontinental tensions than it had for many years. The development of a nuclear capability which provided Pakistan with a way to balance India's overwhelming conventional arms superiority also meant that the threat of mass destruction from a nuclear exchange lay over the subcontinent. The 1990 crisis was, thus, qualitatively different from the subcontinent's previous confrontations.

India's willingness to accept US intervention was in itself a marked departure from past practice. Concern about possible nuclear confrontation, the gradual warming bilaterally between India and the United States, and the emerging reality that, as the power of the Soviet Union faded, the United States was becoming the sole military superpower helped explain this shift in New Delhi's attitude. Gates and Kelly also made clear that Washington no longer backed a UN plebiscite as the preferred way to solve the Kashmir dispute, but instead supported bilateral India-Pakistan talks in accord with the 1972 Simla agreement between the two countries. US Kashmir policy thus corresponded with India's own strongly held preference for bilateral negotiations and was at odds with Pakistan's traditional desire to involve outsiders in settling the dispute. The United States had, in fact, favored this approach ever since the 1972 Simla accord. Because the Kashmir dispute remained quiet until the 1990 flare-up, the shift in the US position had attracted little attention.

The Super 301 Dispute: A New Source of Friction

Even though political relations were becoming more productive, a nasty trade dispute erupted shortly after George Bush entered the White House—the Super 301 problem. Dissatisfied with the Reagan administration's handling of international commercial policy, the US Congress enacted tougher and more protectionist legislation in 1988 for dealing with trade disputes. Paragraph 301 of the Omnibus Trade Competitiveness Act of 1988—known as Super 301—required the President to take retaliatory action against countries that restricted US commerce in instances where, as in the case of India, the United States was running a trade deficit. The volume of Indo-US trade grew gradually during the 1980s to reach $5.8 billion in 1989, with India showing a $690 million trade surplus with the United States in that year. Over time, the United States had emerged as

India's most important trading partner, absorbing about 18 percent of India's exports and providing 11 percent of imports. India, in contrast, was a minor commercial partner for the United States, accounting for less than 1 percent of total US trade.

In June 1989, when the Bush White House issued the first Super 301 watch list, Japan, India, and Brazil were cited as trade offenders with three complaints about India. The first concerned India's policy toward foreign investment, which, in the US view, effectively excluded foreign companies by limiting their equity participation to 40 percent. Although the Indians vehemently denied the accusation, the extremely small size of foreign investment lent credibility to the charge. In 1989, overall investment from abroad was just $200 million, that of the United States only $37 million—a minuscule amount for an economy as large as India's.

The second complaint concerned insurance. Ever since New Delhi nationalized the insurance industry, including foreign companies, US concerns had complained about the amount of compensation and the denial of access to the Indian market. In view of the fact that India nationalized the entire industry, including domestic as well as foreign insurance companies, the basis for a complaint of discriminatory treatment was hard to justify. It appeared as if Washington raised the problem mainly as a sop to US insurance companies.

The third and most contentious dispute related to so-called intellectual property, specifically the length and character of certain types of patent protection, especially for pharmaceutical products. The US drug industry asserted that India's policy of limiting patents to five years, instead of twenty, and of protecting the manufacturing process rather than the actual product, worked unfairly against sales of American pharmaceuticals in the Indian market. The Indian government countered that its drug patent policy had important social implications, enabling India's vast, poor population to have access to medicines at far lower prices than US and other foreign pharmaceutical companies charged.[15]

The US action to put India on the Super 301 list caused a stormy reaction in New Delhi. According to the Congressional Research Office, Washington's move "offended India's deep-seated sense of economic nationalism and long-held views that its status as a developing country entitled it to favorable treatment by the industrialized world."[16] The fact that India, with its low per capita income and almost *de minimis* $690 million trade surplus, was lumped together as a trade policy sinner with wealthy Japan, which boasted an enormous $60 billion trade surplus, further incensed New Delhi.

The upshot was that India, unlike Japan or Brazil, refused to negotiate or even to talk with the United States about the disputed policies. This stance irked US trade negotiators, already annoyed by India's penchant for serving as a self-appointed spokesman for the interests of the world's poorer countries.[17] Upset by Indian tactics, US trade negotiator Carla Hills took a tough line in a speech to the Indo-US Joint Business Council in Washington in mid-April 1990. Calling Indian economic policy shortsighted and flawed, Hills warned that the United States "would not hesitate to retaliate against India" if Super 301 issues remained unresolved. On 27 April, Hills removed Japan and Brazil from the Super 301 watch list, leaving only India. As New Delhi flatly refused to talk about the issues, an unnamed US trade official asked, "How can you not name India and maintain the credibility of our law?"[18] New Delhi responded angrily. Rejecting trade talks, Arun Nehru, Commerce Minister in the V. P. Singh government, told parliament that India was not going to be "intimidated or policed by anybody on the issue of sovereignty or economic independence." In a display of bipartisanship, Rajiv Gandhi's former Commerce Minister, Dinesh Singh, inveighed against the "sheer arrogance of power" of the United States.[19] Because the 1988 Act called for formal retaliation unless circumstances changed, serious bilateral trouble seemed imminent.

Arriving in Washington at just this time, new Indian Ambassador Abid Hussein had his hands full trying to prevent the Super 301 controversy from boiling over. An energetic career civil servant and economic specialist, Hussein was named by V. P. Singh to replace Karan Singh, the heir apparent to the last Maharajah of Kashmir and a Congress Party cabinet minister, whom Rajiv Gandhi appointed as India's envoy in Washington in 1989. Hussein quickly developed good relations with US trade policy officials and succeeded in convincing them that talks in the framework of the multilateral Uruguay Round of GATT negotiations provided a basis for postponing Super 301 penalties. Although in announcing this action, the White House criticized Indian trade practices, it declared retaliation "inappropriate at this time given the ongoing negotiations on services and investments in the Uruguay Round of global trade talks."[20] Hussein found US Special Trade Representative Carla Hills "understanding," but believed some Americans needed to realize that "India is a place where if you try to push in the door, the tendency is to push it right back."[21] The White House decision cooled off the Super 301 dispute even though the underlying issues remained unresolved.

· One sidelight of the fracas was to highlight the tiny size of foreign investment in India. As bad as the figures were for 1989, they were worse in 1990. With political instability and rising violence further damaging the investment climate, foreigners put only a paltry $76 million in India. US investment shrank to a derisory $19 million. The only positive US investment note during 1990 was Indian government approval for Pepsico to enter the Indian market in a food processing/soft drink venture. Accepting the 40 percent ownership restriction, the US conglomerate agreed to a joint venture with Tatas to produce and market its soft drink and other food products. The V. P. Singh government, as weak as it was, held fast against lobbying by domestic Indian soft drink interests, who were fearful they would lose market share to the better-known foreign brands.[22]

The Indian economy, both under the Congress and National Front governments, remained relatively closed to the outside world with high levels of protection for domestic industry and an investment climate that foreign business judged as unfriendly. The lengthy and bitter legal controversy that followed the tragic 1984 industrial accident at the Union Carbide chemical plant in Bhopal—involving vast reparations claims and criminal charges against US-based Carbide executives—hardly reassured American investors.

Overall Indian economic growth more than kept pace with the increase in population, but was far less dynamic than that of the "young tigers" of Asia—Thailand, Malaysia, Indonesia, Hong Kong, Taiwan, and South Korea—or of Communist

China. The large public sector industries, developed in the heyday of Nehruvian socialism, continued to run large deficits, proving a major drag on the economy. Much of the private sector, working in close harness with government officials and politicians, enjoyed large profits from a protected and highly controlled domestic market. *The Economist* spoke of India's condemning itself to "the Hindu rate of growth."[23]

In the 1950s and the 1960s, when US aid represented a significant portion of India's external financial help, Washington had unsuccessfully urged a more market-oriented policy approach. In the 1980s and 1990s, the United States limited its bilateral actions to dealing with instances where it believed US trade interests were being harmed. In the World Bank and IMF, however, the United States continued to urge a more liberal economic policy, as did both the Bank and Fund themselves. Although indirect assistance through the US share of multilateral lending remained as high as $1 billion annually, the tiny bilateral program of $20 million placed the United States way down on the donor list—a far cry from the 1950s and 1960s.

1990-1991: Indian Politics in Turmoil— Persian Gulf War

Prime Minister V. P. Singh, as anticipated, had trouble holding his minority government together. Initially, the biggest problem came from the internal rivalries in his own Janata Dal. In an effort to strengthen his leadership position, Singh in mid-1990 precipitously announced acceptance of a plan—the Mandal Commission Report—to favor India's backward social classes, the lower castes in Hindu society, by guaranteeing them a larger share of government jobs. The action backfired when the Hindu nationalist BJP, seeing Singh's move as an effort to challenge its appeal to Hindu voters, launched a highly emotional campaign in northern India to strengthen overall Hindu consciousness against the Muslim minority. The BJP's vehicle was a drive to replace a mosque at Ayodhya in the state of Uttar Pradesh—supposedly located on the birth site of the Hindu God Ram—with a Hindu temple. Massive demonstrations in favor of the demand brought the BJP leadership national attention, in the process heightening communal tensions between Hindus and Muslims.

When V. P. Singh tried to suppress the Ayodhya agitation, a BJP-Janata Dal showdown led to the collapse of Singh's government. After the BJP withdrew the support of its 85 members of parliament, V. P. Singh's own governing Janata Dal fell apart. A rump group of fifty deputies, led by Chandra Shekhar, was able to form an even shakier minority government, but could stay in power only at the sufferance of Rajiv Gandhi and his 195 Congress Party deputies, the single largest group in parliament and arch-rivals of both the BJP and V. P. Singh.

Originally from Bihar, Chandra Sekhar first achieved note in the late 1960s as a young leftist leader in the Congress Party. By the early 1970s, he left the Congress and became an important figure in the Janata Party. When V. P. Singh put together the Janata Dal, Chandra Shekhar served as party president. Outmaneuvered by Singh in the contest for the prime ministership after the 1989 elections, Chandra Shekhar realized his ambition a year later. Opposed on the right by the BJP and to the left by V.P. Singh's Janata Dal and their Communist allies, the new government was extraordinarily weak. Chandra Shekhar staggered from crisis to crisis through the winter, as Rajiv and the Congress sought to pull the strings without the responsibility of office. In March 1991, the Prime Minister finally gave up, calling for fresh general elections in May.

India, thus, found itself in domestic political disarray throughout the Persian Gulf crisis. After the trouble began with Iraq's seizure of Kuwait in August 1990, the V. P. Singh government's first concern was the fate of nearly 200,000 Indian nationals trapped in Kuwait and Iraq. Traditionally, India and Iraq had friendly relations. Baghdad was a major supplier of petroleum, backed India on Kashmir—unlike most Arab states—and, like India, had close ties with the Soviet Union. Foreign Minister I. K. Gujral made an early visit to Iraq to seek favorable treatment for early evacuation of Indian nationals. As part of the diplomatic effort, Gujral effusively embraced Iraqi dictator Saddam Hussein, provoking controversy in India and abroad. In the event, no special treatment was accorded Indian nationals—though the Indian Air Force performed remarkably in ferrying thousands of stranded Indians out of the Gulf without mishap.

Despite the initial kowtowing to Saddam Hussein, India did not want to be seen as rewarding aggression and decided to join the international consensus in support of UN economic sanctions against Saddam. The fact that the Soviet Union was working in harness with the United States in the first post-Cold War crisis doubtless eased India's decision, which also reflected the improvement of relations with Washington.

In the fall, the V. P. Singh government took another step toward the United States, allowing US military aircraft on supply runs from the Philippines to the Persian Gulf to refuel at Indian airports. Washington appreciated the gesture which, by reducing the amount of fuel the planes needed to carry, increased cargo load.[24] Since New Delhi did not publicize its decision, the media and most politicians were unaware that US military aircraft were refueling in India.

When Chandra Shekhar replaced V. P. Singh, his government maintained India's support for UN action against Iraq and agreed to continued US refueling even after diplomatic efforts to resolve the crisis failed and the bombing of Iraq began. Chandra Shekhar's basically supportive stance drew increasing criticism from his main bulwark, Rajiv's Congress Party, which thought by taking a different tack it could bolster prospects for new elections anticipated in 1991. Rajiv felt restless about India's being on the sidelines, playing no role in the Persian Gulf crisis, and calculated that his party would gain at the ballot box by playing to a combination of nonalignment, Indian nationalism (i.e. opposing superpower domination), and Indian Muslim support for Iraq. Like coreligionists elsewhere in Asia, some Muslims in India sympathized with Baghdad, especially after the air attacks against Iraq began in January 1991.

Into this charged atmosphere exploded the accidental discovery by an Indian press photographer that a US military transport was refueling on the tarmac at Bombay airport.[25] Once the Indian media revealed that refueling was taking place on a regular basis, a political storm broke over Chandra Shekhar's head. With Rajiv Gandhi taking the lead, the entire Indian political spectrum, except the BJP, denounced the government's continuing to grant the United States refueling rights when bombs were raining down on Baghdad. Charging betrayal of nonalignment, Gandhi threatened to withdraw Congress support from the government. The Rajiv who stridently criticized US bombing attacks on Iraq in 1991 hardly sounded like the man that, as Prime Minister from 1984 until 1989, was eager for better relations with Washington. A cornered Chandra Shekhar had no choice but to ask the United States to end refueling stops. Understanding the political bind in which the Prime Minister found himself, Washington agreed quickly, seeing no advantage in trying to force the issue.[26] Since the war ended just a day or so later, the loss of refueling facilities had little impact on the US supply pipeline.[27]

In part as a way of expressing its thanks for the Chandra Shekhar government's cooperation, the United States played a positive role in supporting New Delhi's quest for a large emergency loan from the International Monetary Fund to meet the financial drain caused by the Gulf crisis. This 180-degree switch from the negative stance the United States took when India sought help from the IMF in 1981 was also facilitated by the Indian government's promise to undertake major economic reforms. The dire straits in which the Indian economy found itself was another factor.[28]

After India joined the UN Security Council in January 1991 as one of the rotating, non-permanent members, New Delhi gained an important voice in deliberations on the Persian Gulf crisis. India's weak government also found itself—like all Security Council members—under great pressure from the Bush administration to join the consensus for keeping Saddam's Iraq out in the cold. In a show of hardball diplomacy over Security Council votes, Secretary Baker announced cessation of US aid to Yemen, after that country—along with Cuba—supported Iraq and voted against US favored resolutions. To Washington's annoyance, India seemed to be leaning toward Yemen and Cuba in its initial 1991 vote to oppose proposed reparations.

In a more important subsequent vote on 3 April, however, New Delhi changed its position, dropping its opposition and voting for the key resolution that spelled out the groundrules for dealing with Iraq. This important switch in the Indian stance, for which the US government pressed hard, came only after a tough internal struggle within the by-then caretaker Chandra Shekhar government between those who stressed good relations with the United States and others leery of doing the US bidding and worried about the precedent of UN infringement of Iraq's sovereignty.

1991 General Elections—Assassination of Rajiv Gandhi

India's tenth general election since independence, and the second in two years, focused almost entirely on domestic issues. The 1991 polling was unprecedented in that three major and distinct political groupings were viable contenders. The right-wing BJP appealed to Hindu nationalism and fundamentalism. V. P. Singh's center-left grouping of the Janata Dal and the Communists urged radical social change to help the middle and lower castes. Straddling the center, the once all-powerful Congress Party campaigned on a platform of stability and support for traditional secularism and opposition to Hindu/Muslim communalism.

Foreign policy played no role in the election campaign. All major parties pledged to continue nonalignment; none defined what this meant in the post-Cold War world. Although intellectual and media circles were beginning to debate how India should shape its foreign policy in the changed circumstances, this question had no immediate spill-over politically. India's voters were completely absorbed in how to deal with the country's growing economic, social, and communal problems.

The gruesome murder of Rajiv Gandhi at a rally in a small town in Tamil Naadu in South India the night of the first day of balloting on May 21—presumably by Sri Lankan Tamil terrorists— stunned the nation and the world. Like the assassination of his mother Indira in 1984, Rajiv's death underscored the rising tide of violence and instability in India during the 1980s. A wave of sympathy voting, particularly in the South, in the last two days of the election—postponed until June—enabled the Congress Party to emerge as the electoral victor. Congress won 215 seats in parliament, short of a majority but enough to form a government.[29] The right-wing BJP finished second, winning 115 seats, while V. P. Singh's Janata Dal-Communist coalition trailed with 85 seats. Professional pundits concluded that had Gandhi not been assassinated, the result—like the first day's voting—would probably have yielded a larger swing to the BJP, leaving the Congress with roughly the same number of seats it had in the previous parliament, just under 200. Forming a Congress government would have been a difficult task.

Shaken by Rajiv's murder, the Congress Party chose as its leader—and hence India's new Prime Minister—P. V. Narasimha Rao, a respected but until then undynamic 70-year-old Congress veteran from Andhra Pradesh in southern India. The former foreign minister, who was still recovering from open heart surgery, paradoxically had not contested the elections and was planning to retire from politics.

The new government faced as tough a series of challenges as any since India became independent in 1947. Prime Minister Rao confronted a severe financial and economic crisis, continuing unrest and violence in Kashmir, Punjab, and in the northeastern state of Assam, the threat of communal disturbances in the populous Hindi heartland, and the need to reform a Congress Party dominated by the Gandhis and their entourage for two decades with no semblance of internal democracy.

In foreign policy, the new government faced a major intellectual challenge—how to come to terms with the end of the Cold War and the emergence of the United States as the sole superpower, in effect victorious over India's longtime friend, the Soviet Union. Although both V. P. Singh and Chandra Shekhar as Prime Ministers pronounced India's intention to renew the Indo-Soviet Treaty, the relationship with Moscow in either economic or security terms was of increasingly questionable relevance. Under Rao, the treaty was quietly extended with a routine exchange of notes.

For the first time since independence, India thus had to consider the basic assumptions of its foreign policy—not an easy task at any time, particularly difficult in the summer of 1991 for a country confronted by so many threatening domestic problems. The remnants of the battered pro-Soviet lobby urged a policy of redefined nonalignment, focusing on India's role as the rhetorical leader of the world's poorer nations against the United States and other industrialized countries. The prevailing view rejected this approach, recommending strengthened ties with Washington and, at the same time, a greater effort to build bridges to Western Europe, Japan, and the economically successful nations of Southeast Asia. Yet, despite satisfaction over the US freeze on arms aid to Pakistan, uneasiness still lingered about American policy toward South Asia.

New Delhi was much at sea in adjusting to the new realities in the wake of the collapse of the familar Soviet counterweight. Regionally, India remained the dominant power, but relations with Pakistan continued to be tense and nerves frayed over the belief that Islamabad was fanning the flames of unrest in Punjab and Kashmir. At the same time, the possibility that an armed showdown with Pakistan—something discussed more than occasionally in New Delhi political circles—might become a nuclear confrontation lent a new and far greater danger to the India-Pakistan rivalry.

For Washington, George Bush's first two years as president brought the enormous satisfaction of seeing the end of the Cold War and the threat posed by the Soviet Union. The United States emerged as the sole superpower, its ideology of democratic capitalism victorious over Marxist communism. The successful conduct of the Gulf crisis was further source for satisfaction, even if Saddam Hussein remained in power. Despite the US global success and India's economic policy shift toward market forces, the Bush administration showed little inclination for closer bilateral engagement even though Washington wished India well in dealing with its enormous domestic problems. In contrast to the heavy traffic during Ronald Reagan's second term, not a single US cabinet level officer visited India in the first two years of the Bush presidency. Vice President Dan Quayle represented the United States at the funeral of Rajiv Gandhi in May 1991, although that hardly counted as an official visit for substantive talks. The one issue that continued to get high-level attention in Washington was the threat of nuclear confrontation between India and Pakistan.

A half century of diplomatic relations between the United States and India concluded in the summer of 1991, the end point of this history. In New Delhi, there was a desire for better relations with the United States after the end of the Cold War. The Indian authorities seemed, however, unsure how to go about this and more broadly how to define India's foreign policy after the collapse of the Soviet Union. In the United States, there was a similar lack of clarity about US policy toward South Asia and toward India. Washington seemed unsure how it wanted to relate to India in the changed global environment and where India fit into President Bush's "New World Order." Bilateral ties between Washington and New Delhi were thus superficially friendly, but considerable uncertainty lay just below the surface.

NOTES

1. By this time, Pakistan was the fourth largest recipient of US aid, after Israel, Egypt, and Turkey.

2. *The Statesman*, 10 March and 4 August 1989.

3. Ibid., 12 June and 14 October 1989.

4. Ibid., 20 October, 4 November, and 22 November 1990.

5. Ibid., 22 March 1989.

6. *India Abroad*, 22 February 1991.

7. Interview with Ambassador P. K. Kaul, 23 January 1991.

8. When Ms. Bhutto became Prime Minister, she replaced Neill as Pakistan's lobbyist with Mark Siegel, a personal friend. As soon as the Nawaz Sharif administration gained power in Pakistan, it fired Siegel and rehired Neill.

9. *India Abroad*, 2 April 1989; *The Statesman*, 4 May 1989.

10. *Washington Post*, 28 May 1989; *India Abroad*, 10 November 1989.

11. *New York Times*, 20 August 1989; *The Statesman*, 20 January 1990.

12. *India Abroad*, 21 December 1990.

13. *Washington Post*, 19 April 1990; *New York Times*, 22 April 1990.

14. *New York Times, Washington Post*, 16 May 1990; Interview with Indian Ambassador Abid Hussein, *Economic Times* (New Delhi), 25 December 1990.

15. *Business India*, 28 November-11 December 1988, pp. 131-32; *Indian Express*, 15 December 1988; and *India Abroad*, 23 June 1989.

16. Report by Congressional Research Service quoted in *India Abroad*, 9 February 1990.

17. According to a senior US official who preferred to remain anonymous, one reason India found itself on the Super 301 list was the irritation US officials had in their dealings with Indians in international trade discussions.

18. *New York Times*, 27 and 28 April 1990.

19. *Washington Post*, 11 May 1990; *India Abroad*, 11 May 1990.

20. Press Release by the White House Office of Special Trade Representative, 14 June 1990.

21. *The Statesman*, 15 June 1990.

22. *India Abroad*, 13 April 1990; *New York Times*, 26 February 1990.

23. *The Economist*, 12 January 1991.

24. *India Abroad*, 8 February 1991.

25. The US aircraft in question was delayed in Bombay because of a technical malfunction and photographed outside a hangar at the airport.

26. *The Statesman*, 21 February 1991.

27. Paradoxically, in view of the uproar Rajiv caused over refueling in 1991, his mother had quietly permitted US Navy vessels to refuel at Cochin during the Vietnam War.

28. *Washington Post*, 17 February 1991.

29. The practice in India is to spread the elections over three days in order to allow the security forces to shift around to ensure adequate protection against election violence. Roughly one-third of the country votes on each day with results not counted until balloting is complete.

Chapter XII

Concluding Thoughts

In 1941, India and the United States initiated diplomatic relations when India's Agent-General Sir Girja Shankar Bajpai and US Commissioner Thomas Wilson presented their letters of introduction to President Roosevelt and Viceroy Lord Linlithgow. India was already engaged in World War II at the behest of the Viceroy and without the consent of the Indian people. The United States would be at war before the year was over. By the end of the decade India would become free, but in the process lose a quarter of its population to the newly created state of Pakistan, with which it would fight three wars. After the defeat of the Axis powers, the allied wartime coalition would crumble and the United States would find itself engaged in a global struggle with the Soviet Union that lasted forty-five years.

In this environment, a half-century of relations between India and the United States have been uneven—on occasion friendly, sometimes hostile, but, more often, just estranged. Given their different historical, social, and economic experiences, India and the United States were almost certainly destined to adopt conflicting policies on many issues. Their differences, however, might not have been as jagged in the absence of more profound sources of friction. Why have these two nations, both democracies, so often found themselves at odds with each other in the international arena? What lies behind their difficulties in getting along politically?

This history suggests that the root cause can be found in the clash over national security issues of major importance to each country. For India, the principal stumbling block has been the US-Pakistan relationship. In arming and aligning itself with Pakistan, the entity born of the traumatic partition of British India, the United States linked arms with the country which independent India considered its principal security threat. For the United States, the decisive problem has been India's attitude toward the Soviet Union. In establishing the policy of nonalignment under Nehru, India annoyed the United States by refusing to agree with America's perception of the Soviet threat. Under Mrs. Gandhi, India went much further, establishing close security and political ties with Moscow, making common cause with the nation which the United States regarded as the major threat to its security and to global peace and stability.

Given these disagreements on issues tied to national survival and the time they lasted, it is not surprising the bilateral relationship between New Delhi and Washington has been so uneven and difficult; indeed, it is surprising the estrangement has not been worse. Until the mid-1960s, Indo-US policy differences were, to some extent, offset by the perception of India's strategic importance as a democratic alternative to Communist China, and by the large-scale commitment of US resources to support India's economic development. Since then, the fact that the United States and India have shared few important security interests has contributed, albeit in a passive manner, to the sense of mutual estrangement. The two countries have had little in common other than their adherence to political democracy.

Certain factors have, however, limited how far Washington and New Delhi have been willing to let their relationship deteriorate. For India, the United States has had great economic importance—for two decades, from 1951 until 1971, as the major donor of bilateral aid and, more recently, as a result of US influence over the decisions of international financial institutions. The United States has become India's largest trading partner and an important source of investment and technology—even though, conversely, India has played only a minor role in US external commerce. Politically, also, especially after the signing of the Friendship and Cooperation Treaty with Moscow in 1971, India needed at least the semblance of a working relationship with the United States to lend credibility to its policy of nonalignment and to avoid being tagged as a Soviet camp follower.

For its part, as a global power pursuing global interests, the United States has needed India less than India has needed the United States. Ever since Washington lowered the priority accorded South Asia after the 1965 India-Pakistan war, this unbalanced equation of needs has been a fact of life. The United States, however, has not been able to ignore New Delhi. With one-sixth of the globe's population, India's on-going and—despite all its domestic troubles—so far largely successful experiment in democracy has obvious relevance for the United States and the entire community of nations. Until the collapse of communism in the Soviet Union, half of the people under democratic rule were Indians. Its geographical location astride the strategic oil supply routes of the Indian Ocean and along the southern rim of China has reinforced India's own sense of national importance as heir to one of the world's great civilizations. Growing military power has also made India a factor to be reckoned with as the preeminent force not only in South Asia, but in the Indian Ocean region at large.

As the fifty years reviewed in this history of Indo-US relations concluded in 1991, the global strategic environment underwent a fundamental change. Gorbachev's reforms and the accelerating disintegration of the Soviet Union and its version of Communism brought to an end the Cold War which had decisively shaped US and Indian policies. The United States emerged as the sole superpower, its ideology of democratic capitalism victorious over Marxist communism.

US relations with India slowly improved during the 1980s, but a legacy of suspicion and mistrust remained. Although Washington wished New Delhi well in tackling its enormous domestic problems, the United States showed little disposition to rethink its relationship with India. Washington seemed uncertain—some would say uninterested in—how to fit India into the post-Cold War policy framework. It was almost as if the United States did not know what to make of India. The continued poverty of a majority of the country's vast population of 850 million contrasted with the rising affluence of the burgeoning middle classes. Unrest and terrorism in Punjab and Kashmir and Hindu-Muslim communal tensions contrasted with the re-silience and strength of Indian democratic institutions. India's growing military power, the world's fourth largest army, the beginnings of a blue water navy, and the presumption of a nuclear weapons capability contrasted with an economy that continued to progress far more slowly than most other Asian countries and remained hobbled by bloated and inefficient public sector industries.

If Washington lacked interest, New Delhi seemed hesitant as it tried to address relations with the United States in the midst of domestic turmoil and after the disappearance of its long-time anchor, the Soviet Union. Many foreign policy and security specialists and economists were in favor of building on the gradual improvement in relations with Washington during the 1980s in order to press ahead with the development of friendlier ties, including expanded security cooperation. The rapid growth of the Indian immigrant community in the United States, numbering some 850,000 in the 1990 US census—almost three times the 1980 count—reinforced this view. An alternate approach, reflected in the outburst of anti-US sentiment during the Gulf War, was for India to remain antagonistic to the United States. Washington was seen as continuing to be unfriendly, trying to "keep India down," and unwilling to respect India's position as the preeminent power in South Asia or as spokesman for the world's poorer nations.

Whatever policy conclusions Washington and New Delhi ultimately draw, the end of the Cold War should in theory have a positive influence on Indo-US relations. By removing or reducing the significance of the two principal sources of past frictions—US arms to Pakistan and India's close ties with the Soviet Union—the altered international environment has offered a new point of departure. Indo-US relations need no longer be hostage to US-Pakistan and Indo-Soviet relations. Whether the two countries will take advantage of this opportunity remains uncertain. The history of past estrangement has left its scars. Public opinion, of particular importance in the case of democracies such as India and the United States, poses an obstacle to improvement in relations. The same is true for the often negative attitudes among the foreign policy and national security establishments.

Indians and Americans are each given to moralizing, yet suffer from having thin skins. Just as Americans need to realize that the voice of New Delhi is no longer Krishna Menon or Indira Gandhi. Indians need to realize that John Foster Dulles and Richard Nixon no longer direct US foreign policy. If India makes US-bashing a national political pastime, progress toward better relations will probably be impossible. If Washington functionaries continue to have an almost knee-jerk negative attitude of distrust toward India, it will be difficult to advance relations. Were those concerned with foreign policy and national security affairs in Washington and New Delhi to accept that their opposite numbers are not per se anti-American or anti-Indian and that pursuing respective national interests can bring the two countries closer together on many issues, a constructive rather than an estranged relationship may yet prove attainable.

For Washington, the most logical policy would be to continue along the trail begun in the late 1970s and resumed in the mid-1980s: to treat India as a significant Asian power with which the United States should seek friendly relations, including expanded security cooperation. India and the United States now have a shared interest in stability in the Indian Ocean region and a viable balance of power in Asia. India is large enough, and economically and militarily of sufficient importance, that the Indo-US relationship could have strategic importance in its own right.

There is one essential pre-condition—and here the lessons of the past are transparently clear. The United States needs to respect India's security sensitivities and to avoid actions, in particular a renewal of a major arms relationship with Pakistan, that New Delhi finds threatening to its vital interests. India's apprehensions about a military threat from Pakistan—a country with one-eighth India's population and a greatly inferior military capability—may be irrational and illogical; they are, nonetheless, real for Indians.

In the economic area, the United States should show more understanding of India's enormous problems and poverty, especially in relation to trade policy questions. Expanded commercial and economic ties, however, lie largely in India's hands. Unless the Indian government vigorously carries through with its economic reforms, genuinely modifying India's economic policies to open the country to the rest of the world and to give greater scope for market forces, US business is unlikely to show much greater interest in India than it has in the past. New Delhi also needs to understand that investment and other commercial decisions are in the hands of the US private sector, with the government's role at best a modest one.

For India, a better relationship with the United States requires a strengthening of the approach initiated by the Janata government in the late 1970s and resumed after Mrs. Gandhi's 1982 visit to Washington. Without the double burden of the US-Pakistan and the Indo-Soviet relationship, the pace of improvement could quicken if encouraged by the government of India. But relations are unlikely to become more cooperative if India decides almost viscerally that opposing the United States is the natural state of affairs for Indian foreign policy. Related to this is the future of nonalignment, after the end of the Cold War more a slogan than a guide to policy. The prospects for improved relations would dim should New Delhi redefine nonalignment in North-South terms—positioning itself as a leader of the Third World in a strident struggle against the United States and the industrialized West.

One of the most difficult issues before the two countries in the 1990s is the nuclear question. With both India and Pakistan now acknowledged as nuclear weapon capable countries, the proliferation issue and the related problem of missile capability are certain to remain major bilateral preoccupations. This development has made conflict-avoidance between the two antagonists a key US regional security interest in South Asia. The goal is to avoid a crisis that could lead to nuclear war between India and Pakistan, and, if possible, to induce New Delhi and Islamabad to renounce nuclear weapons. The quasi-nuclearization of the subcontinent could, indeed, mark as important a change in South Asia as the end of the Cold War. A nuclear Pakistan has, in effect, achieved strategic parity with India, something it could never have hoped for with conventional weapons. How effectively and calmly Washington and New Delhi deal with this difficult and dangerous problem is certain to have a major impact on the future course of the US-Indian relationship.

The first half century of relations between the United States and India, in retrospect, has been disappointing. The clash of interests that began during World War II when Indians and Americans differed on basic priorities continued through the more than forty years of the Cold War. The two countries found themselves on opposite sides of major foreign and security policy issues despite their common adherence to the democratic system. With the Cold War over, Indo-US relations could become more positive. It is uncertain, however, that the two governments will take advantage of this opportunity. Even though past problems are for the moment out of sight, they are not out of mind. New Delhi and Washington need to study and absorb the lessons of the past five decades if India and the United States are to forge a more constructive relationship in the years ahead.

BIBLIOGRAPHY

Official Records and Document Collections

Mansergh, Nicholas, ed. *The Transfer of Power, 1942-1947*. London: His Majesty's Stationary Office, 1970-1983.

Selected Works of Jawaharlal Nehru. New Delhi: Orient Longman, 1972-1982 (Vol. 1-14).

Selected Works of Jawaharlal Nehru, Second Series. New Delhi: Jawaharlal Nehru Memorial Fund, 1984-1991 (Vol. 1-11).

US Department of State, *Foreign Relations of the United States*. Washington: Government Printing Office.

US Presidential files at the Harry S. Truman Library, Independence, Missouri; the Dwight D. Eisenhower Library, Abilene, Kansas; the John F. Kennedy Library, Boston, Massachusetts; and the Lyndon Baines Johnson Library, Austin, Texas.

Note on US official documents: In researching this book, the author used only unclassified or declassified US government documents available through a variety of sources, including requests through the Freedom of Information Act. For the years through 1960, documents were primarily found in the *Foreign Relations of the United States* series. For the following decade, most came from the collections at Kennedy and Johnson libraries. Some documents were also located through the *Declassified Documents Catalogue* (Woodbridge, CT: Research Publications, 1977-1991) available in the State Department Library. This service lists and provides copies of national security documents declassified under the Freedom of Information Act. Finally, a few documents cited in the text were referred to or quoted in memoirs and other studies that touched on Indo-US relations.

Memoirs

Acheson, Dean. *Present at the Creation*. New York: W.W. Norton, 1969.

Azad, Maulana Abul Kalam. *India Wins Freedom*. New York: Longmans, Green and Co., 1960.

Bowles, Chester. *Ambassador's Report*. New York: Harper & Brothers, 1954.

——————— *Promises to Keep, My Years in Public Life, 1941-1969*. New York: Harper & Row, 1971.

Brzezinski, Zbigniew. *Power and Principle*. New York: Farrar, Straus & Giroux, 1983.

Chagla, M.C. *Roses in December, An Autobiography*. Bombay: Bharatiya Vidhya Bhavan, 1973.

Chakravarty, B. N. *India Speaks to America*. New York: The John Day Company, 1966.

Churchill, Winston S. *The Hinge of Fate*. Boston: Houghton Miflin Company, 1950.

Dalvi, Brig. J. P. *Himalayan Blunder: The Curtain Raises to the Sino-Indian War of 1962*. Bombay: Thacker and Co., 1969.

Dutt, Subimal. *With Nehru in the Foreign Office*. Calcutta: Minerva, 1977.

Eisenhower, Dwight D. *The White House Years, Waging Peace 1956-61*. Garden City, NY: Doubleday, 1965.

Freeman, Orville L. *World Without Hunger*. New York: Praeger, 1968.

Galbraith, John Kenneth. *A Life in Our Times: Memoirs*. New York: Ballantine, 1981.

——————— *Ambassador's Journal*. Boston: Houghton Miflin Company, 1969.

Gandhi, Indira. *My Truth*. New Delhi: Vision, 1981.

Gundevia, Y. D. *Outside the Archives*. Hyderabad: Sangam Books, 1984.

Harriman, W. Averell and Elie Abel. *Special Envoy to Churchill and Stalin, 1941-1946*. New York: Random House, 1975.

Hull, Cordell. *Memoirs*. New York: Macmillan, 1948.

Jha, C. S. *From Bandung to Tashkent: Glimpses of India's Foreign Policy*. Madras: Sangam, 1983.

Johnson, Lyndon Baines. *The Vantage Point, Perspectives of the Presidency, 1963-1969*. New York: Holt, Rinehart, and Winston, 1971.

Johnson, U. Alexis, with J.O. McAllister, *The Right Hand of Power*. Englewood Cliffs, N.J: Prentice - Hall, 1984.

Kaul, Lt. Gen. B. N. *The Untold Story*. Bombay: Allied Publishers, 1967.

Kaul, T. N. *Reminiscences Discreet and Indiscreet*. New Delhi: Lancers, 1982.

_____ *The Kissinger Years: Indo-American Relations*. New Delhi: Arnold-Heinemann, 1980.

Khan, Mohammed Ayub. *Friends Not Masters*. London: Oxford University Press, 1967.

Kissinger, Henry A. *The White House Years*. Boston: Little, Brown and Company, 1979.

McGhee, George. *Envoy to the Middle World*. New York: Harper & Row, 1983.

Moynihan, Daniel Patrick. *A Dangerous Place*. Boston: Little, Brown and Company, 1978.

Mullik, B. N. *My Years with Nehru: The Chinese Betrayal*. Bombay: Allied Publishers, 1971.

Nehru, Jawaharlal. *A Bunch of Old Letters*. Bombay: Asia Publishing House, 1958.

_____ *Discovery of India*. London: Meridiau Books, 1956.

_____ *Independence and After*. New York: John Day Company, 1950.

_____ *Visit to America*. New York: The John Day Company, 1950.

Nixon, Richard. *RN: The Memoirs of Richard Nixon*. New York: Grosset & Dunlap, 1978.

Pandit, Vijaya Lakshmi. *The Scope of Happiness, A Personal Memoir*. New York: Crown, 1979.

Phillips, William. *Ventures in Diplomacy*. Boston: Beacon Press, 1952.

Rusk, Dean. *As I Saw It*. New York: W.W. Norton & Company, 1990.

Subramaniam, C. *The New Strategy for Indian Agriculture*. New Delhi: Vikas, 1979.

Truman, Harry S. *Memoirs*. Vol. 2, *Years of Trial and Hope*. Garden City: Doubleday & Company, 1956.

Zumwalt, Elmo R. *On Watch: A Memoir*. New York: Quadrangle/New York Times Book Co.. 1976.

Secondary Works

Ambrose, Stephen E. *Eisenhower, The President*. New York: Simon and Schuster, 1984.

_____ *Nixon, The Education of a Politician 1913-1962*. New York: Simon and Schuster, 1987.

_____ *Nixon, The Triumph of a Politician, 1962-1972*. New York: Simon and Schuster, 1989.

Anderson, Jack, with George Clifford. *The Anderson Papers*. New York: Random House, 1973.

Bandyopadhyaya, Jayant. *The Making of India's Foreign Policy*. New Delhi: Allied, 1970.

Barnds, William J. *India, Pakistan and the Great Powers*. New York: Praeger, 1974.

Bhagat, G. *Americans in India, 1784-1860*. New York: New York University Press, 1970.

Bhatia, Krishnan. *Indira*. New York: Praeger, 1974.

Blechman and Kaplan. *Force Without War*. Washington DC: The Brooking Institution, 1978.

Bradnock, Robert. *India's Foreign Policy Since 1971*. London: Royal Institute for International Affairs, 1990.

Brandon, Henry. *The Retreat of American Power*. Garden City: Doubleday & Company, 1973.

Brands, H. W. *India and the United States, The Cold Peace*. Boston: Twayne Publishers, 1990.

_____ *The Specter of Neutralism, The United States and the Emergence of the Third World, 1947-1960*. New York: Columbia University Press, 1989.

Brecher, Michael. *India and World Politics: Krishna Menon's View of the World*. London: Oxford University Press, 1968.

_____ *Nehru, A Political Biography*. London: Oxford University Press, 1959.

Brines, Russell. *The Indo-Pakistani Conflict*. London: Pall Mall Press, 1968.

Burns, James MacGregor. *Roosevelt: The Soldier of Freedom*. New York: Harcourt Brace Jovanovich, 1970.

Caroe, Olaf. *Wells of Power*. London: Macmillan & Co., 1951.

Carras, Mary. *Indira Gandhi, In the Crucible of Leadership*. Boston: Beacon Press, 1979.

Chopra, Pran. *India's Second Liberation*. Cambridge: The MIT Press, 1974.

Choudhury, G. W. *India, Pakistan, Bangladesh and the Major Powers*. New York: The Free Press, 1975.

_____ *The Last Days of United Pakistan*. Bloomington: Indiana University Press, 1974.

Cohen, Stephen P. ed. *The Security of South Asia*. Urbana: University of Illinois Press, 1987.

Cohen, Stephen P. and Richard L. Park, *India: Emergent Power?* New York: Crane, Russak & Company, 1978.

Crocker, Walter R. *Nehru: A Contemporary's Estimate*. New York: Oxford University Press, 1966.

Crunden, Robert M. ed. *Traffic of Ideas Between India and America*. New Delhi: Chanakya, 1985.

Dagli, Vadilal. ed. *Two Decades of Indo-U.S. Relations*. Bombay: Vora & Co., 1969.

Damodaran, A.K. and U.S. Bajpai, eds. *Indian Foreign Policy: The Indira Gandhi Years*. New Delhi: Radiant, 1990.

Das, Durga. *India From Curzon to Nehru & After*. London: Collins, 1969.

Denoon, David D. H. *Devaluation under Pressure*. Cambridge, MA: MIT Press, 1986.

Donaldson, Robert H. *Soviet Policy toward India: Ideology and Strategy*. Cambridge: Harvard University Press, 1974.

Eldridge, P.J. *The Politics of Foreign Aid in India*. New York: Schoken Books, 1969.

Embree, Ainslee, "Anti-Americanism in South Asia." In *Anti-Americanism in the Third World*, Alvin Rubinstein and Donald Smith, eds., 137-150. New York: Praeger, 1985.

Evans, Humphrey. *Thimayya of India, A Soldier's Life*. New York: Harcourt, Brace and Company, 1960.

Ferrell, Robert H. ed. *The Eisenhower Diaries*. New York: W.W. Norton and Company, 1981.

Fisher, Margaret W., Leo Rose, and Robert Huttenback. *Himalayan Battleground: Sino-Indian Rivalry in Ladakh*. New York: Praeger, 1963.

Ganguly, Sumit. *The Origins of War in South Asia*. Boulder, CO: Westview Press. 1986.

Ganguly, Sivaji. *U.S. Policy Toward South Asia.* Boulder: Westview Press, 1990.

Garthoff, Raymond L. *Détente and Confrontation: American-Soviet Relations from Nixon to Reagan.* Washington: The Brookings Institution, 1985.

Gopal, Sarvepalli. *Jawaharlal Nehru, Volume One, 1899-1947.* London: Jonathan Cape, 1975.

_____ *Jawaharlal Nehru, Volume Two, 1947-1956.* London: Jonathan Cape, 1979.

_____ *Jawaharlal Nehru, Volume Three, 1956-1964.* London: Jonathan Cape, 1984.

Gould, Harold A., and Sumit Ganguly, eds. *The Hope and The Reality: U.S.-Indian Relations from Roosevelt to Bush.* Boulder: Westview, 1992.

Gupta, Bhabani Sen. *Rajiv Ghandhi: A Political Study.* New Delhi: Konark, 1989.

Gupta, Sisir. *Kashmir, A Study in India-Pakistan Relations.* Bombay: Asia Publishing House, 1967.

Haendel, Dan. *The Process of Priority Formulation: U.S. Foreign Policy in the Indo-Pakistani War of 1971.* Boulder: Westview Press, 1977.

Hare, Paul. *A Diplomatic Chronicle, Middle East and South Asia: Biography of Ambassador Raymond A. Hare, 1924-1966.* Lanham, MD: University Press of America, 1992.

Harrison, Selig S. *The Widening Gulf: Asian Nationalism and American Policy.* New York: Free Press, 1978.

Harrison, Selig S., ed. *India and the United States.* New York: MacMillian, 1961.

Harrison, Selig S., and K. Subrahmanyam, eds. *Superpower Rivalry in the Indian Ocean: Indian and American Perspectives.* New York: Oxford University Press, 1989.

Heimsath, Charles H., and Surjit Mansingh. *A Diplomatic History of Modern India.* New Delhi: Allied, 1971.

Hersh, Seymour. *The Price of Power: Kissinger in the Nixon White House.* New York: Summit Books, 1983.

Hess, Gary R. *America Encounters India, 1941-1947.* Baltimore: Johns Hopkins University Press, 1971.

Hoffmann, Steven A. *India and the China Crisis.* Berkeley: University of California Press, 1990.

Hope, A. Guy. *America and Swaraj*. Washington: Public Affairs Press, 1968.

Horn, Robert C. *Soviet-Indian Relations*. New York: Praeger, 1982.

Isaacs, Harold. *Scratches on Our Mind*. White Plains: M.E. Sharpe, 1980.

Jackson, Richard L. *The Non-Aligned, the UN, and the Superpowers*. New York: Praeger, 1983.

Jackson, Robert. *South Asian Crisis: India, Pakistan and Bangladesh*. New York: Praeger, 1975.

Jauhri, R.C. *American Diplomacy and Independence for India*. Bombay: Vora & Co., 1970.

Jensen, Joan M. *Passage from India: Asian Indian Immigrants in North America*. New Haven: Yale University Press, 1988.

Jones, Rodney W. *Nuclear Proliferation: Islam, the Bomb and South Asia*. Beverly Hills: Center for Strategic and International Studies, Georgetown University, 1981.

Kalb, Marvin and Bernard Kalb. *Kissinger*. Boston: Little, Brown and Company, 1978.

Kamath, M. V. *The United States and India*. Washington: Embassy of India, 1976.

Kapur, Ashok. *India's Nuclear Option: Atomic Diplomacy and Decision Making*. New York: Praeger, 1976.

Karunakaran, K. P. *India in World Affairs, 1947-50*. London: Oxford University Press, 1952.

_____ *India in World Affairs, 1950-53*. London, Oxford University Press, 1958.

Kaufman, Burton I. *Trade and Aid, Eisenhower's Foreign Economic Policy, 1953-1961*. Baltimore: Johns Hopkins, 1982.

Kavic, Lorne J. *India's Quest for Security*. Berkeley: University of California Press, 1967.

Khera, S. S. *India's Defense Problem*. New Delhi: Orient Longmans, Ltd., 1968.

Korbel, J. *Danger in Kashmir*. Princeton: Princeton University Press, 1954.

Krishnan, T. V. Kunhi. *The Unfriendly Friends: India and America*. New Delhi: Interculture Associates, 1974.

Lamb, Alistair. *The China-India Border: The Origins of the Disputed Boundaries*. London: Oxford University Press, 1964.

_____ *The Kashmir Problem.* New York: Praeger, 1966.

_____ *The Sino-Indian Borders in Ladakh.* Columbia: University of South Carolina Press, 1975.

Lewis, John P. *Essays in Indian Political Economy.* Princeton: Princeton University Press, (forthcoming).

Limaye, Satu. *U.S.-Indian Relations: The Pursuit of Accomodation.* Boulder, CO: Westview Press, 1992.

Louis, W. Roger. *Imperialism at Bay, The United States and the Decolonization of the British Empire, 1941-1945.* New York: Oxford University Press, 1978.

McMahon, Robert J. "Choosing Sides in South Asia." In *Kennedy's Quest for Victory,* ed. Thomas J. Patterson, New York: Heath, 1989.

Malhotra, Inder. *Indira Gandhi: A Personal and Political Biography.* London: Hodder & Stoughton, 1989.

Mansingh, Surjit. *India's Search for Power, Indira Gandhi's Foreign Policy 1966-1982.* New Delhi: Sage Publications, 1984.

Masani, Zareer. *Indira Gandhi: A Biography.* London: Hamish Hamilton, 1975.

Maxwell, Neville. *India's China War.* New York: Anchor Books, 1972.

Mellor, John W., ed. *India: A Rising Middle Power.* Boulder: Westview Press, 1979.

Menon, V. P. *The Transfer of Power in India.* Princeton: Princeton University Press, 1957.

Merrill, Dennis J. *Bread and the Ballot: The United States and India's Economic Development, 1947-1961.* Chapel Hill: University of North Carolina Press, 1990.

Misra, K. P., ed. *Janata's Foreign Policy.* New Delhi: Vikas, 1979.

Moore, Robin J. *Churchill, Cripps and India.* Oxford: Clarendon Press, 1979.

_____ *Endgames of Empire.* New Delhi: Oxford University Press, 1988.

Moraes, Dom. *Indira Gandhi.* New York: Little, Brown and Company, 1980.

Moshaver, Ziba, *Nuclear Weapons Proliferation in the Indian Subcontinent.* New York: St. Martin's Press, 1991.

Nanda, B. R., ed. *India's Foreign Policy in the Nehru Years.* New Delhi: Vikas Publishing House, 1976.

Nayar, Baldev Raj. *American Geopolitics and India*. New Delhi: Manohar, 1976.

Nayar, Kuldip. *India, The Critical Years*. New Delhi: Vikas Publications, 1971.

Paarlberg, Robert L. *Food Trade and Foreign Policy: India, the Soviet Union and the United States*. Ithaca: Cornell University Press, 1985.

Palmer, Norman D. *South Asia and United States Policy*. Boston: Houghton Mifflin, 1968.

_____ *The United States and India, The Dimensions of Influence*. New York: Praeger, 1984.

Pandey, B. N. *Nehru*. London: MacMillan, 1976.

Pillai, K. Raman. *India's Foreign Policy*. Meerut: Meenakshi Prakashan, 1969.

Prasad, Bimal, ed. *India's Foreign Policy: Studies in Continuity and Change*. New Delhi: Vikas, 1979.

Rajan, M. S., *India in World Affairs, 1954-6*. New Delhi: Asia Publishing House, 1964.

Reid, Escott. *Envoy to Nehru*. New Delhi: Oxford University Press, 1981.

Roosevelt, Elliot. *As He Saw It*. New York: Duell, Sloan, and Pearce, 1946.

Rose, Leo E., and Richard Sisson. *War and Secession, Pakistan, India and the Creation of Bangladesh*. Berkeley: University of California Press, 1990.

Rosinger, Lawrence K. *India and the United States, Political and Economic Relations*. New York: The MacMillan Company, 1950.

Rostow, Walt W. *Eisenhower, Kennedy and Foreign Aid*. Austin: University of Texas Press, 1985.

Rubinstein, Alvin, ed. *The Great Game: Rivalry in the Persian Gulf and South Asia*. New York: Praeger, 1983.

Rudolph, Lloyd I., Susanne Rudolph, et al. *The Regional Imperative*. Atlantic Highlands: Humanities Press, 1980.

SarDesai, D. R. *Indian Foreign Policy in Cambodia, Laos and Vietnam, 1947-1964*. Berkeley: University of California Press, 1968.

Schaffer, Howard B., *New Dealer in the Cold War: The Role of F. Chester Bowles in U.S. Foreign Policy*. Washington, DC: Institute for The Study of Diplomacy, forthcoming.

Schlesinger, Arthur M., Jr. *A Thousand Days, John F. Kennedy in the White House.* Boston: Houghton Miflin Company, 1968.

Sen Gupta, Bhabani. *Rajiv Gandhi, A Political Study.* New Delhi: Konark, 1989.

Seton, Marie. *Panditji: A Portrait of Jawaharlal Nehru.* New York: Taplinger, 1967.

Sherwood, Robert S. *Roosevelt and Hopkins.* New York: Harper & Brothers, 1950.

Singh, S. Nihal. *The Yogi and the Bear, Story of Indo-Soviet Relations.* New Delhi: Allied Publishers, 1986.

Singh, Diwakar Prasad. *American Attitude Towards the Indian Nationalist Movement.* New Delhi: Munshiram Manoharlal, 1974.

Sorenson, Theodore C. *Kennedy.* New York: Harper & Row, 1965.

Spector, Leonard, with Jacqueline Smith. *Nuclear Ambitions, The Spread of Nuclear Weapons, 1989-90.* Boulder, CO: Westview Press, 1990.

Stein, Arthur B. *India and the Soviet Union: The Nehru Era.* Chicago: University of Chicago Press, 1969.

Talbot, Phillips and S. L. Poplai. *India and America.* New York: Harper and Brothers, 1958.

Tewari, S. C. *Indo-US Relations, 1947-1976.* New Delhi: Radiant, 1977.

Tharoor, Shashi. *Reasons of State.* New Delhi: Vikas Publishing House, 1982.

Thomas, Raju G. C. *Indian Security Policy.* Princeton: Princeton University Press, 1986.

_____ *The Defense of India.* Meerut: Macmillan, 1978.

Thorne, Christopher. *Allies of a Kind, The United States, Britain and the war against Japan, 1941-1945.* London: Hamish Hamilton, 1978.

Van Eekelen, W. F. *Indian Foreign Policy and the Border Dispute with China.* The Hague: Martinus Nijhoff, 1967.

Veit, Larence, *India's Second Revolution: The Dimension of Development.* New York: Council on Foreign Relations, 1976.

Venkataramani, M. S., *The American Role in Pakistan, 1947-1958.* New Delhi: Radiant Publishers, 1982.

Venkataramani, M. S., and B. K. Shrinavastava. *Quit India, The American Response to the 1942 Struggle.* New Delhi: Vikas Publishing House, 1979.

_____ *Roosevelt, Churchill and Gandhi.* New Delhi: Radiant Publishers, 1983.

Vertzberger, Yaacov, Y. I. *Misperceptions in Foreign Policymaking, The Sino-Indian Conflict, 1959-1962.* Boulder: Westview Press, 1984.

Weintraub, Sidney, ed. *Economic Coercion and U.S. Foreign Policy: Implications of Case Studies from the Johnson Administration.* Boulder: Westview Press, 1982.

Whiting, Allen S. *The Chinese Calculus of Deterrence.* Ann Arbor: University of Michigan Press, 1975.

Wolpert, Stanley. *Roots of Confrontation in South Asia: Afghanistan, Pakistan, India and the Superpowers.* New York: Oxford University Press, 1982.

Woodman, Dorothy. *Himalayan Frontiers.* London: Cresset Press, 1969.

Wright, Denis. *India-Pakistan Relations (1962-1969).* New Delhi: Sterling Publishers, 1989.

Yager, Joseph, ed. *Nonproliferation and U.S. Foreign Policy.* Washington: The Brookings Institution, 1980.

Ziring, Lawrence, ed. *The Subcontinent in World Politics: India, its Neighbors and the Great Powers.* New York: Praeger, 1982.

Journal Articles

Banerjee, Jyotirmoy. "Moscow's Indian Alliance." *Problems of Communism,* 36 (January-February 1987): pp. 1-12.

Banerjee, Sanjoy. "Explaining the American "Tilt" in the 1971 Bangladesh Crisis: A Late Dependency Approach." *International Studies Quarterly* 31 (June 1987): pp. 201-216.

Barnds, William J. "India and America at Odds." *International Affairs* 49, no. 3 (July 1973): pp. 371-384.

_____ "Indian Concepts of Asian Security." *Asian Forum,* 8 (Autumn 1976): pp. 85-96.

_____ "The Indian Subcontinent: New and Old Political Imperatives." *The World Today* 29, no. 1 (January 1973): pp. 24-33.

Brecher, Michael. "Nehru's Foreign Policy and the China-India Conflict Revisited." *Pacific Affairs* 50 (Spring 1977): pp. 99-106.

_____ "Non-Alignment Under Stress: The West and the India-China Border War." *Pacific Affairs* 52, no. 4 (Winter 1979-1980): pp. 612-630.

Chadda, Maya. "India and the United States: Why Détente Won't Happen." *Asian Survey* 26 (October 1986): pp. 1118-1136.

Chellaney, Brahma. "South Asia's Passage to Nuclear Power." *International Security* 16 (Summer 1991): pp. 43-72.

Chopra, Pran. "India's Foreign Policy." *The Round Table*, no. 275 (July 1979): pp. 227-231.

Clausen, Peter A. "Nonproliferation Illusions: Tarapur in Retrospect." *Orbis* 27 (Fall 1983): pp. 741-760.

Clymer, Kenton J. "Franklin D. Roosevelt, Louis Johnson, India and Anti-Colonialism: Another Look." *Pacific Historical Review* 57 (August 1988): pp. 261-284.

_____ "Jawaharlal Nehru and the United States: The Preindependence Years." *Diplomatic History* 14 (Spring 1990): pp. 143-162.

_____ "The Education of William Phillips: Self-Determination and American Policy Toward India, 1942-45." *Diplomatic History* 8 (Winter 1984): pp. 13-36.

Cohen, Stephen P. "Balancing Interests: The U.S. and the Subcontinent." *The National Interest* (Fall 1987): pp. 74-84.

_____ "South Asia After Afghanistan," *Problems of Communism* 34 (January-February 1985): pp. 18-31.

_____ "U.S. Weapons and South Asia: A Policy Analysis." *Pacific Affairs* 49 (Spring 1976): pp. 49-69.

_____ ed. "India and America: Toward a Realistic Relationship?" *Asian Affairs* 15 (Winter 1988-89).

Cronin, Richard P. "Prospects for Proliferation in South Asia." *The Middle East Journal* 37, no. 4 (Autumn 1983): pp. 594-616.

Gandhi, Indira, "India and the World." *Foreign Affairs* 51 (October 1972): pp. 65-77

Ganguly, Sumit, "Avoiding War in Kashmir." *Foreign Affairs* 69, no. 5 (Winter 1990-91): pp. 57-73

Goheen, Robert F. "Problems of Proliferation: U.S. Policy and the Third World." *World Politics* (January 1982): pp. 194-215.

Haass, Richard N. "South Asia: Too Late To Remove the Bomb?" *Orbis* 32 (Winter 1988): pp. 107-118.

Harrison, Selig S. "Pakistan and the United States." *New Republic* 10 (August 1959).

_____ "South Asia and the United States: A Chance for a Fresh Start." *Current History* (March 1992): pp. 97-105

Hess, Gary. "Accomodation and Discord: the United States, India and the Third World." *Diplomatic History* 16 (Winter 1992): pp. 1-23.

_____ "American Perspectives on India, 1947-1990," paper presented at India International Centre Conference on Indo-US Relations, 7-10 January 1991.

_____ "Global Expansion and Regional Balances: The Emerging Scholarship on United States Relations with India and Pakistan." *Pacific Historical Review* 56 (May 1987): pp. 259-295.

Horn, Robert C. "Afghanistan and the Soviet-Indian Influence Relationship." *Asian Survey* 23 (March 1983): pp. 244-260.

Jaipal, Rikhi. "The Indian Nuclear Explosion." *International Security* 1 (Spring 1977): pp. 44-51.

Kapur, Ashok. "Nuclear Proliferation: South Asian Perspectives." *Pacific Affairs* 57 (Summer 1984): pp. 304-311.

_____ "The Indian Subcontinent: The Contemporary Structure of Power and the Development of Power Relations." *Asian Survey* 28 (July 1988): pp. 693-710.

Kapur, Harish. "India's Foreign Policy Under Rajiv Gandhi." *The Round Table*, no. 304 (October 1987): pp. 469-480.

Keenleyside, T. A. "Prelude to Power: The Meaning of Non-Alignment Before Indian Independence." *Pacific Affairs* 53 (Fall 1980): pp. 461-483.

Kennedy, John F., "A Democrat Looks at Foreign Policy." *Foreign Affairs* 36 (October 1957).

Kochanek, Stanley A. "India's Changing Role in the United Nations." *Pacific Affairs* 53, no. 1 (Spring 1980): pp. 48-68.

Kreisberg, Paul. "The United States, South Asia and American Interests." *Journal of International Affairs* 43 (Summer/Fall 1989): pp. 83-96.

Long, Clarence. "Nuclear Proliferation: Can Congress Act in Time?" *International Security* 1 (Spring 1977): pp. 52-76.

McMahon, Robert J. "Food as a Diplomatic Weapon: The India Wheat Loan of 1951." *Pacific Historical Review* (August 1987): pp. 349-377.

_____ "United States Cold War Strategy in South Asia: Making a Military Commitment to Pakistan, 1947-1954." *Journal of American History* 75 (December 1988): pp. 815-822.

_____ "The Evolution of American Geopolitical Strategy and India, 1947-1965," Paper presented at India International Centre Indo-US Relations Conference, 7-10 January 1991.

Merrill, Dennis, "Indo-American Relations, 1947-1950: A Missed Opportunity in Asia," *Diplomatic History*, 11, (Summer 1987): pp. 203-226.

_____ "The Political Economy of Foreign Aid: The Case of India, 1947-1963," Paper presented at India International Centre Indo-US Relations Conference, 7-10 January 1991.

Mukerjee, Dilip. "U.S. Weaponry for India." *Asian Survey* 27 (June 1987): pp. 595-614.

Nayar, Baldev Raj. "Treat India Seriously." *Foreign Policy*, no. 18 (Spring 1975).

Nehru, Jawaharlal. "Changing India," *Foreign Affairs* 41 (April 1963): pp. 453-65.

_____ "India's Demand and England's Answer." *Atlantic,* 165 (April 1940): pp. 449-55

_____ "Unity of India." *Foreign Affairs,* 16 (January 1938): pp. 231-43

Noorani, A.G. "Foreign Policy of the Janata Party Government." *Asian Affairs* 5 (March/April 1978): pp. 216-228.

_____ "India's Foreign Policy." *Asian Affairs* 6 (March/April 1979): pp. 231-42.

_____ "Indo-U.S. Nuclear Relations." *Asian Survey* 21 (April 1981): pp. 399-416.

Power, Paul. "The Indo-American Nuclear Controversy." *Asian Survey* 19, no. 6 (June 1979): pp. 574-96.

Ram, N. "India's Nuclear Policy: A Case Study in the Flaws and Futility of Non-Proliferation," unpublished Paper prepared for the 2-4 April 1982 annual meeting of the Association of Asian Studies, Chicago.

Rao, R. V. Chandrasekhara. "Searching for a Mature Relationship." *The Round Table*, no. 263 (July 1976): pp. 249-60.

Seth, S. P. "The Indo-Pak Nuclear Duet and the United States." *Asian Survey* 28 (July 1988): pp. 711-28.

Singh, S. Nihal. "Can the U.S. and India Be Real Friends?" *Asian Survey* 23 (September 1983): pp. 1011-24.

Stiegler, Kurt. "Communism and Colonial Evolution: John Foster Dulles' Vision of India and Pakistan." *Journal of South Asian and Middle Eastern Studies* 15 (Winter 1991): pp. 68-89.

Tanham, George, "Indian Strategic Culture." *The Washington Quarterly* (Winter 1992): pp. 129-41

Thornton, Thomas Perry. "American Interest in India under Carter and Reagan." *SAIS Review* 5 (Winter-Spring 1985): pp. 179-199.

_____ "The New Phase in US-Pakistani Relations." *Foreign Affairs,* 68, no. 3 (Summer 1989): pp. 142-159

_____ "The United States and India: The Political Relationship," Paper delivered at the US-India Bilateral Forum, New Delhi, February 1988.

Thomas, Raju G. C. "Prospects for Indo-U.S. Security Ties. *Orbis* 27 (Summer 1983): pp. 371-92.

_____ "Strategic Relationships in Southern Asia: Differences in the Indian and American Perspectives." *Asian Survey* 21 (July 1981): pp. 689-709.

_____ "US Transfers of 'Dual-Use' Technologies to India." *Asian Survey* 30 (September 1990): pp. 825-45.

Thurston, Raymond L. "United States Relations With The Government of India." *Middle East Journal* 1, no. 3: pp. 292-306.

Van Hollen, Christopher. "The Tilt Revisited: Nixon-Kissinger Geopolitics and South Asia." *Asian Survey* 20 (April 1980): pp. 339-61.

Van Praagh, David. "India After the Elections *Asian Affairs* 7 (March/April 1980): pp. 218-32.

Wirsing, Robert G. "The Arms Race in South Asia: Implications for the United States." *Asian Survey* 25 (March 1985): pp. 265-91.

List of Interviews

Names are listed chronologically in terms of the role played in Indo-US Relations

Indian Officials

Braj Kumar Nehru, Aid Coordinator and Ambassador-at-large, 1957-1961, Ambassador to the United States, 1961-1968

G. Parthasarathy, Foreign Policy adviser to Prime Minister Nehru, Mrs. Gandhi, and Rajiv Gandhi

Eric Gonsalves, Deputy Chief of Mission, Washington, 1972-1976; Secretary, Ministry of External Affairs, 1979-1982

C. Subramaniam, Minister of Food and Agriculture, 1965-1967

H. Y. Sharada Prasad, Press Advisor to Prime Ministers Indira Gandhi and Rajiv Gandhi, 1966-1977, 1980-1985

Krishnan Rasgotra, Deputy Chief of Mission, Washington, 1968-1972; Foreign Secretary 1982-1985

P. N. Haksar, Personal Secretary to Prime Minister Gandhi, 1971-1975

T. N. Kaul, Foreign Secretary, 1969-1973; Ambassador to the United States, 1973-1976

Kewal Singh, Foreign Secretary, 1973-1976; Ambassador to the United States, 1976-1977

Jagat Mehta, Foreign Secretary, 1976-1979

Nani Palkhivala, Ambassador to the United States, 1977-1979

George Fernandes, Minister of Industries, 1977-1979

K. R. Narayanan, Ambassador to the United States, 1980-1984

P. V. Narasimha Rao, Foreign Minister, 1982-1985, 1988-1989; Prime Minister, 1991-

K. Shankar Bajpai, Ambassador to the United States, 1984-1986

Romesh Bhandari, Foreign Secretary, 1985-1986

A. P. Venkateshwaran, Deputy Chief of Mission, Washington, 1975-1978; Foreign Secretary, 1986-1987.

A. K. Damodaran, Policy Advisory Committe, Ministry of External Affairs

P. K. Kaul, Ambassador to the United States, 1986-1988

Natwar Singh, Minister of State for External Affairs, 1987-89

Karan Singh, Ambassador to the United States, 1989

S. K. Singh, Foreign Secretary, 1988-1989

Abid Hussain, Ambassador to the United States, 1990-1992

Indian Journalists and Authors

Ajit Bhattacharjee, journalist, Washington correspondent for *Times of India* in the 1960s

H. K. Dua, editor, *Hindusthan Times*

Girilal Jain, journalist, former editor, *Times of India*

Inder Malhotra, journalist, former editor, *Times of India*

Dilip Mukeerjee, journalist, correspondent of *Times of India* in Washington

S. Nihal Singh, journalist, former editor, *The Statesman*

George Verghese, Press Adviser to Indira Gandhi, 1966; former editor *Indian Express*

American Officials

George McGhee, Assistant Secretary of State for Near Eastern and South Asian Affairs, 1949-1951

Henry A. Byroade, Assistant Secretary of State for Near Eastern and South Asian Affairs, 1951-1955

Phillips Talbot, Assistant Secretary of State for Near Eastern and South Asian Affairs, 1961-1965

James P. Grant, Deputy Assistant Secretary for South Asia, 1961-1964

Robert Komer, National Security Council, 1961-1966

John Kenneth Galbraith, Ambassador to India, 1961-1963

Carol C. Laise, Deputy Director for South Asia, 1961-1965

Orville Freeman, Secretary of Agriculture, 1961-1969

Walt W. Rostow, National Security Council, 1966-1969

J. Howard Wriggins, National Security Council, 1966-1967

Eugene V. Rostow, Under Secretary of State for Political Affairs, 1967-1969

John P. Lewis, Director, USAID Mission, 1964-1968

Harold H. Saunders, National Security Council, 1961-1973

David T. Schneider, Officer-in-Charge, India, 1962-1965; Country Director, 1966-1967, 1969-1972, Deputy Chief of Mission, New Delhi, 1972-1976

Christopher Van Hollen, Deputy Assistant Secretary for South Asia, 1969-1973

Daniel P. Moynihan, Ambassador to India, 1973-1975

William B. Saxbe, Ambassador to India, 1975-1976

Jane Coon, Deputy Assistant Secretary for South Asia, 1978-81

Thomas P. Thornton, National Security Council, 1977-1981

Robert Goheen, Ambassador to India, 1977-1980

Howard Schaffer, Country Director for India, 1979-1981; Deputy Assistant Secretary for South Asia, 1981-1984, 1988-1989

Robert Peck, Deputy Assistant Secretary for South Asia, 1984-1988

Senator Charles Percy (R–Ill), 1967-1985, Chairman, Foreign Relations Committee, 1981-1985

Harry Barnes, Ambassador to India, 1981-1985

Dr. Fred Iklé, Under Secretary of Defense for Policy, 1981-1989

Owen Cylke, Director, USAID Mission, 1983-1986

John Gunther Dean, Ambassador to India, 1985-1988

Mrs. Teresita Schaffer, Deputy Assistant Secretary for South Asia, 1989-92

George Griffin, Country Director for India, 1990-1992

William Clark, Ambassador to India, 1989-1992

R. Grant Smith, Country Director for India, 1981-1985, Political Counselor, Deputy Chief of Mission, New Delhi, 1986-1991

INDEX

THE AUTHOR

Dennis Kux has spent more than a dozen years living in South Asia or working on South Asia at the US State Department. A Foreign Service Officer since 1955, Ambassador Kux had assignments in both India and Pakistan in the 1950s and 1960s and was in charge of Indian affairs in the 1970s. From 1986 through 1989, he served as US Ambassador to the Ivory Coast. Other State Department positions included tours as Director for the Center for the Study of Foreign Affairs, Deputy Assistant Secretary for Intelligence Coordination, Deputy Director for Management Operations, and overseas assignments in Turkey and Germany. He researched and wrote *Estranged Democracies* as a visiting Fellow at the National Defense University.

CPSIA information can be obtained
at www.ICGtesting.com
Printed in the USA
FSOW02n0719061216
28224FS